The German Invasion of Belgium & France

The German Invasion of Belgium & France

The Opening Campaigns of the First World War in the West from the French Army Perspective

George Herbert Perris

LEONAUR

The German Invasion of Belgium & France
*The Opening Campaigns of the First World War in the West
from the French Army Perspective*
by George Herbert Perris

FIRST EDITION

First published under the title
The Campaign of 1914 in France and Belgium

Leonaur is an imprint
of Oakpast Ltd

Copyright in this form © 2014 Oakpast Ltd

ISBN: 978-1-78282-339-1 (hardcover)
ISBN: 978-1-78282-340-7 (softcover)

http://www.leonaur.com

Publisher's Notes
The views expressed in this book are not necessarily
those of the publisher.

Contents

Introduction	7
BOOK 1: PREPARATION (AUGUST 4–20)	
The Defence of Liège	21
The Plans Revealed	28
The Terror, from Aerschot to Louvain	57
The "Sacred Union"	70
Paris in August	76
BOOK 2: THE ONSLAUGHT (AUGUST 21–SEPTEMBER 5)	
Behind the Screen	89
The Battle of Mons-Charleroi	98
The Retreat to the Marne	109
Paris Prepares for the Worst	122
The Flight from Paris	127
On the Ramparts	136
The Battle of the Marne (September 6–13)	140
The Turning-Point	168
"Sufficient Unto the Day"	179
On the Ourcq Battlefield	187

In the Ruined Villages	194

BOOK 3: TOWARD DEADLOCK

Back to the Aisne	201
Rheims Bombarded	209
The Eastern Barrier	220
The Battles of the Aisne	228
The North-West Turn	238
The Battles of Flanders	252
Paris, the Austere	275

BOOK 4: ROUND THE FRONT IN DECEMBER

Behind the Western Wall	278
From Furnes to Ypres	283
The Defence of Verdun	293
Under Fire In Rheims	303
The Lines of the Aisne	310
The Government Returns	315
War as It is	323

Introduction

1

It needs but little research to lead the fair-minded student to the conclusion that, behind the immediate causes of the great war, there were others of old standing and wider purport, combinations and divisions of interest which, for many years, had brought upon the European family penalties only less heavy than those of open conflict. Several times of late, the same States had narrowly escaped this calamity; and, in the teeth of a growing desire for settled peace, the preparations for war on land and sea were everywhere steadily increased. These increases of armament (as in the Anglo-German naval rivalry, and the German and French return to three-years army service) were always dangerous, not only as direct threats, but, indirectly, as alterations of the balance of means to ends other than national defence, the most important of which ends were the acquirement of (1) foreign possessions, (2) spheres of special or exclusive economic interest, (3) political predominance, either in Europe generally, or in particular areas.

Every one of the Great, and several of the small Powers had fished in these troubled waters; and there was not one of them that could show perfectly clean hands. Even Belgium, not so long since, was being held accountable for the heritage of misrule in the Congo. There were no angelic States; all had dabbled in the imperial vices, from land-grabbing to diplomatic intrigue. Nevertheless, it may be said that there were many and not inconsiderable differences in the bias of their policy, due, for the most part, neither to original sin, nor to abnormal virtue, but to historical and geographical circumstances for which living people cannot be wholly blamed or praised, and the political constitutions resulting therefrom.

The new German Empire entered the lists under very heavy disadvantages. Late in appearing, and almost landlocked, it must find foreign possessions and trade difficult to get and hold; and the problem of defence on two flanks was aggravated by the fact that the provinces on either side contained large populations conquered and unreconciled. At best, great tact and capacity must be required to overcome these disadvantages. Tact, however, was not a Berlin virtue; and the types of capacity there encouraged were not those called for by the international tasks of the twentieth century. Politically immature, though remarkable in their industrial and civic achievements, the German people had been led into trusting all to State authority and armed force just when the rest of the western world was turning to the opposite ideal of democracy, and free, peaceful co-operation. Bismarck proclaimed the opposition frankly at the outset, and established the combined system of militarism and alliance by which the ambitions of the Central European Powers were to be vindicated.

When France and Russia joined hands over this iron wall, its builders affected to be outraged that force should breed force. Then the present emperor set out to add, to the strongest army in the world, a navy able at least to threaten the strongest navy. England being thus tempted into special association with France and Russia, a cry went up from the Fatherland that it was being "encircled." There was some justice in the complaint, as there was also justice in the retort that if, by phases of action and reaction, Europe had at length been split into two opposed camps, the heirs of Bismarck had chiefly themselves to blame. That the German people were no more satisfied than other peoples with the results of the policy which the conquerors of 1870 had fathered upon them is suggested by the emigrations *en masse* in the early years of the period, by the feverish agitations of the later years, and by the growth of the one party of protest, the Social Democrats, to be the largest party in the Reichstag. Unfortunately, dissatisfaction with the results did not here give rise, as it did in France, England, and other countries concerned, to a decided dissatisfaction with the means, the process of the Armed Peace, the new Balance of Power, itself. Individually, the German people may have desired peace; collectively, they did not will the means to peace, even to the inadequate degree that these other peoples did.

In a speech at Dublin, during the early days of the war, Mr. Asquith stated what he considered *"the end we ought to keep in view."* Taking as his text a phrase used by Mr. Gladstone at the time of the Franco-German War, *"The greatest triumph of our time will be the enthronement of the idea of public right as the governing idea of European politics,"* he proceeded:

> The idea of public right, what does it mean when translated into concrete terms? It means, first and foremost, the clearing of the ground by the *definite repudiation of militarism* as the governing factor in the relation of States and of the future moulding of the European world. It means, next, that room must be found and kept for the independent existence and the *free development of the smaller nationalities*, each for the life of history a corporate consciousness of its own. Belgium, Holland, and Switzerland, the Scandinavian countries, Greece and the Balkan States—they must be recognised as having exactly as good a title as their more powerful neighbours, more powerful in strength and in wealth—exactly as good a title to a place in the sun. And it means finally, or it ought to mean, perhaps by a slow and gradual process, *the substitution for force*, for the clashing of competing ambitions, for groupings and alliances and a precarious equipoise, the substitution for all these things *of a real European partnership*, based on the recognition of equal right, and established and enforced by a common will. A year ago that would have sounded like a Utopian idea. It is probably one that may not or will not be realised either today or tomorrow. If and when this war is decided in favour of the Allies, it will at once come within the range, and before long within the grasp, of European statesmanship.

Whether, or not, they truly described the aim of the Allied Governments in the war, these words did unquestionably embody the ideal of powerful parties and movements in the Allied and other progressive countries, an ideal served by the increasing weight of democratic opinion in their internal constitution. This ideal—everywhere supported by the organized working classes, elaborated by bodies like the Inter-Parliamentary Union and many kinds of pacifist association, and, finally, expressed in The Hague Conferences and the arbitral court and conventions deriving therefrom—offered the only alternative to the ancient method of settling disputes by trial of brute force. It was an alternative, no doubt, difficult for the rulers of the German Empire to accept—nearly as difficult as the concession of democratic rights at home.

Nor did the German people show any will to impose such aims upon their rulers. The Socialists grumbled; a few academic heretics occasionally lauded the idea of international comity; for the rest, the results of two generations of militarist theory and practice appeared in a slavish obedience under which the olden culture of the nation withered, and manly independence, conscience, chivalry, and all high public aims were at a discount. At The Hague, in all the councils of Europe, Germany came to stand nearly always for the reactionary refusal of better things. Despotic Russia had, at least, spasms of righteousness. The *Tsar* would have revolutionary petitioners shot down in the street, but would yield them a *Duma*; would establish a State liquor trade, and then abolish it; would persecute Jews, but liberate Poles; would wage a nefarious war in Manchuria, but establish the world's law courts at The Hague. Behind these inconsistencies flames the soul and genius of the Russian folk, for whom no hopes are too high. There has never been a Russian Treitschke, or a German Tolstoy. France remains, at heart, the land of the Revolutionary formula—liberty, equality, fraternity. England, with all the faults which her children are usually the first to point out, is still the England of Gladstone. Germany has not got beyond the Bismarckian doctrine that might is greater than right. For such a case, the ancient warning was uttered: "*he who lives by the sword shall die by the sword.*"

2

One result of the growth of German power was to revive and stimulate the Austro-Russian rivalry which was an olden curse of the Balkan races. When Austria, in 1908, taking advantage of the situation created by the Young Turk revolution, annexed Bosnia and Herzegovina, in the teeth of Russian protests, Germany insisted upon a refusal to submit this matter to the co-signatories of the treaty under which Austria had provisionally occupied this region. Five years later, as we now know, amid the Balkan conflict, Austria and Germany proposed to coerce Servia, but were restrained by Italy. The summer of 1914 presented what seemed in Berlin and Vienna a final opportunity of finishing Russia's patronage and Servia's independent growth; and again every attempt to assert an interest superior to that of any or all of the parties to the quarrel—the interest of European comity and peace—broke, not upon Russia's, but Germany's obstinate refusal. The risk run was so incommensurate with the immediate stake that the question inevitably arose whether Berlin was not merely repeating the successful bluff of six years before. Against this hypothesis there lies the recklessly clear statement of the German Government that "we were perfectly aware that a possible warlike attitude of Austria-Hungary against Servia might bring Russia upon the field, and that it might therefore involve us in a war." The immediate pretext calls for only a word.

The assassination at Serajevo, on June 28, 1914, of the Archduke Franz Ferdinand and his wife excited universal reprobation. If anyone had thought of this foul crime setting the world on fire, he would have been reassured when, eight days later, the German Emperor sailed quietly from Kiel for his usual summer cruise in northern waters. Did the *Kaiser* know what was afoot, or did the war party seize the opportunity of his absence? However this may be, when he returned to Berlin on July 27, Austria had presented to Servia a thoroughly humiliating ultimatum (July 23); Servia had replied (July 25) in a very chastened tone, which was yet accounted insufficient; Russia had begun to intervene (26th) on behalf of the "little Slav brother"; and Germany had appeared once more beside her ally "in shining armour." England, with the support of France and Italy, was energetically acting as mediator, committed to neither side, deeply alarmed at the speed with which the crisis was developing. Well she might be: for, within eight days of the Servian reply and Sir Edward Grey's first peace proposal, the German Army was marching across Luxemburg to the Belgian frontier.

The chief events of these eight black days revolve round four points: (1) the military preparations, (2) Germany's bids for British and French neutrality, (3) the invasion of Luxemburg and Belgium, and (4) the mediation proposals.

In all these categories, the main facts are now pretty clear. We know that the Austro-Hungarian Army was partially mobilized on July 26; that Austria-Hungary declared war on Servia on July 28; that Russian mobilization in four southern districts (Odessa, Kiev, Moscow, and Kazan) was ordered on July 29; that on that night the Kaiser held a War Council, and sought to obtain British neutrality; that Belgrade was bombarded on July 30; that Austrian and Russian general mobilisations, and German ultimatums to Russia and France, followed on the 31st, German and French mobilisation orders and the German declaration of war on Russia on the next day, and the German invasion on Sunday, August 2. In the diplomatic exchanges, Germany cited the Russian mobilisations as a *casus belli*; but, according to the French Premier (*post*, Chap. 4.), the German Government had itself been engaged in active preparations for war since July 25, before the

Austrian Minister had left Belgrade. Berlin and Vienna were aware as soon as the Servian question became acute that Russia would not permit them to extinguish this small kingdom; and they acted throughout as in face of a Pan-Slav conspiracy. If they had been content to play any part but that of the angry bully, there would have been no war.

M. Sazonof preferred direct conversations with Austria, but "was ready to fall in with the British proposal, or any other proposal, of a kind likely to lead to a favourable settlement." England held back as she had never done before, during the existence of the *Entente*, from espousing the cause of her friends. France, equally disinterested save for the obligation of her alliance, was now doubly restrained by the threatened alternative of losing the friend who could alone help her in the west, or betraying her eastern partner.

Meanwhile, the Austrian Army marched to the Save, and the *Kaiser's* lieutenants set themselves to arrange the most promising kind of offensive campaign. The possibility of a defensive in the west was rejected, or never considered. The need of first crippling France was assumed—though France had not uttered a provocative word. Accordingly, on July 29, after a war council at Potsdam, presided over by the emperor, England was asked to promise to stand aside, on condition that France should be stripped only of her foreign trade and possessions. Sir Edward Grey refused this bargain, but, still hoping to succeed as mediator, refused also to range England with the threatened States. The German chancellor had added, with what afterwards proved a remarkable economy of truth:

> It depended on the action of France what operations Germany might be forced to enter upon in Belgium; but when the war was over, Belgian integrity would be respected if she had not sided against Germany.

To this Sir E. Grey replied:

> The Chancellor also in effect asks us to bargain away whatever obligation or respect we have as regards the neutrality of Belgium. We could not entertain that bargain either (July 30).

On August 1 the German Ambassador in London put to Sir Edward Grey two further questions on the point, on his own responsibility, without authority from Berlin: Would England remain neutral if Belgian neutrality were not violated? "he even suggested that the integrity of France and her colonies might be guaranteed." The reply was that the British Government would keep its hands free. This discussion can hardly be taken seriously. The German declaration of war had already been sent to St. Petersburg; troops had crossed the French frontier; and the value of German promises was already gravely compromised. Indeed, Prince Lichnowsky came back to Sir Edward Grey on August 3 to ask him "not to make the neutrality of Belgium one of our conditions." Luxemburg had, in fact, already been occupied, and an ultimatum was being presented to Belgium demanding a free passage.

So far, Great Britain had taken but one step beyond the path of strict neutrality—a step of great importance for France, but motived also by considerations arising from the naval situation in the Mediterranean, where the French fleet was concentrated, and British communications had little independent protection. This step consisted in an undertaking, on August 2, subject to Parliamentary approval, that, "if the German fleet comes into the Channel or through the North Sea to undertake hostile operations against the French coasts or shipping, the British fleet will give all the protection in its power." This did not involve war with Germany, at any rate until she had come triumphantly through to the French coast. But when the Belgian campaign was openly declared, no room was left for hesitation. On the afternoon of the day on which the assault upon Liège was begun, Sir E. Goschen waited successively upon the German Foreign Secretary and Chancellor to present the British ultimatum. There was now no pretence of French aggression, as there had been in the ultimatum delivered in Paris. Herr von Jagow excused the invasion frankly on the ground that:

> They had to advance into France by the quickest and easiest way, so as to be able to get well ahead with their operations, and endeavour to strike some decisive blow as early as possible. It was a matter of life and death for them, as, if they had gone by the more southern route, they could not have hoped, in view of the paucity of roads and the strength of the fortresses, to have got through without formidable opposition entailing great loss of time. This would have meant time gained by the Russians for bringing up their troops to the German frontier.

On his part, the chancellor "began a harangue which lasted for about twenty minutes." The central phrase will be for long memorable:

He said that the step taken by His Majesty's Government was terrible to a degree; just for a word—neutrality,' a word which in war time had so often been disregarded—just for a scrap of paper. Great Britain was going to make war on a kindred nation who desired nothing better than to be friends with her.

On the same day, speaking to the Reichstag, Herr von Bethmann-Hollweg used other words no less memorable:

> We are now in a state of necessity, and necessity knows no law. Our troops have occupied Luxemburg, and perhaps are already on Belgian soil. Gentlemen, that is contrary to the dictates of international law. . . . We were compelled to override the just protest of the Luxemburg and Belgian Governments. The wrong—I speak openly—that we are committing we will endeavour to make good as soon as our military goal has been reached. Anybody who is threatened, as we are threatened, and is fighting for his highest possessions, can only have one thought—how he is to hack his way through. (*The Times,* August 11, 1914).

3

If any doubt remains of the balance of responsibilities for the catastrophe thus precipitated, there is a simple test that can be applied with very clear results. The violation of the neutrality of Luxemburg and Belgium did not constitute the only, or the chief, breach of treaty promises by the Germanic Powers. Reluctantly, no doubt, they had both signed the Convention for the Pacific Settlement of International Disputes, and had made themselves, in 1899 and 1907, parties to the establishment of regular methods of arbitration, mediation, good offices, and investigation by commissions of inquiry, methods centring, but not exclusively operating, in the Permanent Court at The Hague. From beginning to end, Austria-Hungary, and, still more decidedly, Germany, opposed every attempt to procure a settlement of a friendly, mediatory, or arbitral character, and until the end when, too late, Austria began to resume direct conversations with Russia, insisted upon coercion pure and simple.

It was, they held, "a matter for settlement between Servia and Austria alone," between the lad and the giant. As though there should be no doubt on this point, Germany rejected the conference proposal on the specific (and, of course, quite untenable) ground that it would amount to a "Court of Arbitration." Only forty-eight hours were given to Servia to surrender to the extraordinary demands of the Austrian Note. The reply—which, Sir Edward Grey said, "involved the greatest humiliation that he had ever seen a country undergo"—accepted all of these demands save two, and on these proposed a reference to The Hague Tribunal. The Austrian answer was an immediate declaration of war (July 28), quickly followed by a bombardment of the insubordinate capital. Sir Edward Grey tried one mediatory suggestion after another, always strongly supported by the third member of the Triple Alliance, Italy. Several proposals aimed at gaining time and delaying military preparations; others at joint mediation at St. Petersburg and Vienna by Germany and Italy, England and France; at a Conference of these four Powers to find a solution, or a simple resumption of direct negotiations. The Foreign Secretary told Prince Lichnowsky (July 29):

> The whole idea of mediation or mediating influence was ready to be put into operation by any method that Germany could suggest, if mine was not acceptable.

We have seen that England risked her own international partnership in order that this mediatory *rôle* should not be compromised.

One result of first-class importance was gained: Italian neutrality. On July 30, before the final die was cast, the Italian Premier was reported by Sir R. Rodd as having decided to break the partnership which had lasted for thirty-two years. He said:

> The war undertaken by Austria, and the consequences which might result had, in the words of the German Ambassador himself, an aggressive object. Both were, therefore, in conflict with the purely defensive character of the Triple Alliance. In such circumstances, Italy would remain neutral.

By whatever prudential considerations this decision may have been confirmed, it constituted a verdict by the most friendly of judges; and the impression it made was deepened some months later by the revelation that, in 1913, Germany and Austria had proposed to coerce Servia, and Italy had then declined to act with her Allies in what Signor Giolitti called a "most perilous adventure."

The German people knew nothing of these major facts till it was too late; and, such was the strange mingling of boisterous self-assertion and sense of martyrdom into which they had been trained, it would have made very little difference had they known. No body of men in modern Germany has ever dared to question the wisdom of its warlords as did the so-called "Pro-Boers" in England in 1899. The stern discipline which was the national ideal—free nations would call it servile obedience—showed no breach, no inconvenient outburst of thought or conscience, during the black week when a trivial quarrel that a stipendiary magistrate could have judged was blown out into a cause for world-wide slaughter. History will show few such tragic spectacles as this collective infatuation, upheld, let us say, with a courage, endurance, energy, and organizing power which only needed some moral element to make them sublime.

There has been altogether too much disposition in the west to learn this Teutonic lesson of obedient "efficiency" divorced from high social ends. The efficiency of the German military machine, whatever virtues may have been sacrificed in its service, was essentially damnable. It challenged every liberal and progressive element in European life. The increase of militarism had, indeed, become general; but nowhere else did it take a form so daringly logical, so mercilessly inhumane. The crime of crimes, the original aggression, having been decided upon, no sort of scruple was permitted to prejudice the chances of success.

Every Power has dabbled in the dirty business of espionage; but no other State had imagined anything like the swarm of spies that was suddenly let loose upon Belgium and France. To the last moment, cajolery was kept up in Brussels. Afterwards, men recalled the visit of King Albert to Liège in 1914, when General von Emmich was a guest, and overwhelmed the Belgian ministers with assurances of friendship. They recalled that, on the afternoon preceding the delivery of the German ultimatum to Belgium, the Prussian minister in Brussels, Herr von Below, interviewed by a leading newspaper of the city, had freely professed the friendliest feelings, using the words:

Your neighbour's roof may burn; but your house will be safe.

They recalled that, on the evening of August 1, the German Military *Attaché* in Brussels had called upon the chief secretary of the Minister of War, and congratulated him upon the remarkably rapid execution of the Belgian mobilisation. Not content with this call, he had himself telephoned to a leading Brussels newspaper asking it to publish this compliment. I was in Brussels that day, attending an emergency meeting of the International Peace Bureau, and well remember the state of mind prevailing. Everywhere, the little Belgian soldiers were pouring toward the railway stations to join their regiments. The hope of European peace being maintained was ebbing. Some limited breach of the eastern Belgian frontier was anticipated. But any man who had then said that a devastating descent into the plains of Flanders was an integral part of the German plan of campaign, long prepared and to be ruthlessly executed, would have been dismissed as a raving maniac.

Such assurances as those quoted above, the ties of the Belgian, Prussian, and Bavarian royal families, a thousand commercial and financial bonds, and the commonest feelings of decency and honour, were all against the supposition. The manifest preparation for this aggressive campaign, on the one side, the manifest unpreparedness of the Allies, even for defence, on the other, may be treated by the pure militarist as merely the results of efficiency and inefficiency. By the mass of ordinary folk, who will suffer the burdens of defence, but regard an aggressive war as the worst of crimes, because it includes all crimes, this contrast will confirm the conclusion to be drawn from the diplomatic documents. The German plan of campaign assumed, and the early weeks of the war proved, the invulnerability, in either direction, of the short Franco-German frontier: it proved, that is to say, that Germany had no defensive need to attack France and Belgium.

In an aggressive war on two fronts, however, Herr von Jagow did but echo a commonplace of the Prussian Staff when he said that "to strike some decisive blow as early as possible was a matter of life and death for them." England's entry made it impossible to strike, or help to strike, such a blow by way of the high seas. On the other hand, Germany's land-locked position, which had been so loud a grievance, proved in these circumstances a positive advantage for her defence. On land, the aggressors, for a short time, would have an advantage, both in numbers and concentration of forces; but the advantage would soon pass, and in a struggle of exhaustion the numbers that could ultimately be brought up by Russia and the British Empire must turn the scale. At the outset, Germany could throw a peace strength of 860,000 men immediately into the field.

France, two or three days behind in effective mobilization, would only have 790,000 when her Algerian Army Corps had been got over. Meanwhile, a sufficient guard could be left in East Prussia; and Belgium's little army, only about 60,000 men on a peace footing, could be crushed before the British Expeditionary Corps had time to land. Austria-Hungary would have immediately marched 500,000 men against Russia and Servia. Reserves would now be available. "War footing" is a very elastic phrase; but the Germanic Powers, together, could count on putting man against man of France, and having a surplus of between four and five millions to meet the slow-coming hosts of Russia and England. Strange if, before then, a decisive blow could not be struck.

Such was the calculation; and it came painfully near being justified by the event.

There is a continuity of *mise-en-scène* in history that may too easily lead to pessimism. Much of the European past is, indeed, comprised in the ancient rivalry of powerful neighbours for the lands of the great central highways from the North Sea and Baltic, through the Rhineland, to Italy and the Levant—the endless strife of Merving and Karling, Neustria and Austria, Royal France and confederate Germany, Burgundy and Spain, France and Austria, which has filled with battlefields the line of Alsace and Lorraine, Liège, Brabant, and Flanders. Of this secular antagonism, that of Austria and Russia for dominance in the Danubian lands, and of their financial and political friends for profit in Constantinople and Mesopotamia, may be regarded as a modern extension.

When Sir John French faced north from Mons, a few miles from the field of Waterloo where, a century before, Wellington faced south against the greatest of adventurers, he showed England once more stepping aside from her own paths to help the small peoples of this middle tract of the Old World, and casting her weight against the challenge of an upstart imperialism. Can this insane cycle revolve eternally? In truth, perennial as folly and selfishness seem to be, they also change. The stage remains; the play and the actors are never really the same. Dynastic and religious motives no longer bring nations to arms. Empire can no longer be fed on loot, tribute, and slaves. The Old Hemisphere, with its feuds and poverty, stands in too absurd contrast with the New, united and prosperous. The process that has transformed war itself has begun to subordinate it to the arts and laws of peace. No nation will gain by this war, and every one will lose. We live in a world that reads and writes, that can only subsist by labour and trade, in which open violence is the exception proving the rule of public order, and the peoples begin to determine their own destinies.

The chief institutions of a comity of nations are actually in being. Let them be strengthened by an operative will, and an agreement for mutual defence, and "the substitution for force, for groupings and alliances and a precarious equipoise, of a real European partnership" will soon be achieved. If it bring us to that, the blood-offering of the great war will not have been all in vain,.

London, April 1915.

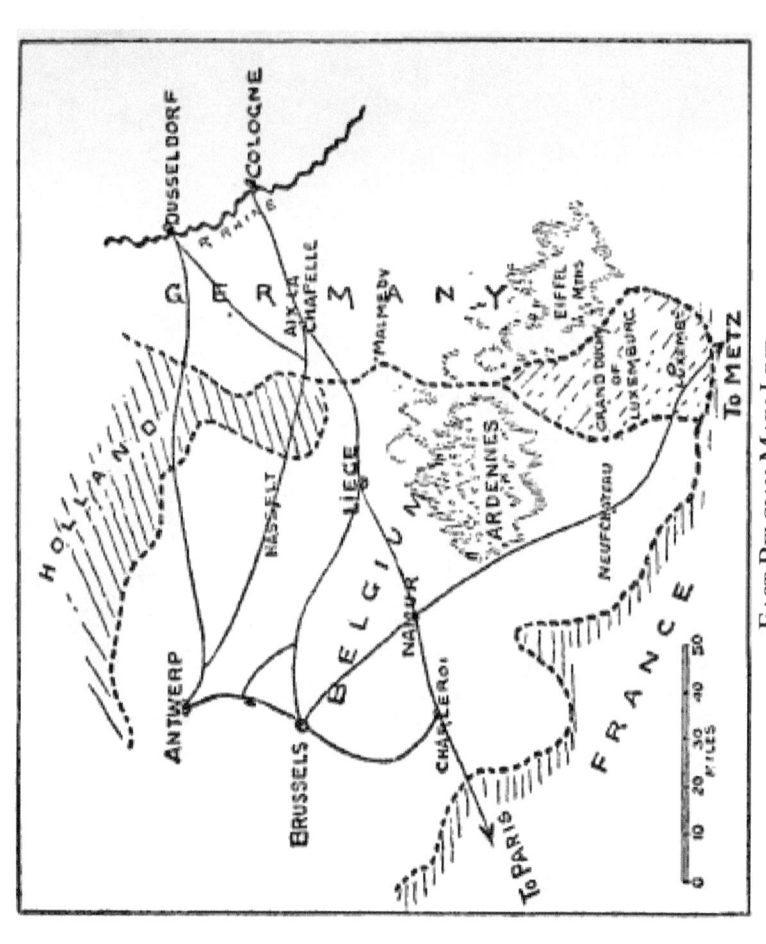

East Belgian Main Line

Book 1: Preparation (August 4-20)

Chapter 1

The Defence of Liège

On the morning of Monday, August 3, immediately after receipt of the Belgian refusal of a free passage, covering troops consisting of the 7th German Army Corps, under command of General von Emmich, advanced from Aix-la-Chapelle, and crossed the Belgian frontier by the narrow tract between the protruding Dutch district of Maestricht, on the north, and the Vesdre Valley, on the south.

This is the only easy road into Belgium from the east, the mountains of the Ardennes and the Eiffel obstructing the roads further south. Hence the importance of Liège, in times both of peace and war. Five main lines of railway cross Belgium from east to west, following, generally, ancient natural highroads. Two of these lines connect the Middle Rhine directly with Antwerp—these were ruled out by the German decision not to violate the neutrality of Holland, for both of them pass through the Maestricht enclave. Another runs northwestward through the Luxemburgs to Brussels, and could thus be used only as a bypath for an attack on France. The remaining two are branches of the great international trunk-lines from Cologne to Ostend and Paris, dividing at Liège, the one for Brussels, the other for the French frontier, a hundred miles away. We shall see that this latter road, through the Meuse-Sambre valleys, was only too obviously the path of a conqueror for whom a little State was merely a little hindrance, a treaty merely a "scrap of paper." Here, therefore, were placed three of Belgium's four fortresses, while the outlet into France was covered by Maubeuge and various lesser works.

Liège, therefore—a great industrial centre and junction of railways, roads, and rivers, guarded by a ring of twelve forts extending across a diameter of eight miles—must first be reduced: it would then be possible to break westward, or to go on up the valley railroad to Namur, or both. It may have been hoped that the Prussian frontier troops could rush this obstacle; at least, the attempt would prevent the strengthening of the works and the arrival of re-enforcements. Two railway lines and three roads served them for crossing the border. The railways, one entering by Gemmenich, and the other by Herbestal, then united to form the Aix-Liège route (forty miles); this was, of course, broken by the retreating Belgians. The most northern highroad passes through Gemmenich, crosses the Meuse at Visé, six miles north of Liège, and then strikes into central Belgium; the other two run, through Herve and Verviers respectively, into Liège. By these three routes the preliminary invasion was effected.

It met with an unexpectedly stout resistance. The position at Visé was defended obstinately all through the 4th and 5th by the Belgian 12th line regiment, with the broad stream of the Meuse, bridged only at one place, in front, the Dutch frontier on their left flank, and the Liège forts covering their right. Pontoon bridges were repeatedly destroyed, but at last a crossing was secured. A number of civilians were afterward seized and shot by the invaders, on the ground that shots had been fired from houses in the little town. The country-people fled inland; many wounded soldiers were taken over the border into Maestricht. The victorious troops marched south upon Liège on the 6th, steadily opposed by General Bertrand's brigade. Meanwhile, other columns representing the main advance body of the invasion, and including the 9th and 10th Army Corps and a brigade of the 4th Corps, had come in by the roads from Eupen, through Herve and Verviers, and from Malmedy-Stavelot, through the Spa, Amblève, and Ourthe valleys on the south. Verviers and Pépinster having been occupied, the army found itself before the first earthworks of the Liège ring. Some of these troops were ill-provisioned and weary from hard marching, a result of incomplete mobilization.

The six major and six minor forts surrounding the city at the great crossways were designed in 1886 by the able military engineer, General Brialmont; and they had been partially reconstructed, in view of the immense increase in the power of siege artillery, under King Albert. Two of them, Forts Pontisse and Barchon, covered the plain towards Visé; three others—Fléron, Evegnée, and Chaudfontaine—faced the hilly approach by the Vesdre Valley; Forts Embourg and Boncelles commanded the Ourthe Valley, southward; the remaining five, from Flemalle to Liers, overlooked the western plain. The largest forts were surrounded by a ditch, within the glacis, or exterior earthen slope; the banquette, or outer wall, of this ditch and the summit of the escarp served as infantry parapets. Above these, within a concrete shell, rose the steel cupolas, moving up and down before and after fire. The structure was pierced with galleries from which machine-guns could be worked under the protection of solid masonry, tunnels for the movements of the garrison, and cellars for ammunition and stores. The ring included four hundred guns; but many of these were at first far from the main field of attack.

Both the strength and the weakness of these works were to receive a quick and tragic demonstration. Thanks to the gallantry of General Leman, the Commandant of Liège, and his men, they secured an invaluable delay for the half-mobilised Allies: but, as fortifications, they revealed two vital weaknesses: the cupola fort gives a prominent mark for the attackers, and the mechanism of the disappearing or oscillating cupola is very liable to disablement. Although the enemy guns could be concealed, if those of the defenders could outrange and overpower them there might be some hope; but no such claim could be made for the Belgian guns. The forts had garrisons averaging little more than a hundred men; and the strain of a week's constant bombardment on a hundred men is indescribable. An army 50,000 strong was needed to hold the intervening fieldworks; but the whole Liège garrison fell greatly below that figure.

The question whether, even in the domain of armed force, numbers and organisation can eclipse the factor of moral inspiration was now to be tried before a breathlessly watching world. The defenders of Liège—the 3rd Belgian Division, re-enforced by militia, reservists, and Civil Guards—a total of, perhaps, 40,000 men—had to face three Russian Corps, about 120,000 men. They had no ground for expecting re-enforcement; England and France were not nearly ready to help them, and the main Belgian Army, which was not yet concentrated, must, even then, wait for its greater friends. General Leman did what was possible—the forts were provisioned, and thousands of civilians helped to dig trenches and put up wire entanglements across the intervals between them. On the night of August 4-5, the German attack began on the south-eastern side, the apparent object being to seize the river crossing, and, after masking Liège, to hasten on to Namur. A full moon shone, and searchlights flashed to and fro over the scene.

While the German field-guns, using high explosive shells of a power unknown to the defenders, from well-concealed positions in the

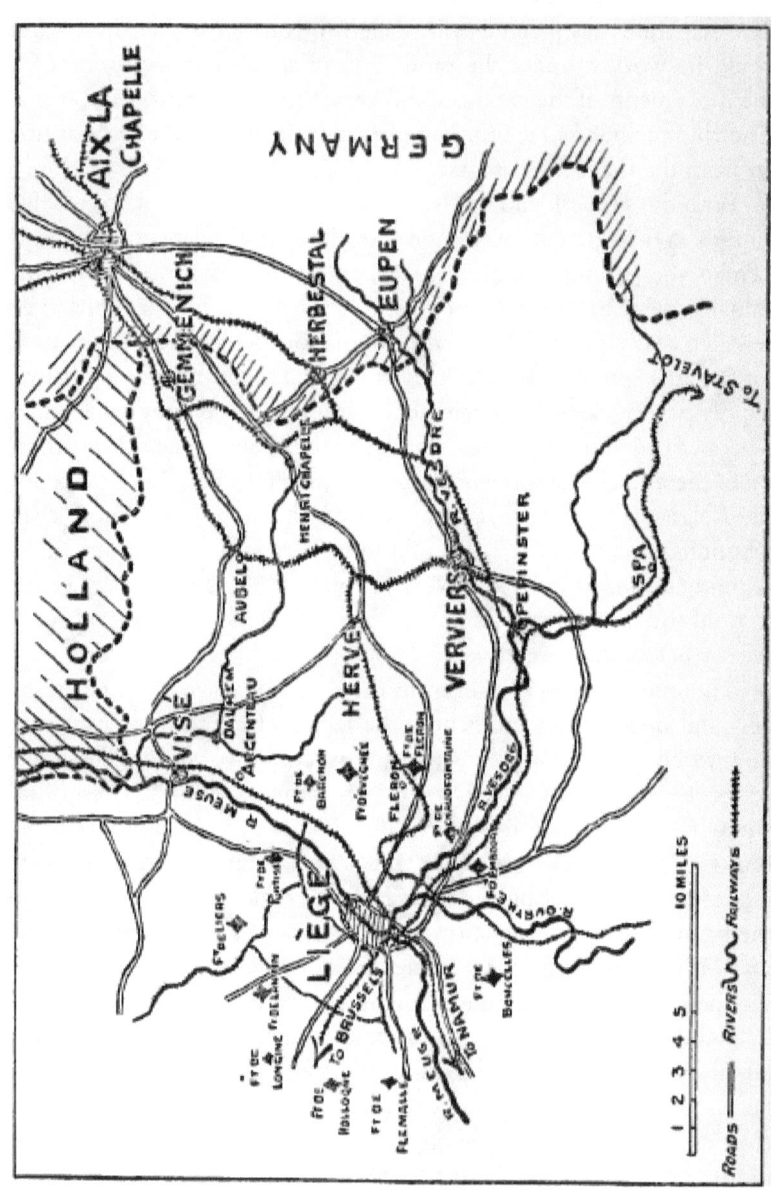

LIÈGE, ITS RAILWAYS, ROADS AND FORTS

wooded hills, made excellent practice against Forts Fléron, Embourg, and Boncelles, masses of infantry in close formation were thrown against the gaps, held by the Belgian 9th and 14th line regiments. Before the trenches, and along the glacis of the forts, they were mown down by fire from above and below; but they still came on. Although the Belgian reports may have been exaggerated, the losses up to this point, a result of the first crude application of the "smashing blow" tactic, were certainly very heavy. The battle continued fiercely through the following day. The defenders, at most one against three, and at last overborne in artillery, had to be moved from gap to gap to meet successive assaults; some infantry sections thus marched for twenty-five or thirty miles in course of the night. At length, they were driven in between Forts Evegnée and Fléron; and the latter was silenced on the morning of the 6th, much of the gun machinery being smashed, and great blocks of masonry, supporting the turrets, shattered. It is understood that the largest German siege mortars were not used at Liège, but were sent on direct to Namur, either because the one task was under-, or the other was over-estimated.

In face of this breach in his line of defence, and as the river crossing had been forced lower down, General Leman withdrew the field troops to the west side of the Meuse, and blew up the two southern bridges, leaving the remaining That morning, a daring attempt was made to kidnap, or, perhaps, to kill the general, half a dozen *uhlans* succeeding in penetrating to his headquarters in the town. Probably, the 3rd Division was already commencing its retreat toward Brussels. During the day, the complete surrender of the fortress was demanded, and refused. The last train, crowded with refugees, left in the afternoon; and at 6 p.m. a short and not very serious bombardment of the town began. In the evening, the German commander proposed a twenty-four hours' armistice to bury the dead and remove the wounded. This was also refused. On the next day, August 7, the attack was resumed. The city, now evacuated, was occupied by Von Emmich. Most of the river bridges had been left intact. General Leman, who had withdrawn into Fort Loncin, continued to direct the resistance of the broken ring.

Not till Sunday, the 9th, was the investment complete and the siege artillery ready. Some of the forts held out for eight days longer, the men dying with Spartan fortitude at their posts. One fort was the scene of a conspicuous act of heroism. Situated near the Chaudfontaine tunnel, it had the special duty of covering the Verviers railway line. When nothing more could be done. Major Mameche, the *com-*

mandant, blocked the tunnel by colliding several engines at its mouth, and then fired his powder magazine, blowing up the fort. For a week the cannonade never ceased; and in further infantry assaults, the Germans suffered very heavy casualties.

The last stage in Fort Loncin was thus described in a diary attributed, apparently with truth, to General Leman himself, and published in Berlin during his subsequent imprisonment at Magdeburg:

> On the 11th, the Germans started bombarding us with 7- and 10-centimetre (3-inch and 4-inch) cannon: and, on the 12th and 13th, they brought their 21-centimetre (8-inch) guns into action. But it was not until the 14th that they opened fire and began their destruction of the outer works. On that day, at 4 o'clock in the afternoon, a German officer approached to within 200 yards of the fort with a signalling flag in his hand; and shortly afterwards, the siege gunners, having adjusted their range, began a fearful firing, that lasted a couple of hours. The battery on the left slope was destroyed, the enemy keeping on pounding away exclusively with their 21-centimetre cannons.
>
> The third phase of the bombardment began at 5 o'clock in the morning of the 15th, firing being kept up without a break until two in the afternoon. A grenade wrecked the arcade under which the general staff were sheltering. All light was extinguished by the force of the explosion, and the officers ran the risk of asphyxiation by the horrible gases emitted from the shell. When firing ceased, I ventured out on a tour of inspection on the external slopes, which I found had been reduced to a rubble heap. A few minutes later, the bombardment was resumed. It seemed as though all the German batteries were together firing salvoes. Nobody will ever be able to form any adequate idea of what the reality was like. I have only learned since that when the big siege mortars entered into action they hurled against us shells weighing 1,000 kilos (nearly a ton), the explosive force of which surpasses anything known hitherto. Their approach was to be heard in an acute buzzing; and they burst with a thunderous roar, raising clouds of missiles, stones, and dust.
>
> After some time passed amid these horrors, I wished to return to my observation tower; but I had hardly advanced a few feet into the gallery when a great blast passed by, and I was thrown violently to the ground. I managed to rise, and continued my

way, only to be stopped by a choking cloud of poisonous gas. It was a mixture of the gas from an explosion and the smoke of a fire in the troop quarters. We were driven back, half-suffocated. Looking out of a peephole, I saw to my horror that the fort had fallen, slopes and counter-slopes being a chaos of rubbish, while huge tongues of flame were shooting forth from the throat of the fortress. My first and last thought was to try and save the remnant of the garrison. I rushed out to give orders, and saw some soldiers, whom I mistook for Belgian *gendarmes*. I called them, then fell again. Poisonous gases seemed to grip my throat as in a vise.

A shell had fallen in the powder magazine, and most of the garrison were overwhelmed by the explosion.

On recovering consciousness, I found my *aide-de-camp*. Captain Colland, standing over me, also a German officer, who offered me a glass of water. They told me I had swooned, and that the soldiery I had taken for Belgian *gendarmes* were, in fact, the first band of German troops who had set foot inside the forts. In recognition of our courage, the Germans allowed me to retain my sword.

In declining to receive it, the German commander is said to have remarked: "To have crossed swords with you has been an honour." In a letter to the King of the Belgians, General Leman narrated the circumstances, adding:

Deign to grant pardon. Sire. In Germany, whither I am proceeding, my thoughts will be, as they have ever been, of Belgium and the king. I would willingly have given my life the better to serve them, but death was not granted to me.

CHAPTER 2

The Plans Revealed

1. Of Certain Uncertainties

If history were reduced to a narrative of events as they are afterward found to have occurred, it would give anything but a true picture of the passage of life with which it is concerned. Not only are motives, opinions, and even prejudices and superstitions, an integral part of this life; one of the essential facts which the historian must present is that his actors did not know the facts as he does, could never see what it is his chief business to see, their development in its length and breadth, could very rarely grasp their significance before it was too late, and so could rarely set a course by their logic. In the history of warfare, where the concealment of facts is general, and systematic deception is frequent, this consideration is of peculiar importance. The governments and commanders know very much more than the newspapers and their readers, as a rule; but it will be safe to suppose that, at any given moment, there were many things, and some considerable things, they did not know which were commonplaces six months later. An aggressor of superhuman foresight, assured of a good start, and backed by a colossal organization, will meet with disturbing surprises. The defence is more seriously handicapped; for its plans cannot be fixed until the nature of the attack is known; and this may not be accurately known until it has already been, wholly or partially, transformed.

Many years may elapse, many of the great actors may be dead, and the blood-lust exhausted and half-forgotten, ere we know exactly and completely what was the original German plan of campaign, with its supporting calculations. To suppose that what occurred was just what had been planned would be to attribute to the Grand Staff in Berlin something like omniscience—an hypothesis plainly contradicted by their failure to comprehend, in particular, the spirit of the Belgian and the British peoples. It is evident that an advance upon France through Belgium was a prominent feature of this plan, because the advance actually made at the outset of the campaign was so strong that it must have been long prepared. The Allied commanders had only to glance at a map to see that the whole of Prussia and the great bulk of the German Empire lie north of the meridian of Paris-Stuttgart, where, in fact, two-thirds of the German army had its stations in time of peace. For a full half of it, indeed, Belgium was the nearest as well as the easiest way to Paris.

But, in civilised States, political and moral considerations weigh more heavily than those of a purely military order; there could be no certainty of a Belgian invasion till it was an accomplished fact; and even then its direction and its dimensions had to be discovered. The Germans, on their part, knew that they had to count with Belgian and British, as well as French, opposition; and, the aggression once decided upon, the importance of striking a crushing blow on this side before turning to the more numerous but slow-moving Russians was evident. Yet they could not know positively where France would make her chief effort, what Belgian resistance would amount to, how many British troops would be landed on the Continent before a crisis was reached, or how soon Russia would seriously threaten their eastern flank.

It is no part of the game of government to confess to ignorance, hesitation, uncertainty; for the historical student, however, these major uncertainties, and others—among them, as to the attitude of neutrals, and the sentiment of the belligerent peoples—are a most important part of the play of forces with which he has to reckon. The inordinate size of the modern war-machine implies a plan of campaign elaborated long in advance, and then very difficult of modification. Nevertheless, in a struggle so complex as this, the second or third week of hostilities, when much more is known than could have been anticipated, must needs be a time of anxious reconsideration among some, if not all, of the directing Staffs. It will be well, therefore, before we reach the period of direct and rapid development beginning with the battle of Mons-Charleroi, to review rapidly the course of events in the whole western land area during and immediately after the investment of Liège, with a view to finding some clew to the relation between what was planned and what actually occurred.

No doubt remains of the purely defensive attitude of France on the eve of the war. This was, indeed, dictated as clearly by prudential motives—the need of British support, of Italian neutrality, and of domestic unity—as by the spirit of the Government and the nation at large. Until the actual outbreak of hostilities, the French troops were kept withdrawn eight kilometres (five miles) behind the frontier, so that there should be no "incidents" to cite as a *casus belli*. One major cause of anxiety immediately disappeared: in all four countries, political and other divisions ceased. The Socialist and Pacifist organizations said their last words at meetings of their respective International Councils in Brussels during the last week in July.

The silent acceptance by four million German Social Democrats of an issue having, to say the least, no favourable relation to their professed principles was conclusive. It might be explained by reference to the national trait of obedience to constituted authority; it could not be harmonized with the traditions of the Red Flag, or any kind of internationalism. To men in other lands who had given years of labour for peace and democratic progress, this was the cruellest blow of all. It dispelled some illusions; destroyed, or indefinitely postponed, many high hopes.

It brought the elemental sentiment of patriotism surging back, like a tidal wave. Leading Socialists—MM. Sembat and Guesde in France, M. Vandervelde in Belgium—assumed Ministerial responsibilities, as Jean Jaures would have done had he lived. Exiled revolutionists returned to Russia to join the colours. Until the German challenge became explicit and unmistakable, there was decided hesitation among British Radicals and Labour men, long devoted to the idea of a reconciliation of the rival Alliances; and, before the last step, Lord Morley and Mr. John Burns had resigned their seats in the Cabinet. Thereafter, no division appeared. Suffragettes had already ceased from troubling. On August 3, Mr. John Redmond declared that the Government might remove all their troops from Ireland, which Catholic Nationalists and Protestant Ulstermen would join hands to defend. The Home Rule Bill was then passed, but its operation postponed till the end of the war. At home, as in South Africa, the spirit of self-government was again justified. All were nationalists now. For good or ill, whatever its original causes, whoever its responsible authors, this was to be in the fullest sense a war of nations. This was, perhaps, the most considerable fact that had emerged clearly before the river crossings and railways of Liège had been lost and won.

"Gaps" of the East Frontier

2. In the Vosges and Alsace

We may now turn to the military plans of the western Allies and their chief enemy, taking France first, as the Power longest acquainted with the threat of a new invasion. The German Empire is bordered on the west, to the extent of nearly two-thirds of its extent, by Holland and Belgium, and to the extent of little more than one-third by France. During the armed rivalry that followed the war of 1870, this short Franco-German frontier—only 170 miles in length, counting all its indentations, from Longwy to Belfort—had been so effectively blocked by systems of fortification, centring in Diedenhofen (Thionville), Metz, Strassburg, and Neu-Breisach on the one side, Verdun, Toul, Epinal, and Belfort on the other, that any rapid invasion in either direction was generally considered impossible. It was, indeed, the prospect of over-pressure of millions of men in the gaps between these great fortresses that German military writers cited as justifying their assumption of a violation of Belgian, and perhaps also of Dutch and Swiss, neutrality.

If these neutral States were barred, the defensive position of the German Empire on the west was very strong—the Italian Alliance apart—the possibility of any serious attack being limited to the gaps between the fortresses on the north of the Vosges (B, C) and the gap of Belfort leading into the plain of southern Alsace (D). We have seen that the German Imperial Government was in no merely defensive mood, but had immediately struck out through neutral Luxemburg and the Liège gap. What was France doing, meanwhile?

She was playing the game on orthodox lines, all warnings notwithstanding. The mobilization progressing smoothly, the chief armies were hurried to the eastern frontier. A minor force was sent north to guard the gates of the Sambre and Meuse and, generally, the line from Maubeuge to Longwy. The western half of the northern frontier was left practically uncovered. An offensive was at once taken from Belfort into southern Alsace, supported by an advance along the crests of the Vosges, under the direction of General Dubail. Evidently, the plain round Mulhouse was only lightly held. Perhaps this French advance was deliberately permitted; certainly it absorbed in Paris and the country at large a great deal of attention which should have been directed elsewhere.

On Friday, August 7, a French brigade, with cavalry and artillery, occupied the town of Altkirch, and on the following morning advanced along the railway across the low country, and, after another stiff

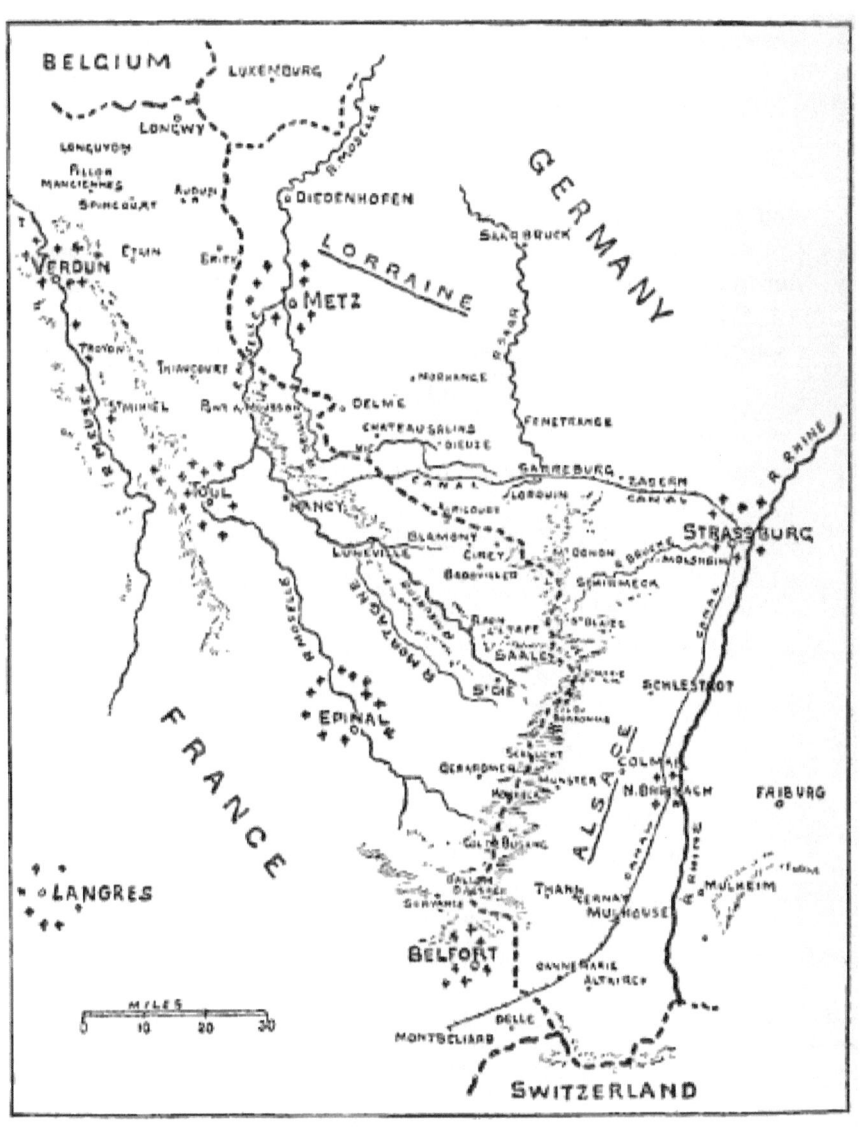

Lorraine and Alsace

fight with the retiring German troops, entered Mulhouse at 5 p.m. This was, politically speaking, a great event. At last, after forty-four years, French soldiers again trod the bank of the "German" Rhine. Much was made of the victorious march of twenty-five miles into Alsace; and General Joffre issued a proclamation in which he said that the magic names of Right and Liberty were inscribed upon the flags of his soldiers, "the first labourers in the great work of *la revanche*."

Correspondingly acute was the disappointment of the following retreat. On August 9, the Austrian Government was reported to be sending troops through southern Germany to Alsace; and it was only then that the French Government broke off relations with the Dual Monarchy. On the same day, Mulhouse was retaken by the German 14th Army Corps and a portion of the 15th, the direct attack being supported by a flank movement against Cernay (Sennheim). The sequel is thus described in a French official statement:

> Our troops were enthusiastically received in Mulhouse by the Alsatians. Some hours were spent in joyous excitement, and for a moment, perhaps too readily, the men forgot that they were in the enemy's country. Beside the Alsatians feting our arrival, there were a number of German immigrants who immediately informed the retreating Germans of our exact position and strength. Mulhouse, difficult to defend against an attack from the north and east, was comparatively easy to recover if vigorously attacked. That is what the Germans did during the night, advancing on the one side from the Forest of Hard and on the other from the direction of Neu-Breisach and Colmar, and marching toward Cernay in order to cut our retreat. If we had remained at Mulhouse with insufficient forces, we would have been in danger of losing our line of retreat toward the Upper Vosges and Belfort. Orders were, therefore, given to retire. Another plan might, indeed, have been conceived and carried out.
>
> The troops we had left at Altkirch had not been attacked. It would thus have been possible to counter-attack the enemy marching on Cernay by utilising our reserves. This plan was not. carried out. Our left was attacked near Cernay by greatly superior forces; our centre was attacked at Mulhouse; and our right was inactive. The battle was badly begun, and the wisest solution was, therefore, to retreat. In order to carry out our

initial plan, it was necessary to recommence the operations on a new basis, and under a new commander. The command was given to General Pau.

When the new start was made in the plain, the chief crests and passes of the Vosges had been captured after hard fighting, and were firmly held. The retirement five miles from the frontier on the eve of the war here involved a peculiarly hard penalty upon the mountain troops. The pass known as the Ballon d'Alsace (Welsche Belchen—4,085 feet), a famous view-point overlooking Thann, was the first to be secured. It is very steep on the Alsatian side, but less so on the French, where, moreover, the summit was commanded by the fort of Servance. From here, the Col du Busang was easily taken. Next, the Schlucht, the picturesque pass between Gerardmer and Münster, and the Hohneck (4,465 feet) were gained, under like advantageous conditions. More to the north, the central Vosges offered much greater difficulties, the French sides being the steeper, so that it was difficult to bring up artillery; while the Germans had been able to strengthen their positions on the narrow, thickly wooded summits by cutting down trees, putting up wire entanglements, and digging trenches.

The Col du Bonhomme (3,120 feet) and the lower Col Ste. Marie, captured after a five-days' struggle before the middle of August, gave protection to the French right in its progress toward Saales, at the head of the valley leading to Schlestadt; but the direct way to Colmar was blocked by German field-works and by heavy artillery on the lower slopes. A further northward advance was, therefore, made along the mountain crests, and artillery was brought down from the head of the Bruche Valley upon the German flank. This operation, in which material losses were sustained, opened the way for the occupation of Mount Donon (3,300 feet), the most northerly of the Vosges summits, on August 14. This quasi-Alpine campaign had been skilfully directed, and met with a deserved success. The numbers of men engaged were not large, varying at first from a battalion of *chasseurs* to a regiment of infantry, and being gradually increased. The most considerable French loss officially named was 600 killed and wounded in the Bonhomme and Ste. Marie passes. Apart from cannon and material, the German losses were believed to be much larger.

The little manufacturing town of Thann had now been reoccupied; and at St. Blaise, a village near Ste. Marie-aux-Mines, in a sharp combat, General von Deimling, commanding the 15th German Army

Corps, was wounded, and the French took their first standard, to the great joy of Paris sightseers a few days later. On August 18, General Joffre issued from eastern headquarters the first dispatch bearing his own signature. It reported steady advance along the Alsatian valleys, and declared that "the enemy retreated in disorder, everywhere abandoning his wounded and material." General Pau had received strong re-enforcements with a view to a "decisive "action. Advancing simultaneously from Belfort and the Vosges, but on a narrower front than previously, with their right supported on the Rhone-Rhine Canal, they had stormed Thanu and Dannemarie, and, bringing the left round toward Colmar, while the centre attacked Mulhouse, threatened the German forces with a serious breach of their communications. After severe street fighting, in which twenty-four guns were taken, Mulhouse was again in French possession on August 20.

The whole of the ground thus gained was abandoned a few days later. This was a grave blow to French pride, and brought a severe punishment upon the Francophile Alsatians. Naturally, the whole southern campaign aroused severe criticism. Several high officers were retired for mistakes in the first advance, which was afterwards officially described as "a mere reconnoissance." If any less eminent soldiers than General Joffre and General Pau had been responsible, there might have been more trouble. But Joffre "the taciturn," the cool-headed engineer whose powers had been tested in many a colonial field, and confirmed in long labours of fortification and organization, and the veteran Pau, who had been second in consideration for the post of *generalissimo*, could not be regarded as reckless adventurers, aiming at a political advantage which they could not hold. The civilian observer presently came to see that, with the evident political advantages of an advance into Alsace-Lorraine—the centre of French hopes and of Prussian oppression—certain important military considerations were joined.

The first raid to Mulhouse was, in fact, a somewhat clumsily handled voyage of discovery, which revealed not only that Upper Alsace was lightly garrisoned, but (this too late) that the only way of profiting by such a situation lies in a rapid, strong offensive, since, with a good railway system behind him, the enemy can bring up large re-enforcements in a few days. General Pau's more substantial expedition was sound, and, in itself, completely successful. It had to be withdrawn because it was not supported by success further north. It did serve, however, for a moment, to detach some German forces from a part of the field where they were more dangerous; carried further, it might have released the troops kept in the Vosges, and have provided a base for an invasion of South Germany. As it was, German Alsace had to be sacrificed to save French Lorraine, and more even than that. We had before us the first great demonstration that, in modern warfare, there are no more independent, free-moving armies, and that every part of a battle-line hundreds of miles long is vitally dependent upon every other part.

3. The Advance in Lorraine

We have seen (a) that the superior numbers available for the German aggression had been further strengthened by a gain of several days in the work of mobilisation; and, as this advantage of time and numbers was not displayed in the southern field, it would evidently be doubly felt elsewhere. (6) The short eastern frontier between the natural obstacles of the Ardennes and the Vosges is covered by extensive systems of fortification, in which the few narrow breaks seem to have been deliberately left to tempt the enemy. From the corner at Longwy, where the territories of France, Belgium, Luxemburg, and Germany meet, to the Col de Saales is a distance of only about 120 miles. In 1870, when the east frontier was thirty miles longer, the strategical deployment of only sixteen German army corps was found to be a matter of difficulty.

Railways and the petrol road-car and wagon have made a great difference in the power of mass movement; but it is at least highly probable that, had the war been limited to this front, the superior German numbers and their great new siege guns (a carefully guarded secret until the campaign was well advanced) would have availed little, and a deadlock would soon have been reached, (c) Reference to the diagram on page 245 will show four gaps indicated by arrows, between the obstructing mountain systems and the groups of fortifications, through which attempts at invasion might be expected. The northernmost and southernmost of these represent the directions of the chief German and French offensives, through Liège and Belfort, respectively, with which we have dealt. We must now follow the course of the movements marked by the arrows B and C, through the north and central parts of the French eastern border.

The first alignment of the opposed armies—apart from the three first German armies and General von Emmich's Army of the Meuse, operating through Belgium, and the 5th French Army, covering the north-eastern frontier from Maubeuge to Mézières—is shown in the accompanying plan:—

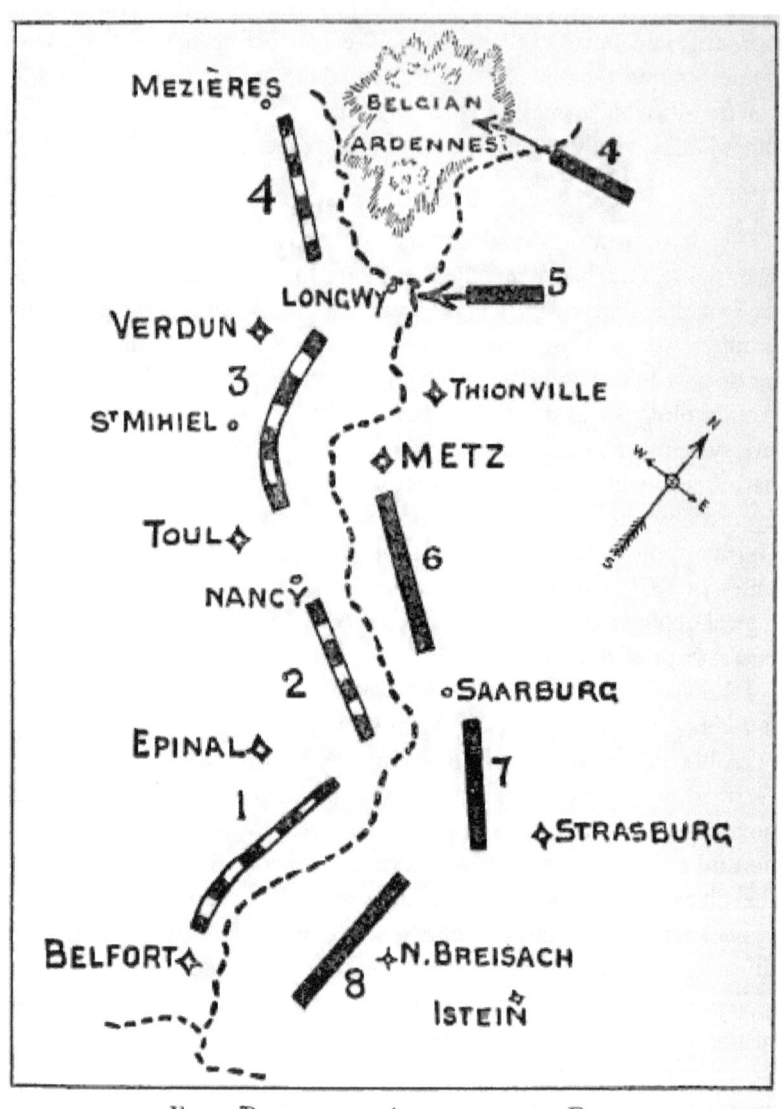

FIRST POSITION OF ARMIES ON THE EAST

FRENCH
1st (General Dubail).
2nd (General de Castelnau).
3rd (General Ruffey).
4th (General de Langle de Cary).

GERMAN
8th (General von Deimling).
7th (General von Heeringen).
6th (Crown Prince of Bavaria).
5th (Crown Prince of Prussia).
4th (Duke of Würtemberg).

There are here five German and only four French groups, two of the former being directed, across the Belgian Ardennes and Luxemburg respectively, against the gap behind Longwy, while the Verdun army watches that of Metz, and the Nancy army watches that of Strassburg. The rate of development of events in this part of the field contrasts strongly with the speed of the blow at Liège, for which a special force had been made ready, and of the raid upon Mulhouse. Many *Uhlan* patrols were quickly upon French soil, with melancholy consequences for the villagers; and the French cavalry occupied Vic, just over the frontier northeast of Nancy, on August 7. It was not till the 12th that the German offensive became marked along the road from Luxemburg to Verdun, at Longuyon and Spincourt, and the French on the roads from Nancy to Saarburg. Longwy, although without serious modern fortification, and having but a small garrison, refused to surrender on August 3, and, after being invested and losing half its effectives by repeated bombardments, capitulated only on the 27th.

The gallant governor, Lieutenant-Colonel Darche, was named officer of the Legion of Honour for this heroic defence. The feat indicates, however, that the German effort in this direction was of a secondary character; and, in fact, it was checked at Mangiennes and Pillon on August 10-12, with a loss of several guns and a thousand prisoners. On this side, Verdun was not to be more nearly approached. A day's bombardment of the little frontier town of Pont-à-Mousson, during which over a hundred projectiles containing large charges of picrite were thrown in by the Metz artillery, resulted only in four civilians being killed and twelve wounded. Two Verdun aviators. Lieutenant Cesari and Corporal Prudhommeau, accomplished more in an air raid upon Metz, where they succeeded in dropping bombs on the military airship sheds, and reached home after an adventurous voyage.

After repelling attacks, and routing a Bavarian corps established on the hills above Blamont and Cirey, east of Nancy and Lunéville, General de Castelnau's army of five corps and reserve divisions now made a bold entry into the Lorraine lowlands. All the signs seemed favourable. The Minister of War boasted (on August 15) that the expected German attack on Nancy had "scarcely been attempted," that the invasion of Belgium had been "foiled," that the movements of the Allied armies had been "perfectly coordinated," and that their supremacy at sea had secured the free passage of the Algerian troops and future foreign supplies. The British Expeditionary Force was known to have crossed the Channel. Mulhouse was lost, but the Vosges passes were won. The *generalissimo* was sure as to the next move; the soldiers had already gained confidence in themselves, their bayonets, and their field-guns, especially their "75's."

It was with a somewhat tart note that M. Doumergue thanked President Wilson for a "new evidence of his interest in the destinies of France" in the shape of a proposal of mediation made on August 6. On Sunday, the 16th, the French troops had a firm hold on Avricourt, the frontier station on the main line from Paris to Strassburg; and at the same time an advance of Dubail's army, by the Bruche Valley, reached Schirmeck and Muhlbach on the Saales-Strassburg railway, and resulted in a capture of twenty guns and fifteen hundred men. During that weekend, Lorquin, a small industrial centre just south of Saarburg, in undulating country where lumbering and sawmills provide the chief normal occupations, was taken, as were Château-Salins (Salzburg), the pondy region west of Fenetrange, and several villages on the Marne-Rhine Canal, on the low borderland of Alsace and Lorraine. Fenetrange, a quaint little place with a ruined *château* and the remains of an ancient church, buried among fruit and walnut trees, was important as threatening the railway communications of Saarburg.

Nearby, in the Saar Valley, are the ruins of the medieval castle of Geroldseck, a gloomy reminder of the Thirty Years' War and the eternal madness of armed feuds. Saarburg was menaced from the north, south, and west. A sleepy town, but an important railway junction, the authorities of the Reichsland kept here a considerable garrison, and the neighbouring hills were defaced with huge barracks. To the south of the town, a strong artillery position had been established. This was taken by assault; and, on August 18, the French entered Saarburg, thus effectually breaking the main railway communications between Metz and Strassburg. Zabern, where Lieutenant von Forstner had so recently executed Prussian military vengeance upon a lame cobbler, which Herr von Jagow had described as "almost an enemy's country," where the Prussian Minister of War had feared "to see life for a German become less safe than life in the Congo"—Zabern, the very name of which cried aloud of the uniformed bully, was only a day's march further east, and Strassburg itself only as much more.

Hope flashed over France like a sudden conflagration. Count Albert de Mun published in Paris the narrative of a refugee priest who declared that Metz was hungry and terror-stricken. It was the anniversary of the Battle of St. Privat; and the old aristocrat and soldier, clerical deputy and philanthropist, presented himself without shame

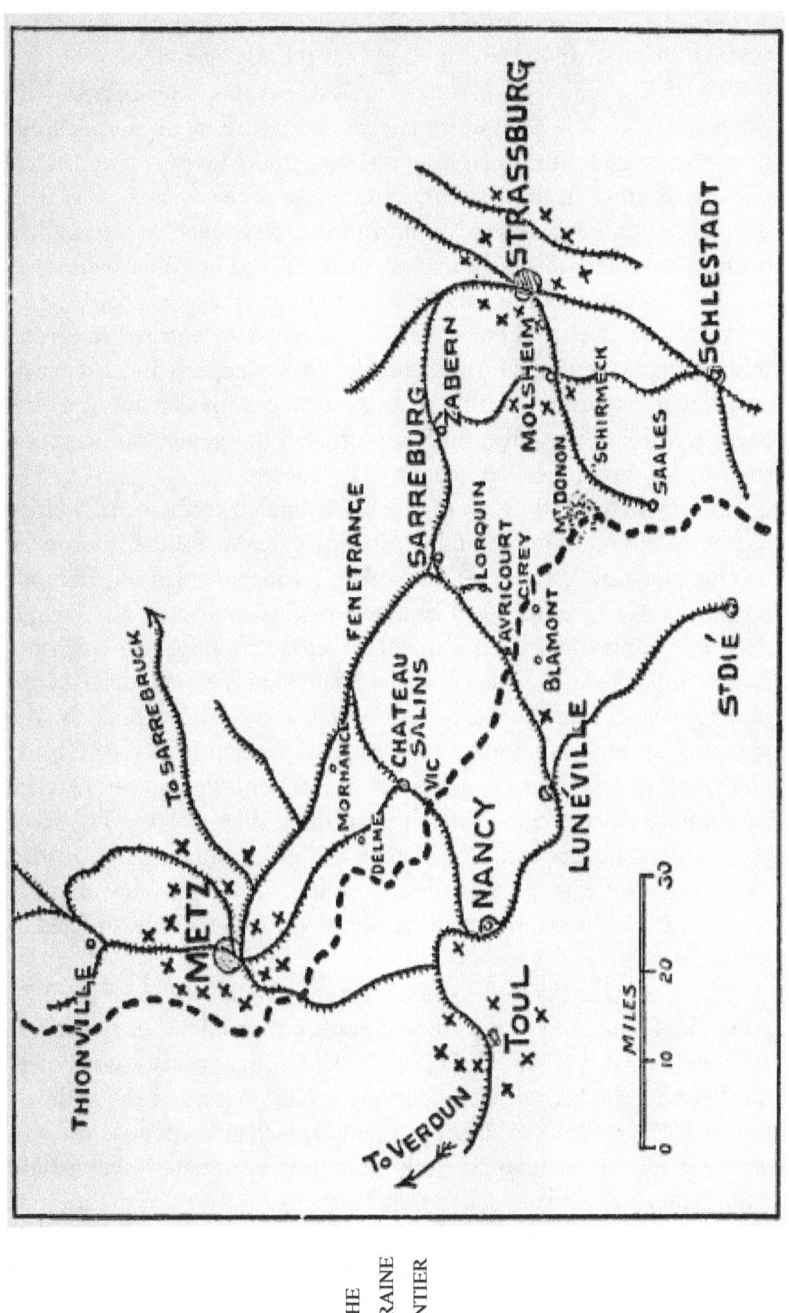

The
Lorraine
Frontier

as standing in the courtyard of the War Office beneath a captured German banner, and thanking God that the day of the long-awaited revenge had come. Gravelotte, St. Privat, Sedan—interspersed with the war news of the day, these anniversaries were a by no means insignificant factor in the consciousness of the opposed armies and nations. General Bonnal, in the *Gaulois*, quoted a prisoner as saying: "It is an officers', not a people's war," and from this concluded that there had been "a complete reversal of roles" since 1870. The Abbé Wetterlé, a notable Alsatian member of the Reichstag, reached Paris on August 19, by way of Basel and Pontarlier, having narrowly escaped arrest and trial for high treason. M. Blumenthal, another deputy, and ex-mayor of Colmar, had also had an exciting journey from that town to the Swiss frontier. Their adventures accentuated the general anticipation that the lost provinces were about to be liberated.

The French positions were quickly extended to the northwest of Saarburg, through Dieuze and Morhange—just such little infernos as had been described some years before in a widely read book, Lieutenant Bilse's *Aus Einer Kleinen Garnison*—to Château-Salins and Delme, decayed country towns on a strategic railway running to Metz, only twenty miles away. Whether they had deliberately tempted Castelnau into this dangerous salient, or had retired only to give time for the bringing up of heavy re-enforcements, the Crown Prince of Bavaria and General von Heeringen were now able, with the aid of the Metz garrison, to fall upon the French from three sides at once. The blow was sudden and decisive. The French 15th Corps, taken by surprise, gave way—some, at least, of these Southern troops tied, but they afterwards bravely retrieved their character—and the whole line had to be withdrawn.

The Germans claimed to have captured 10,000 prisoners and 50 guns. The French questioned these figures, but could not deny a severe reverse. This was on August 20, while the German cavalry was entering Brussels, the French were recovering Mulhouse, and the authorities in Paris were congratulating themselves that, except a corner of land at Audun-le-Roman, the frontier station between Longuyon and Thionville, every part of the national territory was free of the invader. The retreat from Lorraine was arrested for a moment on the line of the Seille and the Marne-Rhine Canal.

On August 22, it had reached the Moselle and the advanced works of Nancy on the left, Badonviller and the Donon on the right. On the 23rd, Lunéville was lost; the French retired to, and at some points

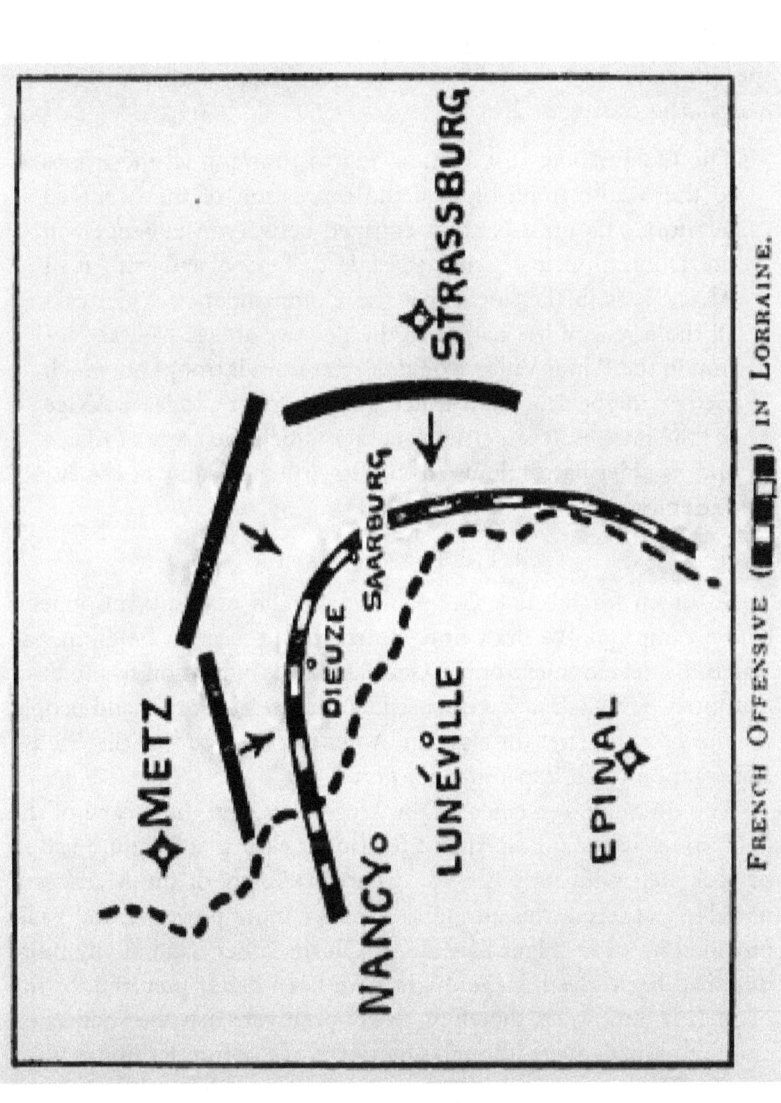

beyond, the Meurthe, the centre of the defence being the ring of hills known as the Grand Crown of Nancy; and the Donon and the Col de Saales were abandoned. On the 25th, Mulhouse was evacuated, and all but the southern passes of the Vosges were abandoned. There was now something more important than Alsace for General Pan to look after. The danger in the north was unmistakable. The change of objective was announced in the following not very happy terms in the Paris *communiqué* of August 26:

> The Commander-in-Chief, having to summon all the troops to the Meuse front, ordered the evacuation of the occupied territory. The great battle is engaged between Maubeuge and the Donon; on it depends the fate of France, and with it of Alsace. It is in the north that the Commander-in-Chief calls all the forces of the nation to the decisive attack. Military action in the Rhine Valley would distract from it troops on which victory might depend. It is necessary, therefore, to leave Alsace for the present. It is a cruel necessity which the army of Alsace and its chief have submitted to with pain, and only at the last extremity.

4. The Fall of Namur

So much for the first German and French offensive movements of the campaign. We must now return to the front in Belgium, and watch the development of the German attack in relation to the three quantities by which it was opposed: (a) the Belgian army and people, (b) the French army, through the Ardennes westward to the Meuse, and (c) the British Expeditionary Force.

The obstinate resistance of the Liège forts, and the escape of the field troops westward on August 6, made it clear that Belgium had to be reckoned with seriously. Von Emmich's Army of the Meuse was not able to prevent this escape, as a slower, more powerful, and well-provided invasion might have done. On the other hand, if any more time had been given, Liège might have been better prepared for the siege. It is impossible, therefore, to say positively that the sudden assault by an inadequate (though superior) force of frontier troops was a mistake. But it was a very expensive way of ascertaining that there are still Davids, as there are Goliaths, among the nations. In the ensuing pause, a screen of cavalry scouts was thrown out far and wide over the country; and, behind this screen, the concentration for the real invasion was hurried forward. Did the Allied Staffs realise the extent of

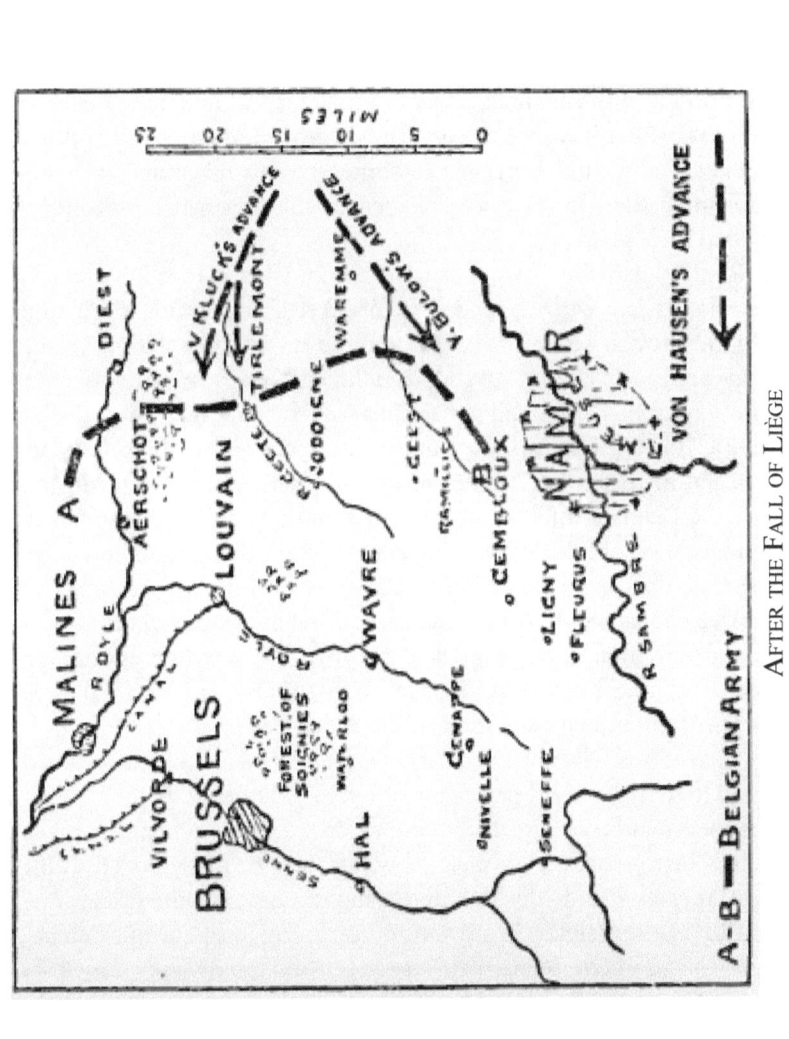

After the Fall of Liège

this concentration?

On August 12, the newly established British Press Bureau issued a statement to the effect that, "of the twenty-six German Army Corps, the bulk have now been definitely located, and it is evident that the mass of the German troops lie between Liège and Luxemburg. The number known to be on the western side proves that, in the eastern (Russian) theatre of war, the frontier, as far as Germany is concerned, is comparatively lightly guarded, unless by reserve troops." Beyond this, nothing was vouchsafed to the public; it was generally believed that the invaders were discouraged, if not broken, and petty skirmishes between *Uhlans* and Belgian detachments were magnified into triumphant battles. In an uncanny secrecy, the German commanders ripened their plans.

The Belgian Field Army was in being, with its headquarters in Louvain, its left wing extended before Aerschot towards Diest, and its right through Tirlemont and Waremme towards Gembloux, where a junction with French cavalry detachments was presently effected. Throughout this line, small test actions were being fought on and after August 10—a guerrilla campaign, of intimidation on the one hand, of delay on the other. At the village of Haelen, near Diest, on the 10th, the Belgians inflicted upon a division of cavalry and an infantry regiment a complete defeat. King Albert might then, honorably, have withdrawn his army into the fortified zone of Antwerp. It is possible that this course would have saved central Belgium from some slaughter and devastation. By removing an obstruction strong enough to check anything but a considerable German advance, it would have worsened the military situation of the Allies.

If, as is possible, but not probable, the German commanders had intended to strike their main blow down the Meuse Valley, the Belgian resistance may have diverted them westward. It is very much more likely that the western campaign which was to prove so costly to the Allies was already decided upon, and, in that case, the gallant opposition of the Belgian Army was in every way justified. To its chiefs, all, at the moment, seemed to rest in a very simple, very unselfish, calculation: how to delay the invader until French and British help arrived. To withdraw seemed to be to abandon not only their country, but their friends and legal guardians. The question was discussed. The young soldier-king would not take the path of evasion; his ministers could not say him nay. It was hoped that the French in numbers, perhaps some British also, would arrive before the main German force was ready.

For four days, the Belgians—at Eghezée, Landen, Waremme, and Diest—beat off all attacks. Then a severe pressure upon their left wing became apparent, the advance proceeding from Hasselt to Haelen and on toward Louvain; while another threatening movement was made from the Hesbaye district, south of Tirlemont, directly toward the capital. These armies evidently could not be for long frontally resisted; and, while the more northerly put the Belgian line of retreat to Antwerp in danger, the other struck at the line of connection with the French before it could be effectively strengthened from the south. Only one decision was possible, for, if the Belgian army could be kept in being in the north-west, it might yet hope to play an influential part in events. So the French columns turned back southward, and the country between Wavre and Brussels was evacuated, the Civil Guards being disarmed, and the villagers left to flee, or to bear as best they might the flood of gray-coated Teutons. First came groups of *Uhlan* patrols, with armoured automobiles and cars full of infantry scouts; then the main columns of all arms—a host such as had never been counted upon, developing an hourly increasing speed and power.

Brussels, whether in the original plan of campaign or not, was now the immediate objective. The property of the Belgian National Bank, and the State papers, had already been sent to Antwerp; on Monday, the 17th, it was known that the queen and the ministers were following. On the 18th, the lines of Waremme, Tirlemont, Louvain, and Aerschot were evacuated, a rear-guard action at the latter place—in which one heroic detachment of 288 men had only seven survivors—being the prelude to a peculiarly atrocious massacre of civilians by the German troops. The road to the capital was thus thrown open; it was, however, still for a moment thought that nothing more than a cavalry raid on Brussels was intended, which the Civil Guard of the city, entrenched across the eastern approaches, would be able to parry. The woods at Soignes and the Tervueren district were, therefore, prepared for a defensive effort; but on the evening of the 19th—from scruples as to submitting an imperfectly armed police force to such a test, as well as from better knowledge of the strength of the invading army—the Guards were withdrawn and sent to Ghent and Ostend, whither a large part of the civil population was already in flight.

While King Albert and the other national leaders accompanied the army under the guns of their one remaining fortress. Burgomaster Max set himself, with rare sagacity, prudence, and courage, to bargain with General Sixtus von Arnim, commander of the German 6th Army Corps, by whom the city was occupied on August 20. They were to have passage through it; but requisitions were to be paid for in cash, public and private property was to be respected, and the Municipal Council was to carry on its work. If any injury were done to the troops, "the severest measures" would be taken; otherwise General von Arnim guaranteed "the preservation of the city and the safety of its inhabitants." The streets where, less than three weeks before, I had watched the Belgian soldiers gathering for mobilisation, were now deserted and silent, a parade march of 40,000 men through the city failing to produce the expected impression. As at Liège, the conquerors established themselves without the gross excesses that had marked their passage through the villages and smaller towns. Instead, they imposed enormous tines—£8,000,000 in the case of Brussels, £2,000,000 in that of Liège—which can only be regarded as ransom in lieu of pillage or arbitrary punishment. Great Britain and France at once advanced to the Belgian Government the sum of £10,000,000 sterling as a loan without interest.

While a part of the German First Army, that of General von Kluck, was thus projecting the right or western wing of the invasion, the Second, under Von Bülow, was crossing the Meuse bridges at Huy, and making for Namur; and the Third and Fourth, under Von Hansen and the Duke of Würtemberg, were penetrating through the difficult Ardennes country, the former toward Dinant and Givet, the latter through Bastogne toward Mézières. The most northerly of the French armies at the beginning of the war, that of General de Langle de Cary, posted across the Ardennes-Luxemburg border, and that of General Lanrezac, from Maubeuge to the Meuse above Givet, had not waited for the enemy, but attempted an offensive which was even less happy than that of their fellows in Lorraine. It was too much dispersed, and, on the most important line, that of the Meuse to Namur, showed neither speed nor strength enough. De Langle's advance from between Mézières and Montmedy through the southern Ardennes, which might have threatened the German communications had it got further, was stopped between Neufchâteau and Paliseul, the French retiring to the south and west.

Lanrezac was at first more fortunate; but his success at Dinant on August 15 left no lasting result. After the check at Liège, the German Staff had decided to bring new forces to the north; and a fresh army consisting of two Saxon corps originally part of the Duke of Würtemberg's army, with the 11th Reserve Corps, and part of the Guard's cavalry, under General von Hansen, was directed to strike across the central Ardennes, and so get behind Namur and catch any French or Belgian body on the Sambre in flank.

The great cross-roads of Namur were then still blocked to the Germans, who were thus forced into various sideways. One of these was the railway from Liège and Huy to Ciney, whence Dinant could be reached either by road, or by railway through Rochefort. Dinant was important as holding one of the direct ways by which the French might relieve Namur, and as having a line of its own, striking west to Charleroi. Hither, then, came at daybreak on August 15 a German force consisting of a division of the Guard, another cavalry division, several battalions of infantry, and some companies of small artillery. A few French infantrymen alone occupied the ancient citadel overlooking the east side of the river; and it was captured during the morning. A struggle for the crossing from the east to the west bank ensued. In the afternoon, two batteries of French artillery and several regiments of infantry arrived. The "75's" quickly dominated the citadel and bridge-head from the neighbouring cliffs; and the assailants were driven back, and dispersed by a cavalry charge. A French captain of infantry, who was wounded in the engagement, afterwards said:

> We were barely two companies strong when we got the order to advance and clear a position for our artillery. Below us, the Germans, who had succeeded in bridging the Meuse, marched confident in their superiority of numbers. A volley caught them, then another, and a third. Within a few seconds, we were close upon them; their machine-guns ploughed through our ranks, but we went on, and, when a second company came to our aid, there was a new hecatomb on the German side. Around me my men held firm, and our comrades, though new to the firing-line, did not hesitate. Their captain, struck by a ball in the chest, could just give his papers to his lieutenant as he fell, uttering the words: 'Take these to my wife and say farewell for me.' Then I remember no more, for a fragment of shell struck me. I learned afterwards that our artillery destroyed the German bridges, and drove many of the enemy into the river.

This success was at once annulled by the failure of Lanrezac's colleagues to the south-east. General Ruffey's left wing had crossed the frontier northward as far as the River Semoy, there to be arrested by the Imperial Crown Prince, advancing from Luxemburg; while the Würtembergers had done as much for De Langle de Cary further west. The two French armies, surprised on several occasions, and outnumbered, retired, and so uncovered Lanrezac's flank. The position in the Dinant Valley became, or was thought to be, untenable—an unfortunate development, for Lanrezac's withdrawal left the troops on the Sambre dangerously exposed, and put an end to any hope of relieving Namur.

During these events, the main body of the French Fifth Army was slowly moving northward between the Sambre and Meuse valleys, and the Belgian Government was strengthening the small garrison of Namur till it at last numbered about 26,000 men. Namur, a much smaller town than Liège, was supposed to be at least as strong a fortress, with its five large and four smaller forts distributed around the confluence of the Meuse and Sambre, and the road and railway bridges which constitute the military importance of this point. The week preceding the battle of Mons-Charleroi is the obscurest part of the whole story of the war; and, in particular, we have little trustworthy information of the events preceding the fall of Namur on August 23. An English journalist, who was in the town on the 13th, describes how the chief streets of the town had been barricaded, and other preparations made for a siege, while German aviators were already soaring above the forts. Areas before these were mined, barbed-wire obstructions set up, and the field of fire was cleared.

Stores of ammunition and food had been accumulated; but the anticipation entertained afar off that the fortress could hold off a German army for several weeks was not shared within; and all eyes looked for the expected army of relief. By the 15th, the railway service had practically ceased, and only one road to the north was open. Next day, the Belgian garrison repulsed a preliminary attack at Wierde, beyond the most easterly fort. Some French troops had been got into the town, including a regiment of "Turcos," whose bayonet charges were already the theme of fearsome story. But when, on the 17th, a German column cut the line of communications with Brussels, and engagements between *Uhlans* and French dragoons or Belgian patrols began to multiply around Gembloux and Sombreffe, the tired troops were in a condition of hardly suppressed panic. The forts were strongly constructed of concrete with armour-plate turrets; but their Gin. guns and 4.7 howitzers were no match for the German 8.4 in, (21 cm.) and 11-in. (28 cm.) siege-pieces—which were able to pour in a continuous torrent of shell from a distance of three to five miles—even if none of the huge Krupp 16.8 in. (42 cm.) siege-pieces were used.

The bombardment, supported by about four army corps, began on the 20th; and, though several forts were not jet reduced, the passage of the Meuse and Sambre was secured by the 23rd. If the surviving defenders had not then fought their way out, there would have been a further heavy loss, without any compensating gain. Whatever explanations of the collapse of the defence may some day be offered, they will probably be found to amount to this: General Michel and his stall could know little of what had happened at Liège, and, in any case, they were even less able than General Leman had been to offer the mobile defence, on an extended line, which, as the world now discovered, could alone save these or any other fortresses against such an attack. On the other hand, the invaders could hardly fail to learn the lesson of Liège. They essayed no feeble preliminaries, but, while the Belgians were waiting for them to come up, prepared behind their cavalry screen an overwhelming blow. They are said to have been favoured by a heavy mist while getting their siege guns into position, just out of range of the much inferior cannon of the forts, and of the entrenched infantry.

The following narrative was given a fortnight later by one of the survivors to Reuter's correspondent at Ostend:

> The Germans at first centred their rain of steel upon our entrenchments. For ten hours our men stood this without being able to fire a shot in return. Whole regiments were decimated. The losses among the officers were terrible; and, gradually, the soldiers, unled, became demoralised. With one bound, they at last rose and fled—a general *sauve qui peut*. Meanwhile, many German guns had been turned on the forts, especially on Maizeret and Marchovelette (which covered the eastern approaches on either side of the Meuse). These could offer but a feeble resistance; and, in fact, Maizeret only fired about ten shots, while it received more than 1,200 shells, fired at the rate of twenty a minute.
>
> At Marchovelette, seventy-five men were killed in the batteries, and both forts soon surrendered. The other works were still holding out when the army left the town. Fort Saurlée resisted from the morning of the 23rd to 5 p.m. on the 25th. The eventuality of a retirement had not been provided for, and great

confusion ensued. Soldiers declare that officers cried out: 'Get out as best you can. The thing is to get to Antwerp.' No provision had been made for the destruction of the immense stores; and all these, with the fortress artillery, and most of the field artillery, the horses being killed, fell into the enemy's hands. At the Cadets' School alone, there was a store of 3,000,000 daily rations. The ambulance corps lost 150 of its 600 men. Our line of retreat was on St. Gerard (south-west, between the Meuse and Charleroi), where we hoped to meet the French brigade which was in retreat from Dinant. They had fallen back by way of Morville, and could only send us two regiments, which bravely fought their way through, and joined us not far from Namur much reduced in numbers.

Our generals had believed that the blowing up of the bridge at Jambes (southern suburb of Namur) would cover our retreat; but the Germans cut it at Bois-les-Villers, and we got through only with heavy losses. Our retreat continued by way of Hirson, Laon, and Amiens, to Rouen; and we were taken from Havre back to our own shores. Of 26,000 men constituting the garrison of Namur and troops sent to occupy the intervals between the forts, those who have returned to Belgian soil number only 12,000.

5. England's Part

The preliminary stage of the land campaign was thus being completed before any British soldiers had come into action—a fact which could not but weigh heavily upon thousands of uninstructed minds, especially among the suffering Belgians. The governments concerned, and studious observers everywhere, knew, however, that England's threefold contribution to the war, while it could not be immediately decisive, would presently become as important as those of the more immediate parties, France and Russia, and all the more important because of its quite different and supplementary character. For England, and England only among the Allies, was in a position to disarm the powerful German fleet, and to deprive its owners of the innumerable military and economic advantages that arise from free sea communications. In a series of relatively small, though positively impressive, engagements in near and distant waters, this supremacy was established before the end of the year, so that only small occasional raids were then to be feared. Meanwhile—the Atlantic and North Sea dominated by British, the Mediterranean by French, ships—the transport of troops, of wounded and prisoners, of supplies and munitions, proceeded uninterruptedly; the colonies and possessions of France and Great Britain were preserved in peace and security, while those of the enemy were seized or threatened; above all, the power of economic resistance of the Allies was maintained at the maximum by the continuance of their foreign trade.

To this *rôle*, England brought, beside her naval power, her strength and weakness as the chief creditor nation of the world, and the first industrial nation in the old hemisphere. Russia, with her vast bulk and population and her primitive rural economy, could hope to stave off any vital injury. Not so the western States. Belgium had the choice of ceasing to exist except as a Prussian province, or becoming dependent upon her treaty guardians, for food and shelter immediately, for re-establishment later. France did what she could amid the ruin of several of her own departments; the people and Government of Holland took hundreds of thousands of refugees into their homes, and cared for them with a generosity that can never be too warmly recognized; the United States sent help both in money and kind. England, while bearing a principal share in this effort, had to constitute herself, to a large extent, the banker and manufacturer of the Alliance. Not only had warships to be made and repaired, cannon and shell, small-arms and ammunition, clothing and food, land and sea transport to be provided in hitherto undreamed-of quantities, without unnecessary disturbance of the normal trade and industry by which the nation lives: the credit necessary to trade had to be maintained; the resources of the State had to be enormously expanded.

The first shock due to general insecurity and the arrest of foreign remittances to British creditors was met by the closing of the London Stock Exchange, on July 31, the extension of the August Bank Holiday by three days, and a simple moratorium postponing pre-war obligations for one month. The State, through the Bank of England, then undertook to provide assistance for the fulfilment of these obligations; and, early in September, it offered like aid in the meeting of post-war obligations. The moratorium, several times extended, did not apply to wages and salaries, rates and taxes, sea freights, or small debts, and it expired in November; but much of its effect was continued by the Courts (Emergency Powers) Act, which gave the law courts power to stay actions for the recovery of debt when the debtor's embarrassment was due directly or indirectly to the war.

By the end of September, Treasury notes of one pound and ten shillings had been issued, largely through the joint stock banks, to the extent of over £28,000,000, a material supplement to the Bank of England's note issues; and, after falling to the lowest point for twenty-five years, the Bank reserve rose steadily through August and September. On August 6, a government credit for £100,000,000 was voted; and, three weeks later, the War Loan Bill enabled the Treasury to borrow whatever money became necessary for the supply services of the following year. The money was easily raised, for the most part by issues of six-months Treasury bills. Repeated visits of the Chancellor of the Exchequer to Paris and of French Ministers to London marked the development of financial, as well as of military and naval, co-operation among the Allies.

In the economic and naval spheres, then, England was able at once to do more than her share. Her only possible military effort at the outset—the dispatch of an expeditionary force of 150,000 men, comprising three eighths of the existing regular army and reserves—was a mere preliminary to the raising of new armies which were to number, counting the votes of August 6, September 10, and November 16, 2,000,000 of men more. The importance of this beginning proved, however, to be far beyond the numerical promise. It represented the best of the voluntary long-service system; and its proof in one of the hardest ordeals recorded in military history constituted, together with the success of the subsequent recruiting, an unanswerable justification of that system. There was a story of a German army order issued by the emperor on August 19 directing that a special effort should be made to "exterminate the treacherous English and walk over General French's contemptible little army." The story was generally credited at the time, for there then seemed to be no bounds to German anger over England's intervention.

It was somewhat tardily denied, and it may have had no foundation; it is certain that this little army excited feelings quite other than contempt among its foes, even when they were driving it before them in the long retreat. It was a title of pride, not shame, to the British peoples that this little army, all that could be spared, until the Indian contingent arrived, from the police duties of a far-stretched realm, could be so spared because, among the hundreds of millions of subjects of that realm, there was not one alien race which wished to weaken the central power in its day of trial. Presently, there came Indians with princely chiefs, Canadians from the prairie, and Australians from the bush. Canada sent a division of all arms and a gift of 100,000,000 pounds of flour. Australia offered her little navy, 20,000 infantry, 6,000 light horse, and a quantity of foodstuffs.

Botha, the ablest of the erstwhile Boer generals, now head of a United South Africa, undertook the suppression of a trivial revolt and the invasion of German South-West Africa, with local levies. India, whose disloyalty German agents had confidently promised, sent at once two infantry divisions and a cavalry brigade, and later, three more cavalry brigades, with various contingents offered from the great native States. The *Maharajas* of Mysore, Gwalior, Bhopal, and other chiefs presented large sums of money toward the cost of the Expeditionary Force; and a dozen or more of them accompanied the Indian contingent to Europe at the head of their men. Though all the majesty of a family of nations can never be exhibited on the battlefield, the world saw in this symbol something of the strength of the invisible bonds woven in years of broadening liberty, and the will that liberty breeds to give up all, if need be, to arrest a great wrong.

The Expeditionary Force, planned during the previous decade, was to consist of five divisions, each of three infantry brigades, one regiment of cavalry, and seventy-six guns, with engineers and other services. There were also five brigades of cavalry, with two horse-artillery brigades attached. Lord Kitchener had, on August 5, accepted the Secretaryship for War for the period of the campaign, recognizing that the organisation of future resources at home was more important than present leadership in the field. Field-Marshal Sir John French thus became the obvious Commander-in-Chief. The 1st Army Corps (1st and 2nd Divisions) was placed under Lieutenant-General Sir Douglas Haig; the 2nd (3rd and 11th Divisions) under General Sir Horace Smith-Dorrien; and the 4th Division under Major-General Snow; while four cavalry brigades formed a division under Major-General Allenby. Hundreds of trains and scores of steamships having been commandeered, the embarkation began, on August 8.

Ten days after the issue of the mobilisation order, by an admirable co-operation between the railways and the navy, the force was landed at Boulogne and other French ports; and on August 15, Sir John French paid a courtesy visit to Paris. It is characteristic of the unintelligence of the press censorship that, while that visit was freely reported in Paris, our telegrams to Fleet Street about it were all stopped. After a short stay in rest-camps on the coast, the 1st and 2nd Army Corps were moved across the Belgian frontier to the region west and east of

Mons. The whole vast movement had been conducted, so far as the general public in England and France was concerned, in complete secrecy. It was carried through without a single hitch. A rare pen would be needed to sum up the emotions excited by this first landing within living memory of a British Army in western Europe, this armed handclasp of races so different, now united in one vital aim. The good folk of Normandy and the Pas de Calais laughed and cried. "Tommy Atkins," generally, in this first expedition, young and unmarried, always trim, straight, clean, and purposeful, was a strangely impressive visitor. It soon emerged that he carried in his pack a final letter from the grim soldier whom he called "K. of K." Lord Kitchener's benediction ran—

> You are ordered abroad as a soldier of the king to help our French comrades against the invasion of a common enemy. You have to perform a task which will need your courage, your energy, your patience. Remember that the honour of the British Army depends on your individual conduct. . . . Be invariably courteous, considerate, and kind. Never do anything likely to injure or destroy property, and always look upon looting as a disgraceful act. . . . Keep on your guard against any excesses. In this new experience, you may find temptations—in wine and women. You must entirely resist both temptations, and, while treating all women with perfect courtesy, you should avoid any intimacy.

Could the witty Frenchman refrain from a smile over this insular bluntness? But it was a very respectful smile.

Sir John French in his first published dispatch said:—

> The concentration was practically complete on the evening of Friday, the 21st, and I was able to make dispositions to move the Force during Saturday, the 22nd, to positions I considered most favourable from which to commence operations that the French Commander-in-Chief, General Joffre, requested me to undertake in pursuance of his plans in prosecution of the campaign.

CHAPTER 3

The Terror, from Aerschot to Louvain

Guilty in its origin and object, and unscrupulous in its design, the German campaign was, ere many days had passed, more deeply damned in the eyes of humane observers all the world over by the appearance of two features which none of the prophets had been cynical or pessimistic enough to anticipate, and which added immeasurably to the pains of this vast catastrophe. In Belgium and France, the path of the invading armies had been prepared by the organization of swarms of spies; and perhaps the greatest mischief wrought by their operations, in which courage and treachery were often strangely mingled, lay not in the acts of betrayal, but in the suspicion aroused, often against quite innocent persons. This evil naturally tended to diminish as the war proceeded; but no information has been made public sufficiently comprehensive and exact to justify us in attempting any further account of the matter in these pages.

With regard, secondly, to the systematic terrorism by which the German commanders sought to ease or consolidate their advance through invaded districts, our difficulty lies in the mass, not the lack, of evidence. Several volumes would be required for even a summary account of the acts of devastation and cruelty by which it was sought to break the spirit of the Belgian people; all that can be attempted here is to cite very briefly a few typical instances out of the many which were investigated by a judicial committee appointed by the Belgian Government, and were the subject of successive reports.

When the first incursion was made at Visé, General von Emmich issued a proclamation in which he said:

I give formal guarantees to the Belgian population that it will not have to suffer the horrors of war; that we shall pay in money for the food we must take from the country; that our soldiers will show themselves to be the best friends of a people for whom we entertain the highest esteem, the greatest sympathy.

On the 9th, General von Bülow was already tiring of this benevolent tone, and warning the Walloons that any attempt to oppose his troops would be severely dealt with. On the following day, a body of German cavalry occupying the village of Linsmeau was attacked by some Belgian infantry, who were accompanied by two *gendarmes*. A German officer was killed in the fight, in which, according to the Belgian authorities, no civilians took part. Later, the village was invaded by a strong German force of cavalry and artillery. Two farms and six outlying houses were destroyed by gunfire or burnt; and the male villagers were then examined. No recently discharged firearms were found. Eleven inhabitants were, nevertheless, placed in a ditch and killed, their heads being broken in by blows from rifle-butts. Many retail cruelties were perpetrated in neighbouring villages during this and the following nights.

The Belgian Government claimed to have issued, immediately after the first invasion, public statements which were placarded in every town, village, and hamlet, warning all civilians to abstain scrupulously from hostile acts against the enemy's troops; and such warnings were also spread broadcast by the newspapers. Since the Belgians are evidently not lacking in love for the homes and the country that had been subjected to a burglarious entry, it is only too likely that the prudential order was sometimes disobeyed. In such cases, punishment was invited, and it would not have outraged the world's sense of justice and humanity. The German officers never pretended to hold themselves within such limits.

When, in the middle of August, their cavalry screen began to move out westward, the "effective occupation" which is the first condition, in international law, of the right to emphasise the difference between civilians and regular soldiers was altogether wanting;. What was imposed was not "law" of any kind, but simply wholesale, deliberate terrorism. The Belgian retreat from Aerschot, on August 18, in course of which the German advance guard suffered heavy losses, has been mentioned. On the following day, the town was occupied without resistance. The remaining inhabitants were ordered to leave their houses.

and, as they did so, a number were shot down. On the following; day, M. Thielemans, the *burgomaster*, his son, a lad of fifteen, and eleven prominent citizens were taken outside the town, and shot. The town was then destroyed by fire. In all, 20 prisoners were shot by the Germans after the fighting at Aerschot. The fifth report of the Belgian Commission of Inquiry says:—

> Whole villages have been wiped out. Their inhabitants who have taken refuge in the woods are without shelter, without food. In the ditches along the roads, the dead bodies of peasants, women, and children murdered by the Germans, are left unburied. Many corpses have been thrown into the wells, contaminating the water, wounded, without distinction of age or sex, have been abandoned, without any attempt to relieve their sufferings. A great part of the male population was commandeered throughout this region. Most of them were compelled to dig trenches and to build defensive works against our troops, in defiance of the laws of warfare. Others frequently were forced to walk in front of the German troops during the fighting.

Tamines, a rich and populous village on the Sambre between Charleroi and Namur, was occupied by detachments of French troops on August 17-19. On the 20th, a German patrol appeared before the suburb of Vilaines: and several *Uhlans* were killed by the fire of the French soldiers and a party of Civic Guards from Charleroi. This is the supposed origin of the massacre at Tamines on the following day. The village was occupied by the Germans in force, the French retiring, on the 21st; and the houses were at once sacked and set on fire. Most of the inhabitants were arrested; but a good many were burnt to death or suffocated in the houses, 264 in number, which were fired.

> On the evening of Saturday, August 22, a group of between 400 and 450 men was collected in front of the church, not far from the bank of the Sambre. A German detachment opened fire on them; but, as the shooting was a slow business, the officers ordered up a machine-gun which soon swept off all the unhappy peasants still left standing. Many of them were only wounded, and, hoping to save their lives, got with difficulty on their feet again. They were immediately shot down. Many wounded still lay among the corpses. Groans of pain and cries for help were heard in the bleeding heap. On several occasions, soldiers walked up to such unhappy individuals and stopped

their groans with a bayonet thrust. At night, some who still survived succeeded in crawling away. Others put an end to their own pain by rolling themselves into the neighbouring river. About 100 bodies were found in the river.

Next day, Sunday, another party of villagers was compelled to dig trenches for the burial of the bodies, soldiers with fixed bayonets standing over them. Fathers thus buried their sons, and sons their fathers. The women of the village were compelled to watch. The German officers were drinking champagne. One man was buried while still alive, on the order of a military doctor. A survivor said:—

> When a soldier, seized with an impulse of pity, came near us an officer immediately scolded him away. I saw German soldiers who could not refrain from bursting into tears on seeing the despair of the women.

The total number of victims at Tamines was over 650. The survivors positively asserted that none of the inhabitants fired on the Germans.

The quaint Flemish town of Dinant, on the Meuse, so well known to British and American holiday-makers, suffered a like fate on the following days. After the French victory on the 15th, there was complete quiet, till the evening of the 21st, when the Germans re-entered in force, shot several civilians, and fired a number of houses. Next day was calm: probably most of the troops had gone west or south.

> On Sunday, August 23, at 6.30 a.m., soldiers of the 108th Regiment of Infantry invaded the Church of the Premonstratensian Fathers, drove out the congregation, separated the women from the men, and shot fifty of the latter. Between seven and nine the same morning, the soldiers gave themselves up to pillage and arson, going from house to house and driving the inhabitants into the street. Those who tried to escape were shot. About nine in the morning, the soldiery, driving before them, by blows from the butt ends of rifles, men, women and children, pushed them all into the Parade Square, where they were kept prisoners till 6 o'clock in the evening. The guard took pleasure in repeating to them that they would soon be shot. About 6 o'clock a captain separated the men from the women and children. The women were placed in front of a rank of infantry soldiers, the men were ranged along a wall. The front rank of them were then told to kneel, the others remaining

standing behind them. A platoon of soldiers drew up in face of these unhappy men. It was in vain that the women cried out for mercy for the husbands, sons, and brothers. The officer ordered his men to fire. There had been no inquiry nor any pretence of a trial. About twenty of the inhabitants were only wounded, but fell among the dead. The soldiers, to make sure, fired a new volley into the heap of them. Several citizens escaped this double discharge. They shammed dead for more than two hours, remaining motionless among the corpses, and when night fell succeeded in saving themselves in the hills. Eighty-four corpses were left on the square, and buried in a neighbouring garden.

The day of August 23 was made bloody by several more massacres. Soldiers discovered some inhabitants of the Faubourg St. Pierre in the cellars of a brewery there and shot them. Since the previous evening, a crowd of workmen belonging to the factory of M, Himmer had hidden themselves, along with their wives and children, in the cellars of the building. They had been joined there by many neighbours and several members of the family of their employer. About 6 o'clock in the evening, these unhappy people made up their minds to come out of their refuge, and defiled all trembling from the cellars with the white flag in front. They were immediately seized and violently attacked by the soldiers. Every man was shot on the spot. Almost all the men of the Faubourg de Leffe were executed *en masse*.

In another part of the town twelve civilians were killed in a cellar. In the Rue en Ile a paralytic was shot in his armchair. In the Rue Enfer the soldiers killed a young boy of fourteen. In the Faubourg de Neffe, the viaduct of the railway was the scene of a bloody massacre. An old woman and all her children were killed in their cellar. A man of sixty-five years, his wife, his son, and his daughter were shot against a wall. Other inhabitants of Neffe were taken in a barge as far as the rock of Bayard and shot there, among them a woman of eighty-three and her husband. A certain number of men and women had been locked up in the court of the prison.

At six in the evening, a German machine-gun, placed on the hill above, opened fire on them, and an old woman and three other persons were brought down. While a certain number of soldiers were perpetrating this massacre, others pillaged and sacked the houses of the town, and broke open all safes, sometimes blasting them with dynamite. Their work of destruction and theft accomplished, the soldiers set fire to the houses, and the town was soon no more than an immense furnace.

The women and children had all been shut up in a convent, where they were kept prisoners for four days. These unhappy women remained in ignorance of the lot of their male relations. They were expecting themselves to be shot also. All around, the town continued to blaze. The first day the monks of the convent had given them a certain supply of food. For the remaining days they had nothing to eat but raw carrots and green fruit. To sum up, the town of Dinant is destroyed. It counted 1,400 houses; only 200 remain. The manufactories where the artisan population worked have been systematically destroyed. Rather more than 700 of the inhabitants have been killed; others have been taken off to Germany, and are still retained there as prisoners. The majority are refugees scattered all through Belgium. A few who remained in the town are dying in hunger. It has been proved by our inquiry that German soldiers, while exposed to the fire of the French entrenched on the opposite bank of the Meuse, in certain cases sheltered themselves behind a line of civilians, women and children.

For a lesser massacre, in the village of Andenne, General von Bülow assumed personal responsibility in a proclamation (August 22) containing these sentences:—

The inhabitants of Andenne, after having protested their peaceful intentions, have taken our troops by a treacherous surprise. It is with my consent that the commanding officer has had the whole place burned, and that about a hundred persons have been shot."

The survivors denied that there was any such provocation; and the Belgian authorities stated the number of victims at over 200. On entering Namur, Von Bülow issued a proclamation announcing that citizens who did not at once give up any hidden French or Belgian soldiers would be "condemned to hard labour for life in Germany," while any soldier found would be "immediately shot." In the small town of Wavre, a German soldier was wounded in the street. Lieutenant-General von Nieber at once issued a notice that a fine of 3,000,000 *francs* must be paid promptly, or "the town will be burned and destroyed, without regard for persons, the innocent suffering with the guilty." The town was, in fact, destroyed, and twenty of the chief citizens were taken away as hostages.

The southern districts of Belgian Luxemburg were the scene of many and extreme excesses. Hostages were usually taken, sometimes maltreated, and often removed to Germany. An official report says:—

> In almost every locality plunder was systematically complete. In Arlon, 47 houses had been sacked before the ransom-money, £4,000, could be raised."

The number of houses deliberately burnt in the province was calculated to be over 3,000. Over 1,000 civilians were executed, including about 300 in Ethe, 157 in Tintigny, 106 in Rossignol, and 111 persons of the communes of Ethe and Rossignol publicly shot at Arlon.

> In most of these villages, the troops did not even allege that they had been attacked by the civilian population. It seems certain that the inhabitants did not commit any hostile act. In many places German soldiers had been shot by French patrols and sentinels, but often destruction of the villages cannot be explained even on this pretence. The inhabitants say that the crimes of which they were victims can only be explained by the soldiers being drunk, by their pleasure in inflicting suffering, or by their anger at the unexpected resistance of the Belgian army, or, finally, by their having received orders for systematic destruction from their superiors.

In this domain of evil, it is impossible to measure one kind of crime against another, and range each in its degree. But a peculiar infamy will attach to the memory of the sack and fire of Louvain, one of the oldest of European seats of learning, and not the least of Belgium's treasuries of art and history. the Commission of Inquiry[1] says:—

> The German Army entered Louvain on Wednesday, August 19, after having burnt down the villages through which it had passed. As soon as they had entered the town and requisitioned food and lodging, they went to all the banks, and took possession of the cash in hand. Soldiers burst open the doors of houses which had been abandoned, pillaged them, and committed other excesses. The German authorities took as hostages the mayor, Senator van

---

1. It was thus composed: President, M. Cooreman, Belgian Minister of State; members: Count Goblet d'Alviella, Minister of State, Vice-President of the Senate; M. Ryckmans, Senator; M. Strauss, Sheriff of the city of Antwerp; Van Cutsem, Hon. President of the Court of First Instance, Antwerp; Secretaries: Chevalier Ernst de Brunswyck, secretary to the Minister of Justice, M. Orts, Councillor of Legation.

der Kelen, the Vice-Rector of the Catholic University, the senior priest, and certain magistrates and aldermen.

A number of outrages were perpetrated in the neighbourhood, but the city seems to have remained quiet for a week. On August 24 and 25, the Belgian troops made a sortie from the entrenched camp of Antwerp, attacked the German Army which was masking it before Malines, and drove it back toward Louvain and Vilvorde. This rout is the only discoverable cause of what followed. At nightfall on the 20th, the retreating German soldiers entered Louvain; and the German garrison appears to have mistaken some of them for Belgians, in the prevailing panic, and to have tired upon them. In order to explain away the mistake, it was then pretended that civilians had fired on the troops—

> A suggestion which is contradicted by all the witnesses, and could scarcely have been possible, because the inhabitants had had to give up their arms to the municipal authorities several days before.

The bombardment and fire followed, a large part of the city, including the ancient Cathedral of St. Pierre, the University buildings, together with the University Library, its priceless manuscripts and book collections, and the Municipal Theatre, being destroyed.

> On the orders of their officers, the German soldiers broke into the houses, and set fire to them with the help of fuses. They shot at the inhabitants who tried to escape from their houses. Many people who sought refuge in their cellars were burnt alive. Others were shot as they tried to escape from the burning houses. A great number of inhabitants who had succeeded in getting out of their houses through their back gardens were led to the Place de la Station, where they saw about ten dead civilians lying about. They were then brutally separated from their wives and children, and stripped of all they had succeeded in carrying away. The women and children remained without food on the Place de la Station during the whole day (August 26). They witnessed the execution of about twenty of their fellow-citizens, among whom were several priests, who, bound together in groups of four, were shot at one end of the square, on the footpath in front of the house of Mr. Hamaide.
> On Thursday, the 27th, at 8 o'clock, order was given to all the inhabitants to leave Louvain; the town was to be bombarded.

Old men, women, children, sick people, lunatics from the asylums, priests, nuns, were driven like cattle about the roads. They were driven in different directions by brutal soldiers, forced to kneel and to lift their arms each time they met German soldiers and officers; they were left without food during the day, without shelter during the night. Many died on the way. Others, among whom were women, children, and priests, who were unable to follow, were shot dead. More than 10,000 of them were driven as far as Tirlemont, fifteen miles from Louvain. Their sufferings are beyond description. The next day, many others were driven further on from Tirlemont to Saint Trond and Hasselt.

The looting began on August 27, and lasted eight days. By groups of six or eight, the soldiers broke into the houses, through the doors or the windows, entered the cellars, drank the wine, ransacked the furniture, breaking the safes, stealing all money, pictures, works of art, silver, linen, clothes, wines and provisions. A great part of the booty, packed on military carts, was then sent to Germany by train. The burning and the looting did not stop until Wednesday, September 2. On this day four more fires were lighted by the German soldiers, one in the Rue Léopold and three in the Rue Marie Thérèse. Without counting the Halles Universitaires and the Palais de Justice, 894 houses were burnt within the limits of the town of Louvain, and about 500 houses within those of the suburb of Kessel-Loo.

The suburb of Herent and the village of Corbeck-Loo were practically entirely destroyed. On August 25, while they were setting fire to houses, the Germans wrecked the fire-engines and fire-escapes; they shot the people who from the roofs were trying to stop the flames. Looting is nearly always followed by fires, which seem often to be prompted solely by the desire to hide the traces of the looting. The houses are frequently set on fire by fuses; at other times they are sprayed over with petrol or naphtha. Sometimes, in order to hasten the action of the fire, the German soldiers use a kind of inflammable tablet, containing nitro-cellulose gelatine.

An eyewitness who left Louvain on August 30, when the fire was still burning, said:—

> The town has the appearance of an ancient ruined city, in the midst of which only a few drunken soldiers move about, carrying

bottles of wine and liqueurs, while the officers, seated in armchairs round the tables, drink like their men. In the streets, swollen bodies of dead horses rot in the sun, and the smell of fire and putrefaction pervades the whole place. Leaving Weert St. Georges, I only saw burnt-down villages and half-crazy peasants who, on meeting anyone, held up their hands as a sign of submission.

M. Paul Delannoy, librarian of the university, was able, in the disguise of a chauffeur conducting a Dutch traveller who had a passport, to visit Louvain while the fire was still burning, and human bodies still lay about the streets and the steps of ruined houses. He said:—

Fire was put to the library and the Cathedral of St. Pierre on the first day. Of the latter, only the walls remain. The library is still burning, and the wind blows hither and thither scraps of burnt or burning paper. The Hotel de Ville is intact, as are several colleges which had been turned into ambulances before the occupation. The poor quarters are also intact, but deserted. The rich quarters were systematically burnt, on different days; for, before setting them on fire, officers and soldiers entered the houses, took the valuable articles, labelled them, and sent them to the station, where trains were ready to take away the spoil. All the horrors related of the bad treatment of the inhabitants are within the reality. The loss of the library is irreparable; many rare and precious works, more than 300 *incunabulae*, manuscripts, and maps, have been destroyed. No pecuniary compensation can mend the loss. If, after victory, the works on the history of the Netherlands in every German University were brought to Louvain, it would not be made good.

On August 27, while the flames of this sacrifice were rising to heaven, the German "wireless" news-supply was ticking out to a horrified world the following sentence:—

The only means of preventing surprise attacks from the civil population has been to interfere with unrelenting severity, and to create examples which, by their 'frightfulness,' would be a warning to the whole country.

Students already knew, indeed, not only that the German Imperial Government was opposed to the extension of arbitral and like methods of settling international disputes, and to experimental steps toward a general arrest of armaments, not only that it took a thoroughly unsympathetic view of the rights of small nations, and of irregular forces particularly, to resist conquest—these things were unmistakably shown at The Hague Conferences in 1899 and 1907; they knew, also, that this same government's faith in force ran even to the point of favouring systematic terrorism and breach of the usages of warfare whenever any kind of military "necessity" could be cited.[2]

Clausewitz, the highest source of German military inspiration, declared that "to introduce into the philosophy of war a principle of moderation would he an absurdity," because "war is an act of violence which in its application knows no bonds." Professor J. H Morgan observes of the book on the Usages of Land Warfare issued by the Great General Staff that "when it inculcates 'frightfulness' it is never obscure, and when it advises forbearance it is always ambiguous"; and the text abundantly justifies his conclusion that "to 'terrorise' the civil population of the enemy is a first principle with German writers on the Art of War," the aim being "to smash the total spiritual resources of a people, to humiliate them, to stupefy them—in a word, to break their spirits."

Preachers and teachers, statesmen and diplomatists, having established the idea of war as a moral necessity, before which ordinary scruples are folly, and prior undertakings may be cast away as so many "scraps of paper," the professional soldier, when his opportunity comes, naturally gives full swing to his most violent impulses. If he be a naturally humane and just man—and there must have been many such in the German armies—he is overborne by the general tradition, now sharply backed by coercive authority.

He may weep in secret, like some of the assassins of Tamines; not having the blood of martyrs in his veins, he carefully conceals his tears from his superiors. There are always superiors, and they have been chosen as tearless men. Was it not the highest of them, the emperor himself, who claimed "the God of armies and of battles" as his "great Ally," and said:—

> The soldier must not have his own way, but you must have only one will, and it is mine; one law, and it is mine.
>
> It may happen, though God forbid, that you may have to fire

---

2. See *The German War Book* (London: Murray, 1915), a full and literal translation, by Professor J. H. Morgan, of the *Kriegsbrauch im Landkriege*, issued by the German General Staff for the instruction of officers. In a critical Introduction, Professor Morgan shows the relationship between this cult of the "mailed fist" and the cynical developments of German diplomacy, politics, and academic teaching, in the last forty-five years.

on your own parents or brothers. Prove your fidelity, then, by your sacrifice?[3]

From Clausewitz to Bernhardi and Von der Goltz, expositions of this monstrous doctrine were familiar to the outer world. Why, then, should the story of Aerschot and Tamines, Dinant and Louvain, produce a thrill of horror throughout the west? The answer can only he that, to citizens of progressive and liberal States, while it was outrageous that such ideas should be proclaimed, it was, also, incredible that they should ever be acted upon by a people that had often boasted itself the spiritual children of Kant, Lessing, Goethe, and Schiller. These ideas seemed to be a part of a modern pose, a very ugly pose—ugly with the sensational-sentimental ugliness of Berlin architecture and the German comic press—a pose strangely compounded of upstart arrogance and ancient servility, a pose very annoying and even dangerous, but by no means to be taken as more than a pose. This is the mistake made by generous minds all over the world. The discovery of the fearful truth, during the third week of the war and afterwards, gave the struggle a new element of abnormality. Possibilities of moderation and mediation, which would early have arisen in any less extreme issues, were decisively excluded.

The unity of the Allies and of every class in every Allied country was sealed anew. England was now pledged as deeply to the utmost efforts as she had been during the Napoleonic wars. The definite breaking of the German war spirit became an aim secondary only to the liberation of the soil of Belgium and France. The Governments of France and England had been far from immaculate in the development of European rivalries during the preceding decade. But in neither of these countries was the State regarded, even in times of stress, as above criticism and above law; in neither were the whole resources of the community, nor could they be, concentrated toward the purpose of an offensive war. In both, the preservation and strengthening of international peace was an aim frequently avowed by leading statesmen, energetically pursued by considerable organisations, and commanding sincere and general support among the people.

In England the complete lack of military forces for such an emergency, in France the strong opposition to three years' service and the neglect of fortresses, are proofs positive, to which many others might

---

3. Other considerations on this point will be found in the author's *Germany and the German Emperor*.

be added, that, grudging even the sacrifices demanded for defence, these nations could not be persuaded to support a clear aggression. Not only was a war destructive of their best hopes, personal and public, forced upon them, but a war of unspeakable savagery, in which it must soon become difficult for the Englishman to preserve his proverbial phlegm, the Frenchman his native gallantry. In the marketplace of Tamines and the bloody streets of Louvain, men who had loved the singers and thinkers of the Fatherland saw, with sickness in their souls, the fruit of the *Kaiser's* partnership with Abdul Hamid, continued through Enver Bey, his palace guards, and his Kurdish levies. Now that the very foundations of civilized society were seen to be in danger, who could hesitate? Three weeks of German terrorism in Belgium braced the will of the Allies—after a pause of sheer incredulity—as nothing else could have done.

Chapter 4

The "Sacred Union"

I came through from Brussels to Paris, on the afternoon of Saturday, August 1, by one of the last normal trains on the direct route. Communications over the German frontiers both of Belgium and France were already broken; but we little thought, and there was nothing to suggest—for the fact that only a few frontier pickets were visible did not then seem significant—that this route would soon become one of the chief lines of supply for conquering German armies. The train was crowded with foreigners leaving Belgium, many of them Americans. We exchanged experiences of petty inconvenience not worthy to be recalled (the difficulty of cashing notes and credit orders was a prominent theme), and speculated anxiously about a future in which there was now no more than a glimmer of hope for the maintenance of peace.

War had been declared by Germany that day, though we did not yet know it, upon Russia, and Luxemburg had been invaded. On the morrow, Sunday, the *Kaiser* presented his ultimatum to Belgium. The peace that had lasted in western Europe for forty-three years was at an end. On Monday, France received the expected declaration of war from her old enemy. And now one question beat insistently upon the British ear: What would England do? It was suggested, I think, less by anxiety as to the fate of France than by the inherent chivalry of the Gallic character, to which it is incomprehensible that anyone should hesitate to step in when a foul crime is threatened. England has never taken any particular trouble to enable her foreign friends to appreciate the gravity of the burden of her imperial responsibilities; and I have surprised many Frenchmen by compelling them to reflect what it must mean to add participation in a European war to the guardianship of 100,000,000 of natives scattered all over the face of the earth.

At the outset, the insular and continental peoples naturally looked at the European conflict from different angles. The facts which were major for the one were minor for the other. It was only on second thoughts that the French realised at all fully how important for them was the British power to keep open sea communications. The Frenchman stood with his face to the east, his back to the ocean. Very soon, however, we heard discussions as to the price of coal and the prospect of importing Argentine meat. The most obvious cause of artificially high prices was removed by the lowering or cancelling of the food duties. The German sea raiders compelled reflection; and the slowly tightening blockade of the German Empire completed the educative process. Long before this, on Tuesday, August 4, England had become a party to the war, and from that day onward there was not in France a responsible voice that expressed anything but warm appreciation of the British contribution to the common cause.

A second matter of anxiety was the attitude of Italy; and her prompt declaration of neutrality not only relieved France of a grave peril, but afforded the simplest and most conclusive exhibition of the aggressive character of Germany's action, and of the inner falsity of the Triple Alliance. Austria-Hungary, the original cause of the universal calamity, was not officially at war with the western Powers until August 10. This was the end of statistical feats in which Austrian and Italian Dreadnoughts were counted together as Germany's instruments in the Mediterranean. Within three days of the outbreak of war there were no active warships there except those of England and France, though several German raiders appeared later on.

For a moment, there had been a yet graver question: Would France herself be united? There has never been a Quaker or Tolstoyan movement in France; but the Socialist party was profoundly international and pacific in sentiment, and had participated recently in many efforts, very ill-supported on the other side, toward Franco-German reconciliation. Its leader, Jean Jaures, struck down in a cafe near the office of their journal, *L'Humanité*, on July 30 by a half-witted royalist, had only just returned from the meetings of the International Socialist Bureau in Brussels, and died struggling to the last moment to avert the European catastrophe. How would his followers regard this sudden breach of all that was promised for the Armed Peace? Perhaps the most emphatic reply was given by a Socialist who had often mocked at Jaurès as a moderate, and who might claim to be the author of the idea of an international labour strike against war—Gustave Hervé.

A more regular, collective answer was afforded at the special session of the Chamber on August 4, when the Socialist deputies applauded the Presidential and Ministerial declarations, and M. Deschanel pronounced a warm eulogy of Jaures, his "magnificent eloquence," his "remarkable cultivation and power of work," his "generous heart, wholly devoted to social justice and human fraternity."

> From the grave of the man who has perished, a martyr of his ideas, arises a thought of union; from his icy lips comes a cry of hope. To maintain this union, to realize this hope, for the fatherland, for justice, for the human conscience, is it not the worthiest homage we can render him?

The working-men of France had already made up their minds on the merits of the case; but words like these certainly helped them to accept what for them, private sacrifice apart, was an evil only less intolerable than another Prussian conquest.

The issue was placed before the nation and the world, on this occasion, by the President of the Republic and the Prime Minister in phrases worthy, by their clarity and eloquence, of a high place in the records of French oratory. M. Poincaré said:—

> France is being made the object of a brutal and premeditated aggression, which is an insolent defiance of the law of nations. Before a declaration of war had been addressed to us, even before the German Ambassador had demanded his passports, our territory was violated. The Emperor of Germany gave tardily, only last evening, the true name to a situation which he had already created.

No act, no gesture, no word could be attributed to France that had not been pacific and conciliatory. She had made up to the last:—

> Supreme efforts to conjure a war of which the German Empire will have to bear before History the crushing responsibility. . . . She will know now, as ever, how to reconcile the most generous pride and the most enthusiastic ardor with that self-mastery which is the sign of durable energies and the best guarantee of victory. In this war, France will have with her Right, of which peoples can no more than individuals with impunity misconceive the eternal moral power. She will be heroically defended by all her sons, whose sacred union before the enemy nothing will break. . . . Already, from all parts of the civilised world, sym-

pathy and good wishes reach her. For she represents today, once again, before the world. Liberty, Justice, and Reason."

M. Viviani rapidly traced the course of events since "the abominable crime" of Sarajevo, dwelling particularly upon the final stage. When, in July 31, Germany proclaimed the *Kriegszufahrstand,* she had already, he said, several days before, prepared the passage of her army from a peace to a war footing.

As far back as the morning of July 25, that is, before the expiry of the period given by Austria to Servia, she had warned the garrisons of Alsace-Lorraine. The same day, she had armed the defence works near the frontier. On the 26th, she had given the railways preliminary instructions for the concentration. On the 27th, she had effected the requisitions and put in place her covering troops. On the 28th, the individual summonses to reservists had begun, and the units distant from the frontier were brought nearer. Such was the situation when, on the evening of July 31, the German Government, which for a week had not participated by any positive act in the conciliatory efforts of the Triple Entente, addressed its ultimatum to Russia. On the same day, this unfriendly step was doubled by clearly hostile acts toward France: rupture of road, railway, telegraph, and telephone communications, seizure of French locomotives on their arrival at the frontier, placing of *mitrailleuses* on the railway, which had been cut, and concentration of troops on this frontier.

From this moment, we could no longer believe in the sincerity of the pacific declarations which the representative of Germany showered upon us. We knew that, under shelter of the ' state of warning of war,' Germany was mobilizing. We learned that six classes of reservists had been called up, and that the concentration transport even of army corps far removed from the frontier was being pursued. The general mobilisation of our land and sea armies was, therefore, ordered. On that evening (August 1), although the Cabinet of St. Petersburg had accepted the English proposition, Germany declared war on Russia. On the morrow, in contradiction to her ambassador's declarations, the German troops crossed our frontier at three points; while the neutrality of Luxemburg was violated, and that of Belgium was menaced. Since then, the aggressions have been renewed, multiplied, and accentuated.

On more than fifteen points, our frontier has been violated. Shots have been fired at our soldiers and customs officers. There have been killed and wounded. Yesterday, a German aviator threw three bombs upon Lunéville. Last night, the German Ambassador asked for his passports, and notified the state of war, alleging, quite untruly, acts of hostility by French aviators in German territory. . . . European opinion has already done justice to these miserable inventions.

M. Viviani then read the Franco-British exchange of letters of November 1912, by which it was agreed that there should be military and naval consultations, without prejudice to the liberty of each country on any occasion to decide for itself whether it would co-operate with the other. He also cited a new declaration of Sir Edward Grey promising that, if the German fleet emerged to attack France, England would intervene, and would then be at war with Germany. This undertaking, which was received by prolonged applause from the Chamber, had been given in London two days before, subject to Parliamentary approval. The appeal of Belgium to England, her response promising support, and the appearance of the first Belgian troops before Liège, were only occurring during this historic session of the French Chamber. The Premier declared in conclusion:—

France, unjustly provoked, did not wish for war. She has done everything to avoid it. We are without reproach. We shall be without fear. To sustain the weight of a heavy responsibility, we have the comfort of an untroubled conscience, and the certitude of duty accomplished.

Before the sitting closed, Ministerial Bills were produced to establish payments to the necessitous families of soldiers, to extend the power of the Bank of France to issue notes, to authorize a moratorium, to suspend import duties on food and necessaries, to set up a state of siege, to admit Alsatians and Lorrainers into the French army, and "to repress indiscretions of the press in time of war."

Long before the dreadful character of the German campaign in Belgium became known, the cause of the Allies had excited the sympathies of neutral nations of a progressive type. There was, indeed, one grave subject of hesitation. This was to be a war against the spirit of militarism, conquest, and arbitrary rule, a war in aid of a great Republic and two little peoples threatened in their independence. What could or would a State so constituted as that of Russia contribute to such ends? Optimists replied that, unlike the less arbitrary, but harder and more heartless, State of Prussia, Russia holds surprising and incalculable powers of sudden progress and moral grandeur which war has liberated before (as in the freeing of the serfs after the Crimean War, and the establishment of the Duma after the war in Manchuria), and may liberate again. No mere promise could suffice to establish this view; but the *Tsar's* appeal to the Poles of Austria and Germany, and his pledge to set up a new Poland, enjoying complete autonomy and freedom of language and religion, which was the greatest news of mid-August, went far to justify the optimists.

The student of history will recognise the irony of this proclamation by the descendant of Catherine the Great at the cost of the descendant of her partner in the iniquity of 1772, Frederick the Great[1]. Like the invitation from the same monarch to the first Peace Conference at The Hague, this bold stroke came as a complete surprise to Europe. Even among the most patriotic Poles, the hope of recovering their national unity and autonomy was the faintest and most visionary. Probably it is as true today as formerly that an absolutely independent Poland could not exist between the three great neighbours who brought about its extinction formerly. But, set up under Russian suzerainty, its position and the numbers of its population might well favour a liberal development which would react upon the condition of all the Slavic lands.

All the Poles were not in the same case. In East Prussia, they had been subjected for twenty years to a systematic, costly, and yet futile course of repression. In Galicia, they had been more fortunate, and, therefore, more loyal. To all, this lightning flash out of the east brought a quickened pulse, a new aim and strength. It was one of the masterstrokes of history; and the day has not come when any man can say where or when the reverberations will cease.

---

1. *Frederick the Great & the Seven Years' War* by F.W. Longman is also published by Leonaur..

CHAPTER 5

Paris in August

These were days, for the young manhood of the Republic, of swift, excited movement, of brave farewells, of journeys too full of dire expectation to be tiresome, of work at unprecedented pressure. For the families left behind, and all mere watchers, they were days of deepening stupefaction. On the busy *boulevards*, or in little seaside and country resorts far from the throbbing centre of political life, we were surprised to find the echoes of a distant disturbance swelling, without apparent cause, into the imminent threat of war in these very streets and fields upon which the sun shone so radiantly. Hour by hour, then minute by minute, the thunder of gathering legions sounded nearer and nearer; curiosity passing into anxiety, astonishment, anger, and at last, when the storm burst, into a dull, bitter impotence of feeling. Taken together, the work of mobilisation and the censorship completed the social transformation. When hundreds of thousands of men of all classes are suddenly enrolled and removed, business life is automatically reduced to a necessary minimum.

Within a few hours half the shops and offices of Paris were closed, three-quarters of the machinery of transport was removed, and an unknown but very large part of the industry of the country came to a standstill. The banks and bourses were idle; therefore there were no financial newspapers. The actors had put on uniform, and there were no theatres. The daily papers were reduced to small single sheets—no more advertisements, no more fiction, no more criticism of art and literature. The Goddess of Fashion had fled. When the night was yet young, a full moon looked down upon a city apparently asleep, except along a few streets leading to the eastern and northern railway stations. These, day or night, and the government offices, were always simmering like the blowholes on the flanks of a volcano.

Thus, Paris rapidly assumed the appearance of a beleaguered city. The mobilisation not only robbed factories, workshops, offices, and shops of most of their adult male workers; it not only required the transfer to the military authorities of the whole of the railways and much of the road and water transport of the country, the telegraphs and telephones, and the main power of the postal service. Into nearly every home in the land it brought warning of wages and salaries stopped, employment of every kind disorganized, and prices of commodities rising. On top of this came the stern announcement of the state of siege, by which military law was made supreme over the destinies of the civil population, or what remained of it. The money famine of these first days, though it had its amusing side, was tragic for hundreds of thousands of the lower middle-class folk for whom small change is not merely a convenience, but a necessity.

The inconvenience continued for several weeks, despite an issue of 20-*franc* and 5-*franc* bank-notes. I heard of a rich traveller who was going about with 20,000 Austrian *crowns*, and for some hours could not raise the price of a meal. In many cases it was possible to change foreign money only at cent. *per cent*, discount. Our civilization now rests so much upon credit and ready exchange that the mind was altogether unprepared for the flood of individual misfortunes which the arrest of retail credit caused. It was like a return to the pre-banking era. At the restaurant, the waiter politely asked at the outset if you could pay in coin; at the *magazin*, the shopman deeply regretted to have to put the same question, but *Monsieur* must pardon him, for he had veritably no alternative. So, howling crowds gathered at the bank doors, and the proverbial messenger from Mars might have supposed that the thriftiest people in Europe had with mysterious suddenness lost all their savings. It was, no doubt, this very thrift made feverish by fear of the unknown future, that created the difficulty.

Even metal money is not the most essential of our needs, and cannot procure everything when the army is in possession. The question of the feeding of Paris loomed threateningly before us. The Prefect of the Seine said:—

> Despite the absorption of railway services by the army, a certain number of trains are reserved for the transport of essential commodities, notably meat, milk, and potatoes, as well as the flour necessary for making bread. The public will continue to obtain these provisions at such retail shops as remain open. As to milk,

special measures are being taken to secure a preferential supply for children and invalids. Persons who wish to avail themselves of this measure must enter their names at the *mairies*, producing such evidence as birth certificates of children, doctor's certificates, etc.

The same officer confessed that the sanitary as well as other public services must sutler from the mobilisation by urging householders to rely as little as possible upon scavengers, and to burn their old paper, bones, foodstuff, and other refuse. Working bakers, it should be said, were exempted from the call to the colons. Several incipient riots against shopkeepers who tried to put up food prices exorbitantly took place. The police promised special measures to secure "loyalty of transactions" in the provision markets, including prosecution of those unamiable persons who used to be called "forestallers and regrators."

At the outbreak of the war, all foreigners in Paris were required to report to the police, who either gave them a permit to remain in the city or an order to leave the country, unless they were sent to a concentration camp. Outside the police commissary's offices one saw, day after day for a whole fortnight, thousands of people of different nationality, class, and age, lined up awaiting admission to the commissary's presence. The weather was still hot, and many of the women and girls who stood waiting on the pavement for hours swooned. In such circumstances the Parisians showed their native kindliness. One evening, a frail German seamstress fainted outside a dairyman's shop. The dairyman's wife and sister, who were caring for her, explained that she had been in line from early in the morning until the police officials closed their doors, and had then been turned away. "Poor things!" said the dairyman's wife. "Of course, we are at war with Germany, but we cannot help pitying them." The little seamstress was not allowed to make any payment, and was escorted home by two residents of the Rue de la Victoire.

There were still, also, thousands of English and American holidaymakers and travellers who had not been able to get away, or had not tried to do so, hoping against hope for peace. For many of them the language difficulty did not exist; but to others the rule forbidding the acceptance of any private telegraphic messages in foreign languages inflicted hardship. At the same time, it was announced that no private telegrams would be accepted at railway stations. In many small places this meant that none could be sent at all. Telephone communications between town and town were altogether suspended; and the Paris-London telephone service, upon which Fleet Street had come to depend more and more, was closed. No telegrams at all were allowed to Germany and Austria; with neutral or friendly countries they could only be sent or received under police sanction.

The museums were permanently closed, and the last traces of Paris the Holiday City disappeared—or, rather, the only remaining traces consisted of cues of distracted English, American, and other visitors at the Consulates and police headquarters seeking the special passports which were now necessary to get out of the country. Many of these people, especially the women, were in pitiful case. It is impossible to convey to comfortable stay-at-home readers any adequate impression of the disturbance and anxiety involved in the mere fact of not being able to obtain any definite information. You wished to get to London. But all regular train services were suspended, and the station-master himself—if you could penetrate into the station, which was completely blocked by troops and by officials wielding military law—could not tell you when it would be possible for a passenger train to leave for the north or west coast.

Meanwhile, you must have money. If you were poor, Heaven help you. Otherwise, there was a double difficulty: it was still extremely difficult to get change for French 50-*franc* and 100-*franc* notes, and restaurants and shops insisted on having small money. On the other hand, the British sovereign was no longer negotiable in the ordinary way, and the banks kept their stock for special customers.

Much of this was to be expected, but few had anticipated a week without news. When the censorship established itself under the shadow of martial law, I thought it impossible that public patience could be long maintained. Yet the memory of the cost of certain newspaper indiscretions in 1870 sufficed to condone it. Up to August 4, the only information from the front allowed to api)ear in the Parisian press—after news of the first German incursions on the eastern border—consisted of three or four trivial items about bomb-throwing from a German aeroplane at Nancy, and patrol raids near Renoncourt and Belfort. What censors commonly fail to appreciate is that news cannot be suppressed—that, if true news is forbidden, false rumours will have a more lively and persistent circulation.

Rumour at this time considerably exaggerated the natural anxiety as to the lot of French residents in Germany, especially in Lorraine, of whom their families had learned nothing since the eve of the war. On the night of August 4, the establishment in Paris of a censor's office and a bureau of official information was announced in the following terms by the Minister of War:

> It is forbidden to publish any news relative to events of war, mobilisation, movements, embarkations, transport of troops, composition of armies, effectives, etc., which have not been communicated by the Press Bureau organised by the Ministry of War.
>
> The *communiqués* will be made three times daily—between 10 and 10.30 a.m., between 2.80 and 3 p.m., and between 11.30 and 11.59 p.m.
>
> The directors of the different daily and periodical publications are invited to inform the Press service at the Prefecture of Police in writing, today, August 4, of their regular day and hour of publication. All special editions are forbidden, as are also announcements cried or placarded in the public streets.
>
> Further, they must transmit to the Ministry of War (Press Bureau) final proofs of each number as soon as the last page is made up.
>
> The newspaper or publication concerned will, otherwise, be free, after sending this proof, to print and sell without other formality. But it will expose itself to immediate confiscation if the examination of the proof reveals the insertion of any military news whatever which has not been communicated by the Press Bureau or Ministry of War.
>
> Messimy.

With the exception of the first, which could not be literally applied, these rules were rigorously imposed. No responsible journalist, so far as I know, either in France or England, has ever questioned the necessity of a censorship of war news; but it would be hard to find a responsible journalist in either country to justify the censorship as it has actually existed and operated. If a general distinction can be made between the experience of the two countries, it is, probably, that opinion was most severely dealt with in France, and statements of fact in England. For a time, the French press was nearly extinguished, and many of the censors' decisions were merely stupid and annoying. Afterwards, there was a reorganisation and some improvement. The official bulletins also became franker, fuller, and more dependable. If there is ever to be another war, however, this question of press censorship should be well considered in consultation with responsible and representative journalists. Meanwhile, in France, as in England, strange and erratic decrees have been accepted with a remarkable loyalty and patience.

During those first days, we lived, as it were, behind an impenetrable curtain. Lacking fresh material, the newspapers repeated the old endlessly, and then dwindled to tiny single sheets in which the official *communiqués*—the first of which was issued on August 5—were eked out with editorial reflections (interspersed with white patches marking the censor's activity) and notes on the aspect of the city. It was an extraordinary thing to reflect that, with a million men at the front, Paris had not the least idea what they were doing. The German declaration of war, received by M. Viviani on Sunday afternoon, August 2, was only published on Tuesday morning, when a thirty-line summary had to satisfy the anxiety of the French public as to what Sir Edward Grey had said in the House of Commons on the previous afternoon. Private and press telegrams, if they went through at all, were subject to long delays; as for letters, we came to regard the Paris Post Office as a vast cemetery, full of the remains of useless journalistic effort. Most of the automobiles were requisitioned for the army.

Moreover, from August 4 the gates of Paris were closed from 6 p.m. to 6 a.m. (the evening hour was afterwards extended to 8.30); and motor-cars were only allowed to leave the Department of the Seine under special and exceptional permits. All newspaper correspondents were turned back from the frontier region, and it was practically impossible to enter what was defined as "the actual zone of the armies." At the same time, foreign war correspondents were encouraged to wait about in the belief that they would soon be authorized and sent to the front. A code of rules was actually issued, on August 10, for their guidance, the chief and severest novelty being that telegraphic dispatches were to be everywhere, always, and absolutely forbidden, and that messages, to be entrusted to the field post, must be written in French. Gradually, the British correspondents drifted back home, tired of waiting.

The measures which isolated the civil population also isolated the army, whose consequent anxieties had to be taken more seriously. On August 11, the military authorities promised to publish a newspaper especially for the troops at the front. This novel enterprise was heralded by an exchange of letters between M. Messimy, the War Minister, and M. Viviani, the Premier—a correspondence interesting to a Brit-

FACSIMILE OF *COMMUNIQUÉ*

Communiqué à la Presse du 1er septembre 1914
(23 heures):

1°.- A notre aile gauche, par suite de la continuation du mouvement enveloppant des Allemands, et dans le but de ne pa accepter une action décisive qui aurait pu être engagée dans de mauvaises conditions, nos troupes se sont repliées partie vers le Sud, partie vers le sud-ouest.

L'action engagée dans la région de Rethel a permis à nos forces d'arrêter momentanément l'ennemi.

2° - Au centre et à notre droite (Woëvre, Lorraine et Vosges), situation sans changement

LES AÉROPLANES ALLEMANDS.
Il a été organisé une escadrille d'aéroplanes, blindés et munis de mitrailleuses, pour faire la chasse aux aéroplanes allemands qui survolent Paris

ish reader as marking the difference in the position of a country that sends an Expeditionary Force and one the whole of whose strongest manhood is gathered on distant frontiers for the defence of the Fatherland. M. Messimy said:—

> Over an immense front of 300 miles, officers and soldiers are subject to momentary impressions, without news of their homes or even of the war. By the *Bulletin des Armées de la République* they will be able to measure their individual share in the national effort. This will create a generous emulation of sacrifice for the independence and greatness of France and in the triumph of right and liberty.

M. Viviani, in the course of his reply accepting the project, said that the children of France, then on the frontier, and on the morrow beyond it, would thus know that their mothers, wives, sweethearts, and sisters watched them with burning eyes.

> Ah, young men, and you, my two sons, among them, look backward, and you will read how France, in her mission of emancipation, has been pursued by barbarian hatred! Look forward, and you will see Europe freed from abject tyranny, peace assured, labour enjoying a happy resurrection. Forward, children of the Fatherland! When you return we will go, by paths which your heroism opened, in pious pilgrimage to bless the tombs where the spirits of the heroes of 1870 have awaited so long the terrible awakening of justice.

The *Bulletin des Armées de la République* duly appeared, a small four-page sheet, containing articles by leading French writers, war bulletins, and other official matter; but it was soon found that effective circulation is not easily procured even when the journal has the State behind it and no revenue is expected. The postal arrangements between the front and the soldiers' families were for some months a cause of bitter complaint. An office was established at one of the Paris barracks where lists of killed and wounded were kept, and families applied for news, no general lists being published. The applicant was told whether a particular soldier's name was on either list, but not the place where he was, or the date, these and other details, however, being sometimes obtainable from regimental officers. Letters for soldiers had to be addressed in the first place to the original station of the regiment; as this might be far away in the south or west, delay was necessarily caused.

FACSMILE OF *SOLDIERS' LNEWSPAPERS*

N° 20. Jeudi 3 Septembre 1914.

BULLETIN DES ARMÉES
DE LA RÉPUBLIQUE
PARAISSANT CHAQUE JOUR

PROCLAMATION DU GOUVERNEMENT

Français,

Depuis plusieurs semaines, des combats acharnés mettent aux prises nos troupes héroïques et l'armée ennemie. La vaillance de nos soldats leur a valu, sur plusieurs points, des avantages marqués. Mais, au Nord, la poussée des forces allemandes nous a contraints à nous replier.

Cette situation impose au Président de la République et au Gouvernement une décision douloureuse. Pour veiller au salut national, les pouvoirs publics ont le devoir de s'éloigner, pour l'instant, de la ville de Paris.

Sous le commandement d'un chef éminent, une armée française, pleine de courage et d'entrain, défendra contre l'envahisseur la capitale et sa patriotique population. Mais la guerre doit se poursuivre, en même temps, sur le reste du territoire.

Sans paix ni trêve, sans arrêt ni défaillance, continuera la lutte sacrée pour l'honneur de la nation et pour la réparation du droit violé.

Aucune de nos armées n'est entamée. Si quelques-unes d'entre elles ont subi des pertes trop sensibles, les vides ont été immédiatement comblés par les dépôts et l'appel des recrues nous assure pour demain de nouvelles ressources en hommes et en énergies.

Durer et combattre, tel doit être le mot d'ordre des armées alliées anglaise, russe, belge et française!

Durer et combattre, pendant que sur mer les Anglais nous aident à couper les communications de nos ennemis avec le monde!

SITUATION MILITAIRE
(2 septembre.)

I. — A notre aile gauche, dans la journée du 1er septembre, un corps de cavalerie allemande, dans sa marche vers la forêt de Compiègne, a eu un engagement avec les Anglais qui lui ont pris 10 canons.

Un autre corps de cavalerie allemande pousse jusqu'à la ligne Soissons-Bouy-le-château.

Dans la région de Rethel et de la Meuse, l'ennemi n'a manifesté aucune activité.

II. — En Lorraine, nous avons continué à progresser sur la rive droite du Sanon; au Sud la situation est inchangée.

En Haute-Alsace, les Allemands semblent n'avoir bâti devant Belfort qu'un rideau de troupes.

III. — Dans la région du Nord, on ne signale pas d'avances à Lille, Arras, Douai, Béthune, Lens.

IV. — Ces nouvelles de Belgique que des fractions appartenant à plusieurs corps d'armée allemands sont restés en mouvement vers l'Est et retournent en Allemagne.

Widespread pain was given, especially in the early months of the war, by the simple impossibility of communicating quickly with absent fathers, husbands, and sons.

Early in August, the Prefect of Police, under powers given by the state of siege, ordered the closing at 9 p.m. of all places where drink was sold. The order was peacefully obeyed, a few minutes' latitude being given to those of us who were snatching a hasty meal. More than once, hurrying Paris-wards by motorcar from the eastern battlefields after nightfall, I wished it would serve to cry, "Curfew shall not toll tonight!" No doubt, the attenuated and wearied staffs of the restaurants rejoiced; but thousands of people who depend upon the *cafés* for their food were sorely tried, as were other thousands by the closing at 9 p.m. of the Metropolitan Railway.

Our greatest satisfaction in this early phase was to know that nothing had been done on the French side, either with intent or by accident, to thwart the pacific efforts of Great Britain. or, afterwards, to prejudice a cause which was already strongly appealing to the conscience of the outer world. Never, perhaps, has there been such complete unanimity in a great nation accustomed to the noisy processes of democratic government. When M. Viviani, the prime minister, appeared on August 4, with Mme. Jaurès on his arm, at the head of the procession behind the remains of Jean Jaurès, the great Socialist leader, it was at once a parable and a command. Months passed, but the truce continued unbroken. Where were the mobs of the older France, now intoxicated with hope, then stricken to a frenzy of desperate anger; now crying "Treason!" "Traitor!" and *anon* hailing some *poseur* as its saviour?

The self-control of the government was very marked; and petty incidents could not obscure the admirable spectacle of the restraint, courage, and intelligence shown by the population at large. There was no "mafficking" in Paris or the provincial cities. It would be unfair to exaggerate the importance of a few attacks upon German shops following upon the news of the German violation of the eastern frontier. The police took precautions against the repetition of such scenes, and the Prefect of Police issued an appeal to the good sense of the people. Riots against tradesmen and market people attempting to obtain the excessive price for provisions were more frequent.

One saw many pale, distraught faces, and women with their eyes red with weeping. The mobilization proceeded with a clock-work smoothness. Soldiers were continually marching through the streets amid a chorus of huzzas and weaving of handkerchiefs by enthusiastic crowds. Apart from the marching of troops, the streets were almost denuded of traffic. An ambulance wagon carrying Red Cross nurses was always the sign for a wave of applause. Old men reflected how different from this comparative calm was the beginning of the tragedy of 1870. Every stage in the events of this first week was unprecedented, incredible. It seemed as though mankind had been stricken with mental paralysis. Hundreds of millions had already been expended before a single battle had been fought, and years of battles across the whole of Europe might be before us. The humblest Frenchman, proudest of patriots as he was, and outraged by an unpardonable aggression, was restrained by this thought. There was no disorder, no intoxication, only a cold white anger, and the sense of a devilish but irresistible destiny.

The most horrible thing in human life, perhaps, is the deadening of sensibility that comes about when we see crime or suffering no longer in retail, but in wholesale, and no longer an evil to prevent, but a fate to endure. The calm of the Parisian people was, no doubt, in part the proud courage of which the Press spoke eloquently—in part, it was a numbness, an incapacity to feel more to which I can myself testify. We were stunned. Into every minute of that first week had been crowded the pain of a normal year. Over a whole continent the tender ties of family and social life, the myriad nerve-threads of industry and business, study and recreation, were roughly torn asunder. A squad of reservists, not yet in uniform, trudged bravely through the streets to the train which would carry it beyond our sight into the zone of death. Husband and wife, lover and lass, mother and son, white-faced but tearless, snatched a farewell kiss.

They felt—because they were for each other familiar living individuals, heart to despairing heart. We felt less and less, because they had become for us a procession, a spectacle, a formula—something infinitely sad and brave and sacred, it is true, our saviours by vicarious sacrifice, but not, like ourselves, beings of flesh and blood who must be rescued, there and then, from injury. Day by day this insensibility would spread and deepen. With it would be mixed elements of frenzy of which we, Englishmen, Frenchmen, Germans, had thought ourselves incapable. There would ho hours of panic, hours of orgy over news of triumph. This—not the material destruction, or even the hideous loss of life—was the cost of war we had most to fear. It was against this deadening of heart and conscience that our preachers and teachers should be directing any moral influence they could yet exert—not either an easy, or always a pleasant, task.

No calamity, perhaps, can quite extinguish the smokeless flame of Parisian wit. From the workman to the aristocrat, everyone had for a time his little joke, most of them represented by the return railway ticket for Berlin, marked "August-September," which was being sold on the boulevards. "I was going to Baden-Baden in September," said an officer, "and I shall still go, but without any Customs House nonsense." A little infantryman, after the last kiss, said to his wife: "Now, don't cry; I'll bring you some German helmets to make flower-pots of." And, in fact, helmets were, within six weeks, the favourite "relics" which wounded soldiers brought home. Old men recalled that in August 1870, after the defeats of Wissembourg and Froeschwiller, "*La Muette de Portici*" was being played at the *Opéra*, "*Lala Roukh*" at the *Opéra Comique*, and other pieces at the *Gaieté* and *Variétés*. Times had changed. On the first day of this mobilisation, there were forty spectators at the *Théâtre Français*, and on the third day the doors were closed. A number of picture theatres remained open for the benefit of the Red Cross. The silence deepened daily; and when the great retreat began, there was no more public joking.

M. Urbain Gohier. one of the extreme anti-militarists of ten years before, pointed out that if, and when, the whole four and a half millions of mobilisable men in France were called out, there would be still plenty of work, as necessary to the State as the military effort, for other hands to accomplish:

> War is not only fighting; it is, above all, a proof of endurance, a succession of unaccustomed effort, fatigue, privation which the young and the strong can bear, but the feeble and the old would collapse under. Everyone can fire a rifle, but everyone cannot walk twenty miles, knapsack on back, in sun and rains, sleeping upon the moist earth, starting off again at dawn, and always maintaining his physical strength. To make ourselves really useful, according to our strength and capacity, without seeking theatrical effect—that is our duty. There are plenty of opportunities to fulfil it. The crops must be harvested, the tramway and railway services maintained, letters transmitted, the police re-enforced, and the daily labour continued in all the workshops and factories in the land. This is, in the truest sense, national service.

The Press presently set up a hue-and-cry against those who appeared—often the appearance was quite fallacious—to be evading military service. On the whole, the call was responded to promptly and willingly, not only by the mass of young men of unformed opinions, but by middle-aged fathers of families, by thousands who could have pleaded physical weakness, by poets and artists, deputies and editors, pacifists, socialists, syndicalists.

Very soon, a large part of the well-to-do classes in Paris and other French cities was engaged in the organisation of relief. The following figures are typical: In the twelfth arrondissement of the capital, 6,500 families were at once thrown on the charity lists, and the distributions of food, clothing, and money were regularly made. In the thirteenth arrondissement 10,000 families were succoured, and in the fourteenth more than 7,000. In the seventeenth, another working-class district, milk was distributed largely to those who required it, and those justified in asking for money help were found to number about 10,000. The Boy Scouts made themselves generally useful. Hundreds of thousands of families, many of them accustomed to a comfortable scale of living, settled down to a bare subsistence upon the legal allowances of a shilling a day to the wife, and fivepence per child under sixteen years of age. Many of the great hotels and business houses were turned into provisional ambulances, or work-rooms where girls were kept at a low wage making hospital supplies or winter garments for the troops. On August 22, the twenty-first day of the mobilisation, there were 1,300,000 Frenchmen under arms, about a half of them on or near the frontiers. Brussels was already lost, Namur was invested, and Nancy threatened. The hour of trial had come.

BOOK 2: THE ONSLAUGHT (AUGUST 21—SEPTEMBER 5)

CHAPTER 6

Behind the Screen

Standing at the critical point where the mobilization of the chief forces is practically complete, and the preliminary phase of the campaign closes, and using our privilege of looking backward and forward, we should now be able to see more clearly, if not quite clearly, what were the original plans of campaign, and how they have been modified as a result of the first shock of arms. There is no mistaking this critical point, which lies between the German victory in Lorraine and the occupation of Brussels, on August 20, and the German occupation of Lunéville and the passage of the Meuse-Sambre at Namur, on August 23. The position thus reached is, indeed, an extraordinary one; and the main problem it places abruptly before us is so important that it will be best to deal with it before resuming our narrative of events. This problem may be thus stated: If, against the trivial Belgian Army almost unaided, the invaders could only get from the northern frontiers past the obstacle of Namur in nineteen days (August 4-23), how was it that they were able, against the French and British armies, to reach the outer forts of Paris in another thirteen days (August 23-September 5), fighting several big battles, holding Belgium and long lines of communication, and overrunning a large part of eastern France, the while?

We may commence with an axiom and two assumptions. The axiom is that we are seeking to discover and explain, not to judge. It cannot be too often recalled that, while the reader is spared the overwhelming labours and anxieties of the combatants, he has before him knowledge which, if the commanders themselves had possessed, this story would not be to tell, but another very different. The assumptions are these: (a) That the defeat and retreat of the Allies were not due to inferiority of soldierly qualities in their men, and that the problem is, therefore, one of numbers, strategy, preparedness, and organization, (b) That, in so far as it is a problem of numbers, it is one chiefly not of total numbers—the German advantage in reserves being soon counterbalanced to some extent by Austrian failures and Russian attacks—but of forces somewhat superior in mass, strategically disposed so as to be markedly superior at certain points at a required moment.

There are, next, two sets of facts to review: (1) The disposition of forces on the eve of the campaign, and (2) their lines of movement from August 4 to August 23 when Namur fell, the Belgian Army was dispersed, and the main onslaught by the north began at Mons and Charleroi.

1. It has been seen that the first dispositions indicated (a) that *Belgium* would resist, her small field army supporting the small garrisons of the Meuse fortresses. Much evidently depended upon how long this resistance could last, if there was to be an effective junction of the Franco-British with the Belgian forces. It seems highly probable that the German commanders expected a shorter resistance. Whatever General Joffre may have intended, and whatever the Belgian Government may have secretly known, the army and people expected the Allies to march north to their aid. (b) The British *force*, landed at French, not Belgian, ports, was only a late participant in the French plan of campaign, which, however, must have been made, or promptly modified, in view of its arrival on the west wing. This could hardly have been expected at an earlier date, or in larger numbers, (c) The *French* plan had to take account of inferior numbers, a relative backwardness, equal perhaps to two or three days, or even more, in real mobilization and frontier concentration, and the difficulties of common action by widely separated Allies.

We have seen that the great effort in fixed defences had been made on the eastern frontier in the double system Verdun-Toul and Epinal-Belfort. On the north, the only considerable fortress was Maubeuge, though there were a number of isolated forts, and Longwy, as we have seen, made an admirable resistance, Lille, La Fère, Laon, and Rheims had not been modernised, and were all abandoned without a serious attempt at defence. Various schemes for a northern system of fortifications had been discussed from time to time; but they had been set aside on account of the enormous expenditure required, and the growth of opinion in favour of mobile defence and increase of artillery. A phrase in the French official bulletin of August 24, 11 p.m., suggests that the original plan of campaign did not contemplate an advance into Belgium, even if it were already invaded by Germany:—

> By order of General Joffre, our troops and the British troops have taken positions on the covering line (*i.e.* the frontier), which they would not have quitted had not the admirable effort of the Belgians permitted us to enter Belgium.

This, in turn, would suggest that a lengthy Belgian resistance was not expected. However that may be, the French frontier west of the Sambre was left undefended, until the arrival of the British, all the armies being ranged around the north-east and east, from Maubeuge to Belfort, with a view to getting contact, and an offensive concentrated in Lorraine and southern Alsace, (d) Of the seven original German Army groups (an eighth appeared later, that of Von Hansen), the aim of five was plain and not easily alterable. The two northernmost armies, those of Von Kluck and Von Bülow (seven army corps in all), were North German troops manifestly prepared to take the nearest way to Paris, the way through Liège—Von Emmich's provisional army of the Meuse was their advance guard for the purpose of reducing this fortress. The two southernmost, consisting of six corps based upon Metz and Strassburg, had to guard almost the whole stretch of the Franco-German frontier, and could not be strong enough for offense there until they had received re-enforcements.

The role of the two middle armies was probably less definitely determined at the outset. The more northerly of these, the Third Army, under the Duke of Württemberg, based upon the railway system of the Lower Moselle, might be sent in any one of four directions, at need: through Malmedy to Liège; through Bastogne and the Lesse valley to the Meuse near Dinant; through the southern Ardennes to the region of Sedan; or due south to re-enforce the Crown Prince of Prussia. Again, the Fourth Army, under the crown prince, consisting of only three corps, Rhinelanders, Lorrainers, and Hessians, and, gathered between Treves and Thionville, might be thrown north-westward into the Ardennes, or westward through the Longwy gap, or it might be sent south to re-enforce the Metz Army under the Crown Prince of Bavaria. In brief, the general prospect was a strong northern offensive, a tentative central movement which might be shifted north or south, and a southern defensive which might be stimulated if and when opportunity occurred. On both sides of the Franco-German frontier, railway communications were abundant, and were successfully used for rapid re-enforcement.

2. The actual course of events on these different fronts during the first nineteen days may be summed up thus:

(a) *Alsace and the Vosges.*—An inadequate French advance reached Mulhouse (August 8), but was met next day by German re-enforcements, and had to be withdrawn. A stronger movement under General Pau secured the Vosges passes by the middle of the month, and Mulhouse on August 20. Immediately afterwards, the turning of the French southern line was threatened by the German victory on the Lorraine frontier; and all that had been gained, except the south Vosges heights, was abandoned. General Joffre's original aim being stated to be "to flank the attack of our troops operating in Lorraine," as the actual outflanking occurred in the opposite direction there can be no disguising the fact that there was here a very bad failure.

(b) *Lorraine.*—On the 12th, a French advance was begun, under Castelnau, through the Nancy gap; and on the 16th this was supported by a northward advance from Mount Donon. Both were directed against Saarburg, which was taken on the 18th, the direct railway communication between Metz and Strassburg being thus broken. This advance, again, was insufficiently strong; but whether its defeat (August 20) was by surprise, or by the arrival of heavy re-enforcements, does not plainly appear. In any case, the German victory was successfully followed up; and, by the 23rd, the French Army had retreated to or beyond the River Meurthe. The movements thus terminated were afterwards explained as designed to hold as many German troops as possible on the eastern frontier, and so weaken the northern attack (*Bulletin des Armées*, December 5, 1914).

(c) *Longwy corner.*—A German offensive of a not very serious character from Luxemburg and Thionville toward Verdun was checked by August 12, and was withdrawn. The check of General Ruffey by the Imperial Crown Prince aided the Würtembergers' advance; but the Longwy gap only became a considerable entry when the retreat of the north-western Allied armies made a general withdrawal of the French lines necessary. Even then, the successful resistance of Verdun greatly reduced its value.

(d) *Belgian Ardennes.*—The operations in this difficult field proved to be of a more important character than was anticipated, or, perhaps, could be anticipated until the nature of the northern attack was revealed. While the crown prince held General Ruffey on the Semoy, and the Duke of Würtemberg attacked and defeated De Langle de Cary at Paliseul and Neufchîteau in the south, a new army under Von Hansen, a development from the possibilities for the German centre indicated in paragraph 1 (d) above, struck through Marche to Dinant, so supporting Von Bülow's investment of Namur, and threatening the French flank. The failure of the French attempt to move eastward from the Meuse through the Ardennes entailed De Langle de Cary's retreat, which, in turn, uncovered the right wing of General Lanrezac's army in the angle between the Sambre and Meuse, and, through it, affected the British position west of Charleroi.

(c) *Northern Belg*ium.—Without any substantial interference except that of the Belgian army and its two fortresses, General von Moltke, then and for some weeks longer head of the Great General Staff in Berlin, under the formal command of the emperor as war-lord, had procured the concentration in northern, eastern, and central Belgium, before the French mobilisation was complete, not of a subsidiary force intended to make a useful diversion from the north, but of rather more than a half of the German armies in the west—those of Von Kluck, Von Bülow, Von Hansen, and Duke Albrecht, comprising in all twelve or thirteen army corps, with seven or eight divisions of cavalry, about 700,000 men in all. In a strategical analysis, this achievement far overtops all the dramatic episodes by which it was obscured at the time. Without casting any shade upon the heroic resistance of Liège, it may be doubted whether such a concentration could in any case have been completed in a shorter time than it actually occupied.

The atrocious treatment of the Belgian villages goes to show how much the invaders feared any delay; but all we can say with any confidence is that to the delay at Liège may perhaps be attributed the safe junction of the French and British armies on the ground chosen. The Belgian field force retired westward from Liège on August 6 or 7. Yet the crossing at Huy was only seized by Von Bülow on the 12th, Brussels was only occupied on the 20th, and the Namur crossing was only obtained on the 23rd. Undoubtedly these steps could have been taken earlier, for they did not need a third of the force available. We must suppose, therefore, that the delay was deliberate. One reason for it, perhaps, was to give time for Von Hansen's flank attack against the Sambre line through Dinant; but probably the chief reason lay in the importance of preventing the Allies from measuring the next move till it was actually taken. Everything was done to conceal what was afoot,

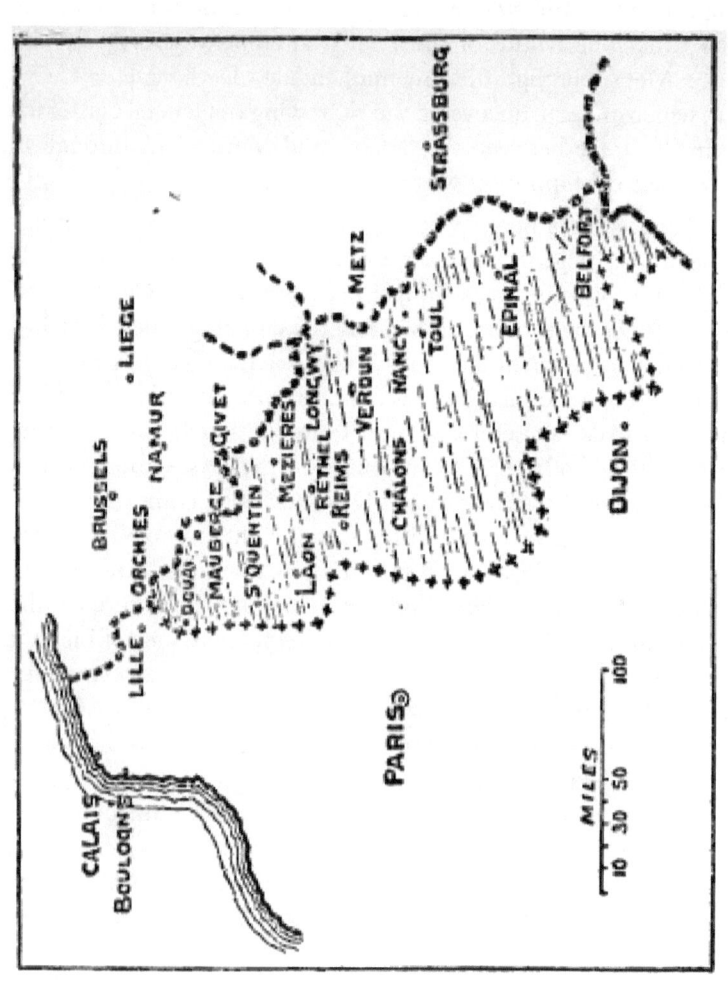

"Zone Actuelle des Armées" (August 10th)

by terrorisng the population, by the ubiquitous activity of the cavalry screen, and, above all, by the delay of the southward and westward advances until everything was ready for a "smashing blow."

How far, then, were the Allies able to see what was coming, to anticipate the numbers and speed of the attack from the north? No full answer can be given to this question until the military archives are opened and the memoirs of the leading actors penned. The difficulties for the French and British staffs were very great. The war had been sprung upon them by an enemy fully prepared. The factor that speeded the aggressor delayed them—they had to wait for Russia, and for the still slower muster of the British Empire. France must, in any case, look first to Lorraine, for there the enemy was always at the gate.

As to the north, the Allies were necessarily dependent for information upon the Belgians, who were in no position to conduct the cool work of reconnoissance and secret service. Whether because they expected first to strike a decisive blow in Lorraine and Alsace which would draw the enemy thither; or because they thought the attack from the north would be smaller and slower, and could be dealt with by the Belgians, two French armies, and the British Expeditionary Force; or because the east must be guarded first, and there were not yet enough men under arms for an equal effort in the north,—or for all these reasons—no adequate preparation was made where the need proved greatest.

The daily bulletins of the Press Bureau of the War Ministry in Paris, which became, after the battle of the Marne, the chief source of public information, gave us at this time no real guidance; but they are not without historical interest. The eastern frontier absorbed attention; Liège was always "still holding out."

On or about August 10, we received a set of rules for war correspondents, and with them a large skeleton map on which a thick black line marked off the "present zone of the armies" (shaded portion of the above map). The western limit of this zone, on the Belgian frontier, was at Orchies, sixteen miles south-east of Lille, and fifty-six miles of Dunkirk. When the Germans were flooding through Orchies and occupying Lille, we recalled this map, with its uneasy advice: "*La Limite de Cette Zone Peut Varier au Cours des Opérations.*" The armies, then, covered two-thirds of the border from the sea to Longwy, and left open the western third, including the great city of Lille, seat of the 1st Army Corps, once a formidable fortress, and only recently dismantled and declassed.

On August 12, the British Press Bureau announced it as "evident" that "the mass of the German troops lie between Liège and Luxemburg." The movement to the left of De Langle de Cary's and Ruffey's armies had now begun, to support the advance of Lanrezac between the Meuse and the Sambre, and the position arranged for Sir John French, from fifteen to thirty miles due east of Orchies. When these movements were complete, there was no force in Flanders or northwestern France, except two divisions of Territorials at Arras, under General d'Amade, On August 15—when Sir John French was in Paris—the French bulletin announced that the invasion of Belgium was foiled, and that the movements of the Allied armies were "perfectly coordinated." A more noteworthy fact is the presence of General Joffre at the "headquarters of the eastern armies" as late as August 18. A swift change, accentuated by the defeat in Lorraine, is then discernible.

On August 19, the night bulletin announced that "very important German forces" had crossed the Meuse between Liège and Namur. On the 20th. the invasion of the Ardennes was reported as reaching the line Dinant-Neufchâteau, and it was added that Brussels was occupied, "important columns pursuing their movement on this side." On the 21st, while the British troops were being brought into position, the Paris Press Bureau was congratulating itself, for the last time for many a long day, that "there is no longer any point of French territory occupied by the enemy," except a little corner near Briey, a fact "the moral value of which it is good to signal." Next day, the Germans were through Namur; and on the evening of the 23rd, faced by "most unexpected "numbers, the great retreat of the Franco-British forces began. On the 20th, when they were at Cambrai-Le Cateau-Landrecies, forty miles south-west of Maubeuge, the Paris *communiqué* stated, in one breath, that "the great battle is engaged between Maubeuge and the Donon on which depends the fate of France," and that German cavalry were at Douai, sixty-five miles west of Maubeuge.

These citations suggest that not only the numbers and speed, but the direction also, of the northern invasion were most imperfectly appreciated. The north western advance of Von Kluck's army from Liège was, no doubt, motived by the need of driving back the Belgian army and masking it after it had retired to Antwerp, and by the moral value for the Germans at home of a demonstrative occupation of the capital. But there was another important object which these proceedings helped to conceal. This was to carry a large marching wing far to the west without exciting suspicion, preparatory to a dash toward the unprotected extremity of the French frontier. Liège and

Namur have always exercised an hypnotic influence upon discussions of a possible German violation of Belgian neutrality. Their importance was, of course, great—that of Liège as the necessary doorway to both west and south. Namur as the second doorway to the straight roads up the Sambre and Meuse, of which the former had a third door at Maubeuge. This seemed to be the obvious way because it pointed a straight line to Paris, with a first rate railway: hence the three fortresses. If the invasion of Belgium had been only a supporting operation to a main advance elsewhere, this might have been the only road taken (except those through the Ardennes).

The tearing up of the "scrap of paper" might then have been comparatively easily forgiven, for, though the country would have been injured, it would not have been ruined. The destruction of Belgium was due mainly to the overrunning of the Flanders plain, which was due mainly to the desire to practice the favourite German manoeuvre in the shape of an enveloping movement against the weak western wing of the Allies. No human scruple was allowed to obstruct this design; and. though complete success was not achieved, it was a leading factor in determining the precipitate retreat on Paris.

The question with which we started—Why should the Germans take nineteen days to pass Namur, and only thirteen more to reach the outskirts of Paris?—may, therefore, be provisionally answered thus: A longer period is naturally occupied in preparing than in delivering what is intended as a "smashing blow." The dominating feature of the preliminary phase of the campaign was not any of the events which at the time loomed large and red in the public eye, but was the secret preparation of a force calculated by the numbers, speed, organization, and directions of its attack to overwhelm all possible opposition. A secondary, but important, feature was the successful westward movement through the Ardennes toward the Sambre. On all these heads, the Allies were ill-informed. But they were also ill-prepared in the north for reasons arising from the political character of the war and Germany's advantage as the aggressor; from weakness of immediately available numbers, due partly to the prior need of a strong defence on the east, partly to the choice of Alsace for an offensive; and from necessary economies in the past as illustrated in the disarmament of the entrenched camp of Lille. The immediate penalty fell with disproportionate force upon the small British army which formed the extreme left or western wing; and to its more than Spartan endurance and vigour was largely due the later turn of fortune.

Chapter 7

The Battle of Mons-Charleroi

The plain of central Belgium lies between the middle courses of the two great rivers which sweep round it to Antwerp and Rotterdam respectively, the Scheldt and the Sambre-Meuse. Rising near each other in northern France, they are firmly divided by the hilly region which forms the southern boundary of the plain, between Condé-on-Scheldt and Charleroi on the Sambre. This region, after being for many centuries one of the cockpits of Europe, had become during the last generation one of its busiest industrial districts, the seat of Belgium's greatest coalfields and ironworks. The two alien characteristics are marked all over the countryside, the one in many famous battlefields, ruined castles and abbeys, and names that have the ring of a bugle-call; the other in crowded and towering mine-heads, furnaces, foundries, glass-works, and the close network of railways and canals needed for their service.

The little River Haine (hence "Hainault") trickles westward to the old fortress town of Condé, crooning to itself some song of bygone chivalry; but the straight line of the Mons-Condé Canal rather seemed to typify the material purposes of the twentieth century, until the cannon woke again the echoes of the past. Hither came once more armed hosts to seize the gates of the fair fields of France; and, to save them, Sir John French stood upon the hill, Mons, where Caesar pitched one of his *castra* against the Gauls, while General Lanrezac held the bridge-head that Vauban had fortified for Louis Quatorze. Jemappes, Waterloo, Fleurus, and Ramillies lay before them, for remembrance.

Rising from these hills, and ultimately to join the Scheldt, four lesser streams run northward across the plain, with roads and railways beside them—the Dendre (to Alost), the Senne (to Hal and Brussels), the Dyle (to Wavre and Louvain), and the Gette (to Tirlemont), Four railroads from these towns, beside the main line of the Meuse-Sambre Valley, were soon, if not immediately, available, in addition to the great highways, for the three German armies which, rested and ready to the last button, were now flooding south, with cavalry and motor-car parties flung out far to the west by Oudenarde and Ghent toward Lille, as well as forward of the central advance. The parade through Brussels of 40,000 picked troops had been a very successful blind. A day later—August 21—these were moving on, the mass of troops, who had never entered the city, well in front of them.

It is noteworthy that the German staff resisted every temptation to touch the Channel coast during the effort to cut British communications on that side. Maubeuge (through Charleroi), Valenciennes (through Mons), and Lille (through Tournai) are the main Belgian routes to Paris; and these were the routes of the western invasion. How bold and skilful it was, in design, preparation, concealment, and execution, was recognized only when too late. The French War Office had just been advertising the enemy as an insane "horde of unbridled savages." It now learned that these savages were capable of an unprecedented effort of military organisation. The nations concerned began to realize the full gravity of their task, and the sacrifices it involved.

From Meuse to Scheldt, half a million men—on foot and horse and in motor-buses, with guns, light and heavy, and ammunition wagons, armoured automobiles, columns of food and other supplies, engineer corps, aeroplanes, field telegraphs, pontoons, ambulances, and officers' cars—moved south with machine-like regularity and speed. We have seen that the French had failed to hold their positions in the Ardennes, and, before the fall of Namur, had fallen back up the Meuse toward Givet, so that Namur was left isolated, and the left wing of the Fifth Army, on the Sambre, uncovered. All the week beginning August 16, the French on the Sambre had been in touch with flying columns of the German screen, as far north as Gembloux. On Thursday evening, August 20, the pressure to the northwest of Charleroi was perceptibly increasing.

The northwest was still relatively free; and Mons was not threatened, although numerous bodies of *Uhlans* had been found about Nivelles and Hal, and the railway from Mons to Brussels (thirty-five miles) was cut midway. Early on Friday morning, the 21st, a column of *Uhlans* broke into Charleroi, whose garrison was strengthened by a battalion of the line, some *Chasseurs d'Afrique* and Turcos, with artillery. Whether because they were mistaken in the thick mist, or because

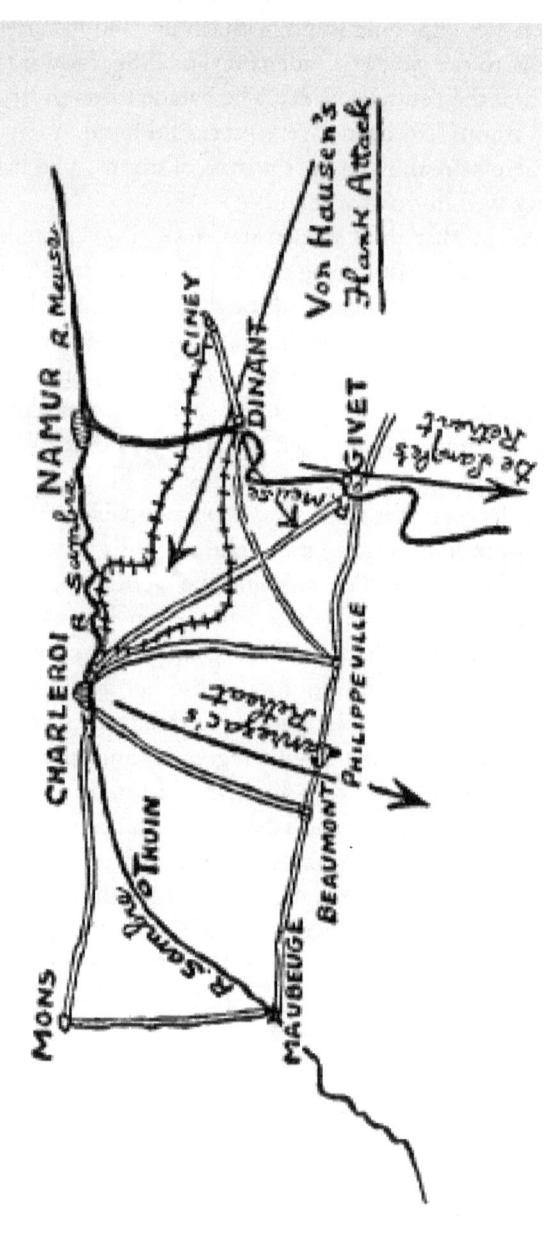

The French defeat at Charleroi

they claimed to be such, the *Uhlans* were hailed as British troops.

That afternoon, the first shells fell on the railway station. All the northern approaches to Mons and Charleroi were swarming with bodies of the invaders on Saturday, and the serious fighting had begun. Artillery posted to the south of Charleroi checked the first advance on the town and the Sambre bridges above and below. Infantry regiments were brought up, but not in sufficient numbers to make a pursuit possible. By Sunday evening, the position was very precarious. Charge after charge had been made by one side and the other under a continual bombardment, the town being repeatedly taken and retaken. In one of these encounters, the Turcos inflicted heavy losses on the Prussian Guard Corps. But the French were steadily losing ground. Some buildings had been destroyed by the German artillery, others deliberately fired by the attackers; and, before it had been decided to retire, the place had become uninhabitable. No full account of the battle of Charleroi has yet been permitted to appear; but, six months afterwards. General Joffre was reported as saying to a French friend: "We ought to have won it. Our army was numerous. We lost through our own faults—faults of command."

Probably the gravest was an over-sensitiveness to the threat on the eastern flank. However this may be, it was known at French headquarters on Sunday afternoon, August 23, that the resistance of Namur was broken, that two of Von Hausen's three corps were advancing on the east flank, that Von Bülow held the passages of the Sambre between Namur and Charleroi, and that the attack in the west was very much more powerful than had been anticipated. The British commander-in-chief was informed, after some unexplained delay; and the withdrawal of the French troops towards Beaumont and Philippeville began. Meanwhile, the British army—of whose movements we have precise and authentic information in Sir John French's dispatch of September 7—had been holding its own more successfully. It was, as yet, only two army corps strong, and the concentration of these was only effected on Friday, August 21.

During Saturday, positions were taken up and entrenched, the 2nd Corps, under Sir H. Smith-Dorrien, holding the line of the canal from Condé (5th Division, General Ferguson) to Mons (3rd Division, General Hamilton), and the 1st Corps, under Sir D. Haig (1st and 2nd Divisions) extending eastward to Binche, where the 5th Cavalry Brigade (Sir P. Chetwode) covered the right. The four brigades of the Cavalry Division, under General Allenby, formed a reserve pending the arrival

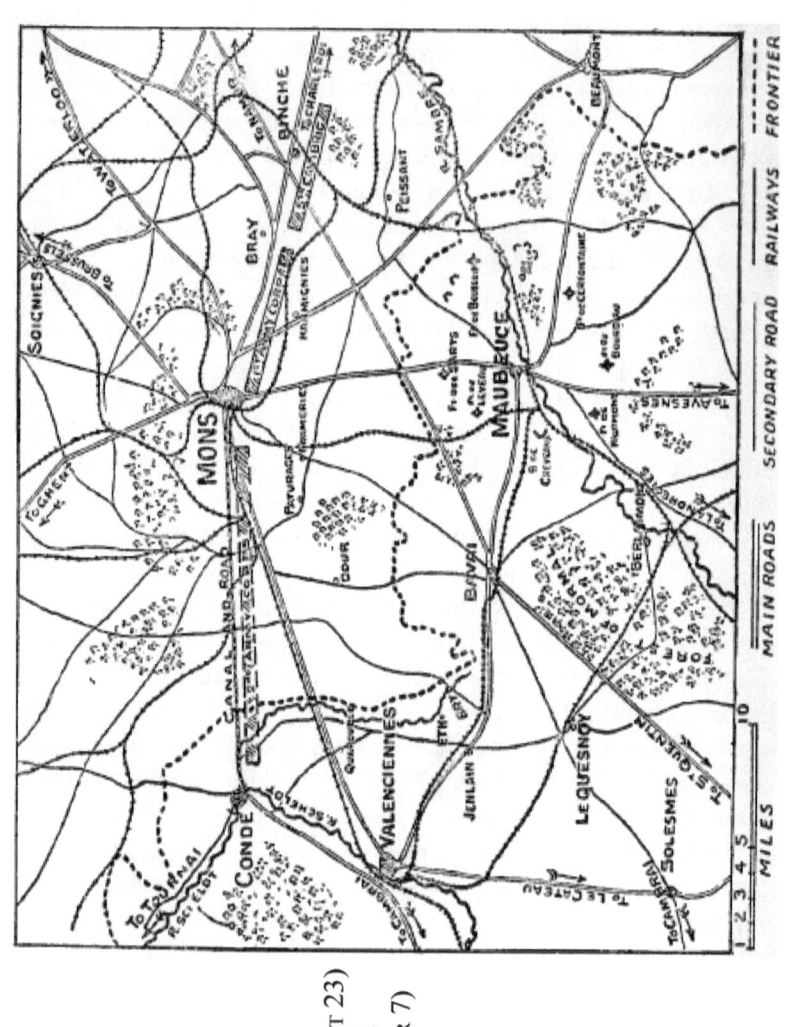

BATTLE OF MONS (AUGUST 23)
SIEGE OF MAUBEUGE
(AUGUST 25-SEPTEMBER 7)

of the 3rd Army Corps, and also aided Sir P. Chetwode in scouting work on Saturday and Sunday, when skirmishes took place as far north as Soignies, on the Brussels road. Saturday passed quietly in and behind Mons in preparatory work. Mr. Atkins stripped to the waist for his morning tub; and one imperturbable British soldier, who had tied a fishing-line to the end of his rifle, was seen playing Izaak Walton in the unlikely waters of the Scheldt-Sambre Canal. Parties were sent out to blow up the canal bridges—Captain Theodore Wright, of the Engineers, afterwards received the Victoria Cross for gallantry in this work. Lieutenant Dease and Private Godley, of the 4th Fusiliers, and Lance-Corporal Jarvis, of the Engineers, for defending the passage. Meanwhile the infantry and artillery occupied points of vantage overlooking the valley. In several villages, in order to establish good zones of fire, a number of houses had to be destroyed, the inhabitants taking refuge with their neighbours. Hundreds of them helped the soldiers to dig trenches and build barricades.

The German attack began on Sunday morning, the 23rd. At that time. Sir John French's information from General Joffre seemed to be confirmed In' his own patrols and aeroplanes—"that little more than one, or at most two, of the enemy's army corps, with perhaps one cavalry division, was in front of my position, and I was aware of no attempted outflanking movement." The first serious attack came that afternoon on the right wing. Before this, the 1st Corps drew back to high ground south of Bray, Chetwode's cavalry evacuated Binche, which the Germans at once occupied; and before dark Mons, now "a somewhat dangerous salient," was abandoned, General Hamilton's division, the centre of the line, being drawn back behind the (own. The Royal Irish and Middlesex regiments, part of this division, forming the right wing of the 2nd Army Corps, suffered heavily from a surprise attack of artillery and infantry on the east of Mons, but, with the aid of the Gordon Highlanders, beat it off, and held their position till 9 p. m., when orders were received to retire.

One of the aforesaid villagers, who watched the battle from the centre of the British line at Paturages, afterward a refugee in Paris, gave me an exceptionally intelligent account of the events of these three days; and a part of his story may be here transcribed:—

> The British were still busy strengthening their positions when, on Sunday morning, we were surprised by a sudden attack. The Germans were coming out of the woods to the north-

west of Mons in numbers greatly superior to the British. At the same time, another considerable force of the enemy assailed the French positions beyond. The first German rush on the British advance posts near the canal was quickly repelled; and we could see them falling back into the woods. The distance between the two armies would then be about three miles. From our higher positions we could follow the whole movement of the invaders as they emerged into the plain from the shelter of the trees. It appeared to me to be the British tactics to cease fire abruptly all along the line until the Germans, supposing that there was a weakening of the defence, swarmed out of the woods and made rapidly toward the canal. Then, when the distance seemed right, the British artillery would open upon them a devastating fire, which was echoed by that of the rifes in the trenches. Thousands of Germans fell.

By nightfall on Sunday, they had not made any progress, and their dead and wounded were scattered over the hills between the canal and the forest. The German shells, on the other hand, were not very effective, and the British losses were comparatively small. The fighting slackened during the night, but was resumed at daybreak more violently than ever. The Germans had evidently received large re-enforcements. Advance parties of dragoons and *Uhlans* tried to reach the canal. Most of them were killed by the guns, but some were made prisoners. Then an advance was made *en masse*, and, although whole ranks were mowed down by a well-directed fire, the main body managed to reach the north bank of the canal, and began to build bridges, without which they could not get at the British positions. Ten several times the Germans succeeded in throwing pontoons over the water, and ten times the British artillery destroyed them. Closer and more desperate fighting took place in the village of Jemappes on the west. The British occupied a part of the place, and for a time held it against an attack, in the course of which whole columns of German infantry fell, so that, as a friend who witnessed the engagement told me, the bodies of the dead were piled one upon another at several points, completely blocking the streets.

The courageous conduct of two Belgian doctors on this occasion became, properly, the matter of after-notice by the Belgian Government. An ambulance had been established at the villages of Hornu and Wasmes, between Paturages and the canal; and hither came Dr. Lecocq and Dr. d'Huart to tend some wounded among the British infantry and artillery in the neighbourhood. Some colliery buildings were first used; but the German gunners got the range, and poured in a rain of shrapnel and shells. One of the ambulances being hit, another building was chosen; but this also was soon under fire. Nevertheless, the doctors and their assistants continued steadily at their work. One of them afterwards said:—

> From a top attic, I could keep count of the shells that fell among the buildings to the right, to the left, in front, and behind. Tiles and windowpanes of the ambulance station flew in fragments; pieces of the sides of the house fell away; and the dust of the ground and of the plaster mingled with the yellow smoke of the great shells. The colliery chimney had covered all the space around it with broken bricks.

At 5 p.m. on the 23rd, General French learned that the attack was being made by forces more than twice as large as those reported in the morning, and that Charleroi was being evacuated. General Joffre's "most unexpected" telegram stated that "at least three German corps, *viz.*, a Reserve corps, the 4th Corps, and the 2nd Corps, were moving on my position in front, and that the 2nd Corps were engaged in a turning movement from the direction of Tournai." A retirement of the whole line about fifteen miles due south, to positions which had already been reconnoitred, just beyond the frontier, between Maubeuge and Jenlain, was at once decided upon. This movement began at daybreak on Monday the 24th. To cover it, the 1st Division, from about Harmignies, advanced as though to retake Binche, the 2nd Division supporting it about Peissant. The 2nd Corps was thus enabled to withdraw to the line Quarouble-Dour-Frameries; but its right, the 3rd Division, suffered heavily during the operation by a German pursuit from Mons.

Sir Douglas Haig then gradually withdrew the 1st Corps, which reached its place between Maubeuge and Bavai without much further loss by 7 p.m. The chief German strength during this afternoon seemed to be directed against the British left. Early in the morning, indeed, General Allenby had been summoned urgently to bring cavalry toward the wing retiring from Condé to Quarouble, the 5th Division being very hard pressed. This was effected; but the 9th Lancers and 18th Hussars, part of General de Lisle's 2nd Cavalry Brigade, were pulled up by wire obstacles during a charge upon the German flank, and lost heavily. Though themselves in a serious plight, a squadron of the lancers succeeded in bringing away a battery of guns that had been put out of action. Captain Francis Grenfell afterwards received the Victoria Cross for this feat. Smith-Dorrien had, according to General French, two German army corps on his front, and one on his flank. It is not surprising, therefore, that the retirement was costly. On the evening of the 24th, the 2nd Corps halted between Jenlain and Bavai, and the 1st between Bavai and Maubeuge. The arrival of re-enforcements, the 19th Infantry Brigade, had somewhat strengthened the position on the left. But if there had ever been an idea of resting here, it was quickly dispelled by two decisive considerations—the continued retirement, on the east, of the armies of Lanrezac and De Langle, up the Sambre and Meuse valleys, pressed by Von Bülow and Von Hansen, and the ever more imminent threat of envelopment on the west.

Uhlan patrols were, in fact, boldly raiding over a wide area. One such body crossed the frontier near Condé on this night, the 24th, traversed the neighbouring towns and villages, doing some small damage, and was at last caught by a French artillery column, at Bouchain. A similar patrol of dragoons was stopped near Roubaix, north of Lille, on the morning of the 23rd. Yet another was captured at the gates of Courtrai by a detachment of mounted *chasseurs*. Its chief officer was found to be a Lieutenant Count von Schwerin, a connection of the *Kaiser*; the young man's blood-stained sword was found, by an inscription upon it, to be a present from the emperor himself. One of the purposes of these raids, no doubt, was to spread alarm throughout the countryside; and in this they were so successful that, during the next few days, the French Government had to cope with a vast civilian exodus from the north, in addition to a foreign invasion. The retreat of the French and British armies was no little embarrassed by the plight of the frightened villagers.

The refugee, a part of whose story I have quoted, was one of a party of some hundreds, men, women, and children, who were being taken through Paris on the night of August 27 to one of the concentration camps in the west of France. Most of them were peasants and workpeople; and they carried little bundles of clothes and food, all they had been able to save. As they passed down the *boulevard*, a torrential downpour of rain fell. It was as though the heavens would wash away the mist of blood that enveloped us; but I thought of Lady Macbeth's futile cry, for, guilty agents or guiltless victims, not in the lifetime of any of us can the "damned spot" of this imperial crime be wiped away. The policeman who guided the wretched exiles hurriedly drew them into the covered entry of the underground railway near the Madeleine; and it was there we found them.

My informant concluded so:—

The British troops told us, at about 2 p.m. on Monday, to make our escape while we could. They spoke in English; but their gestures and meaning were plain enough, and fifteen hundred of us gathered hurriedly a few things, and while we were doing so an English officer, who spoke French, directed us over the frontier, and at Berlaimont (fifteen miles south of Paturages) we got train for Paris. Many of the peasants, especially the women and children, could not fly with us, but hid in their cellars. We knew that, after the capture of a village, the Germans ransack the cottages, and fire volleys at the terrorised people hidden inside. Some they take out and drive before them as a protection. The English might have better opposed the advance of some German columns, but that they would not sacrifice our folk by firing through them.

With this, the rainstorm having passed, my Belgian friend hoisted on to his shoulder one big bundle, while his wife, who seemed very tired, took up another hardly less heavy. But, as the party came out into the street, one of the police stepped up to her, and took the burden, saying: "Give it to me; it is too heavy for you. I'll carry it."

It was in such tales as these that the people of France received the first serious premonitions of the approaching storm. The influx from the northern frontier began on August 26. It being evidently impossible to leave such an emergency to be dealt with by private societies, the Prefect of Police intervened; and the Cirque de Paris, situated between the Invalides and the Eiffel Tower, was turned into a refugee camp. The stalls and boxes, galleries and corridors of this large building overflowed with human jetsam. Instead of children's happy laughter over clownish jokes, the rotunda was filled with a ground-swell of lamentation, broken by the sharp cries of babes. Their eyes red with weeping, their faces drawn with fatigue, the elder exiles sat dumb; only here and there was one calm enough to tell a clear tale.

A woman from Frameries, one of the villages in the British lines by Mons said:—

"My husband is with the Belgian Army, and I was left with my three babies in our cottage. When the Germans came on Monday, they sacked and destroyed every house, and nothing remains of our poor village but ruins. I saw one of these bandits strike one of my neighbours in the breast with his sword, and then flourish the bloody blade, as though proud of the feat."

A housekeeper from Chatelet, near Charleroi, said that she, with her mother and five children, had had to walk for seventy miles forward and about, before she reached the train that brought her to Paris. Another woman, from Péronne, near Binche, had started out with a neighbour who carried a young child at her breast. On the way, the mother suddenly found that the little one was dead. She could not bear this new shock, and became mad. When she was helped out of the train on reaching Paris, she still held, and was crooning over, the body of her child.

Through the broken sentences of these martyrs of war appeared a dim image of a land ruthlessly invaded and ravaged. We could see the headlong escape from burning villages in the night; the terror of the unknown worse even than that visible in horizons riven by flashes of murderous fire; the barefooted children crying because they could not run fast enough; the old folk left by the way. All ordinary distinctions had been lost in the despair of the random flight. There were now no more "gentlemen" and "workmen," "Protestants" or "Catholics," "Flemings" or "Walloons." All were simple paupers, filled today with a dumb fear, that would too often crystallise tomorrow into a lasting hatred. Was this to be the fate of France, also?

Chapter 8

The Retreat to the Marne

The position on the night of August 24-25 is thus described by the British commander-in-chief:—

The French were still retiring; I had no support except such as was afforded by the fortress of Maubeuge; and the determined attempts of the enemy to get round my left flank assured me that it was his intention to hem me against that place and surround me. I felt that not a moment must be lost in retiring to another position. I had every reason to believe that the enemy's forces were somewhat exhausted, and I knew that they had suffered heavy losses. I hoped, therefore, that his pursuit would not be too vigorous to prevent me effecting my object. The operation, however, was full of danger and difficulty, not only owing to the very superior force in my front, but also to the exhaustion of the troops.

Sir John French does not say, but it is apparent, that General Joffre had already determined upon a retreat of the northern armies to the line of the Marne, or even to that of the Seine, a movement pivoting upon Verdun, the north end of the eastern line of defence, and bringing the west wing swiftly round to lean upon Paris. It needed a bold mind to conceive a scheme involving so large an abandonment of national territory, and good men to execute it. A lesser intelligence would have relapsed into day-to-day expedients, fighting rear-guard actions from one defensive position to another, till the armies were divided and broken up, and the German host could strike at Verdun and Nancy from the rear, and, by opening that road for reinforcements, complete their task at will.

If the interior line of fortresses—La Fère-Laon-Rheims—had been in fact, as was generally supposed, capable of resisting modern siege artillery, they might have afforded at least a temporary line of arrest. Soldiers may find abundant room for speculation in the possibilities of such a situation. Whatever may be said of the first advances into Alsace and Lorraine, the plan of escape from the northern peril proves that the genial taciturnity of Joseph Jacques Joffre covered a cool, clear brain, capable of large and delicate combinations, a rare knowledge of the terrain of central France, and a firm belief in the willingness of his men to respond to the extraordinary demand now to be made upon their endurance. France had not begun well; and the full force of the invasion was upon her, like a tornado. Few commanders have ever held such a responsibility; but, in the supreme crisis, this captain did not fail.

Before tracing the course of the retreat, it will be well to note some of the strategical considerations of which the opposed commanders had to take account. Subject to the immediate aim of pursuing the retiring armies, the German plan of campaign opened an evident alternative: a leftward turn against the rear of the Verdun-Toul-Epinal line, by way of opening a direct line of communications with central and southern Germany, preparatory to a more formidable advance; or a more immediate concentration against Paris. Doubtless under fear of Russia, the latter way was chosen.

The accompanying skeleton map shows two sets of natural features of northern and eastern France—the chief rivers, and the densely wooded hills called the Forest of the Argonne; and two artificial features—the eastern fortress barrier, and the chief railway lines, which may be taken as sufficiently indicating the direction of the great highroads also. It will be seen that the whole system of communications radiates fan-wise from Paris, northward to Lille, eastward to Nancy. Within these two lines, the serious operations of the campaign were to be limited. Between them, three trunk roads, each with many feeders, lead to the French capital. The most northerly and most important comes down the Oise Valley, uniting, at the important junction marked by the old fortress of La Fère, tributaries from the Ardennes through Hirson, and from Mons by Valenciennes, with the main line from Cologne through Liège, Namur, and Maubeuge.

The second line makes a long detour from Luxemburg to Mézières. and there divides, one branch going through Laon to Paris, the other through Rethel to Rheims. The third is the direct route from Metz to Paris, through Verdun, the Argonne, Châlons. and the Marne

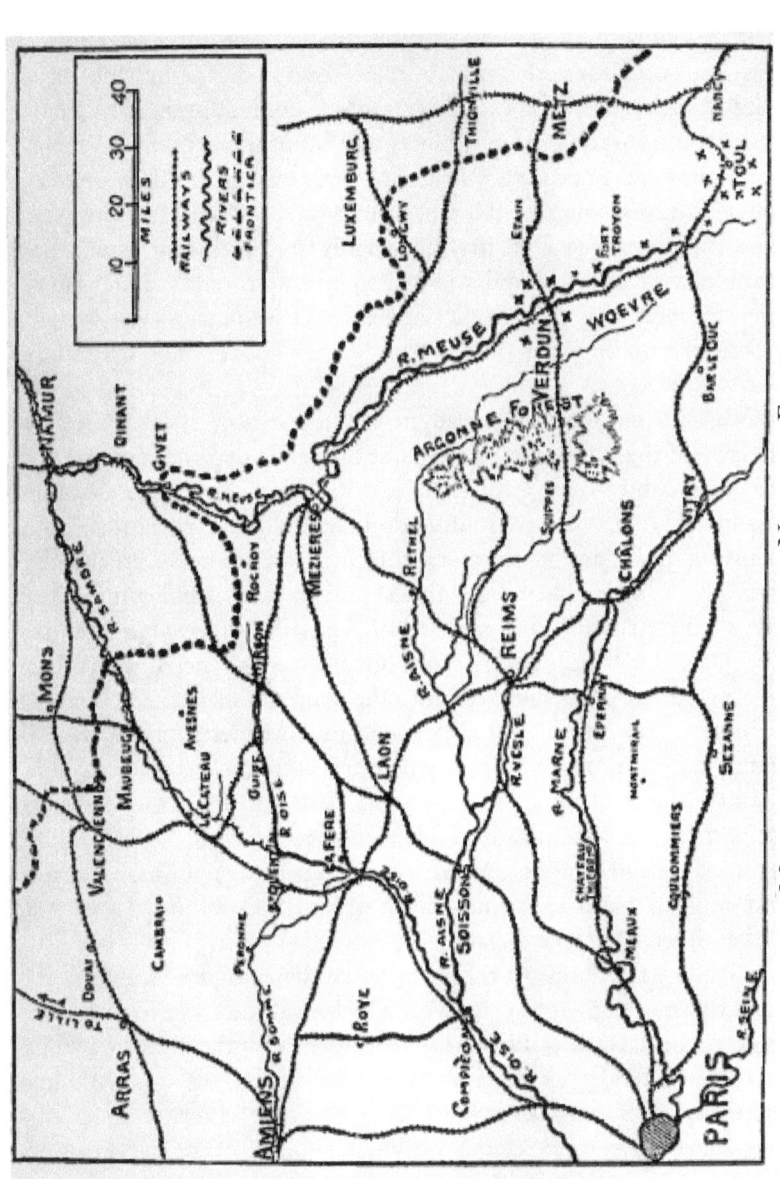

Main railways and rivers of Northern France

Valley, with a feeder touching Rheims and Soissons. Except for a few days, this last remained in French hands, and became the real "line of the Marne" on which the Allies were based. After Paris, Rheims and Amiens are the most important centres of communications, the former dominating the middle plain, and the latter the coast. There is a general south-westerly trend of roads toward the capital; but three main ways run nearly due south: (1) from Cambrai through St. Quentin and Soissons to Château-Thierry and Montmirail; (2) from Vervins to Rheims and Epernay; (3) from Mézières to Châlons. The area between the west wing of the fan, from Mons to Paris, and the base, from Paris to Bar-le-Duc, may be roughly described as an equilateral triangle, with sides 145 miles long, and an eastern entry, about Mézières, 50 miles below the upper angle. The excellence of the French highroads is an important factor. The weather was very hot, with some heavy showers.

We shall see that the onslaught was remarkably synchronised to fall around the whole French front at once, but that the resistance of the Verdun and Nancy armies, the essential condition of General Joffre's manoeuvre, was successful. Verdun could do little more than hold its pivotal point and its southern communications, however; and the crown prince was able to cross the Meuse and advance down the east side of the Argonne toward Bar-le-Duc without serious resistance. The Duke of Würtemberg's army, on the west of the Argonne, had greater difficulty in its progress into the plain of Châlons. The French turned on their pursuers at Charleville, near Mézières, on August 25; and there was more hard fighting before Rethel was reached, at Signy l'Abbaye and Novion-Porcien, on the 28th and 29th. General von Hansen came due southward from Hirson to Rheims; but before the crisis was reached his command seems to have been absorbed in the 2nd and 4th German Armies, those of Von Bülow on its west and Duke Albrecht on its east flanks.

All the importance of the invasion lay with the two western armies, those of Von Bülow and Von Kluck; and these we must follow more particularly. A glance at the map will show the risks of a front so widely extended as theirs was. Considering that the western wing had to cover about twice as much distance as the eastern, contact was kept remarkably well. Yet the weakness could not but declare itself in time. While the Allies were concentrating upon a line with two strong terminals, admirable railway services, easy access to supplies and re-enforcements, and tactical positions known to every student of

Napoleon's campaigns, the invaders were prolonging their supply lines and their fighting front in a gamble on the chance of enveloping the retreating armies on the west, or smashing their centre at one blow.

The greatest mass and capacity were engaged in the former effort; and it was the honour of Sir John French's little army, hardly maintained by re-enforcements at its first strength of about 80,000 men, to bear the main stress of this attack by greatly superior numbers through the three decisive days. The retirement from the positions between Maubeuge and Jenlain began early on the morning of August 25, the direction being south-west, toward a line that was partially entrenched in preparation, from Landrecies, through Le Cateau, toward Cambrai, a march averaging over twenty miles. The 4th Division, under General Snow, had just detrained from the coast at Le Cateau, a welcome element of new strength to compensate for heavy losses. It was at once sent to the west flank, and did good service there. Sir John French says that he had grave doubts about stopping at this point, owing to the continued withdrawal of the French on his right, and "the tendency of the enemy's western Corps (2nd) to envelop me."

But the men could go no further. The 1st Corps, under Haig, pursuing the road by the eastern border of the Forest of Mormal, reached Landrecies at 10 p.m., the 1st Division having been extricated with difficulty in the darkness from a rear attack near Maroilles, with the help of some neighbouring French troops. About the same time, part of the German 9th Army Corps, coming up, probably, by the road on the other side of the woods, entered the narrow streets of Landrecies, where a desperate struggle took place during the night, the 4th (Guards Brigade) at length driving the assailants back with very heavy loss. There had been time to put up some barbed-wire defences; four machineguns covered the entry to the little town; and rows of infantry lay and kneeled across the road. Charge after charge was delivered, and once a gun was lost for a short time. The attack was made in close order; and the German casualties were estimated at from 800 to 900. After two or three hours' sleep, the British troops were roused to resume their march toward Guise.

Meanwhile, on the evening of the 25th, the 2nd Army Corps had reached Le Cateau by the more westerly route, and had taken their posts just south of the Cambrai road. Some battalions had marched thirty miles in the day, and dropped to sleep without waiting for food. For the officers, this was an anxious night. Sir John French had earnestly requested the aid of General Sordêt's Cavalry Corps, which was

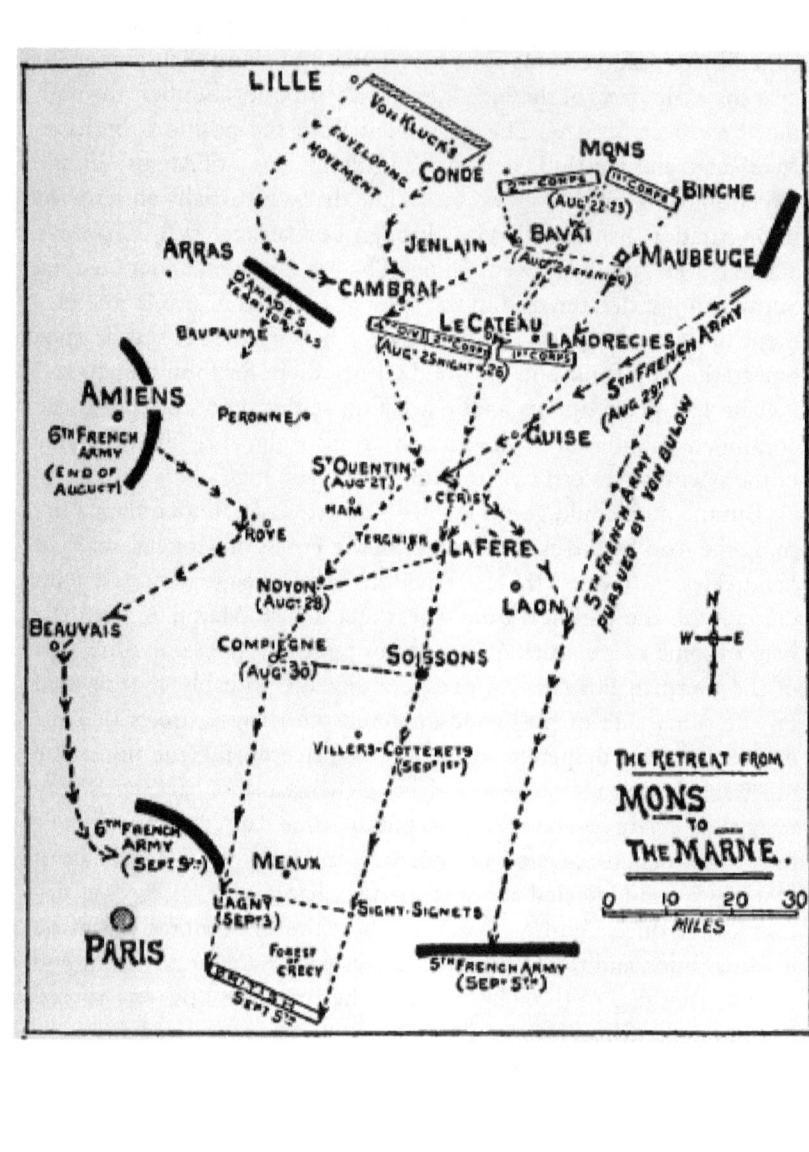

near Avesnes; but the horses were too exhausted to move. The British force was not now absolutely unsupported on its west flank. The French were gathering together toward the coast the elements of the new army which General Maunoury was to use so ably in the battle of the Marne. This was concentrating in the Amiens district, and being joined by fragments of various Territorial units which had put up an ineffectual resistance to the German onrush at Lille, Béthune, Arras, Cambrai, and Bapaume. General d'Amade, of Moroccan fame, lay between Arras and Cambrai; and during the next few days his 61st and 62nd Reserve Divisions were able, as were Sordêt's cavalry, to relieve the pressure upon the sorely-tried British columns.

Wednesday, the 26th, proved to be "the most critical day of all." Field-Marshal French says:—

> At daybreak it became apparent that the enemy was throwing the bulk of his strength against the left of the position occupied by the 2nd Corps and the 4th Division.

Allenby had concentrated two brigades of cavalry south of Cambrai, whence the line ran through Serainvillers to Caudry (4th Division), and on to Le Cateau:

> At this time, the guns of four German army corps were in position against them; and Sir Horace Smith-Dorrien reported to me that he judged it impossible to continue his retirement at daybreak (as ordered) in face of such an attack. I sent him orders to use his utmost endeavours to break off the action and retire at the earliest possible moment, as it was impossible for me to send him any support, the 1st Corps being at the moment incapable of movement. There had been no time to entrench the position properly, but the troops showed a magnificent front to the terrible fire which assailed them. The artillery, although outmatched by at least four to one, made a splendid fight, and inflicted heavy losses on their opponents.

One of many thrilling incidents in this stand of one corps, one division, and two cavalry brigades, against five corps, including some of the best German troops, was a charge of the Prussian Guards Cavalry Division upon the British 12th Infantry Brigade, "when the German cavalry were thrown back with heavy loss and in absolute disorder." By the afternoon, the weight of repeated infantry attacks—concentrated upon parts of the line which could not be strengthened, as there were no reserves—had become intolerable. It was:—

> .... apparent that, if complete annihilation was to be avoided, a retirement must be attempted; and the order was given to commence it about 3.30 p.m. The movement was covered with the most devoted intrepidity and determination by the artillery, which had itself suffered heavily, and the fine work done by the cavalry in the further retreat from the position assisted materially in the final completion of this most difficult and dangerous operation. Fortunately, the enemy had himself suffered too heavily to engage in an energetic pursuit.

Another incident may serve as a type of many. All the officers and men of one battery had been killed except a subaltern and two gunners. These continued to fire one of the guns, and emerged from the battle unscathed. Five Victoria Crosses were granted for this day's work—to Major Yate and Lance-Corporal Holmes, of the 2nd Yorks Light Infantry, the few survivors of which made a desperate charge; and to Captain Douglas Reynolds, and Drivers Luke and Drain, of the 37th R.F.A battery, for bravery in covering the retreat.

Sir John French, in his dispatch, regarded "this glorious stand " as the last phase of" a four-days' battle," in which, heavy as were the British casualties—between 5,000 and 6,000 men—those of the enemy were very much heavier. It was one of the defeats which have all the glory and some of the effects of victory. It had saved the west flank of the Allied armies, and so stiffened the whole retreat. It had checked an onrush on which the success of the invasion depended. It had saved the great body of the British force, and that of General Maunoury. Von Kluck did not immediately draw in toward his colleagues on the east; but, when he saw Smith-Dorrien escape him on the evening of the 26th, he must have known that a direct attack upon Paris was now impossible. Officers and men of all grades had well earned Sir John French's praise and congratulations.

> I say without hesitation that the saving of the left wing of the army on the morning of August 26 could never have been accomplished unless a commander (Smith-Dorrien) of rare coolness, intrepidity, and determination had been present to personally conduct the operation.

The Flying Corps had furnished "must complete and accurate information, which has been of incalculable value," and, incidentally, "by actually fighting in the air, succeeded in destroying five of the enemy's machines." But the most remarkable service of all was the dogged endurance of the rank-and-file, now half-dead for lack of rest.

While Von Kluck was thus sweeping round westward, Von Bülow's army advanced from Charleroi, by Maubeuge, toward Guise and Laon, with the heavy siege guns from Namur in its train. The resistance of Maubeuge is worthy of comparison with that of Liège; and the delay of twelve days which it procured at this important point on the main line of railway was probably one of the chief reasons for the German decision to postpone the attack upon Paris. The first German troops arrived before the place on the 25th. For three days and four nights, they had only heavy mobile artillery (28 cm.) to bring to bear upon the ring of forts; but these pieces were moved about so skilfully that their positions could not be detected by the defenders. On August 29, the large siege howitzers (42 cm.) were got into position five or six miles to the northeast.

Only two of the six forts had been strengthened with concrete and steel cupolas; but the garrison had been increased to 30,000 men, by detachments from Lanrezac's force. It was not till September 7 (while the issue was being decided on the Marne) that Maubeuge surrendered, and full possession of the trunk railway was obtained. A story widely current at the time, that the gun emplacements had been prepared in advance by secret German agents, was afterwards shown to be unfounded. On September 7 the Minister of War sent, on behalf of the French Government, a message of admiration to the Governor of Maubeuge.

The retreat of the British army from Cambrai and Le Cateau was continued through the 27th and 28th by the St. Quentin and Guise roads. The former day witnessed a disaster to the 1st Army Corps, the 2nd Munster Fusiliers being cut off and killed or captured. On the 28th, the retreat lay along the Oise Valley from La Fère, westward through Chauny, to Noyon. It was hoped that the weight of the pursuit had been thrown off; but, on the evening of the 28th, the cavalry brigades covering the retreat were overtaken by large mounted forces of the enemy, General Gough's 3rd Brigade south of the Somme, near Ham, and the 5th Brigade under General Chetwode, near Cérizy, halfway between St. Quentin and La Fère. Both attacks were repelled, Gough driving back the *Uhlans* of the Guard with heavy loss, and the eastern column "suffering very severe casualties and being almost broken up," as General French afterwards reported, by a headlong charge of the 12th Lancers and the Scots Greys.

The gravity of the position could, however, scarcely be exaggerated. The men had marched about ninety miles in four days, fighting several serious engagements, skirmishing continually, leaving villages just as the enemy entered them, and getting very little sleep. Many men, naturally, fell out of the ranks, lost themselves, and were either hidden for a time by the remaining inhabitants till they could find their way south, or were captured. The marvellous thing is that the line of supplies and communications with the coast was never lost. The base had to be twice changed—first to Havre, then to St. Nazaire, with an advance base at Le Mans. The short German occupation of Amiens did not otherwise inconvenience the British force.

Happily, General Joffre was now able to make dispositions which finally relieved it of the peculiarly onerous and perilous part it had had to play. These he explained during a visit to General French at 1 p.m. on August 29. The latter wrote to Lord Kitchener:—

> I strongly represented my position to the French commander-in-chief, who was most kind, cordial, and sympathetic, as he has always been.

The plan was three-fold: (1) the western wing had to be more effectually guarded; (2) new forces had to be gathered for the intended recoil; (3) in the meantime, the retreat was to be continued to the Marne, the eastern armies conforming to the western movement. The first requirement was met by bringing General Maunoury's new 6th French Army (composed of the 7th Corps, four reserve divisions, and Sordêt's Cavalry Corps) into touch with what had been the British left from near Amiens to Roye; while the 5th Army (General Lanrezac), which was behind the Oise, between La Fère and Guise, was moved west across the British rear against the German advance from about Péronne. While these steps were being taken, the British force retired without interference to positions to the north of the Aisne between Compiègne and Soissons. Though Von Kluck seemed to have completely recovered from the check at Le Cateau, and attacked on three lines with undiminished vigor and a largely superior strength, the French counter-offensive was partially successful, and wholly served its purpose. Against the four corps of the 5th French Army, on the Oise. there were five or six German corps marching from the Somme. Sir John French says:—

> At least two corps were crossing the Somme east and west of Ham.

Three or more corps were directed against Maunoury further west. The French right met the first shock between St. Quentin and Guise, on the 29th, and inflicted a severe defeat upon the Guard 10th and Guard Reserve Corps, which were driven back in disorder, with heavy loss, by the 1st and 3rd Corps, the north wing of the 5th French Army. The left about Roye and Ham was less successful; and, threatened with being cut off. General Maunoury retired from Amiens and the Somme to Beauvais, blowing up railway bridges on the line to Paris, and road bridges, as he did so.

General Joffre, we may suppose, had two particular preoccupations at this juncture. The first was to watch over the integrity of the line of the Allies,—for the maintenance of the line was essential to an effective recoil—a task of great difficulty under the pressure of speed and superior numbers which an extraordinary organisation enabled the German commanders to maintain. A strong stand, as at Guise on the 28th and at Rethel on the 29th, checked a dangerous sagging of the long front (or rear) at these points; and the actions west of Le Cateau and Guise had served the further purpose of pressing the heavy enveloping movement outward toward the west, so that it would presently itself be broken against the fortifications of Paris, or would have to be drawn in eastward under very disadvantageous conditions. There is no reason to think that a stand upon the old fortress line La Fère-Laon-Rheims was ever thought of. The armies were not yet in a condition to turn and stand. Their re-enforcements were not at hand.

Above all, General Joffre had a better plan. The million-headed civilian began at this moment to be obsessed by the fear of a new siege of Paris, or an assault which might multiply a hundred-fold the horrors of Liège. Joffre knew that he was getting Von Kluck upon the horns of a dilemma of which it would be difficult to say which would be the more fatal, the assault upon Paris, with all the Allied armies intact, or its refusal. It was for the other end of the line, rather than for this upon which the eyes of the world were concentrated, that the *generalissimo* must have felt most anxiety. Would the eastern wall, from Verdun, down the lesser forts of the Meuse, through Nancy and Toul to Epinal, hold firm? The French had abandoned the line of the Meuse between Verdun and Mézières on August 26.

The Imperial Crown Prince would hardly be given the least important role in the invasion. Suppose that, coming down the east of the Argonne, and joining hands with the Duke of Würtemberg in southern Champagne, he should be able, if not to cut through the armies of General Ruffey (now passing under the command of General Sarrail) and De Langle de Cary, at least to press them so far south as to make it impossible to keep up the communications of Verdun, to compel the withdrawal of De Castelnau from Lorraine, and so to open the road from Metz to the Marne?

In face of such risks, amid such preoccupations, General Joffre prepared for the day when the retreat would end and the reaction begin. While General Gallieni was making ready the army and defences of Paris, and General Maunoury was concentrating to the north-west of the fortified ring of the capital, a new army, consisting of three corps from the south, was brought into the space between the right of the 5th Army (which now passed from the command of General Lanrezac to that of General Franchet d'Espérey) and the left of the 4th, that of General de Langle de Cary. It will be remembered that the corresponding part of the German front was weakened about this time by the disappearance of Von Hansen's separate command. This new 7th [1] French Army, under one of the ablest officers of the Republic, General Foch, constituted, therefore, a considerable relative strengthening of the Allied centre.

At Compiègne, forty-five miles from Paris, the south-westward direction of the British retreat was changed to due south, to bring the force below the Marne, with its left resting upon the eastern defences of the city. Rearguard actions were repeatedly fought, for the pursuit had not flagged, though most of its weight fell elsewhere. On September 1 the 10th Cavalry Brigade and the 4th Guards Brigade were overtaken by German cavalry in the thickly wooded tracts south of the Aisne known respectively as the Forest of Compiègne and the Forest of Villers-Cotterets. The former column momentarily lost a Horse Artillery battery, 165 of its men being killed or captured; but some detachments from the 3rd Army Corps—which had now arrived at the front, under General Pulteney—were brought up, and not only were the guns recovered, but twelve German guns were also taken.

Captain Bradbury, Sergeant-Major Dorrell, and Sergeant Nelson won Victoria Crosses in this action. The 4th Guards Brigade, a part of the 1st Corps which had come through Soissons, was less fortunate, and lost about 300 men killed and wounded. It was regarded as worthy of note on this occasion that "the Germans were seen giving assistance to our wounded." The following day was one of compara-

---

1. I adopt the usual French numbering. Sir John French in his dispatches speaks of this army as the 9th, and some English writers have followed him.

tive quiet; and, on September 3, Sir John French's columns lay south of Meaux (between Lagny and Signy-Signets), having destroyed the Marne bridges behind them at the request of the French commander-in-chief. This proved to be insufficient for General Joffre's purpose. The trap must be made a little deeper.

So, while Von Kluck's and Von Bülow's horsemen dashed across the river by hurriedly constructed bridges at La Ferté and Château-Thierry, the British fell back to the River Seine, and there waited. They had hardly been on French soil for three weeks, had fought in that time two great battles and many smaller engagements, and had lost nearly a fifth of their original strength, about 15,000 officers and men. Well might there be tears in many an island home. But these men embraced their task without fear, and, cheered by new drafts to fill the gaps in their ranks, cheered more by the rumour that the retreat was ended, turned grim faces toward the north.

The more easterly part of the French line was coincidently drawn back till it had crossed the series of westward-flowing rivers of central France—the Oise, Aisne, Vesle, Ourcq, Marne, Petit Morin, and Grand Morin. Here it was arrested on the line Meaux-Coulommiers-Esternay-Vitry-le-François-Revigny-Verdun. The anniversary of Sedan, September 1, had come and gone, a great disappointment for Potsdam.

CHAPTER 9

Paris Prepares for the Worst

On August 27, the reconstruction of the French Ministry, as an enlarged Government of National Defence, was announced. M. Viviani retained the premiership; M. Millerand succeeded M. Messimy as Minister of War; M. Briand went to the Ministry of Justice, M. Delcassé to the Quai d'Orsay, and M. Ribot to the Ministry of Finance. M. Sembat and M. Guesde were also included in this strong combination. M. Clémenceau remained prominently outside, as did M. Caillaux, who later on accepted an administrative mission to South America. The changes were favourably received, though the censorship put all demonstrations out of the question.

The appointment, on the same day, of General Gallieni as Military Governor of Paris excited keener interest, for it bore more directly upon the question that was now beginning to fill most minds. On the day of the first air-raid, when the Germans were as near as Birmingham is to London, Paris presented an appearance of complete calm. It seemed to me that there were more shops open than there had been; rows of chairs had reappeared before the chief cafes; and the return of a radiant sunshine, after some days of gloom and rain, typified the smiling stoicism which is the strength of the French genius. There was no scare; the question was inevitable, and was intelligently discussed. Probably a half of the families in the city had some relative in the retreating armies. We were constantly meeting wounded soldiers, or refugees from the north, or families returning tardily from their holidays on the coast (15,000 such passengers were said to have come into Paris on one day, the 27th).

Cool heads remarked that an attack upon Paris while the Allied armies were intact would be madness. That, however, could hardly be conclusive—to the good patriot, the enemy is usually mad; and this particular enemy had lately shown no scruple about bombarding large towns. Evidently, General Gallieni did not think the question needless, for his "Army of Paris," with thousands of civilians helping, was busy night and day strengthening the fortifications; and the Bois de Boulogne and neighbouring lands had been turned into a vast cattle and sheep farm, and large supplies of wheat stored, against the possibility of a siege.

The ring of outer forts has a circumference of nearly a hundred miles, extending thirty miles from east to west between Chelles and Marly, and twenty-three miles north to south, from the Domont to the Palaiseau Fort. The shortest distance between these works and the boundaries of the city is about eight miles. Admitting that the great body of the population would be out of reach of bombardment from the first German positions, how could the defenders hold a line of a hundred miles, and, against the concentrated attack that had reduced Liège, Namur, and Maubeuge, prevent a breach from being made? No doubt, the forts were now connected by a system of trenches and barbed-wire entanglements, and the suburban railway system would serve to convey flying bodies of troops from point to point. If, nevertheless, the circle of forts were broken through, would the city surrender, and a war-tax be agreed to, or not? Governing persons themselves were not completely unanimous in their answers to such questions; probably no authoritative answer could be given till the last moment, when all the circumstances could be weighed. My own impression was that the "smashing blow" was impossible as things stood, but that, if it should come, the people would fight from street to street, and from house to house, at however frightful a cost, rather than tolerate a surrender. Paris, we said to ourselves, may not be a Tchatalja or a Port Arthur; but neither is it an open town to lie honourably abandoned, like Brussels, or a half barbarian Moscow, which the inhabitants can burn before they take refuge in the neighbouring forests to wait for "General Hiver."

At the city gates, on the line of the old ramparts, gangs of men were digging trenches, setting up screens of small trees, and preparing other works of arrest. I was watching one of these groups when an ugly machine, like a huge yellow pot on an automobile chassis, came past. Four dirty soldiers were crowded inside, and there was an ominous little tube sticking out in front. It was an armoured machine gun. Troops, mounted and on foot, constantly passed through the town to the northern suburbs. In the other direction, a growing stream of wheeled traffic from the nearer invaded districts was pouring in. Lost or wounded soldiers, French and British, continually arrived by railway and road. One night, when the post-office had become useless, and we had not yet established a daily courier service to London, I went to the Nord Station to find a passenger willing to take a letter. A convoy of 140 British soldiers wounded in the lighting in the Oise Valley was brought into the crowded great hall, and was the object of a touching demonstration of sympathy, A number of Belgian infantrymen crossing their path, the two parties exchanged hearty salutations. Sometimes we met two or three "Tommies" near the city gates waiting to get in or out, each surrounded by a crowd of women in transports of hero-worship.

"Having a good time?" I shouted to a tired but happy-looking lad in khaki, who was conducting a commissariat wagon and a van marked with the name of a Canterbury laundry company guaranteed for "high-class work."

"Rather too good!" he replied, with a grin.

But these fellows could only tell of isolated incidents, and a general sense that all was going well. Some of them had lost touch with the fighting line, and, after various adventures, found their way to Paris partly on foot, partly by rail. There was one particularly poignant case of this kind. A French officer found a British infantryman exhausted and hungry by the roadside to the north of Paris, and took him to an inn. Returning a little later, he found the man weeping like a child. He had lost his regiment, and could not get it out of his overwrought brain that he would be suspected of having run away, and be court-martialled.

A lady who lived in one of the villages to the north-east of Paris until the approach of the Germans told me an episode out of which, by adding here and subtracting there, an artist would construct a thrilling romance, but whose sting will touch the intelligent mind more sharply if I tell only the naked truth. The village lies not far from Chantilly racecourse, with the smoke of Paris visible on one hand, and a countryside of parks and mansions on the other. Four lost Tommies turned up, and asked for shelter. They had been chased by *Uhlans*; and the *curé* probably realised the risks he ran in taking them into his little house. Early next morning, sure enough, a German patrol rode into the place, summoned the inhabitants together, and demanded the surrender of the Englishmen, threatening dire penalties. Everyone knew where they were, and turned to their spiritual guide. Instinct saves us from reason in such crises. The good *curé* lied boldly, in a loud voice, so that his flock should understand. He had not seen the Englishmen. No doubt they had gone on toward Paris. The German soldiers rode on. What most struck my informant was the exceeding deliberation with which the Atkins four performed their toilet, and brushed their hair and clothes, before making their escape. The *curé* then left for a safer place. When they returned and found all the birds flown, the *Uhlans* took their revenge by burning his house down.

The first of a series of air-raids upon Paris took place in the forenoon of Sunday, August 30, when five bombs were thrown by an aviator who, in a message which he dropped, said: "The German Amy is at the gates of Paris—you can do nothing but surrender," and signed himself "Lieutenant von Heidssen." Two women were wounded, and a number of windows were broken. The exploit alarmed no one but the families which suffered directly. The rumour of what had occurred ran quickly through the city; but the spirit of exaggeration which would have decorated such an outrage in normal times was lacking now. Madame and the children continued their Sunday walk, promising themselves that Jean and his fellows would dispose of these birds of prey. "Attila's visiting card" was not a bad *mot* for Heidssen's letter-case.

M. Henri Bérenger, addressing the German aviator wrote:—

Go back to your Pomeranian Grenadiers. Mimi Pinson is not for you. We don't want your *Kaiser*, nor your *kultur*, nor your *kolossal*. You are not even original, wretched Prussian cuckoo. Where did you get your wings, your motor? Who invented aviation, Germany or France? Who first crossed the Channel or the Alps, a German or a Frenchman? What did you bring under your wings that we should surrender to you—intelligence, or liberty, or justice, truth, or love? Nothing of the kind. You brought death—a bomb—that is all. That is why you will never have Paris. Paris is civilisation in its beauty. You are barbarism in its ugliness. Possibly you may bombard us—burn our city—but we shall never surrender. Paris will be wherever the French flag floats, and in the end Chanteeler will crow over the bloody nest of your crushed tyrants.

On the following day, another German aeroplane appeared over the city, and, after letting off three bombs, which did no material damage, made its escape. On September 1, there was a still bolder raid.

This time the aviator reached the centre of the city, and threw, among others, two bombs which exploded behind the great stores known as the Magazin du Printemps, and in the Avenue de l'Opéra. No great damage was done, strange to say. A gun had been mounted on the roof of the Crédit Lyonnais, and fire was opened there. Two British privates also fired from the *boulevard*, but without effect, the aeroplane being out of range. That night it was announced that a squadron of armoured aeroplanes provided with machine-guns had been organized to pursue such intruders. Accordingly, on Wednesday, September 2, the sportive Parisian was on the *qui vive* for the next German visitor, expecting that the long-promised "battle in the air" would be brought off for his delectation.

The raider duly came, at about six o'clock that evening; and, for at least twenty minutes, he carried out a series of cool evolutions, first over the Invalides, on the south side of the river, where he threw one bomb, if not two, then over the Elysée, and finally over the grand boulevards. I had the privilege of witnessing the performance from a royal box, as it were. I happened to be leaving the British Embassy, and was crossing the courtyard, when the familiar British accents of the porter's voice called out a warning and an invitation to take refuge in his lodge. From this shelter, we watched the daring turns of the aviator over the Elysée and its neighbourhood. Rifle-shots and fire from some kind of small machine-gun were then already being directed at the aeroplane, evidently by men posted in advance on the roofs of various buildings.

The outline of the machine was clearly visible; but, although hundreds of shots were fired, none seemed to hit. I walked back past the Madeleine to the top of the Boulevard des Capucines, and watched the war-hawk make off steadily and disappear to the northeast. Thousands of Parisians witnessed with ironical smiles what seemed rather like a pigeon-shooting match, except that all the chances favoured the pigeon.

Chapter 10

The Flight from Paris

On the night of Monday, August 31, I received privately the alarming news that the Government of France was abandoning its capital, the first city of Continental Europe. At four o'clock on that afternoon, 1,200 of the 1,500 employees of the Ministry of War, of all grades, had received notice, first to send their families into the country immediately, then to go themselves to Tours, taking with them what they could of the material for which they were responsible. The loading of automobiles with office documents, typewriters, and other effects was then proceeding at full pressure. Many of the men had already left. At other Ministries, there was the same scene of hurried packing in corridors full of boxes, and a rapid succession of motorcars carried away the official property as soon as it was ready. Some was taken to the Quai d'Orsay and Austerlitz stations; other motorcars had gone southward by road. The decision to abandon Paris and to shift the seat of Government to Bordeaux was come to on the Monday afternoon at a Cabinet Council, of which a usually trustworthy official gave me a grievous account. This climax had been reached so rapidly, and it is so easy for the stolid Englishman to misunderstand the French temperament—in which wild gesticulations are perfectly consistent with an heroic courage—that I will not repeat my informant's words, lest it should be supposed that there was a flagrant hour of sheer panic. Suffice it that the ministers were not agreed whether to go or stay, but that it was ultimately decided to go.

It is difficult now to recall the sense of impending calamity that then seemed so real, and lay hourly more heavily upon us. At the Central Telegraph Office that Monday evening, I was told that, since the early morning, there had been no communication with London. Letters were three days late. We were, or appeared to be, nearly isolated.

There might have been a great defeat. We did not know. When I went to the War Office at eleven o'clock that night to receive the usual late *communiqué*, I already knew the facts cited above, and had, beside, a bundle of rumours hot enough then to set the Seine on fire; but not now. The officer in charge of the Press service did not usually come in person, but sent an orderly with a parcel of type-written sheets which were distributed without comment. There had been an unusually long *communiqué* at 5 p.m.—a *réchauffé* of the former news which did not indicate any new defeat or cause for anxiety. At 11 p.m. Commandant Thomasson came to us himself, and, after announcing that no official bulletin would be issued, made a short statement, in course of which he admitted that a second aeroplane had appeared over Paris that day and left the usual missiles. Not a word as to what many of the responsible French journalists present must, like myself, have been thinking about. And therefore no guidance in the next morning's papers for the hundreds of thousands of anxious hearts in a city that had been at full stretch of its nervous powers for a month.

Or, rather, there were two notes, faintly struck, in either of which some comfort might be found, but that neither had any apparent authority, and they were quite irreconcilable. Paris is all right, said the one voice; she can stand a long siege, and by that time the Russians will be in Berlin. Paris may be invested, said the other voice, and it is evidently inadvisable for the ministry to be locked up or captured by the enemy. Naturally, it will retire, as the Belgians retired from Brussels to Antwerp. Putting aside for a moment the question of the power of the city to resist assault and to bear a siege, it will be seen that the analogies were unsound. It was supposed that, if the Russians reached Berlin, everything would be over but the shouting, while, when the Germans reached Brussels and Paris, the governments would move away and the resistance be maintained as if nothing had happened. An impartial observer Would say that, if the Russians continued their successful march, the Prussian Government would leave Berlin—and the German people would not lose much by that.

The Belgian Government was in being; but there was this great difference between Brussels and Paris—Brussels was an open town, and could not be defended. Paris had a double ring of fortifications, and we had been told, with every kind and degree of positiveness, that it would resist capture to the last. Evidently, the Government, or the main body of it, should be moved whenever there was any danger of its being captured; but a premature movement of the kind could not but be a severe shock to the Parisian public, and it was a matter of no little local importance that shocks should be avoided if possible, apart from any general effect upon the feeling of the nation.

No news more alarming than statements that the defences were being put in readiness, and that it was advisable for people having relations in the country to send their women and children thither, had been allowed to appear in the Paris Press for a week past. Yet an exodus, now much accentuated, had begun on Saturday, August 29; throughout that and the following days, lines of cabs, many of them filled with household goods, were racing through the *boulevards* to the southern and western railway stations; and a very large part of the population of the city was engaged in discussing whether, and if so how, it should remove itself. A lady who had arranged some time before to leave Paris on the Saturday night for Biarritz had to be content at the last moment with a seat on a rough bench in a cattle truck, into which thirty passengers or more were crowded, without a glimmer of light. The train carried nothing but third-class and trucks, and, stopping at most stations, it took about thirty hours to reach its destination. I went down to the St. Lazare Station on the Sunday morning to see how it was with the British and American passengers leaving at 9.30 by the Havre route. A quite orderly, but tired, anxious, and uncomfortable crowd of about a thousand persons surrounded the entry to the platform, and more were constantly arriving. At noon there were 10,000 persons in and around the Mont Parnasse Station, trying to get train for Rennes, St. Malo, and Brest; and at the Invalides Station, which had been more carefully reserved for military use, the officials said that enough passengers had been booked in advance for Brittany to fill all the trains for a week.

The odd thing was that there was an inflow as well as an outflow, though not on so large a scale. First, there was an uninterrupted stream of refugees from the immediate scene of fighting—the region of Mons, and then the region around Laon. More than 30,000 of these poor people were landed at the Nord Station on the 29th. Many of them were carrying oddments of property with them, and some of the children had been allowed to bring a favourite dog or canary. All of this vast social disturbance was not directed upon Paris. A lady who had a summer cottage near Pontoise described vividly the abandonment of many of the villages on this north-western road by their inhabitants, who had not yet seen the Germans, and were resolved not to see them. Add to the influx of refugees that of wounded soldiers—all the hospitals of the city were not full, but even when expecting a siege, Paris is a great distributing centre—and a smaller number of German prisoners; then offset against these the flight of Parisian families and foreigners, and there is given a problem of social migration that would be very grave even if there were no urgency about getting troops mobilised and to the front. So far, the railways had worked marvellously; and it was not till Sunday, the 30th, that some little effervescence was perceptible among the people of Paris. The cool courage with which the agonies of the past month had been borne deserved every word that the best living French prose writers (there was here no tendency to cheap versification) said in its praise. But this patient loyalty could not safely be abused; and the migration problem could not safely be allowed to be aggravated by an open alarm.

There were various and potent warnings of the gravity of the situation other than the statements of refugees and wounded soldiers. On the evening of August 30, the president of the City Council, M. Mithouard, made a statement advising residents having friends in the country to send their women and children thither, as a siege would mean privation, whatever efforts were made to assure the food supply. On the same day, the papers were forbidden to issue more than one daily edition; and news became scantier than ever. Englishmen, getting through with difficulty by Dieppe and Beauvais, and arriving many hours late, reported that the enemy was at Compiègne, and rumour added falsely that this town, only 45 miles away, was in flames. The War Office admitted that the French Army was continually retreating, but gave no details. It was safe to conclude that the enemy was within two days' march. All round the northern suburbs and outlying districts of Paris, the inhabitants were ordered to get away immediately; and many of these were pouring into the city by the Maillot, St. Ouen, and Clignancourt gates, while others more sensibly took suburban roads to the south. The telegraphs were working subject to many hours' delay, and to England only two wires, *via* Havre, were open on September 3. Orders had been given for all the wounded to be removed outside the "entrenched camp of Paris." Those in hospital at Versailles, sufficiently recovered to be moved, were taken by train to such distant points as Rennes and Nantes.

Secrets, like bombs, are a worrying cargo; and it was with a sigh of relief that I read over my coffee and crust (no fancy rolls in these days!), on the morning of September 3, the proclamation announcing the shifting of the Government to Bordeaux, It was couched in the following terms, and signed by M. Poincaré and all the ministers:

Frenchmen! For several weeks, our heroic troops have been engaged in desperate combats with the enemy. The valiance of our soldiers has given them at some points a marked advantage. But, in the north, the onset of the German forces has constrained us to fall back.

This situation imposes upon the President of the Republic and upon the Government a grievous decision. In order to guard the national safety, it is their duty to move, for the moment, from the city of Paris. Under the command of an eminent chief, a French army, full of courage and spirit, will defend against the invader the capital and its patriotic population. But the war must be pursued at the same time on the rest of our territory.

Without peace or truce, without stay or default, the holy struggle for the honour of the nation and the reparation of violated right will continue. None of our armies is crippled. If some of them have suffered heavy losses, the gaps have been immediately filled from the depots, and the calling up of recruits assures us for tomorrow new resources in men and energy.

To hold out and to fight must be the word of command for the Allied armies, British, Russian, Belgian, and French! To hold out and to fight, while on the sea the British help us to cut our enemies' communications with the outer world! To hold out and to fight, while the Russians continue to advance to strike a decisive blow at the heart of the German Empire! It is for the Government of the Republic to direct this obstinate resistance. Everywhere, Frenchmen will rise to defend their independence. But to give this formidable struggle all its vigour and efficiency, it is indispensable that the Government should retain its freedom of action.

On the demand of the military authority, therefore, the Government is temporarily removing its residence to a place where it can remain in constant relations with the whole of the country. It invites members of Parliament not to remain far away, so that they and it may form the guard of the national unity.

The Government is quitting Paris only after having assured the defence of the city and the entrenched camp by all means in its power. It knows that it need not recommend calm, resolution, and sangfroid to the admirable Parisian population. They are showing, every day, that they are equal to the highest duties.

Frenchmen! Be worthy of these tragic circumstances! We will obtain victory in the end. We will obtain it by a tireless will, by endurance, and by tenacity. A nation which is determined not to perish, and, in order to live, recoils before no suffering or sacrifice, is sure of victory.

Not a hint of this grave step had appeared in the Paris Press till now, although thousands of officials knew of it, and a number of journalists had scented sensation afar off. I had learned that an announcement would be issued before midnight on Thursday, September 3; and this was my excuse for troubling the British Embassy with a call. The great door in the Rue du Faubourg St. Honoré, surmounted with the royal arms, was closed, and the porter had received orders, on this sad and busy day, not to admit any visitors. The reason was soon apparent; indeed, two furniture vans and many half-packed cases in a corner of the courtyard, the unusual bustle on the stairs and in the upper rooms, and large labels showing that many boxes of papers and other property would be left in charge of the American Ambassador, told the whole story so eloquently that there was no need for me to do more than wish the courteous secretary *bon voyage*. All the same, there was something very grievous about this retreat—something, for a civilian, like what the soldier feels when he witnesses a forced retirement on the battlefield.

On Wednesday evening, September 2, their various Excellencies left the Quai d'Orsay Station; and none who saw it is ever likely to forget the scene. Groping my way in the deep, narrow streets about the War Office, on the south side of the river, during the past few nights, I had conceived a perfectly practical affection for the much-slandered moon. You see, they were saving coal and electricity; moreover, it is advisable to give no guidance to hostile airships. So, off the boulevards, the streets were hardly lit at all. We may see again a mild alarm such as had carried scores of thousands of Parisians southward in these critical days; but we are never likely again to see the abandonment of the first city of Europe at dead of night by a cosmopolitan crowd of diplomatists. There was Sir Francis Bertie, in black suit and bowler hat, and Mr. Graham, very tall and fair, talking to the Marquis Visconti-Venosta—the Italian Ambassador himself, Signor Tittoni, being another distinguishable figure, in gray and a soft felt hat.

Mr. Myron T. Herrick, the United States Ambassador, had come down with his wife to say goodbye to his *confrères*, and M. Isvolsky, the *tsar's* envoy, was chatting with the Spanish minister, who, like Mr. Herrick, was remaining in Paris to perform the duties of courtesy that fall upon neutrals at such a time. The windows of each carriage of the special train were labelled with the names of the countries whose representatives it was carrying off—there was even an inscription for the more or less imaginary Republic of San Marino; but no one appeared to answer to this honorific name. There was the Persian minister, and M. Romanos, the black-bearded Greek, and a Russian military *attaché* in uniform, and some Belgians, and all sorts of servants, including a Chinese nurse feeding a yellow baby, with coal-black eyes. And, at last, a soft horn was blown, and the train rolled away. Whatever might be said about the adventurous Herr Taube, and the possibly approaching legions of his still more reckless *Kaiser*, it was no pleasant thing to see the world's delegates pack up their traps, and leave the splendid city of Paris to its fate.

President Poincaré accompanied by all the members of the ministry, left for Bordeaux at 5 a.m. on Thursday, and they were followed in two special trains by the presidents and members of the Senate and Chamber of Deputies, with other official persons. The main body of the staff and the reserves of the Banque de France had already been removed. Of the major embassies, only those of Spain and the United States remained, and the neutrality of the American Republic was oddly marked by the fact that Mr. Herrick had taken charge of the records of the British, the German, and the Austrian Ambassadors. A like transfer of the higher legal machinery of France had been made by sending to Bordeaux fifteen magistrates selected from among the three sections of the Cour de Cassation. During the day, the Presidents of the City Council and the Council of the Seine Department formed a committee, under the authority of the Military Governor, the Prefect of Paris, and the Prefect of Police, for the government of the capital.

A new Prefect of Police, M. Laurent, was appointed in place of M. Hennion, a change warmly welcomed, and connected by rumour with official discussions as to whether, if a breach were made in the line of forts, the city should be surrendered. Thousands of people continued to crowd into the southern railway stations, but there was still no panic. The quietude of the population was a worthy reflection of the courage of the children of the Republic under arms. As one writer said, "*It was a moment for those who act, not those who talk*"; and General Gallieni enjoyed unbounded confidence, both as organizer and as soldier.

Thus was Paris derobed of her accustomed majesty. Long afterwards, we learned that many of the treasures of the Louvre and other museums and public galleries had been secretly removed. Other monuments, and those the most characteristic, if not the most precious, remained only because they could not be shifted. The perspective of the Champs-Elysées was no less glorious because the presidential palace was closed. We could walk among the flowerbeds, the plashing fountains, and the statuary, of the Tuileries gardens, and reflect upon the hollowness of worldly hopes, or discover with a more genuine surprise that nothing avails to extinguish love's young dream. A column of *chasseurs* click-clacked along the Rue de Rivoli: what were they thinking of it all? Perhaps only that the thin moonshine was worth a hundred searchlights to General Gallieni, now master of our immediate destinies. To me, the vague mist of light made all that had seemed so terribly real a few hours before most unreal; and I saw only the ghosts of the soldiers of olden times, called from forgotten graves by the sound of cannon and the cry of the blood-lust, the ghosts of the conquering fighters who built these palaces and arches—and, far behind, under one blue star, the pale ghost of a man who was crucified....

The *chasseurs* passed, and then a regiment of infantry; a little donkey-cart piled with the poor property of a workman's home passed; and a procession of such refugees urged onward to the south through the dead city. With the early daylight, some of the shutters fell, the doors opened, and through these miles of streets, men and women awoke to ask what news there was from Compiègne, whether they too must go into exile, how they could gather together a few shillings for bread upon the journey, and what would happen when that was eaten.

Did I say Paris had lost something of her majesty? But she had gained a majesty higher than the glitter of any official uniforms can give. Let me confess it. I had feared, half expected, trouble in this still crowded population. *Rien du tout!* Where had the volatile, explosive, rather vicious Parisian of forty-four years ago gone? There was no sign of him today. I have no belief in easy generalisations—you do not know much of the mind of two millions of people by observing the faces of two thousand, or by a closer knowledge of two hundred. But, without over-estimating the worth of such evidence as one man can gather, it must yet be said that the quietude of the city, the appearance of a grave confidence and resolution, the perfect order in public places, were things to impress the most sceptical. So far, I do not believe that any human society in time of peril could display in a higher degree than Paris was doing the virtues of calmness, courage, loyalty, and endurance. Used to enjoy her powers and amenities in perfect security, she had suddenly become a frontier town, imminently threatened with a blow hardly less grave in its effect on the national spirit than in its material injuries. Pride and calculation, it is true, combined to throw a ray of light upon this prospect. Many of these Parisians, elders who had given their last and dearest for the national defence, recalled 1870, and could see that it was not now as it was then with France, that the daily work of industrialism and of political democracy, the progress of education and humane influences, have created a new Republic, more sober, stable, and strong.

As for the Government, they were not indifferent to its departure, and they did not hurl after it the open scorn reserved for more wealthy and less responsible fugitives. They watched stoically, sure of the future. Many old Parisian traditions are dead; new and better have grown, and the city has no peer in the Latin world. To imagine Westminster and Whitehall taken out of London does not give an adequate analogy of this situation; for Paris has always played a larger part proportionately in the crises of French history than London in ours; and the tie between the national Government and the city, under the French system of centralised bureaucracy, is much closer. The departure of the President of the Republic, the ministries, and the diplomatic corps, broke many political nerve-threads. It was not a heavy price to pay for the revelation of a city more lovely and lovable than we had yet known, the beautiful home of a family sorely wounded, threatened with worse calamity, but whole in heart and will, and, as I felt, invincible in its faith.

Chapter 11

On the Ramparts

Paris, September 9.

A brief diary of a Parisian day may illustrate the strange mixture of the normal and abnormal in our life. The first thing is always to make sure, for another twenty-four hours at least, that one's concierge and servants are not going to make a sudden departure, whether under orders, or from—ahem! let us call it conversatism. Large numbers of male artisans, shop assistants, and servants of all kinds are always awaiting the call to the colours; and, now that nine shops out of ten, and a large proportion of the houses, flats, and workshops of the city, are closed, it becomes evident that the exodus of the past week has very greatly reduced the female population also.

The next business, after laying in some necessary stores, is to secure one's line of retreat, or, in the present case, one's line of communications. The telegraphic service with England being practically at an end, the postal service much delayed and very uncertain, and the train services, so to speak, on their last wheels, one naturally thinks of that engine which has perhaps more than any other proved its utility during the present crisis—the motorcar. The latest triumph of the most famous makers would be worthless, however, without the various kinds of passport which are necessary to get out of Paris, to stay in Paris or any other town, to pass from one town to another, or to leave the country. We make our way, therefore, to the Prefecture of Police, just opposite Notre Dame.

After hours—or so it seems—of wandering through the interminable corridors, up and down the endless staircases, of this huge barracks (you could put New Scotland Yard down in the central quadrangle with room to spare), I have conceived the liveliest opinions about the Parisian police system; but that is another story, to be told in cooler moments. M. Hennion has just been replaced by M. Laurent; and it is like a change of ministry—familiar faces are gone, and the new masters are only just settling down. At long length, the right man is found, the papers of the chauffeur are shown, and the necessary pass is made out for two persons to go by road to Bordeaux at some time within the next month. Later in the day, all this effort proves to have been wasted, for several reasons, only one of which need be named here. The permit is made out for specified persons, a specified destination, and a specified automobile. But it turns out that the large firm from whom our car is hired will not allow it to go further than Orleans; and that would cost a special fee—£20. But Orleans is no better than Paris for our purpose. Very well, we can buy the car—£450. That may be necessary presently, but not at the present moment.

Motoring being impossible within the military zone, we decide to run round the inner fortifications, that line of grassy hills which girdles Paris with a belt of playground thirty miles long. To reach the Porte de Versailles as a starting-place, after resting a little in the many-coloured shades and the blessed coolth of Notre Dame, we have to cross the Latin Quarter. Poor, desolate Bohemia, where now are thy students of so many races scattered? A few bookshops are still bravely open, as, by the riverside near the Louvre, a few old-book merchants still keep their zinc boxes on the parapet, though they can sell nothing but maps, and histories of the war of 1870. Science, art, letters, what are they when the nations rush into the gulf of war? Tell me not of compensations! And yet it is near here that Mlle, de Roze, whose brother is one of the most daring of French aviators, has her home for poor workmen's children—for the Quartier is also a workmen's district, and this part of its desolation is the more painfully, if less aesthetically, interesting. Here there is no excitement of passing uniforms, no sunny vision of dainty *midinettes*, no *boulevard* glamour to relieve the tension of endless anxiety.

The Sorbonne glowers upon streets of shuttered shops. The workmen are on the battlefield; the schools are closed; and Mlle. de Roze—a modern saint in the manner of Jane Addams of Chicago—is trying to save a few of the little victims from the extremities of suffering. More than five hundred girls, she has already sent away to homes in the country; others—among them, children of fugitives from the north—are kept here for the present. "I do not know how it happens," she says, with her serene smile, "but the 550*f.* which I had at the beginning of the war are still in the bank. I begin to think *le bon Dieu* wishes them to stop there. I'm only sorry a little that He does not increase them, for then I could do more."

The Ecole Polytechnique is now a Red Cross hospital, under Mme. Messimy's particular care. As I walked through the roomy corridors and the quiet little garden I could not but regret that only officers enjoy the hospitality of this great establishment. One peculiarly sad case was pointed out to us—a man sitting under the trees with a companion. Some shock has affected his brain, and he has to be constantly watched lest he should commit suicide. There are, perhaps, more cases of mental injury in war-time now than of old. Some weeks ago, I heard of an officer who, before he bad seen any fighting, suddenly went mad in the barrack-square, asked his men why they did not rush at the enemy, and then began firing his revolver at them. The story was told by one of the men, who received a shot in the leg.

It is a strange scene along the long line of the old ramparts, and at the numerous gates, of iron or stone, by which vehicles and foot passengers pass between the city and the suburbs. At each gate there is a real control of traffic, and a mild show of armament. That is to say, the roadway, except a central passage, has been blocked with small and leafy trees, and behind this screen shallow trenches have been dug. I imagine that the only intention is to stop the entrance of odd cavalry raiders who might conceivably get through the line of modern forts. There are no real fortifications now along the lines of 1870, but only a continuous grassy mound, open to the roadway on the town side, and, on the other, supported by a wall perhaps 30 ft. deep. The lads and old men gather on the edge of the wall by the town gates, and watch the trench-digging, or gaze over to the aerodrome at Issy-les-Molineaux, or northward to see if another 5-o'clock raider is coming down the sky. The women sit in little groups about the grassy slope, bareheaded, with the delightful neatness, the indescribable air of competence, that characterize the Parisian women—never more than now, when they have to fend for themselves. And, while they sew and knit with a calm intentness, the children who are spared their cruel knowledge play innocently in the blazing sunshine.

There are many barracks and some recruiting offices around the ramparts. Normally, it is a lost and happy byway, aloof from the roar of the great city thoroughfares. Here and there are high buildings of flats where, for £50 a year, one may make a comfortable nest, with glimpses of country upon the horizon. Elsewhere, as at Auteuil, it is villadom and relative opulence. Today, (1915), all this green belt shows the strangest mixture of the ways of war and peace. There was something in the sight of those hundreds of women gravely knitting upon the grass-grown redoubts of the last war that will never pass from my memory. At the Henri Martin Gate—where a stronger barrier was being built of thick planks pierced for riflemen's use—we turned inward to the *Etoile* and the wonderful *vista* of the Champs-Elysées. There is no bustle of fashionable traffic now. The great hotels and most of the private mansions are closed. Some of the automobile houses have been converted into Red Cross work-rooms. No more the old *flâneurs* ogle the governesses in the shady walks by President Poincaré's abandoned palace. The Place de la Concorde is an echoing desert by day, and by night a pool of darkness broken only by the shifting arm of the searchlight on top of the Automobile Club.

Up by the Madeleine, I saw a white-faced workwoman. So queenly she looked; and of a sudden the empty street was filled with the ghosts of her children. Why should I feel shame to mix my tears with the tears of France? "*Madame,*" I would have said—but she had no eyes for me—

> Madame, we have gone mad, we men. We have dreamed a mad dream, and we are punished. Save us from ourselves. Tame us. Help us to build better. Open our sight to the divine pity. Teach us that, in war or peace, gain is nothing, and only what we lose can give us a little nobility.

CHAPTER 12

The Battle of the Marne (September 6-13)

1. THE STRATEGIC IDEA

From Paris to Verdun, by the main-line through Châlons, is 174 miles; and, without including the connected operations east of the Meuse, this figure gives us approximately the length of the line of that series of actions which, because they were so closely articulated, and because it was there, or near there, that the chief decision was won, we may continue to call the Battle of the Marne. Four German armies, and part of a fifth (Von Hansen's), one British, and five French armies, were involved in this terrific encounter—not much short of two millions of men, in all. It will be marked in history not only by these unprecedented dimensions, the magnitude of the stakes, and the proportionate horror of lives lost or maimed, but by the fact that, for a single week, the ponderous modern war-machine was subjected to a definite strategic idea. A running narrative, with incidental details, of the simultaneous struggles all across central France would effectually drown this general idea. We shall put it (or our conception of it) first, therefore; then sketch briefly its fulfilment in the western and the central portions of the field; and add afterwards several chapters of personal experience which may in some measure restore suffering humanity to its rightful place in the picture.

The strategy is essentially, we may almost say exclusively, that of the French commander-in-chief, General Joffre. The governing ideas of the German camp—the "smashing blow" and the enveloping movement—were exhausted during the retreat from the Sambre; and so little was their place supplied by a new dominant idea that it is impossible, till the Great General Staff explains, to state positively what was the objective Von Kluck and Von Bülow were pursuing when they reached their furthest south on the plateaux of Brie and Sézanne. The most probable supposition is that—ignorant of the French reserves, and misconceiving the morale of the Allied armies—they were aiming at a concentration midway between Verdun and Paris preliminary to a serious attack upon the capital, and hoped meanwhile to deliver the "smashing blow" at the French centre, while the Metz army and the crown prince, together, were breaking through the fortified barrier of the Meuse. They had had the advantage, in their first onslaught, of preparation carried to a point that no other State had imagined.

They were now beginning to pass the point to which this advantage carried, and to feel what it meant to have four disparate Powers directly across their path. France had been unprepared, many of her forts worthless. But Maubeuge resisted till September 7, thus keeping back the siege-pieces without which (at least) Paris could not be attempted. On September 1, the Austrian army suffered a crushing defeat; two days later, Lemberg fell. Five or six army corps, including some of Von Hansen's, were at once hurried off to the eastern frontier—an act of nervousness which was possibly confirmed by the aforesaid under-estimate of the resisting power of the retreating French and British armies. Before he reached Compiègne, Von Kluck knew better; but it was then just too late. Perhaps, the generals in the field were overruled by their political masters.

Belgium continued to contribute to the confusion of the German plans during these critical days, despite terroristic penalties like the burning down of Termonde. The army made constant demonstrations toward Brussels; and a more serious action took place before Ghent on September 6. This city was surrendered two days later, largely out of regard for its ancient monuments. The troops of the victorious General von Boehn were then sent off to France; but they had to be called back again to deal with a sortie from Antwerp by which Alost, Aerschot, and Malines were retaken, and Louvain and Brussels were threatened. After heavy losses on both sides, the Belgian Army was driven into its refuge on the Scheldt, having again gravely retarded the southern flow of German re-enforcements.

There were outside factors favourable to General Joffre's calculations. His plan, however, was quite independent of them, and of any adventitious aid (one adventitious element, in the shape of a violent rainstorm, did, as we shall see, materially aid it). It was the designed sequel to the plan of the great retreat, which was essentially a manoeuvre for advantage of position and numbers. Such advantages, of which we will speak directly, and the fighting qualities of French and British soldiers which he knew he could count upon, were to be used in a particular manner, that is to say, by a combination of the methods of the strategic reserve and the flank assault. The former, a favourite French method, is only a larger, more emphatic form of the usual retention of a reserve behind the fighting line, and General Joffre's strategical reserve consisted of three different elements: (1) The new 7th Army under General Foch, of which the German commanders could know nothing till they struck it, at the French centre. (2) The presence of the 6th Army (Maunoury) between Paris and the Ourcq was known to Von Kluck before he passed across it to the Marne and beyond. But it was then strongly re-enforced from Paris. (8) The British army was known to Von Kluck, but sadly misconceived. It, also, was now re-enforced; and it may be said to have been used as a strategic reserve when, having been withdrawn to the Seine, and then brought back within the covering woods of Crécy-en-Brie, it was suddenly unleashed upon Von Kluck's head columns.

The flank assault is an obvious expedient, probably more dangerous in modern than in ancient circumstances because, with its large numbers and delicate marching mechanism, the army of today, (1915), cannot very easily turn its flank into a front. What was designed in the present case may be called a cumulative, or recurrent, flank assault. This may be illustrated by supposing, as in the accompanying diagram, four armies, E, F G, H, to be meeting the attack of four other equal armies, A, B, C, D. If, in the first phase of the struggle, army A can by any means be disabled or removed, it should be possible for E, F, G, H to dispose of the three remaining opponents by a recurrent combination of flank and frontal attack. Thus, in the second phase (A having disappeared), E turns against the flank of B. which is frontally held by F. B has, therefore, to retreat; and, while E carries on the pursuit, F is able to turn against the flank of C, which is frontally held by G. C has now to fall back, with F in pursuit. Finally, G and H can deal in like manner with D, and, perhaps, turn the whole retirement into a rout. It is a powerful, but delicate, manoeuvre which can rarely be possible in modern conditions.

With opponents of equal quality, it requires a preponderance of total as well as of local "Recurrent Flank Attack." numbers (for army A is not to be abstracted by magic); and it asks for, if it does not positively require, advantages of total, as well as of local, position.

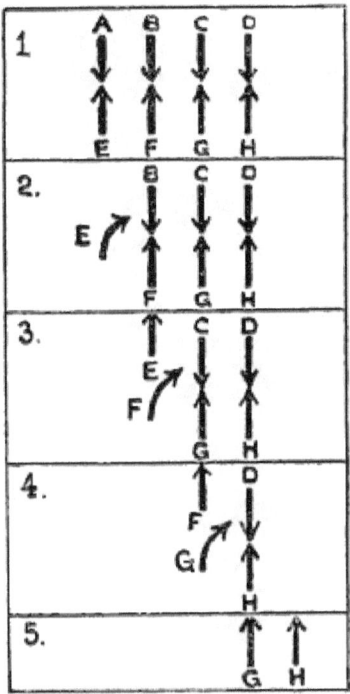

"Recurrent Flank Attack."

All these advantages General Joffre had played for, and had won, by the retreat from Belgium to a line falling a little south of the great main road from Paris to Nancy.

The whole alignment of forces from Paris to Belfort was, on September 5, as follows:

German	Allies
	Army of Paris (Gallieni).
1st Army (Von Kluck).	6th French Army (Maunoury).
2nd Army (Von Bülow).	British Force (Field-Marshal French).
Saxon troops.	5th French Army (D'Espérey).
4th Army (Duke of Würtemberg).	7th French Army (Foch).
5th Army (Crown Prince of Prussia).	4th French Army (De Langle de Cary).
Garrison of Metz.	3rd French Army (Sarrail).
6th Army (Crown Prince of Bavaria).	2nd French Army (De Castelnau).
7th Army (Von Heeringen).	
8th Army (Von Deimling).	1st French Army (Dubail).

We are not immediately concerned with the position of the armies east of the Meuse; but it should be said that General von Deimling's force was only a detachment, and that the 1st French Army had also been reduced to very small proportions. The Metz garrison is named because it undertook certain independent field operations. In the western and central field, the army of Paris took only a passive, though influential, part in the Battle of the Marne. The Army of Verdun, on the other hand, could give but a portion of its strength to the attack on the west. On the German side, we may now regard the remainder of Von Hansen's Saxon army as a detachment divided between the commands of General von Bülow and Duke Albrecht. Although no exact numerical comparison can be made, the Allies would seem to have had a superiority about equal to that of their armies—5½ to 4½ (excluding Paris, counting the British Force as a full army, including only a half of the army of Verdun, and reckoning the Saxons as ½). The greatest mass of forces, and of the Allied superiority, was gathered in the west.

The long retreat was dictated primarily by the necessity of obtaining re-enforcements before the issue was decisively joined, and of gaining time for the general adaptation of the original plan of campaign to the exigencies of the unexpected attack from the north. But it gave important advantages of position, also, both general and local. It did not actually shorten the front of the Allies: from Condé-on-Scheldt, through Charleroi and the southern Ardennes, to Verdun is about the same distance as from Paris to Verdun. But it brought that line very much nearer to the main bases of supply and re-enforcement; it may be said to have effected a concentration of national resources (beside which the lengthening of British communications was a small matter). On the other hand, it greatly prolonged the German lines, abstracting from the fighting ranks large numbers of men, and immensely aggravating the labour and anxiety of the road and base services. It brought the German armies on to ground which, with all their studies—and it was chiefly their studies of the terrain that saved them from a complete rout—the German commanders could not know as well as the French.

Coolly dangling the precious prize of Paris before the Teuton eye, it, in fact, presented a deadly choice: to assault a powerful position, with five armies free and unconquered beside it, and, in case of success, the task of managing two millions of enraged people; or to abandon Paris (and Western France with it) and pursue the said five armies on to the defensive ground they had themselves cho.sen.

The most important advantage of position, therefore, was that it compelled the invaders either to stop the pursuit, or to enter a wide *troucé* in which they would have the army of Paris on one flank and the army of Verdun on the other. When, in parallel columns, they passed east of Paris and west of Verdun, a further portion of their strength would have to be abstracted to guard their wings and lines of communication. But for the excessive strain upon Verdun, the pivot of the whole manoeuvre, the retreat might have been continued to or beyond the line of the Seine and Aube, with a more completely satisfactory result.

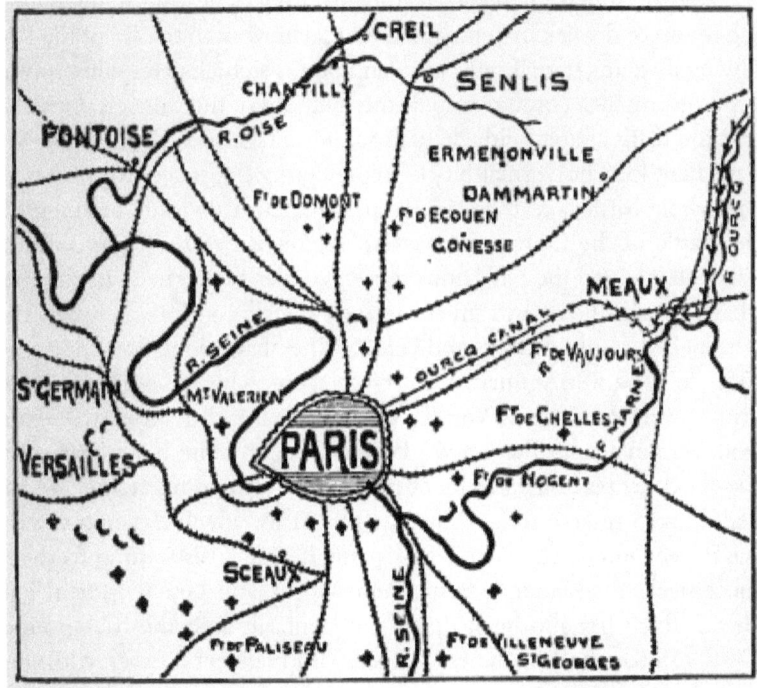

THE DEFENCES OF PARIS

As it was. General Sarrail's army, hanging round its fortified ring down into the Woevre on the east of the Meuse, and nearly to Bar-le-Duc on the west, was hard put to it to keep touch with the Government and the rest of the armies. This might have proved impossible, but for two things: the indifferent talents of the Crown Prince of Prussia, and the obstruction offered to military operations between the plain of Champagne and the Meuse by the obstacle of the Argonne Forest. Coming through the Longwy gap, the crown prince had hardly a third the distance to travel that Von Kluck covered; and the Imperial father must have keenly felt his failure in a task of peculiar importance. His next colleague to the west, the Duke of Würtemberg, once free of the Ardennes, had a long southward march over flat plains, with few towns, roads, or railways to help his supplies. When General Foch's new army fell upon him, the difference between fresh, well-fed, and tired, ill-fed troops must have been very marked. In the western part of the field, the most important physical feature is the series of westward-flowing rivers obstructing the route of the armies—the Oise, Ailette, Aisne, Ourcq, Marne, Petit Morin, Grand Morin, and Aubetin.

Skeletonising what occurred along the front of nearly 180 miles during the second week in September, we may now, with the aid of the following diagram, state briefly the plan upon which General Joffre solved his problem, by a combination of the methods of the strategical reserve and the flank assault, with the various advantages described above. We have here four horizontal blocks, representing the successive phases of the whole battle; and there is one perpendicular division, marking off the Battle of the Ourcq, the western region where the chief decision was obtained (to the left), from the remainder of the field. In the first phase, the 4½ German armies are seen marching south between the entrenched camps of Paris and Verdun. They have three French armies (5th, 7th, and 4th) immediately before them; while Maunoury's (6th) army covers Paris against Von Kluck. and Sarrail's (3rd) army strikes out from Verdun against the Crown Prince. General Joffre has prepared for the shock by placing an army of new troops (7th) at his centre. He has kept a small reserve (R) behind the 6th Army, which is facing toward the River Ourcq, while Von Kluck passes it south-westward, and crosses successively the Ourcq, Marne, Petit Morin, and Grand Morin. The British force has also been drawn momentarily into the background. Thus, Von Kluck (I) becomes engaged with Franchet d'Espérey (5); and the second phase opens.

The French 6th Army is swung round against Von Kluck's right flank, on the Ourcq; while the British force, emerging from the Crécy woods, dashes at the more advanced part of the long German line, and its fore-guard is disposed of by the left of the neighbouring French army (D'Espérey). Von Kluck is badly outmatched; but he fights desperately to avoid a rout. He first brings re-enforcements from his rear, and with them endeavours to envelop by the north and to break the French flank attack on the Ourcq. He nearly succeeds; but Joffre fetches up, at the critical moment, the last part of his tactical reserve, the 4th Corps.

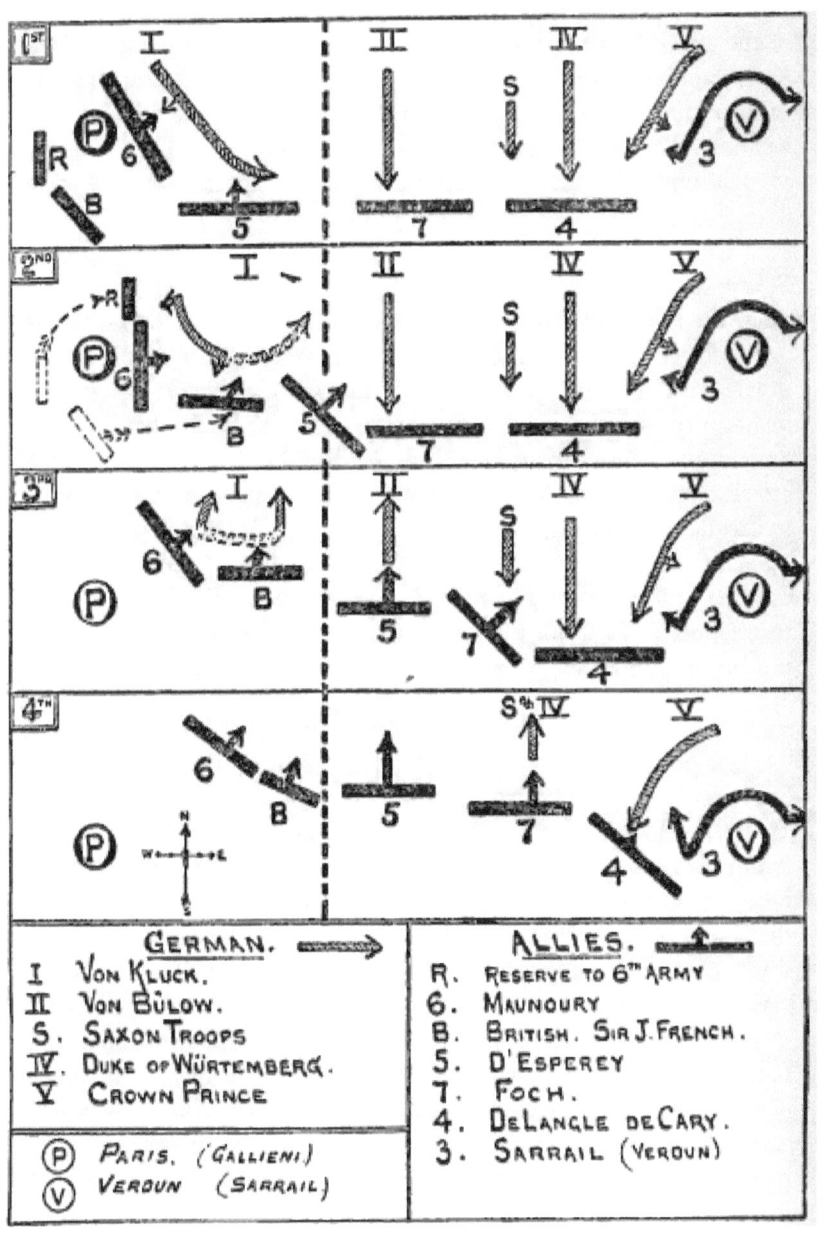

Strategical Plan of the Battle of the Marne

In a final counter-effort to delay his fate, the German commander withdraws a corps from the British front, and flings it against the north end of the attack. But the French stand firm till the British come up. Von Kluck holds out long enough for his forward columns to turn north-eastward, and come abreast of his flank guard on the Ourcq: then it is a headlong flight of the whole army for the Aisne.

The rest of the story is that of a wave-like repetition of the same manoeuvre—combined flank and frontal assault. The pursuit of the First German Army being left in the main to the 6th French and the British armies, D'Espérey is free to turn north-eastward against the uncovered flank of Von Bülow (II), who is frontally faced by the left wing of the 7th Army (Foch). Taken on two sides. Von Bülow retires north, with D'Espérey at his heels (third phase); and Foch is now free, in his turn, to wheel north-east against the uncovered flank of the Saxons and Würtembergers, already held by De Langle. This double attack compels their retreat; and, in the last phase, the crown prince has to flee in like manner, before the 4th and 3rd Armies, from the scene of some of his most miserable exploits. Paris is saved. Verdun and the line of the Meuse are saved. Still larger expectations are destined to disappointment. But the fame of Joffre as strategist and tactician is put beyond doubt.

2. West Wing: Battle of the Ourcq

The position on the left wing of the Allies on the morning of September 5 was as follows:

The defence of the districts to the west and north of Paris had been left to General Gallieni and the forts. Maunoury's (6th) army had been brought round to the north-east of the capital, between the suburbs and the woods of Chantilly and Ermenonville; and it had spent there a quiet day of preparation. Its left, the 7th Army Corps, under General Vaulthier, was at the village of Louvres, on the road and railway halfway to Senlis or Chantilly, and under cover of the guns of Fort Ecouen behind it. A Reserve corps, under General de Lamaze, lay immediately to the south-east, at Mesnil-Amelot; and, southward to the Marne about Lagny, territorial detachments kept up a loose contact with the British army. This had continued its retirement to the Seine on the 4th, evidently with the idea of tempting Von Kluck's advance guards to extend themselves to the south-east as far as possible without taking alarm. It was only on the morning of the 6th that Sir John French's force was brought back north to fill the gap between the French 6th and 5th Armies. The latter, that of General Franchet d'Espérey, extended over the Brie plateau, with its centre north of Provins, and its right at Esternay. Allenby's and Conneau's Cavalry Corps covered the gap between French's right and D'Espérey's left, and made a show of resisting the German advance about Coulommiers.

The German armies concerned in this part of the field were that of Von Kluck (1st) and a part of Von Bülow's (2nd). The latter had come due south through Laon, Soissons, and Château-Thierry. Von Kluck's force, consisting of the 2nd, 4th Reserve, 4th, 3rd, and 7th Army Corps with the 2nd and 9th Divisions of cavalry, in its crescent-like detour, had gone, near Amiens, well to the west of Paris, and was now drawing in toward a point fifty miles east thereof—a very considerable deflection.

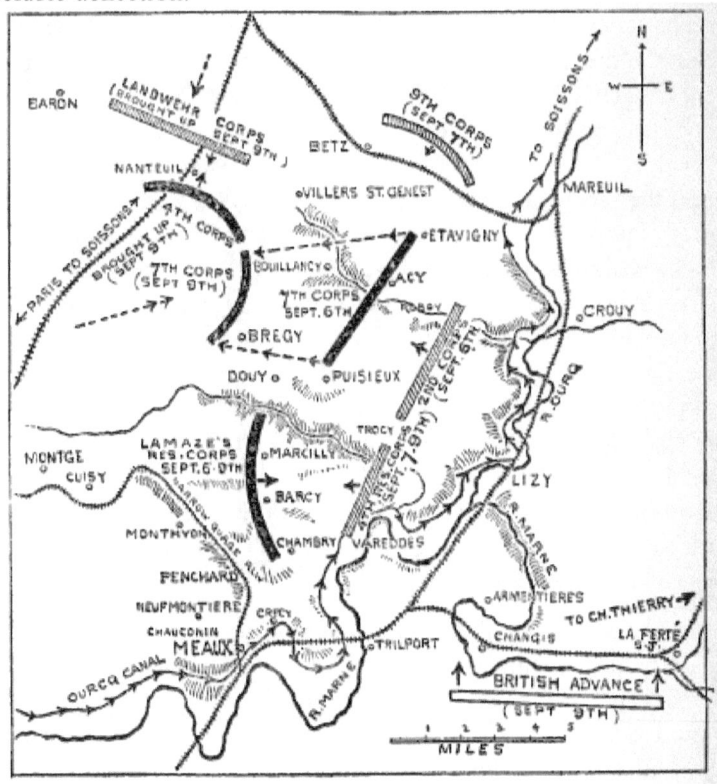

BATTLE OF THE OURCQ.

French 6th Army (black): 7th Corps, positions on September 6th and 9th; Lamaze's Reserve Corps, position September 6th to 9th; 4th Corps, September 9th.
German 1st Army (shaded): 2nd Corps, September 6th; 4th Reserve Corps, September 7th to 9th; 9th Cavalry Div., September 7th; Landwehr, September 9th.
British advance toward the Ourcq and Château Thierry.

The 2nd Corps pursued the main road from Creil to Meaux, through Senlis and Nanteuil-le-Haudouin; the 4th Reserve that from Compiègne through Crépy-en-Valois. The whole, or the greater part, of these were left on the Ourcq; while the 4th, 3rd, and 7th Corps, coming south mainly through Villers-Cotterets and Château-Thierry, went on across the Marne in pursuit of General d'Espérey, with the two cavalry divisions on their right. The furthest point reached by Von Kluck's advance guard, on September 6, was the little village of Courchamp, just north of Provins—thirty miles south-east of Meaux, and sixty miles south-south-east of Compiègne. To the east of Von Kluck, the four corps (9th, 10th, 10th Reserve, and Guards) of Von Bülow were aiming at D'Espérey's right and the newly constituted French 7th Army under General Foch.

The statement of these positions indicates the nature of the counter-stroke the Allies were now able to deliver. When Sir John French went to General Joffre's headquarters at Claye, on the road from Paris to Meaux, on Saturday, September 5, the general strategic idea was so evident and simple a deduction from the positions and balance of forces that everyone must have been feverishly anxious lest the wonderful opportunity should be snatched away at the last moment. Von Kluck's main body was to be caught in the angle of the Ourcq and Marne by means of the strategical reserve, and struck at once in flank and face, while the fore-part of his line was being crumpled up thirty miles away on the Brie plateau. If he should retreat eastward, he would upset Von Bülow's ranks; if due north, he would draw Von Bülow with him. In either case, the intended concentration of attack upon the French centre would be checked, and the benefit would extend to the other armies. The French troops went into this momentous action with the words of the following pointed *ordre du jour* by the *generalissimo* ringing in their ears:—

> At the moment of the opening of a battle upon which the safety of the country depends, it must be recalled to every man that this is no time to look backward. All efforts must be made to attack and repel the enemy. A troop which can no longer advance must, at whatever cost, hold the ground won, and let itself be killed on the spot rather than retreat. In the present circumstances, no failing can be tolerated.

On Sunday, the 6th, General Maunoury began his attempt to turn the German right rear; while the British and the French 5th, 7th, and

4th armies faced round against the front of their various pursuers, and the 3rd Army attacked westward from Verdun. First, on the extreme left, General Lamaze advanced his Reserve Corps from Mesnil-Amelot to the line of the narrow-gauge railway on the hills above Meaux. Here he came upon the German 4th Reserve Corps, posted on the heights above the villages of Montgé, Cuisy, Monthyon, and Iverny. One by one, these points were taken; and, at night, the French had reached the villages of Chambry, Barcy, and Mareilly, directly north of Meaux. The 7th Corps, under General Vauthier, had advanced to Lamaze's left, and, by evening, continued the front north-eastward from Puisieux, through Acy-en-Multien, to Etavigny, pushing back the outposts of the German 2nd Corps on the west side of the Ourcq.

During the morning, the British force, now strengthened to five divisions, with five cavalry brigades, advanced from the Seine to positions between Villeneuve-le-Comte and Jouy-le-Châtel (on the road from Lagny to Provins), where it was more or less concealed by the forest of Crécy. In the afternoon, it moved rapidly forward to the northeast, sweeping through the cavalry which covered Von Kluck's flank; and during the night, after several hours' fighting in the streets, its centre was established in the market-town of Coulommiers. The German commander now knew that his army was in danger of being cut in two, divided from its line of communications, and extinguished piecemeal. He could not save everything; that he saved so much is proof of great skill and energy, and a remarkable courage and endurance in his exhausted troops. His reply to the threat was to draw back in a north-easterly direction, toward Château-Thierry, the three forward corps which were at grips with the British and 5th French Armies, and to strengthen the stand of the 2nd and 4th Reserve Corps against the attack amid the watercourses of the Ourcq-Marne angle. Unfortunately for them, the Germans on the Ourcq could not make a double front—westward against Maunoury, and southward against the advancing British.

On the morning of September 7, Maunoury at first made further progress toward the Ourcq. Then the German 4th Reserve Corps advanced, and entrenched itself between Trocy and Vareddes. Its right was supported by the 2nd Corps, the two facing west over the rolling fields, with the wooded ravine of the Ourcq behind them, and the hill running down to Meaux on their left. Later in the day, the German 9th Cavalry Division, withdrawn from the British front, was brought back over the Marne, and, through Lizy-sur-Ourcq, round toward Betz. The French north wing was thus seriously menaced. The 7th Corps was dislodged from Acy by an attack of the German 2nd Corps; and, at nightfall, its exposed left was threatened at Etavigny. The fighting continued through the night; and, on the 8th, while Lamaze's Reserve Corps maintained its positions, the 7th Corps was compelled to fall back to Bouillancy and Villers-St. Genest. The German artillery was in great strength; destroyed villages and fields torn with shell-fire marked the fierceness of the struggle.

While the success of the first phase of General Joffre's manoeuvre was thus in doubt, the second phase opened in the next area to the east. On September 7, the British force strode on from Coulommiers, its left toward the Marne, its right toward the Petit Morin, General de Lisle's Cavalry Brigade, with the 9th Lancers and 18th Hussars, showing especial vigour. In covering the German retreat, the 2nd, 9th, and Guard Cavalry Divisions were severely punished. The German retirement on this side opened to attack the right flank of the advanced neighbouring force. This was the opportunity of the French 5th Army. Swinging his left forward over the Brie plateau, D'Espérey reached the Grand Morin, at La Ferté Gaucher and Esternay, on the 7th; and on the 8th. supported by the British offensive, he drove forward to the Petit Morin.

D'Espérey's attack was now quickly turned against the open flank of Von Bülow; and the 2nd (German Army, driven frontally by the 7th French, was quickly retreating beside the 1st. Thus, as we shall see. General Foch, at the French centre, was enabled to carry on the general movement.

On the west, the progress of the British force was maintained throughout the 8th, against stout opposition by the enemy rear-guards on the Petit Morin. Sir John French wrote:—

> The First Army Corps encountered stubborn resistance at La Tretoire, north of Rebais. The enemy occupied a strong position, with infantry and guns, on the northern bank of the river; they were dislodged with considerable loss. Several machine-guns and many prisoners were captured, and upward of two hundred German dead were left on the ground. The forcing of the Petit Morin at this point was much assisted by the cavalry and the 1st Division, which crossed higher up the stream. Later in the day, a counter-attack by the enemy was repulsed by the 1st Army Corps, a great many prisoners and some guns

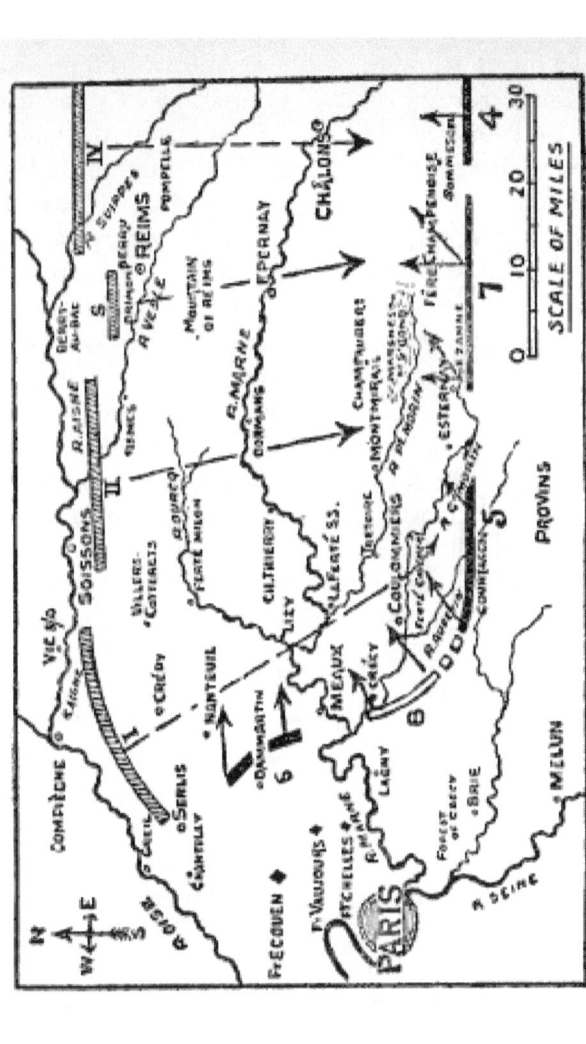

THE BATTLE OF THE MARNE.

German Armies: I, Von Kluck; II, Von Bülow; S, Saxons; IV, Duke of Würtemberg.
Allies: 6th French Army (Maunoury); B. British (Sir J. French); 5th French Army (D'Espérey); 7th (Foch); 4th (De Langle de Cary).

again falling into our hands. On this day, the 2nd Army Corps encountered considerable opposition, but drove back the enemy at all points with great loss, making considerable captures. The 3rd Corps also drove back large bodies of infantry and made some captures.

The French on the Ourcq were now, however, very hard pressed, their attempt to break the German flank being completely arrested. The crisis of the battle on the Allied left was reached on the fourth day, September 9, when masterly handling of the situation on Von Kluck's flank and front (or rear, as it was becoming) decided the issue. The morning of that day found the French 6th Army in great difficulties. The moment had come for General Joffre to play his trump, which was also near being his last, card. An army corps (the 4th) of troops from the west had been gathered under General Boelle, and rushed up from Paris by railway, and by a great fleet of taxicabs and miscellaneous automobiles hurriedly requisitioned by General Gallieni, to Nanteuil—save one division, sent to the aid of the British. Von Kluck had also strongly re-enforced his flank guard on the Ourcq; and the new arrivals, including a corps of *Landwehr*, coming up by way of Compiègne, were thrown round the north end of the French lines. While the 4th French Corps held out at this side, just south of Nanteuil facing north, the 7th Corps and Lamaze's Corps, facing east, stood firm through Brégy and Barcy until, in the evening, the British advance from the south brought decisive relief.

Sir John French had placed his 3rd Corps at the difficult point on his left centre—difficult because the narrow street' crossing of the Marne at La Ferté-sous-Jouarre was resolutely held by a strong rearguard of artillery and infantry. This passage of the river was not won till night. By that time, part of the 3rd Corps had got across further west at the village of Changis, and had begun to bombard the nearer German positions on the Ourcq. The 1st and 2nd Corps gained the north bank to the east at Charly and Château-Thierry and, continuing their progress, threatened to cut in between Von Kluck's and Von Bülow's lines. The British commander says:—

> During the day's pursuit the enemy suffered heavy losses in killed and wounded, some hundreds of prisoners fell into our hands, and a battery of eight machine-guns was captured by the 2nd Division.

At Château-Thierry, the British were in close contact with General d'Espérey's left, which had cleared the road from Montmirail, "after most serious fighting," of bodies from both the 1st and 2nd German Armies.

During the night of September 9, the German retreat from the Ourcq to the Aisne began. There was no longer any reason to hold this line, since the main armies were in full retreat; and there was every reason to hurry back beyond the Aisne to what is one of the strongest natural defensive positions in France. There was no possibility of an immediate resumption of the offensive. The troops were thoroughly exhausted by three weeks of uninterrupted marching and fighting. Lines of communication, supply, and re-enforcement must be re-formed. The "smashing blow" had not been delivered; the famous enveloping movement had failed; a new plan of campaign must be thought out. Russia was demanding more and more attention; Austria-Hungary must be helped, or disaster might ensue. Verdun and Nancy had proved invulnerable. For the moment, at least, there was nothing for it but a simple defensive; and, for that, what better centre could there be than the Laon Mountains?

On the morning of September 10, the retreat from the Ourcq was undisguised. The red tide of battle ebbed from the stubble-fields and coppices on the hills above Meaux; but burning farmsteads and haystacks, broken bridges, shattered churches and houses, many unburied dead, and piles of abandoned ammunition and supplies still spoke of the frightful frenzy that had passed over a scene but lately marked by quiet charm and happy labour. In the orchards and folds of the open land, the bodies of invader and defender lay over against each other, sometimes still grappling. Every here and there, horses rotted on the roads and fields, presently to be burned on pyres of wood, under fear of a pestilence arising. The human victims had been generally buried in the trenches where they had fought; little wooden crosses sometimes marked these great common graves.

On September 10, General Joffre addressed to his 6th Army a message of congratulation and thanks in which he said:—

> The struggle has been hard; the losses under fire, and from fatigue due to lack of sleep, and sometimes of food, have surpassed what could be anticipated; you have borne it all with a valour, firmness, and endurance that words are powerless to glorify as they deserve. Comrades! the commander-in-chief asked you,

in the name of our country, to do more than your duty: you have responded even beyond what seemed possible. Thanks to you, victory crowns our flags. Now that you know the glorious satisfaction of it, you will not let it slip away. As for me, if I have done some good, I have been repaid by the greatest honour that has been granted me in a long career: that of commanding such men as you.

Some of Von Kluck's columns went due northward through Villers-Cotterets and Pierrefonds to Vie-sur-Aisne and Attichy. For several days, there was much scattered lighting on their west flank, in the wooded district between Dammartin and Senlis, It was hardly realised by the Allies that the enemy was not so badly beaten as to forget the importance of holding, about Noyon, his main line of railway communications. The main body of the two first German armies raced north-eastward, through La Ferté-Milon or Oulchy-le-Château, to Soissons, spreading out thence to right and left over the hillsides; or through Braisne and Fismes (on the Vesle) to Vailly and the Craonne plateau. The chase was hard, fast, and bloody. In one day, the British 1st and 2nd Corps and cavalry took thirteen guns, seven machine-guns, about 2,000 prisoners, and quantities of transport. The Royal Flying Corps did invaluable service, as General Joffre testified in a special message to Sir John French. In the woods north of Château-Thierry and around Villers-Cotterets, small parties of desperate Germans fled and hid themselves, in hope of reaching their fellows under cover of night. Many, no doubt, succeeded in doing so; others were hunted down, or came out and surrendered in a half-starving condition.

The spoil brought into Paris during the next few days from different parts of the vast battlefield included 60 cannon. 30 *mitrailleuses*, about 40 gun-carriages, trainloads of arms, ammunition, and other material, three aeroplanes, and a number of motor-wagons. But the spectacle of booty, always fallacious, was in this case peculiarly so. The main body of the German host was intact. It was checked, but not routed; driven back, but not dispersed. The skill and speed of the retreat were very remarkable; and still more so was the preservation of the long German line, to the other parts of which we must now turn.

3. CENTRE: THE RETREAT IN CHAMPAGNE.

It will be convenient to consider this section of the field in three parts: (a) The western, bounded on the west by a line running due north from Esternay on the Grand Morin, through Dormans on the

Marne, and Fismes on the Vesle, to Berry-au-Bac on the Aisne; and on the east by a line drawn northward just beyond Fère-Champenoise, Epernay, and Rheims. The southern portion of this area is the plateau of Sézanne, which falls abruptly on the east into the plain of Champagne; its chief physical feature, for our present purpose, has been mentioned: the half-reclaimed marshland from which the Petit Morin rises, known as the Marais de Saint Gond. The northern portion contains the great city of Rheims, and, on either side of it, the eastern end of the Laon Mountains, at Craonne, and the wooded massif called the Mountain of Rheims, both, like the Sézanne plateau, falling abruptly on the east into the bare flatland called La Champagne Pouilleuse. Here the 7th French Army, under General Foch, faced the left of Von Bülow's army, including the Prussian Guard, and some fragments of the Saxon Army lately under Von Hansen. (5) The plain of Champagne extending northwards from Vitry-la-François through Châlons, to the River Suippe. Here General de Langle de Cary faced the army of the Duke of Würtemberg. (c) The eastern area, consisting of the sub-alpine Argonne Forest and the hill region about the west bank of the Meuse, including its great fortress Verdun only so far as operations on the west are concerned. Here, with some help from General Sarrail, the left of the 4th French Army, had to meet the attack of the Duke of Würtemberg's army, to which most of the remaining Saxon troops were appended, while its right coped with that of the Prussian Crown Prince.

(a) Foch had instructions to maintain the defensive until the result of the first phase of the Battle of the Marne was declared; and, based upon the Esternay-Vitry highroad and railway, between Sézanne and Mailly (just south of Sommesous), he fought for three days an obstinate defensive action against Von Bülow's left wing and some of the Saxon troops. It is difficult to see how a piercing of the French line at this point would have redeemed the German position, though it would, of course, have encouraged new efforts. At any rate, Von Bülow spared no sacrifice; and on September 8 the right of the new French army was pressed back as far as the village of Gourgançon. Early on the following morning it fell back a mile or two further, the attacking forces coming on from both sides of Fère-Champenoise. They consisted, in the main, of picked troops. The Prussian Guard Corps, 30,000 strong, with 75 cannon and 200 machine-guns, had hurried south, chiefly by the two highroads which run from Rheims

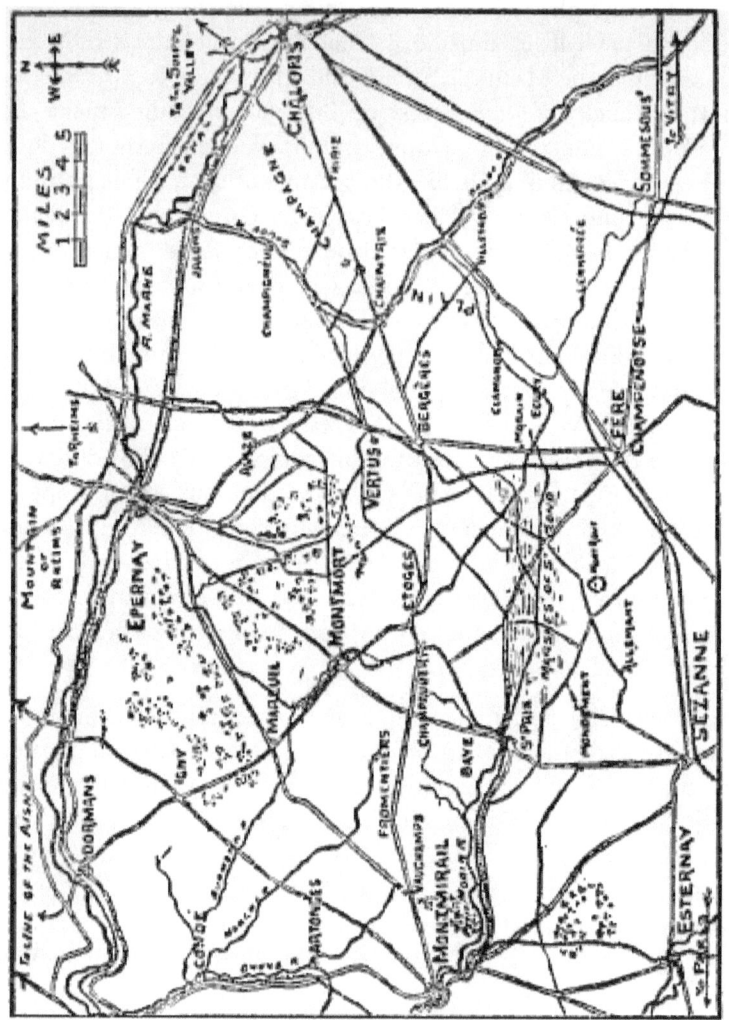

The Centre: Scene of Foch's success

to Sézanne and Fère-Champenoise, but necessarily, also, by lesser intermediate country roads. Of the latter, several cross the St. Gond marshes between St. Prix and Morains. Being checked, between St. Prix and Sézanne, and finding here a firm clay surface under the long grass, the Guards dug trenches and placed their guns. The position on the morning of September 9 was this: on the west, General Franchet d'Espérey had reached Montmirail (13 miles north-west of Sézanne) on the previous day. The right flank of the Guards was thus completely exposed, while the German left was extended to the south-east of Fère-Champenoise. Foch immediately saw and took advantage of the weakness of the position.

First his Moorish Division was sent charging up the Sézanne-St. Prix road; and in the evening his left army corps followed. This bold assault at once relieved the pressure on the right, which joined in the offensive. And now there happened one of those historic "accidents" as we call them, or "miracles" as the ancients would have said confidently, because of the abnormality of result. We had had several showery days at the end of August and the beginning of September. That Wednesday evening, it blew a half-gale, and poured cats-and-dogs, along the Marne Valley and the Sézanne plateau. The clay pocket of St. Gond immediately became a quagmire; and, when Foch came down on their flank, by the solid main roads, the gunners were up to their knees, and their gun-carriages up to the axles, in muddy water. A fearful slaughter by the French "75's" and larger guns followed, in which thousands of the picked German troops were overwhelmed. A week after the battle, peasants crossing the marshy roads found wounded men still alive amid their dead fellows. The horror of the scene is not to be described.

Joffre and Foch knew, of course—did they remember, when they planned their victory?—that this was an ancient death-trap? Nearly all the place-names of the battle of the Marne of 1914 are to be found in the histories of Napoleon's campaign of 1814 "from the Rhine to Fontainebleau," as Ségur called it. Blücher retreated from the Ourcq to Soissons, and there escaped, to the enragement of a greater than Joffre; and both the French and the Allies of a century ago learned to their cost the treachery of the Petit Morin marshes. It was shown in the beginning of that extraordinary week in which Napoleon, against overwhelming numbers, won the victories of Champaubert, Montmirail, Château-Thierry, and Vauchamp. The name still survives, though little else, between the villages of Fromentières and Champaubert, of the Bois du Desert, into which Blücher beat his retreat, not knowing its boggy character. Three thousand Russian grenadiers were here slain or captured by Marmont's *cuirassiers*; two hundred were drowned in the marshes; and fifteen hundred more gave themselves up to the peasants.

A few days afterward Blücher, Kleist, Kapsewicz, and Prince Augustus of Prussia themselves narrowly escaped capture in the neighbouring woods of Etoges. A month later, "Marshal Vorwaerts" was back from Laon, attacking on the old ground as though memory brought no fears to him. Marmont and Mortier were in full retreat along the highroad to Fère-Champenoise, their men harassed on every side, and blinded by a storm of rain. Pachod turned north to the marshes of St. Gond, as to a refuge. The Russians and Prussians soon surrounded them—10,000 cavalry and 80 guns, against 2,000 soldiers of the line and 4,000 National Guards. The Emperor Alexander directed his own troops. A few hundreds only of the French escaped by the St. Prix road. "Splendid misfortune!" exclaims Ségur:—

> Guards truly National! Noble victims! In what monument will the Fatherland offer to your descendants the memory of a devotion more sublime?

The great stone column in the fields at Champaubert—which the Prussians of our day passed, but did not touch—commemorates, in fact. Napoleon's victories, not any "splendid misfortune" of his victim subjects. So it will ever be while men pursue this maniacal vision of armed conquest. Today, with a little difference, history repeats itself; and the bones of some thousands of German and French peasants and workmen rot, as the bones of other thousands of their forbears rotted a hundred years ago, in the bogs of the Sézanne plateau, while we discuss the butchery as though it were a move in a game of chess.

(b) Meanwhile, on Foch's right, the Duke of Würtemberg's army was in a hardly less grave predicament. It had reached further south than its neighbours, beyond Vitry; but the Saxon troops on its west wing were a very weak element. Foch's right had been engaged with them for two days when the Prussian Guard, perhaps to relieve them, entered the St. Gond marshes. The little town of Fère-Champenoise and the village of Sommesous (source of the Somme), between which the hardest fighting took place, have a certain military interest as road and railway junctions on the great Paris-Nancy highway, with lines from Troyes and the south running through the former to Epernay, through the latter to Châlons. Vitry-le-François, an ancient and once fortified town of 9,000 inhabitants, on the Marne and the Rhine-Marne Canal, is a more important place. Here the Duke of Würtemberg had his headquarters, and good road communication with those of the Crown Prince at Ste. Menehould, the gate of the Argonne.

The 4th French Army (De Langle de Cary) lost Vitry on September 6, but resisted continually, and kept touch with the south-western end, now most dangerously extended, of the army of Verdun. Repeated assaults were made upon the Würtemberg positions, as well as upon those of the Crown Prince, whose men (if we may judge by results) were largely occupied in sacking the villages around Revigny. There are indications that the French artillery was particularly powerful, and that these German armies were experiencing, as would seem natural, difficulty in bringing up supplies. That they realized the critical character of the next actions is testified by an army order issued in Vitry on the night of September 7, and signed by Lieutenant-General Tülff von Tschepe und Weidenbach:—

> The object of our long, hard marches has been attained. The chief French troops have been forced to accept battle after their continual retreat. The great decision is at hand. . . . I expect every officer and man, notwithstanding the hard and heroic fighting of the last few days, to do his duty unswervingly and to the last breath. Everything depends on the result of tomorrow.

The words echo those of General Joffre: the difference—and it is vital—lies in the dates. It is the difference of the two days in which the first two German armies had been turned back. The centre had discovered the crisis two days late. It was dangerously late when, on the morning of September 10, General Foch was driving the remnants of Von Bülow's best troops like chaff before him along the roads from Sézanne and Fère-Champenoise which converge at Rheims. This victory was so swift and complete that it left strength for another bold operation; and Foch immediately threw a large body eastward over the edge of the Sézanne plateau against the flank of the Würtemberg army, now weakened by the withdrawal of the exhausted Saxon regiments. On the same day, De Langle de Cary was re-enforced by an army corps, and took the offensive. Perhaps Duke Albrecht had by now received orders to fall back to the line of the Aisne, parallel with Von Bülow and Von Kluck; he should certainly know that Von Bülow's army was already retreating far to the north-west. There was, in fact, no time to win a victory, even if he had power to do so, for in a few hours the northern roads would be cut off. To check the immediate threat, a bloody struggle was maintained throughout the day, between Fère-Champenoise and the Marne; during the night, the men were withdrawn from their trenches, and started upon a forced march over the plains to the Suippes Valley, fifty miles north of Vitry.

At 7 a.m. on September 12, a patrol of French *chasseurs* re-entered Châlons, and during the morning General Foch followed. The town had been held since the afternoon of September 4, under General von Seydewitz, who took several leading citizens as hostages, and extorted, in addition to daily rations for his troops, a war contribution of 506,000 *francs* (about £20,000). During the week, there was a good deal of pillaging of shops and houses; but no part of the city was destroyed, and the acting-mayor afterward testified that there had been no acts of violence against women. Von Bülow's troops had all reached Epernay on September 9, 10, and 11, and had retired on the latter day to the north of Rheims, which was then reoccupied by the French. The later German fugitives at Châlons, therefore, must all have gone north-eastward to Suippes, and to the railway line running across the plain of Champagne from Bazancourt to the northern end of the Argonne at Grand Pré and Varennes. In this region they soon dug themselves in as securely as did Von Kluck and Von Bülow in the more favourable ground to the west.

(c) The crown prince's army entered the small town of Revigny, on the River Ornain, twenty miles south of Ste. Menehould, twenty-five miles west of the Meuse at St. Mihiel, and thirty miles south-west of Verdun, on September 6. It was a dangerous position, between the army of Verdun and the garrison of Toul on the east, and De Langle de Cary's army on the west, with a frail line of communications behind interrupted by the forest block of the Argonne. But how tempting for a bold and able soldier!

Sitting behind the veil of the censorship in Paris, the eastern danger seemed to me so plain that it must dominate the German plan of campaign. I wrote on September 7:—

> As, at the beginning of the war we had our eyes too closely fixed on the eastern frontiers, so, more lately, we have thought almost exclusively of the north-west of France and the long line of communications round Brussels to Aix-la-Chapelle. Next, the possibility of a siege of Paris hypnotised us; and the Ger-

man advance seemed to shape itself as a wedge, a triangle with its base reaching from Lille to Sedan, and its sides compressed inward till they met at an apex just northward of Paris—the objective of the whole movement. Little was known of what was going on outside this imaginary triangle, except that there were few Germans to the west (the Dieppe-Paris trains have never stopped) and that, far to the east, what we may call the armies of Nancy and Metz were engaged in a vast deadlock. Such was the conception. It flattered us. It was a wrong conception.....An incidental aim (of Von Kluck's turn south-eastward) may be to reach the southern and somewhat less fortified side of Paris. But I think the whole idea is something much larger and bolder. Let us ask what are the chief necessities of an army situated as this now is?

They are (1) to get out of reach of the Belgians now waiting in Antwerp), (2) to keep as far away as possible from the ever-increasing British contingents, (3) to immobilise the army of Paris, (4) to reduce the long line of communications and recover direct touch with the Rhineland, (5) while accomplishing these ends, if possible to smash the other French armies, and then (6) when the German armies are united, to march toward either Berlin or Paris, as circumstances direct. The avoidance of Paris and the double concentration toward the south-east appear to meet the requirements of this analysis. The army which has come south from Mons and Charleroi will presently join the other army or armies coming from the Ardennes and Luxemburg.

But this junction will mean that there is no longer a German Army isolated in the west, with an intolerable train behind it, but only a still stronger army in the east having a direct line to its bases in Luxemburg and the Middle Rhine. This immense strategical overturn may involve the abandonment of Belgium and northern France by the Germans. In revenge it immediately threatens the French armies before the Vosges with a rear attack. If they resist, they must fight on two fronts. If they fall back to the south-west, as would seem probable, the German hosts will join hands, and a new war will begin.

We shall see presently that, at this critical moment, the French line of the Meuse was very near being pierced, by the fall of Fort Troyon;

and it is highly probable that, if the crown prince had been an abler and more daring commander, it might have been broken through, Verdun completely invested, the French army of Lorraine compelled to retire south, and the whole complexion of the campaign changed. Instead, his men were burning down and pillaging the small towns and villages between Vitry and Bar-le-Duc, in the intervals of assault by De Langle de Cary and Sarrail. Not that the power of these attacks can be depreciated. There was a four-days' battle near Triaucourt on September 4-8; and, just south of Revigny, hard fighting took place, from Sermaize on the west through Vassincourt to Mogneville, on the 10th. The retirement northward then began, the last German troops leaving Revigny on September 12. The strategical importance of the Argonne now declared itself, as it had not done when the Crown Prince had only retreating armies before him, and when he held the southern as well as the northern roads round this region, and the rare roads through it.

Counting from the Gap of Grand Pré on the north to the Villers-Triaucourt road on the south, the Argonne stretches twenty-three miles nearly north-to-south (the portion beyond Grand Pré, and the woods of Belval and Belnoue near Triaucourt, we need not now consider). This range of thickly forested clay hills constitutes an important obstacle, secondary to the Heights of the Meuse, to an invasion of France from the east; and, though it does not equally obstruct invasion from the north—its average width being only six miles—it compels the invader either to neglect the plain eastward toward the Meuse, or to divide his forces.

When the German retreat began, the French at once resumed possession of the Triaucourt road to the Meuse; but the great highway from Paris to Verdun was still beyond them. The Germans not only held the Gap of Grand Pré, where the Aire, coming up the east side of the Argonne, joins the Aisne, coming up its west side, and where two lines of railway unite after crossing Champagne from the Rheims-Rethel mainline. They held also the direct Paris-Verdun highroad and railway, which penetrate the Argonne by the defile of Les Islettes, and the only two other practicable roads across the Forest (between Ville sur Tourbe and Varennes), the importance of which was to appear later in the campaign. The western entry to the defile of Les Islettes is at the small, ancient town of Ste. Menehould; the eastern is at Clermont-en-Argonne. Whether the crown prince's chief instructions were to advance south, or to attack Verdun, we do not know. But his headquar-

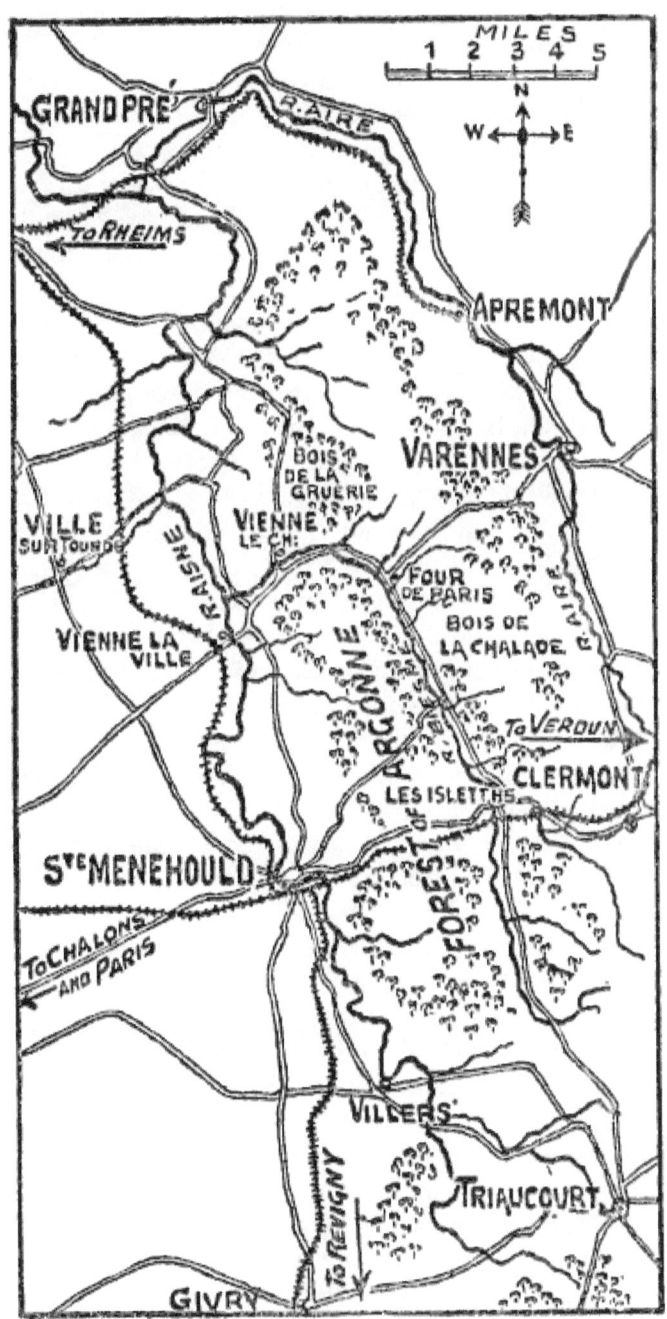

THE ARGONNE

ters at Ste. Menehould were just equidistant from Verdun, which he never attained, and the villages near Revigny, which he left in ruins.

When the retreat of the western German armies to the Aisne was determined, we must suppose the consequential movement in Champagne and the Argonne to have been carefully considered. Could a line sloping slightly southward beyond Rheims, along the Suippes Valley, to the Les Islettes ravine, be held—the main road from Rheims to Ste. Menehould? Only so could the western attack upon Verdun be maintained. But Rheims, in French hands, would have made a dangerous salient, and Ste. Menehould would have been open to attack from west, south, and east at once. The decision was to draw the armies of the Duke of Würtemberg and the crown prince back to a line running from Berry-au-Bac to the Aisne, through Souain, Ville-sur-Tourbe, and Varenne, to the district north of Verdun.

Here they would have behind them the two railways which unite to run through the Gap of Grand Pré. But the hope of reducing Verdun, or of breaking through the chain of the Meuse forts, was abandoned—perhaps, the most momentous of all the results of the Battle of the Marne. The crown prince pitched his tent on the feudal eyrie of Montfauçon. General Sarrail picked up his direct communications with Paris, drew in his western wing, and faced round to Metz. On this side of France, at least, the worst days were over.

Thus, all along the line of 170 miles, the Battle of the Marne was a success for the Allies. The offensive of Maunoury and Sir John French, on September 6, almost immediately determined Von Kluck's retreat, though he defended his flank on the Ourcq till the night of the 9th. By that time, D'Espérey was at Montmirail, and Foch's offensive was beginning. On the night of the 10th, the retirement of the Würtembergers began; and two days later the Imperial Crown Prince followed. As a French official statement says:—

"Each army, opening the road to its neighbour, and at the same time supported by it, took in flank the adversary, which the day before it had attacked in front."

Thus, the whole victory was due chiefly to the strategical idea upon which the recoil was planned. This conclusion destroys the belief, with which I approached the subject, that, in modern warfare, any bold, large strategy had become impossible; but the facts do not seem open to any other interpretation than that given above. Only in one other episode did the western campaign of 1914 show any considerable accomplishment of strategy—the defeat of Lanrezac's army on the Sambre by the combined northern and eastern attack. Joffre's feat, however, is incomparably the greater of the two, and entitles him to lasting fame in the sphere of military art.

Chapter 13

The Turning-Point

Gagny, east of Paris, Monday night, September 7.

I have spent a day of crowded and thrilling interest with the rear columns of the most westerly of the armies that are at this moment engaged in meeting the German attempt to break through by the south-east into the heart of France.

In this little town, the broken remains of several French regiments were resting and re-forming after the retreat from Belgium. We went eastward through Gagny, and returned, after a long detour, tonight. A vast change had happened during the day. In the morning, the town was pretty full of men of the 103rd and 104th Infantry. Many of them were in possession of the *cafés* of the town, inside and outside of them; others lay in siesta on the grass in the gardens of the villas. The elementary school playground formed a little camp, with pyramids of rifles stacked up one side, knapsacks lying about in piles, and a barber busy by the doorway. Several soldiers sitting at the little tables before the restaurants had children on their knees, and beside them a wife or sweetheart who had brought a basket of provisions.

A young trooper offered a girl, who came up to wish him good luck, a piece of light gray cloth off a German military cloak. "We have one here," he said.

"One what?"

"An *Uhlan*, of course!"

"Do you mean a dead one?" the girl asked.

"Why, no; he's very much alive."

"Where have you shut him up?"

"He isn't shut up, either," the man explained. "We took him prisoner near Rheims, and since then he has become servant to our junior officers."

"But he will escape," cried the girl.

"Not at all! He's a very good fellow. He's married and has two children, and isn't at all anxious to see any more fighting."

As we went north and eastward, my comrade and I, afraid that every sentry and outpost with bayonet ready would put an end to our unauthorized expedition, I will not deny that we felt the panoply of war to be rather less terrible than we had expected. The actual fighting was six or eight miles away in front, and not by any means to be come at. The great city and its myriads, now in flight or anxiously awaiting the decision, lay twelve miles behind. Here, the sun shone hot upon crowded town and deserted countryside. It was a strange alternative of bustle and stillness, both abnormal; but there was, so far, not even a Red Cross wagon to remind us of the hidden cause.

So we went on through the dust of the empty fields and shuttered villages, passing here and there a marching column, an automobile carrying a group of officers, a motorwagon of the field telegraphs going at breakneck speed, a cyclist dispatch-rider, a battery of guns in trucks in a railway siding, and, oddest of all, a flock of sheep, with a shepherd in infantry blue and red and a rifle under his arm, and another uniformed shepherd at the tail of the dusty procession.

At one wayside inn, mine host regaled us with an unexpected, if not a horrifying, yarn. Several regiments had passed, he said, yesterday and today, and were now fighting "'*là bas*." Yesterday they arrested three spies here. One was dressed as an English soldier, another as a French infantryman, a third as a woman.

"There was a regular outbreak of spy-mania. One old reservist who had been sent down to do detective duty was so excited that he stopped everybody in the village—they were mostly women and children—and demanded their 'papers.' When our village constable tried to calm him, the angry reservist threatened to use his rifle; and he was only with difficulty placated by *M. le Maire*."

It was when the moon was getting up in the east, and we were beginning to think of the night's lodging, that we suddenly struck the graver side of the business. We were watching a small encampment in a wooded by-road. The men had built a fire between the wagons, and were having a pleasant rest out of the sun, when a rider dashed up at a speed that must have made it very uncomfortable for him to smoke his short briar pipe. At once a bugle blew, and in a moment the glade was like a swarming bee-hive. We watched them leave, while the birds sang their evening chorus. Then we went on our way.

Presently, as I have said, we were back in Gagny, only just in time to witness the departure of our friends of the morning for the firing-line, now brought to a full army corps by large re-enforcements that had arrived during the day. The town was boiling from end to end. In the main street a regiment was already marching out to the hills above Meaux, to strengthen the attack on the German flank which had been proceeding for the last two days. Neither here nor elsewhere did we see anything of a regimental band (except some drums); possibly the matter has now become too serious for musical accompaniment.

Looking at these fine figures and bronzed faces, one realised anew the wickedness of the waste of warfare. But they were, beyond doubt, happy and confident. A thin line of country folk watched them, the women—many of them come from a distance to see the last of their men—waving handkerchiefs, the girls running beside the ranks to give some handsome lad a flower. Up the side roads, other battalions stood at ease, or sat on the edge of the pavement waiting their turn. A few tired fellows had curled themselves up, and were asleep, against the houses; and there was one who lay at full length on the ground—over-exhausted by the sharp march of twelve miles which they had already made. As the ambulance took charge of him, a *piou-piou* said to us, "You see, the chaps of forty have to keep up with the lads of twenty."

We talked to them for an hour or more. A young officer, of marked intelligence, told us that his men were all who remained of two infantry regiments in a disastrous engagement at Eth, near Valenciennes, after the Battle of Mons-Charleroi—one of the many affairs of which we have heard little or nothing. He said:—

> It was a regular butchery. We were a full army corps, moving eastward from Eth, when the Hussar regiment which served as our advance guard charged a regiment of Prussian cavalry. Our Hussars were splendid; but they had no sooner routed the first body of the enemy's cavalry than they found themselves faced by another. We were, in fact, flanked by overwhelming numbers, while the German artillery cannonaded us from a distance of several miles. What could we do, one against three? True, we punished them, and, after a moment of panic—for the attack had been sprung upon us—we retired in good order. But of 1,000 men of the 103rd only 180 escaped, and the other regiment suffered hardly less.

The success of the Germans is due to their undoubted superiority in heavy artillery, and to their skilful and daring reconnaissance work. We French have the best artillery in the world, so far as the ordinary guns and the '75' pieces go; but we cannot fire beyond 9,000 or 10,000 yards, while the German heavy guns will do 11,000. This has been a factor since the beginning of the war. Then they send out cavalry scouts eight or twelve miles, and sometimes more, in advance. When these patrols find and report our first lines, they send aeroplanes to examine our positions, especially those of our cavalry and artillery. And in less than an hour their shells are beginning to fall upon us from several miles' distance. So it is under a rain of fire that we have to advance to enable our artillery to get into action. Happily for us, the German shells burst too soon, and the fire is often very badly measured. Once our '75' cannon gets the range, things take a very different turn. Generally the Germans cannot stand it, and move away.

While we were searching for something to eat and drink, we came upon yet another surprise, in the shape of a long line of taxicabs stretching through by-roads out of sight. Fifteen hundred of them there were, they told us, in the neighbourhood—requisitioned in haste to carry forward needed re-enforcements to the French left before the Ourcq.[1] In my innocence, I had supposed that infantrymen must march, and cavalry ride, while wagons bring up supplies. But the internal-combustion engine is changing many things. For a quick retreat, or a quick advance, or the transfer of cartridge cases from one wing to another, there is nothing, it appears, like the common or city taxi. So now I know why we have to put up with old-fashioned *fiacres* on the *boulevards*.

The troops I met today were full of news of a victory between Creil and Meaux, which latter place is about twenty-seven miles from the gates of the capital. There has been considerable fighting around Dammartin to the north of Meaux. To the south of the Marne, on its tributary the Grand Morin, the right wing of the German advance has been met by a French army prepared for this diversion, and by Sir John French's army, which had apparently escaped notice in the woods behind Crécy-en-Brie. The Germans seem to have reached Coulommiers and La Ferté-Gaucher. This is a land of deep valleys and

---

1. Without doubt, the critical movement of reserves referred to earlier.

thickly wooded hills, a very favourable terrain for an army at home and on the defensive. It forms, in fact, a part of what is called the Falaise de Champagne, extending from the Forest of Fontainebleau to Rheims.

Paris, Wednesday Morning, September 9.

Where are the jolly boys whose march out to the firing-line I watched on Monday evening? Dead, some; wounded, others; lost, a few, perhaps; and the remainder happy in their victory. How great a victory, or what exactly is its bearing upon the position in the whole wide field, it is still too soon to say. The official record of the series of actions on the French left and German right wings to the east of Paris is brief and not too clear; but their main purport is unquestionably cheering. The facts which are clear are that the German right in its southward advance has been stopped both on the west and south, has been compelled to retire, and is being ceaselessly harried—a fact even more important for its consequences further east than in its local effects. It would be altogether premature to suppose that the main German movement is yet decisively checked. That may take some time.

M. Dausset, an active member of the Paris Municipal Council, happened to be near Coulommiers yesterday, and has an interesting story to tell of what he saw and heard:—

> By sheer accident, we found ourselves in the midst of the district occupied by the British troops. In one village, the *curé* alone had remained with a few of the more helpless people when the others abandoned their homes. The Germans had been there a few hours before (that is, yesterday morning). Pushing forward, we reached a village where the British troops were resting. At the railway crossing, near by, we came across the body of a black horse lying across the road. We got down, and questioned the crossing-keeper, a good old fellow who was there with his wife. He told us that that very morning the *Uhlans* had come down to the railway, cut the telegraph-lines, and gone away again. Soon afterwards a body of British cavalry, commanded by an officer and guided by the village chemist, had crossed the line. Some of the Germans, it then appeared, had stayed, hiding on a wooded slope, from which they fired on the British column. It was then that the black horse was killed. The officer, seriously wounded, was carried by the old crossing-keeper to his cottage. He was in horrible suffering, but all he asked for was a

cigarette. Soon the British ambulance came up, and took him away. We learned afterwards that the chemist was also seriously wounded.

We soon came to another village; and I shall never forget the spectacle we saw. The place was absolutely deserted; only three women and a boy remained. They told us that the Germans came in large numbers on Sunday. They occupied the whole village and the neighbouring farms. They looked harassed, as if they had been marching for days without a stop. Nearly all the houses being shut up, they broke open the doors; but they respected the few cottages that were still inhabited. I went to the *mairie* to see for myself, and found it in indescribable disorder. In every room there were mattresses, sheets, and bundles of straw, on which men had been sleeping; remnants of food, half-empty bottles, drawers piled on the floors, chests open; in the yard eiderdowns, mattresses, and pillows, and the like on the village square. In the church, more straw, where men had been sleeping; the remnants of rabbits, fowls, and pieces of meat.

In the large but not very luxurious country-house, which they call the *château*, all the rooms had been occupied by the higher officers. In the large dining-room, the table was covered with fine white cloths, vases full of fresh-cut roses, and dishes showing that several courses had been served. There even remained two serviettes folded in mitre-shape before two chairs that had not been occupied. An oil-lamp was still burning, and a number of candles guttered over the empty bottles into which they had been stuck. The invaders had drunk champagne from the cellars of the house—a good deal of it. The women who accompanied me said that nearly all the officers spoke French. They did not hurt anyone, but took away all the provisions they could lay hands on. The first thing the officers asked for was a bath. They had certainly intended to remain; and, in the bedrooms which I visited, they had carefully drawn the blinds, as though for a long sleep. At 2 a.m. they received a sudden signal to leave, and the district was evacuated immediately. There must then have been stiff fighting, for on our return we passed the bodies of thirty horses and some fresh-made graves.

At Massy-Palaiseau and other south-eastern suburbs of Paris there is a constant succession of trains today taking British and French troops toward the front, and bringing wounded and prisoners back.

Behind the British Lines, on the Grand Morin.
Thursday, September 10.

It would be near Guignes, thirty miles south-east of Paris, that I first struck a British detachment, and learned that the line of battle had moved rapidly northward. They were lads of the Army Service Corps, resting in the shade of one of the long poplar avenues, awaiting orders, in charge of a line of commissariat wagons, and commandeered carts bearing the familiar names of great English trading firms. Some of the men were more red of face than brown, others swarthy with work in the continuous sunshine of the last month. Glad, perhaps, to hear a new English voice, and certainly glad to get a taste of English tobacco, they quickly thawed, and launched out into stories such as would have seemed incredible six weeks ago, and are now the common talk of every day over half the Continent.

A little later, at a crossroads in the dead black heart of one of the forests of the Brie plateau, full of mysterious sounds in the gloom of nightfall, I came across a British motorcyclist of the engineer branch of the corps, keeping his lonely watch. He was too full of the morning's advance to think about his eerie surroundings. But one of his words stayed in my mind. He had been telling me of a narrow escape he and some of his fellows had just had. They suddenly found themselves, with a file of wagons, between two German columns, within sight of both. What do engineers do in such a case? They take out something he called, I think, the fusible plugs—safety plugs in some part of the wagon engine—and then they bolt.

"So the Germans got the wagons?" I asked.

"Yes," he replied; "but they couldn't move them, and we expect soon to find them again."

And then he added, very modestly, the word to which I have referred—to the effect that this rear work of supplies and communications is as important as the fighting line itself, although little is heard of it. There was not the faintest suspicion of a complaint in the good fellow's voice—he was simply stating a fact that every soldier knows. But it came home to me almost as a rebuke. How often and easily we forget the high aim and the whole design of a defensive war in the wild glamour of its central struggles!

Yet even in the narrow view of the military art itself, the feeding and transport of the troops assume a larger and larger part in modern warfare. Napoleon closed a chapter of history; there can never again be a single man equal to the direction of the multitudes now thrown into the field. He began the transformation; it has since gone so far that nearly all the impressions we get from narratives of the old campaigns are false to the facts of today. This has been called an "anonymous war" because, on the French side especially, great secrecy is maintained as to the whereabouts of the commanding officers, and their individual part in the campaign is never mentioned. In a larger sense, all warfare has become "anonymous," partly because of the fear of giving any useful information to the enemy, and partly because the individual mind counts for less, the prearranged scheme, the system, the total organisation, the obscure engineering operations, count for more.

When we entered the village of Rozay-en-Brie, we found the street deserted save for an old lady who from her garden gate watched curiously the approach of another foreigner. But the word "English" counts for much now in these parts.

"*Ah, monsieur, les Anglais!*" And for the moment she could add nothing but a beaming smile to this exclamation. The dear old thing had stuck to her little home all through the double inundation. "There were 12,000 of yours here on Sunday," she continued. "My daughter, who has lived in London and learned to speak English, acted as interpreter for your 'Tommies.' Go on two miles to Lumigny, Pezarches, and Touquin, and there you will find the battlefield."

Perhaps that is too large a name for what at this particular point was only a rather serious skirmish, covering a few miles of stubble-fields and broken forest, and several small villages. In one of these fields, as we drove up, six or eight peasants were digging a pit in which to bury the carcases of two horses that lay near by. They had already buried fourteen others. They pointed out the woods in the distance to the east where the Germans had taken cover; the British were posted along the roads by which we had come. These grave-diggers seemed happy at their gruesome work—just such sententious fellows as Shakespeare took for his models in an immortal scene three hundred years ago. So little does raw humanity change! I should have to translate their words into some one of our own provincial lingoes to give its flavour; and that would overpass the limits of true reporting.

But presently there came through the stubble a neat cart conveying a somewhat superior person of rubicund visage, who introduced himself as the Mayor of Pezarches, M. Couple, at your service; and he was able to give a more full and consistent explanation of what had happened.

> We knew that the Germans were at Coulommiers on Saturday, and so we were expecting them. About 8 o'clock that evening, I was trying to eat my dinner, when suddenly I heard the sound of horses' hoofs, and said to my wife: 'It is they.' Outside the door I found a score of German dragoons. Their lieutenant called out: 'Where is the mayor?' 'I am the mayor,' I said. 'What do you want?' On this he came up to me, put the revolver which he had in his hand to my head, and said: 'Bread for my men, and oats for the horses. And,' he added, ' in five minutes at latest!' I replied that I would get what oats there were, but there had been no bread at the baker's since morning. He retorted, more imperiously than ever: 'Get it how you can, but bread I must have.'
>
> I managed to get together 75 kilos of oats and 15 kilos of bread. The officer seemed satisfied, gave me a signed receipt, and said it would be paid. That night the Germans passed behind the villages, putting their guns in position there. The British, who were in force, had established themselves behind the little wood you see at the end of this field. On Sunday morning they opened fire. One shell went through a villager's cottage; but happily he and his were hidden in the cellar and no harm was done. Later on, the Germans retreated, and the British have followed them closely ever since.

I asked whether the losses were serious.

> The Germans seemed to suffer greatly here," replied our friend the mayor; "they had many wounded. But the English were well covered; they lost only two killed and thirty wounded. They buried the two bodies over there on the border of the wood; if you will come, I will show you the place.

I shall never forget that humble grave amid the fields of the Brie plateau. No stone marks the place where two sons of England, someone's beloved, rest after their labour and sacrifice. There is nothing but a pile of brown earth in the bottom of a small chalk pit, surmounted by a couple of brown sticks tied together with string, to make a rough cross. A thicket looks over the hollow, and all around are rolling hills from which the corn has just been garnered. It is one of thousands of anonymous graves in this "anonymous war." If these lines should meet the eyes of any to whom those two lads were dear, let them be brave to hear the worst, and happy to hear the best, that I can say. The good mayor told us he had taken trouble to strengthen the mound. But Nature is inexorable; life, and ever more life, is her supreme law. Such graves may be lost before they can be found. Yet I cannot think of any more fortunate resting-place than on the edge of this wood among the wheat-fields, with its fringe of flowers, and the pure sky above, where the birds will always sing *matins* and evensong, and the children of the village will come and speak of how the two lads from distant England helped to save their home and Fatherland.

We must bow to the law of life. Already they are ploughing the upper ridge of the stubble-field where the battle was fought. Already, while the grave-diggers are still at their task, at the farm on the other side of the road a threshing-machine is working; and, as we leave, a procession of great harvesting carts, full of women and children sitting on top of their household goods, is bringing back a first party of fugitives to the homes they abandoned a fortnight ago. The harvest of death gives way already to the harvest of life.

Down in the village, they showed me holes in some of the houses made by the artillery fire. They are just recovering, as it were, from a frightful dream; and the women are reaching the loquacious stage following upon such an experience. In the village inn, *Madame*, an upstanding woman of about thirty, told us her part of the story, with many lively gestures.

> *Imaginez-vous, monsieur!* When the Prussians came, we took them for Belgians. As we had been warned that there would be a battle, everybody took refuge in their cellars. On Sunday morning, my mother had gone to church, and I remained at home with my father and my little boy. My father had left us to get some tobacco. Going out for a moment with my child, I saw a group of horsemen in the street, and said to myself, 'We are saved. It is the Belgians!' When I returned, to my surprise, they were in the house, sitting in my room and in the *café*. An officer asked me to cook him a couple of eggs. I noticed that one of the men was wounded, and asked if it was painful. He nodded, and I went to the kitchen. There I saw, on the window-sill, a spiked helmet. I nearly fainted! So they were Germans!
>
> I managed to take in the eggs. Then the officer very politely asked me to show him my left hand, and, pointing to the

wedding-ring, said, 'You are married?' 'Yes,' I replied, trembling. 'Your husband is a soldier?' 'Yes.' 'You have a child?' 'No, I have no children,' I said. 'But I saw him. You are hiding him because you have heard that the Germans cut off the hands of French children. That is false. We never hurt women or children. Bring your little boy.'

But as I persisted that it was not my child, he said no more. He and the others paid for what they had in German money, and left. A quarter of an hour later the firing began.

CHAPTER 14

"Sufficient Unto the Day"

Château-Thierry, Saturday, September 12.

We first realised yesterday, in the little town of Brie, which lies east of Paris between the Seine and the Marne, how difficult it is to get food in the rear of two successive invasions. As in every other town in the region, all the shops were shut, and nearly all the houses. It was only after a long search that we found an inn that could give us lunch. There, in a large room with a low, beamed roof and tiled door, our stout landlady in blue cotton produced an excellent meal of melon, mutton, macaroni, and good ripe pears. The dogs and cats sprawled around us, and a big bowl of roses spoke of the serenities that are now in general eclipse.

At a neighbouring table, a group of peasants, too old for active service, were discussing, not the battle that has just passed their doors, but their business grievances. A farmer had refused to sell something to one of them, who thought he should be forced to do so. Another angrily protested against this view; while a third declared that it was monstrous to offer straw at 45*f.* "You may be old," retorted the other, "but there are people older than you," meaning cleverer. But at the end of the table there was a big, fat man who showed the greater wisdom; he went on with his meal, and said nothing.

At the railway crossing just out of town, we were blocked by a train of about a dozen big horse-trucks and two passenger carriages, carrying wounded and prisoners to Paris from the fighting lines. It had been a gloomy morning, and the rain now fell in torrents. Nevertheless, the townsfolk crowded up, and for half an hour managed to conduct a satisfactory combination of profit and pity by the supply of big, flat loaves, bottles of wine, fruit, cigarettes, and jugs of water, to those in the train who had money, and some who had none. One very old lady in white, with a little red cross on her forehead, turned up to take advantage of the only opportunity ever likely to fall in her way. A great Turco, in *fez*, blouse, and short, baggy breeches, was very active in this commissariat work. Some of the Frenchmen on board were not wounded sufficiently seriously to prevent their getting down on to the roadway; and you may be sure that they were not ashamed of their plaster-patches and bandaged arms.

There were about 300 German prisoners in the train. We got glimpses of them lying in the straw upon the floor in the dark interior of the big trucks. I got on to the footboard, and looked into the open door of one wagon. Fifteen men were stretched upon the straw, and two soldiers stood guard over them, rifle in hand. They all seemed to be in the extremity of exhaustion. Some were asleep; others were eating large chunks of bread. In the middle of the wagon, a young soldier, who spoke French fairly well, said that the German losses during the last three days had been enormous; and then, stopping suddenly, "Would it be possible, sir, to get a little water for my fellows and myself?" A man belonging to the station, who was passing with a jug said at once that he would run and get some. The prisoner thanked him, and added with a sigh, "They're very good fellows here."

Beside one of the roads running through the numerous forests of the region, we came upon a Tate's sugar-van left stranded in the ditch, with the engine smashed. It was the first of many abandoned motor-vans, lorries, and cars that we were to find during this day's journey. Some of them had, no doubt, merely broken down; and it was thought advisable to make them useless in case they were captured by the enemy. In other cases, the danger of seizure was more immediate; and they were put out of action and left. These incidents, often repeated, impressed upon us at once the importance of motor transport in modern warfare, and the great wastage to which it is liable—a wastage, however, probably much less than would have occurred in the old horse-transport days.

We thought that we were going to be shipwrecked as unhappily ourselves, for, in the middle of the Forest of Chaumes, we completely lost ourselves in pouring rain, and at last came to a full stop in a slough of mud. Happily, our labour and anxiety were of short duration; and in the evening we reached the quaint and very ancient town of Provins, normally of 9,000 inhabitants, on the edge of a rich given valley beneath the Brie plateau. It is odd today to think that Provins. which was once proud and great, was nearly ruined by English invaders in the fifteenth century, whose descendants have now saved it from a German invasion. An Englishman is, therefore, as such, a welcome visitor; but everywhere in the wake of the war civilian visitors are suspect. So we stuck to the one hotel that was open, and did not attempt to visit the remarkable twelfth-century keep which is called "Caesar's Tower." or the medieval ramparts. This big hostelry was being run by four women who, despite a natural courtesy, were evidently quite unprepared to receive ordinary guests. They let us hang our wet clothes among the brass pans in the kitchen, however; and then we sat and smoked around the charcoal fire in the linen-room, with piles of napkins and sheets around us. At the dinner-table, beside ourselves, there were only a captain of *gendarmerie*, several army officers, and half a dozen of the more substantial refugees from the neighbouring district. We went to bed along ghostly echoing corridors, with a feeling that the house must have antedated Caesar's Tower itself.

This morning we had decided to make an early start northwards; but, when we had paid our bill and were ready to go, a venerable, but not otherwise very impressive, French officer came up, and informed us that he proposed to requisition our car for an hour. He seemed so gentle, and he might so well have turned crusty had we refused, that we promptly gave way, returned to the breakfast-table, and waited until the car had come back from the station.

Then we struck upward through fields and orchards on to the plateau; and within hair an hour we had reached the first of the ruined villages which mark the southward limit of the German advance.

In Courchamp, a number of houses had been burnt down, and the neighbouring fields showed that there had been fighting there. But it was Courtaçon, halfway between Provins and La Ferté-Gaucher, which presented the most grievous spectacle. Eighteen of the two dozen houses—small, modern brick buildings, not old cottages of wood and thatch—had been completely destroyed by fire. The walls were partly standing, but the floors and the contents of the rooms were completely buried under the debris of the roofs that had fallen in. In the little post-office, the telegraphic and telephonic instruments had been smashed. Just opposite is a small building, including the *mairie* and the village school. The outside of the building and the outhouses were littered with straw, upon which the *Uhlans* had slept. In the *mairie* itself, drawers and cupboards had been broken open, and their contents scattered, with the remnants of meals, upon the floor.

It is the scene in the little village school that will longest remain in my memory as a flagrant exhibition of brutality and malice. The low forms, the master's desk, and the blackboard stand today as they did on July 25, which was no doubt, the last day before the summer vacation, as it was also the last week before the outbreak of the war. On the walls, the charts remained which had reminded the children daily that—

Alcohol that is the Enemy,

and had summoned them to—

Follow the Path of Kindness, Justice, and Truth.

The windows were smashed. Broken cartridge cases lay about, with the wings of birds and other refuse. Just near the door, I saw chalked up, in an evidently German handwriting, the words, "*Parti Paris*"—"Left for Paris." The really speaking message that had been left lay, however, in the piles of burnt straw with which it had been deliberately sought to burn the place to ashes. There was one pile under the school bookcase, the doors of which had been smashed, and some of the books thrown about. They could not even—these ruffians—respect the little museum, consisting of a few bottles of metal and chemical specimens. And when I turned to leave, I suddenly perceived, written across the blackboard, in bold, fine writing, as the lesson of the day, these words:

À Chaque Jour Suffit sa Peine.
Every day brings pain enough

Or in the familiar words of our English version, "*Sufficient unto the day is the evil thereof.*" No fictionist's imagination could have compassed the biting irony of these words; but the deepest bitterness of this irony lies in the fact that such an outrage could be perpetrated by men belonging to a nation one of whose boasts was that they have been the pioneers in Europe of elementary schooling.

One of the villagers gave me the following narrative of their experiences during the past week:—

It was last Saturday (September 5) that about 1,500 *Uhlans* arrived in the village, with the intention of marching on Provins on the morrow. They probably learned during the night that the British and French lay in force across their road; and perhaps they may then have received orders to fall back in any case. At any rate, early on Sunday morning, they started to retire, when they met at the entrance to the village a regiment of Chasseurs.

This was the beginning of fighting which lasted all day. Under pretext that we had learned of the presence of French troops, and had helped them to prepare a trap, the Germans sacked the whole of the village. Naturally, there was a panic. All the inhabitants—mostly women and children, because, since the mobilization, there have only been nine men in Courtaçon—rushed from their cottages; and many of them, lightly clad, fled across the fields, and hid themselves in the neighbouring woods. In several cottages, the Germans, revolver in hand, compelled the poor peasants to bring matches and themselves to set fire to their homes. In less than an hour, the village was like a furnace, the walls toppling down one by one. And all this time the fighting continued. It was a horrible spectacle. Several of us were dragged to the edge of the road to be shot; and there we remained for some hours, believing that our last day had come. A young village lad of twenty-one years, who was just going to leave to join the colours, was shot. Then the retreat was sounded; the Germans fled precipitately; and we were saved.

I asked whether the cottages had not been fired by our artillery. He replied pointing to the ruined street:—

Not a cannon-shot fell here, all that was done by incendiaries. Last Tuesday, two French officers came in an automobile, and brought with them a superior German officer, whom they had made prisoner. They compelled him to become a witness of the mischief of which his fellow-countrymen had been guilty.

As we spoke, a peasant woman passed, pushing a wheelbarrow containing some half-burned household goods, and followed by her two small children. "Look," she said, as we turned to her, "at the brutality of these Germans. My husband has gone to the war, and I was alone with my two little ones. With great difficulty we had managed to gather our crop; and they set fire to our little farm, and burnt everything."

Half an hour later, we were at La Ferté-Gaucher, a small town on the Grand Morin, now first made famous by the fact that it was here the German fight began, after severe fighting, last Monday. The invaders had only arrived on the Saturday, and had the disagreeable surprise of finding that the river bridges had been broken down by the then retreating French. The German *commandant* informed the municipal officials that, if the sum of 60,000 *francs* (£2,400) were not produced, he would burn down the town. He then compelled the people to set about in building the bridge; and they worked day and night at this job, under the eyes of the soldiers with revolvers and rifles ready to shoot down any shirker. The relief to these people of the return of the Allies may be imagined. Here, as elsewhere, some houses had been burned down; otherwise, the damage did not appear to be very serious.

The chief bridge being destroyed, the invaders crossed southward by boats, and over some small private bridges that had been overlooked. The villagers say that they advanced with loud cries of "*Nach Paris!*" There seems no doubt that even the officers shared the illusion that the capital was besieged, and that already their comrades might be camped in the Place de l'Opéra. When they learned something of the truth, they were stupefied. This fact and the rainfall help to explain the suddenness and completeness of their breakdown.

We now went onward to the north-west, through Rebais to La Ferté-sous-Jouarre, at the junction of the Petit Morin and the Marne. This is a larger place, normally of 5,000 inhabitants, situated forty-one miles east of Paris, mainly in a turn of the fertile, well-cultivated, and beautiful valley of the Marne. As we rode in, it was occupied by a large French detachment. We were immediately pulled up at the broken bridge, the fragments of which partially dammed the stream of the larger river. On the top of the ruins of the bridge itself, in the river-bed, lay several motorcars, which had, no doubt, been used as barricades before and during the bombardment. The roofs and walls of many of the houses, especially on the north bank of the Marne, were shattered, and some completely destroyed, during the attack on the retiring German columns last Wednesday. They had defended this passage hardily. From the ferryboat that carried us over, we could still see, on the parapets of a pretty terrace overlooking the stream, the sandbags, mattresses, pillows, and cushions from behind which the German riflemen had commanded the bridge-head on the opposite side. A few hundred feet only had separated them from their British pursuers.

The Germans were here for a week; and during that time they ransacked every shop in the place. The staff put up at the best inn, the Hôtel l'Epée, a title the proprietor is now probably out of love with. His good lady told me that, by way of celebrating their arrival, the officers—there were sixteen of them—demanded a good brand of champagne, as they had only had inferior sorts of late.

I told them our cellars were empty. They then sent men to search the town; and these presently returned with a case of Moët and Chandon. At the end of the dinner-party, they were all drunk, and set about kicking and whipping some of their servants and men. One day, an officer, whom I understood to be the commandant, ordered me to prepare a special dinner. 'But,' said I, 'I have no butter, and there is none to be got in the district.' 'Get a knife, and come to my room,' he replied. This was not very reassuring, as you may imagine, for these men went about giving orders with revolvers constantly in their hands. When we got upstairs, he showed me a large lump of butter, and told me to take a little. I took it; but I may confess, now, it was grease I used for his meal, and the butter for our own.

One evening, a party of soldiers burst in and asked me, with their usual threats, for some good wine. I said I had nothing but *ordinaire*. They wouldn't believe me, and told me to bring a light and show them to the cellar. At the bottom of the steps they shouldered me away; but when they found the bottles which— (this with a shrewd smile—I had been careful not to hide, they declared they had only wanted champagne, and left in a very angry mood. Undoubtedly, there is not now a bottle of champagne in La Ferté, for the Germans stole and drank thousands of bottles during the few days they were here.

We had now to make a long detour by the village of Méry in order to get over the Marne; and, pursuing our way through lovely vineyards—the first of the vineyards of Champagne—and desolate villages, we reached Château-Thierry.

A long French Red Cross convoy followed us into the town, and, thereafter, endless strings of British supply-wagons. A few washerwomen by the riverside seemed to be almost the only remains of the civil population; but the normal roll of 5,000 people must have been fully made up by soldiery of the two allied races. They were *laagered* in every available space, beneath the ruins of the ancient castle, and the birthplace of La Fontaine of the *Fables*, around the square before the town hall and theatre, everywhere and anywhere.

I had some interesting chat with several British soldiers, including a member of the Flying Corps, who confirmed my impression of the difficulty of distinguishing friendly from hostile aeroplanes at any height, and said it was no good shooting at interlopers—our own 'planes must always be up and ready to tackle them.

A brief encounter with a French *gendarme* officer was less pleasant, but not as anxious as the question of petrol. Thanks to a kindly doctor, we at last renewed our stock, and went north into the villages behind the battle front, where the fainter and fainter sound of the cannon proclaimed the continued success of the great recoil. How the old ghosts from all past sieges of Soissons—they go back to Caesar's day—will walk tonight; and with what blazing lights and horrid shadows the elder Dumas, whose birthplace has rung today to the sound of combat, would have glorified the story! Sir John French himself, happy and fit-looking, was in these villages only yesterday, saying a bracing word to his men.

But, for me, with the fresh mounds of earth, and the long train of British wounded going south, blinding my eyes, the only words that I can add—and they are as true in the hours of victory as of defeat—are the words of the schoolmaster who wrote, on breaking-up day, upon the blackboard in the ruined village of Courtaçon—unconscious instrument of the omnipotent and eternal Irony—"*Sufficient unto the day is the evil thereof.*"

CHAPTER 15

On the Ourcq Battlefield

Paris, September 14.

I have only now been able to run out to Meaux, and obtain a clear impression of the battlefield of the Ourcq. These motor-trips behind the lines, involving long detours, because passes are given only for some place beyond the zone of operations, are something of an adventure—not that an arrest can involve any great discomfort, but because, for a journalist, the heaviest penalty is simply to be shut out of the field of action. I hear that three British and two American pressmen have just been stopped on the Marne, and politely conducted south to Tours. Naturally, the pickets posted behind their barricades of logs, stone, and wire, along the main road running due east out of Paris, are particularly exacting. British officers have, apparently, received still stiffer orders—in fact, if all orders were literally interpreted, there could be no public record of the war beyond the meagre official bulletins; and, within the British lines, the scrap of pink paper issued, after interminable formalities, by the Prefect of Police and the Military Governor of Paris has no value. When these difficulties have been overcome, there always remains the possibility of being held up by some excited subordinate as a spy.

We were pelting homeward along a narrow lane between Villers-Cotterets and La Ferté-Milon. It was near nightfall, and we had to get to the gates of Paris by 7.30 p.m., on pain of being shut out. Suddenly a couple of men in khaki, with fixed bayonets, loomed before us, with a sharp summons to halt. Lengthy explanations were received with stolid incredulity, perhaps because my companion and chauffeur were manifestly not Britons. We were taken a few yards back to a large motor-wagon, in which we were surprised to see half-a-dozen wounded men lying. One of them was the sergeant; and to him—though he was evidently out of action—the matter was loyally referred, the Tommies standing around while I repeated my explanations. He replied that we could not go on, as they were hunting German fugitives out of the woods just beyond, and it would not be safe for us to pass. No, we could not go backward, either. The man-hunt was, then, a pretext for delay. But they were very good fellows; and I was presently busy writing postcards for the wounded men, to assure Mrs. Atkins at home that all was well with them. Then they let us go, by an eastward side-road.

Between Meaux and Changis, the Marne makes a northward loop, and at the head of this loop it is joined by the Ourcq, which has flowed from the western spurs of the Mountain of Rheims, through La Ferté-Milon. This little country town, the birthplace of Racine, has two fine ancient churches, and is overshadowed (we can no longer say "dominated" in these days of big guns) by the immense rectangular walls and flanking towers of the *donjon* of Duke Henry of Orleans. Two months ago, these things would have taken all our interest. Now we are absorbed in examining the wreckage of a small general shop— the only one open in the place—and in hearing the story of its miserable owner. No! he had no food to sell us. He had a single bottle of country wine hidden; but he dare not give us that, lest the soldiers, who had taken everything, should charge him with concealing provisions. Some infantrymen were watching us as we spoke; so, to save the man from suspicion, we moved away.

From Ferté-Milon, the Ourcq flows southward to the Marne through a narrow, wooded ravine. On both sides stretch rolling wheatfields, broken by small woods and orchards, and farmsteads and villages that have bought with their modest substance a fame like that of Hougomont and Mont St. Jean. The French Army covering Paris stretched from the Marne toward Senlis; and the outposts of Von Kluck's army were also on the west side of the Ourcq when the battle began, his main columns being on the east bank, along the roads between Villers-Cotterets and Château-Thierry. The plateau slopes down southward to the Marne Valley, the descent into Meaux being rather sharp. Meaux is a quiet little town of 14,000 inhabitants, twenty-seven miles east of Paris, on the main road and the railway to Châlons. It is a market-town for Brie cheese and other country produce; it is also the meeting-place of main roads from Senlis, Compiègne, and Soissons. Immediately to the east, there is a tangle of water-ways; and it is difficult to understand how the invaders could allow themselves to get involved in such a region.

Thus, the Paris-Châlons road crosses the Ourcq Canal before entering the town of Meaux. On leaving it, it crosses the canal twice, and the Marne once, before reaching Trilport. It then runs south of the river to La Ferté-sous-Jouarre, where it crosses the Petit Morin; while a north-east road there crosses the Marne to reach Château-Thierry. You get from the north to Coulommiers either by a road through Meaux, crossing the Ourcq Canal and the Marne, or by roads from Trilport and La Ferté. We found all Meaux shuttered up, and practically depopulated. But no harm was done in the town; some Germans entered it, but it was not occupied.

The chief stress of the battle fell among the villages in the angle between the Marne and the west bank of the Ourcq, beyond the shoulder of the rise from Meaux. Five days have passed, but the scene is still painful beyond description. We went up the road which strikes north between Meaux and Trilport, leaving Vareddes and Lizy on our right, Penchard, Chambry, Barcy, Etrepilly, and Acy on our left. The road is bordered by a fine avenue of Lombardy poplars. Many of the tree-trunks have been completely severed; others have great branches lopped off, which lie about the road; yet others show gaping wounds where shells have struck them. We wandered about the orchards and coppices, the patches of potatoes and maize, beside the highway, and beyond these into the fields of stubble and grass. Everywhere are to be seen the ruts of gun-carriage wheels, and wide holes torn out by shrapnel or shell fire, metallic patches in the red earth showing how the soil has been fused by the explosion.

Everywhere scraps of clothing, old letters and unwritten postcards, presumably thrown out when the dead were being buried; masses of used cartridges in abandoned trenches, scraps of French "75" shells, a long lint bandage, a broken spectacle-case—the most trifling things eloquent of overwhelming horror. Where the German guns have made a rear-guard stand, there is a pile of live projectiles, and the elaborate wicker baskets in which they are carried, left in the hurry of retreat. Nearly all the human remains in this district have now been buried, the trenches being used for common graves; but dead bodies of horses lie along the road and over the fields, poisoning the air for miles around. As we came home, the gloom was broken by dozens of fires by which these carcasses are being incinerated.

Shattered and still burning farm buildings, gutted houses in the villages from Chauconin northward, torn and charred hayricks, broken motor-carts, and all sorts of litter mark the track of the storm. The hardest fighting seems to have occurred between Penchard, Barcy, and Vareddes, during the earlier part of the battle, and between Acy and Betz when the Germans tried to turn the French flank by the north. At Penchard and Vareddes, there were terrible bayonet charges, under the unceasing blaze of artillery. At the entrance to Acy village, Frenchmen and Germans fell in hundreds together. At Chauconin, Congis, Penchard, and Barcy, the German soldiers deliberately set fire to a number of houses, without any known excuse. French engineers are now busy patching up the broken bridges. Convoys of prisoners and wounded pass south; re-enforcements and supplies go north. Otherwise. the countryside between Meaux and Soissons is almost uninhabited, and almost uninhabitable.

No food or lodging is to be obtained, so far as we could find, except at Villers-Cotterets; and this pretty little town has the disadvantage of being full of troops. After nearly tumbling into the midst of the *quartier-général*, naturally established in the best hotel, we turned about quickly, and found refuge in a third-class inn. This place, also, was overllowing with soldiers, including a number of sub officers who were discussing, in a very calm and intelligent way, the massacre at Senlis. There is no longer any doubt of the barbarities of the invasion. The Germans have pillaged Crépy-en-Valois; they have burned down a large part of Choisy-en-Bac; they have committed wholesale robbery in Creil and Compiègne, and many personal outrages. But the case of Senlis calls for a special judgment. When General von Kluck's men entered the town, on September 2, they were fired upon, as the natives say, by retiring *Zouaves*; as the Germans aver, by some of the inhabitants. That night, the town was set on fire by means of hand-grenades and other incendiary apparatus, over a hundred houses being burned down. Other houses were sacked.

A number of hostages were then taken, among them the mayor, M. Odent, who seems to have shown great dignity under cruel treatment. After a mock trial, M. Odent and six other citizens were shot, A dozen other inhabitants, or more, were murdered in the streets. How much the French officers to whom I was listening knew of these facts did not appear. The question had been raised whether civilians were in any case justified in resisting invaders entering a town; and no lawyer could have been clearer than those French patriots that they are not. Needless to say, they would not have justified so barbarous a revenge, even if it were proved that some of the inhabitants of Senlis were *francs-tireurs*.

An officer of a Highland regiment, a veteran of the Boer War, now lying wounded in Paris, told a French relative that if the British Army, comparatively few in numbers, had been able to give very important aid in the crises of this war, it was because they had learned a lesson from the Boers.

> Formerly, we did not know how to use either artificial protection or the lie of the land to get shelter from the enemy's fire, and we charged in close formation against the best marksmen in the world. The Boers were our teachers; and now there are no soldiers in Europe who know as we do how to find cover. This time, we have to meet only mediocre, not to say bad marksmen, and they employ mass tactics. So, if the numbers are equal, we beat them; and if they have the larger force we can hold our own with small loss. Also, before charging, our men watch the effects of the artillery fire. These, briefly, are the secrets of our success.

The following notes by a French writer, M. André Paisant, written on Saturday at Nanteuil-le-Haudouin, thirty-five miles north-east of Paris, may be read as a pendant to my last messages:—

> They were fighting here on Thursday night. On the railway, we found the body of a little Frenchman. The telegraph-lines are all down, and the houses show gaping holes. On the avenue between the station and the town, a sickening odour of dead horses and food left by the flying Germans strikes us. The lampless streets were full of troops till early this morning. Dogs wander disconsolate about the empty houses. Inside, chests of drawers have been upset, cupboards broken open, curtains and cloths cut to pieces, and all sorts of refuse left about. At Boissy Levignon, only four walls of the railway station were left. I found here a circle of litters on which lay the bodies of five dead *Uhlans*, stiff, bare-chested, and their wounds clotted with blood. They had been brought here alive, and were then abandoned during the fight. One of them, with fine hands and a face still speaking of energy, was strikingly handsome.
> Some soldiers stood at a tap between the corpses, drawing water. In a shed next door, with shattered roof, there were more bodies. One of the dead men was sitting upright, with open eyes and outstretched hand, like a figure at Mme. Tussaud's; but a figure of flesh, not wax. The railway-crossing keeper told me

how the Germans suddenly stopped their advance, then turned and lied, abandoning everything. At Peroy-les-Gombries, little mounds with crosses show where most of the dead were buried. At the entrance to the village, three Germans were sitting in a ditch, with French maps in their hands. A shell intermitted their studies. I returned with some prisoners. They were very much afraid; but the captain said, 'The French are kind; you are safe,' and I saw their lips quiver. Some soldiers brought them water to drink. War is a horrible thing, yet the heart expands to see such acts as this.

It is remarkable that the Germans have not attempted to defend the line of the Marne south-east of Rheims, or to hold that city. We shall now be able to learn what has been happening there during the past fortnight. To the west, Amiens has been abandoned; and we may hope for a resumption of the Boulogne and Calais boat services to England. At many places, including Montmirail, the retreat was so sudden that the papers of the general staff, as well as all sorts of munitions, were captured. At the village of Fromentières in particular, ten miles north of Sézanne, whole batteries of guns were taken. Both prisoners and horses seemed utterly worn out. The campaign of "smashing blows" has, in fact, smashed its authors, and this kind of offensive, which was much in favour recently among soldiers who had learned in the Prussian school, must be regarded as correspondingly discounted. The centre is always a very difficult situation, and here, around Vitry-le-François, some of the most desperate of the fighting has taken place. All along the line the heavy rain of Fridays helps to account for much of the German artillery losses.

Best of all, perhaps, is the news of the German abandonment of the Nancy region and the French reoccupation of Lunéville, to which it is added this afternoon that beyond Lunéville and St. Dié a number of points have been recovered on the Alsatian frontier, including Pont-à-Mousson, Nomeny, Baccarat, and Raon-l'Etape. It is over a fortnight since Lunéville was occupied, and considerable anxiety has been felt for the Nancy forces. When the *Kaiser* went to the battlefield before Nancy the other day, it may be presumed that he still entertained certain expectations now destined to remain unfulfilled. This is not the moment to think of that strange life, so often covered with flattery, so hard to understand, the victim of an evil heritage, now faced with a prospect of disgrace and ruin. Let me rather say a word in praise of the admirable calm with which, after the long news of misfortune, the people of Paris have heard the news of victory. The sober-sided *Journal des Débats* says:—

> This calm is not in our French temperament; it is the fruit of experience.

No doubt this is true, and let us not forget that this experience includes a mass of sorrow beside which the whole of the battles of 1870 were a small matter. The song of triumph is stilled by the thought of those nameless graves all over the plains and hillsides of the north.

Chapter 16

In the Ruined Villages

Paris, December 10.

Since I followed in the wake of the Battle of the Marne, and saw the havoc wrought among the thriving little communities on the Brie plateau and from there to Soissons, I have seen much of what General Sherman called "the hell of war," but nothing quite like the ravaged region in southern Champagne.

It is difficult to maintain anything like a judicial temper when face to face with wrong of this character and extent. Our law-courts are conducted upon the supposition, probably justified, that very few men make good witnesses. If it be so in normal times, how much more so amid this great unloosing of passions, this agony of sufferings immeasurable. The observer coming from a distant isle, which has not known for centuries what invasion means, may easily discern that there are here all kinds and degrees of wickedness; and—still believing, as we did a few months ago, that there is no such thing as a nation of criminals—he may seek for those instances of generosity and pity which, however exceptional, would allow him to maintain his faith in human nature, with all its tangle of good and ill.

There must be German soldiers and officers who are ashamed of what has been done in Belgium and France, as Frenchmen and British and Belgians would be ashamed if any such devil's work were to be wrought in Germany. But it is useless to search for evidence of such scruples amid the ruins of beloved homes; and it is asking too much of human nature, when it has lost all that made life tolerable, if not happy, to rise to the height of impartiality which is the ideal of the Courts of Justice.

The peasants, many of whom we have examined and cross-examined, speak with manifest sincerity. But what they have heard has become a part of what they have seen; and how (for instance) is a simple civilian to distinguish what report calls " incendiary pastilles "from the little squares of modern gunpowder a packet of which lies before me, picked up in the trenches on the Ourcq? No complete and trustworthy account of these things can be made at present; I doubt if it will ever be possible to make one. But some general facts are beyond doubt; and they are sufficient to justify us in saying that the normal cruelty of war has, in considerable portions of the present campaign, been so far exceeded as to doubly damn the original German aggression, and eclipse all the previous evil of Prussian militarism. There is nothing, so far, in French experience to equal the fire and sack of Louvain, the massacres of Aerschot, Tamines, and Dinant, and the retail butchery in many Belgian villages. But there have been foul deeds the memory of which will live, to the shame of the German Army, for generations to come.

From Châlons to Verdun, it is chiefly the crown prince and his men who must bear this burden. But rumour attributed to this unfortunate youth an impossible ubiquity, sometimes evidently confusing him with his brothers. There is no doubt about the pillage of the Château of Baye, on the eve of the Prussian disaster in the neighbouring marshes of St. Gond.

The Baron de Baye is an explorer and collector of historical and artistic objects; the *château* is known to the guide-books for his rich collections, as well as for remains of a twelfth-century Cistercian monastery, hard by. The Baroness de Baye says:—

> Breaking all the numerous glass-cases in a gallery forty-five yards long, he (the crown prince), has stolen the arms, medals, precious vases, carved gold cups, all the splendid presents given by the *tsar* to M. de Baye as souvenirs of his journeys to Russia. In the Museum of 1812, he has stolen jewels, icons, tapestries, miniatures . . . furniture, priceless pictures. But he had to abandon the last boxes in the precipitation of the retreat. Our faithful old servants wept.

(*Matin*, September 21).) When this letter was published, a vague denial was issued by the German Embassy in Rome. The baroness de Baye then added some details: the thieves had compelled the village locksmith to help them in packing their loot, and in driving the wagons to Rethel. Some high officers must be held accountable for this deed; but there is no trustworthy evidence identifying the crown prince.[1] In the same district, the Château of Montmort, a remarkable square building flanked by pepperbox towers, dating from 1580, and the Château of Beaumont, near Montmirail, belonging to the Comte de la Rochefoucauld-Doudeauville, were both pillaged. In the latter case, a door was chalk-marked for a Count Waldersee.

Responsibilities in Champagne are divided. In the Argonne, the Crown Prince's troops had their own way, which is graphically illustrated by the blackened skeletons of brickwork that tower above the site of the thriving holiday centre, Clermont.[2] This picturesque little town, of 1,200 inhabitants, set upon a hill overlooking the Aire Valley, at the junction of the Paris-Verdun and Bar-le-Duc roads, was occupied by the Germans early on the morning of September 5, after hard fighting on the Verdun side. The sister superior of the hospital had evacuated the wounded soldiers by train the day before, but had herself refused to leave because some forty old and infirm civil patients remained. At 5 a.m. three officers forced an entry into the hospital, but this brave woman withstood them till they had promised to do no harm. On the morrow, some houses were fired, and, the hospital being threatened, she asked that some firemen should be sent to protect it. This was done. A large part of the town was burned down, including the church; and the remainder was sacked.

Châlons, as I have already shown, came off very lightly. The Germans were there just a week, from September 4. The city was not bombarded. A ransom of £20,000 was demanded and paid; and the officers and men freely looted wines, liquors, jewellery, and clothing, especially from closed houses. A few miles eastward, we came to L'Epine, the two striking towers of its church rising prominently

---

1. The French Commission of Inquiry says: "Baron de Baye's room must have been occupied by a person of very high rank, for on the door there still remains a chalk inscription, 'J. K., Hoheit.' No one could give us exact information as to the identity of this 'Highness'; however, a general who lodged in the house of M. Houllier, town councillor, told his host that the Duke of Brunswick and the Staff of the 10th Corps had occupied the *château*." This Commission of Inquiry consisted of MM. Georges Payelle, First-President of the Cour des Comptes; A. Mollard, Minister Plenipotentiary; G. Maringer, Councillor of State, and E. Paillot, Councillor in the Court of Appeal. Its report, presented to the French Government on December 17, 1914, contains many specific allegations of outrages upon women. This is a class of crime as to which I should require particularly convincing evidence. For this and other reasons, it is hardly mentioned in the present volume.

2. The French Commission of Inquiry states that Clermont-en-Argonne was occupied by the 13th Würtemberg Corps, under the command of General von Durach, and by a troop of *Uhlans* commanded by Prince von Wittenstein.

on the road. Here, one side of the main street was burned out, only a few broken walls still standing. On September 5, a Prussian brigade took possession of the village. Most of the inhabitants had fled; their houses were ransacked, and then set on fire with petrol, torches, and grenades—except those in which the officers were billeted. The church, which is a place of pilgrimage, owes its immunity to the fact that 300 wounded German soldiers were sheltered there. On one of the shattered walls at the entry to the village, there still hangs the French Touring Club's warning to motorists—another note of irony—"Think of the children. Thanks."

The worst lies in the triangle between this village, Vitry-le-François, and Bar-le-Duc, and especially between the last two. Proceeding from Bar to Vitry, we had already passed through several villages of which only piles of bricks and plaster remained, through fields marked by huge holes where shells had exploded, and by wayside graves bearing thin wooden crosses, with the soldier's cap or a few faded flowers hanging on them. Perhaps these communities were victims of "legitimate" warfare; at any rate, our guides passed them by.

Villers-aux-Vents, lately a jolly hamlet, sheltered behind trees on the southern edge of one of the rolling plateaux of the region, is a spectacle no man could lightly pass by. Its name is now tragically appropriate. It is, indeed, open to all the winds. It is destroyed from end to end. Out of about a hundred houses—recently built, by the appearance of the bricks—only one remaius partially habitable. Within a few crazy, charred fragments of wall, or areas that had been walled, I climbed about the piles of broken stone and brick, examined protruding pieces of twisted iron, bedsteads, tools, kitchen things, and shattered fragments of pottery. The woodwork had disappeared, save a few black bones of rafters, tables, and chairs. The inhabitants were told to leave their houses before they were set on fire. The only reason I can find alleged is that several French soldiers had disguised themselves in civilian clothes, or that (alternatively) there was a "wireless" installation in the village.

The beautiful church has better borne the torture by fire. The spire is broken, the timbers of the roof have gone, the two big bells lie upon a heap of debris, and a hole in one of the walls shows where a shell broke through during the battle outside the village. A dozen human beings are still living in this wilderness, most of them in yawning holes which were once the cellars of their homes. Just outside the hamlet, they show the deep, covered trench from which the crown prince is supposed to have watched the battle.

After Villers, we visited Brabant-le-Roi, a rather larger place. It has suffered less; but we heard grievous tales of old folk taken hostage (including a woman of sixty-five, now supposed to be kept prisoner at Sedan), and of the heartless theft of the peasants' few pieces of silver plate and jewellery. A woman and her three children are said to have been killed at the nearby hamlet of Sommeilles, burned down by the 51st Infantry Regiment, as it is supposed because they did not give pleasing answers to some of the soldiers' questions.

The market town of Revigny, on the other hand, seems to have been scientifically destroyed. One wonders how so many solid stone houses could be broken up; but it is clearly evident here, as at Villers and other places, that it is the result not of bombardment, but of systematic incendiarism. The central street presents an extraordinary scene of devastation. Nothing remains except parts of the lower walls, and, within, deep masses of stone, brick, and mortar, broken small, with scraps of iron and charred wood. The town hall, a graceful building in French classic style, has about a half of its outer fabric standing. The church, which is of historical interest, is roofless and much injured within.

The Germans entered the town on September 6, and remained for six days. The few inhabitants who remain of the original 2,000 say that they used two kinds of incendiary stuff, one being explosive. The town was first pillaged, then fired. At once the streets became a flaming furnace. Some German officers angrily declared that the people themselves had set it on fire. The mayor, M. Gaxotte, on the other hand, says that motorcars brought up tins of petrol and packets of inflammable substance, that the German soldiers placed this stuff along the houses, and, at a signal, threw in hand-grenades. "The cellars," he says, "had already been emptied, and pianos and valuable furniture had been piled on motor-wagons to be taken to Germany."

A boy of fifteen was shot on suspicion of having communicated information to the French. Three elder citizens were taken away as hostages, and nothing is known of their fate. It would be interesting to know what General von Ethel (commanding the 3rd Brigade of Cavalry) has to say about these proceedings. The crown prince entered the town, but was not content with the rooms prepared, and went to a neighbouring country house. Possibly the exploit of a French aviator, who dropped a bomb on Revigny on the second day of the German occupation, killing eleven soldiers and thirty-five horses, may have had something to do with this barbarity.

Usually, one finds traces of a general policy, and two particular pretexts, in the ravaged villages. The policy is that of terrorism which heads of the Prussian State have more than once openly stated; the pretexts are that inhabitants have tired upon the German troops, or have given information to the French. But I suspect another partial explanation of the peculiar ferocity of the crown prince's army. It had advanced from the north-eastern frontier, by the line Ste. Menehould-Revigny, and, on September 6, reached the villages just west of Bar-le-Duc. So far, the French had steadily fallen back. The crown prince began to see himself as an irresistible conqueror entering Paris at the head of an invincible army. The awakening from this dream was so sharp and sudden that it may well have produced a fit of murderous temper. On that Sunday of the beginning of the great recoil, the French guns worked a slaughter, the exact extent of which will, perhaps, never be known. The precipitate retreat has also been attributed to a breakdown of transport, involving a shortage of ammunition. It went fast and far. It was the downfall of German hopes and the ambitions of the *Kaiser's* heir.

The battle between Vassincourt and Mogneville, on the 10th, was one of its episodes. The demolition of these villages, of Laimont and Neuville-sur-Ornain, of Andernay and Sermaize, of Huiron and Hassimont, of Sommesous and Sompuis, was their revenge—at least, this seems the most reasonable explanation of the facts, if there can be said to be any reason in them. And this would explain how Vitry-le-Francois and Châlons escaped the fate of Revigny and Rheims. The routed troops destroyed on the line of their flight; but sometimes they had no time to give themselves this pleasure, or to do the work thoroughly.

At Vassincourt, I wandered about in the debris of farmers' houses whose big blocks of limestone seemed strong enough to have borne a siege. The quaint old chimney corners gaped over remains of irons and kitchen ware polished by many generations of faithful housewives. An ancient cupboard-bed, finely carved, was broken and covered with filth and empty bottles. The half-dozen villagers remaining gathered round us, and told the story of a woman who had dared to hide two silver dishes when the officers she had had to entertain were preparing to depart. One of them missed the dishes; at first the old woman denied that she was the owner of any such wealth. But, when she and her husband were tied by the hands and put against a wall, she confessed, and, on producing the treasured heirlooms, was spared. There is a story of another kind of officer who, catching three drunken soldiers threatening an innkeeper, made them kneel down in the bar in an attitude of supplication, and kept them thus for an hour. It sounds like Prussian army discipline; but even Prussian officers—if they entertained such unusual ideas of honour—would rarely dare to impose them in face of a general policy of terrorism dictated from above.

One scene stands out in my memory. Sermaize-les-Bains was a pleasant town of 4,000 inhabitants, on the Saulx, with a mineral spring, a large sugar refinery, and a handsome old church. It had been demolished from end to end by fire. Of 500 houses, only two or three are now standing. Except a few chimneys and pieces of wall, the rest is a rubbish heap. In the middle of the town, there is rather a fine fountain; from this crossways you look down four streets—a perspective extraordinarily like Pompeii before it was cleared up by the antiquaries. There was an iron-monger's shop; you can trace it by the masses of molten metal and what I can best call clotted nails. There was a glass-and china shop; you can trace it by the lumps of milky coagulate that stick out among the brick litter. Most of the townsfolk had lied; a number were taken prisoner, and carried away; a few still inhabit their cellars; you see them—women, children, and old men—carrying home large, rough loaves of bread, or wheeling barrows of firewood. Two enterprising tradesmen have built shanties where they sell a few necessaries of life. The church is roofless, gutted, and littered with fragments of stone.

A little way from it is the presbytery, or *curé's* house, also burned out. Behind this lies a garden, unusually pretty for France, with a tiny fishpond and fountain in the centre, and statues of the saints, turned a rusty brown by the smoke of the great conflagration, along the paths. And in the middle of the grass plot stands a white statue of the Virgin, turning clasped hands towards the ruins of this house of peace and charity.

BOOK 3: TOWARD DEADLOCK

CHAPTER 17

Back to the Aisne

Château-Thierry, Sunday, September 13.

The ever fainter boom of the big guns over the fields and woods to the north tells me in most emphatic language that the grand *débâcle* has begun. Most of the *Kaiser's* armies in France are in full retreat. Many prisoners, guns, and quantities of impedimenta are being captured daily. The French re-entered Soissons at 6 p.m. yesterday.

Since the retreat has now continued for four days, the rejoicing which fills the French and British armies can hardly be called premature. On the other hand, it would be dangerous, as well as foolish, to encourage extravagant hopes. A lightning withdrawal may, in certain situations, be the best strategy. True, this retreat has been marked by heavy losses; but, again, the German Great Staff has never shown itself tender toward its own men. If there is a plain object in view, it hurls its forces forward, indifferent to the death-roll. The retreat means the abandonment of the hope of attacking Paris, at any rate in the near future. But it does not mean that the flight is altogether hopeless and useless. From Courchamp, which was set on fire by a party of angry *Uhlans* on Sunday last, to Soissons, is fifty-three miles as the aeroplane might fly. In such a retreat, it is natural that there should be many stragglers. They give themselves up in a starving condition in parties of fifty or a hundred; and, all over the route of this central advance, in the woods that cover the Brie tableland and the rolling country north of the Marne, groups are still known to be hiding.

Sometimes they snipe at passers-by—we were repeatedly told that it was unsafe to pass through such or such a wood—or attempt a feeble resistance; but most often they give themselves up, half-dead from lack of rest and food, to the rearguards who are inexorably waiting for their surrender. Generally speaking, along this fifty miles of almost continuous battlefield, all you can find of the dead, except the horses, on the day after the fighting, is a line of mounds of fresh brown earth. There are reports that, near Montmirail, the Germans' simply piled their dead in great heaps and turned them to ashes. Usually each army buries its fallen at once; but I am told there are many Germans dead of hunger, wounds, and fatigue in the woods to the south, and that some days must pass before the country is completely cleared.

It is useless to exaggerate the loss of oddments when it is evident that the main armies have saved themselves. Nevertheless, there is evidence of exhaustion, and of something more than physical weariness. Many of the British and French troops were exhausted at the end of the fortnight's retreat from Belgium. Two Englishmen I have just seen may be taken as typical specimens. One was a young lancer, whom we met at La Ferté, while we were hunting vainly for a meal. He had lost his horse and his sole grievance was that he must go back to a depot for another, and would then have some difficulty in finding his regiment. He looked thin and frail, after a touch of fever; but there might never have been anything but victory so far as his spirits were concerned.

The other fellow, a Cockney infantryman, was lying along a bench in the shade of the *mairie* of the little town of Montreuil-aux-Lions, a modest building, which has been transformed into a British field hospital. Two other boys in khaki sat beside him, and, thinking him ill or wounded, I came up to inquire. The odour of an English cigarette brought him promptly to a sitting posture. He was played out, but perfectly happy, with never a shadow of doubt about the justice or success of his job, and he possessed more confidence than ever, now that he has seen them through days of trial, in the competence of his chiefs.

To come to the crucial spot at the crucial moment, and to carry all before you, is what raises good men to their best. Contrast this condition with that of the wretched gangs of prisoners whom one meets in the rear camps, or sees lying in the straw in the darkness of the railway vans. Prussian pride is obstinate enough; but the pride of infatuated militarism is no match for the quiet confidence of men who are defending a people from outrage. An imprisoned aviator, guarded by two Tommies, cheekily offered one of them two *marks* for a coat-button, as a souvenir. The Briton did not smack him across the face—so far as I can find, the prisoners are treated well, and often very kindly—but simply declined the transaction.

"You are as proud as a Frenchman," said the prisoner, evidently a man of certain education.

"Right you are," was the smiling reply; "we are all Frenchmen while we're here."

As you move along these grievous roads, where the ditches have been deepened for trenches, and a litter of straw and empty tins marks last night's encampment, or a malodorous mound speaks of yesterday's battlefield, one thing that strikes you is the monstrous silly malice of some of the damage done by the retreating enemy, and especially his cavalry wings. In general, the northern campaign of intimidation by outrage has not been repeated in the centre of France. But when they found themselves suddenly blocked by the British on the Brie plateau, the anger of the enemy knew no bounds; and villagers suspected of giving information were first compelled to set fire to their own houses, and were then shot. War must always be outrageous. The Marne and other bridges were necessarily destroyed by the Allies in their retreat, and one's own towns must be bombarded if the enemy occupies them. But there are much smaller injuries than these that horrify by their positive indecency.

When one sees the traces of such crimes, when one recalls the spectacle of the famishing prisoners, seemingly astonished to find themselves in British instead of French hands, and hears them tell of the frightful losses on their southern march, one realizes what a gulf separates demoralisation from exhaustion and the defeat that yet leaves hope in the heart and light in the mind.

They are by nature more docile and enduring than the British and French; but now the iron has entered their souls. I never heard a profounder truth than that which one of the Tommies put to me this morning, in these simple words: "I'm sorry for the poor devils. They had to march. It wasn't their fault." Such a campaign could not last. For the common soldiers, the light of despair broke upon them when they found themselves within a single march of Paris, and then suddenly, without explanation, diverted to another objective. But, to anyone of greater intelligence and education, it was precisely this other objective which must have completed their disillusionment. For I cannot believe that Von Kluck and Von Bülow had any hope of getting round for an effective attack on Paris by the east and south. If they had, their intelligence department must have been badly lacking. Every instructed German officer and private must have felt the cold hand of Fate upon him last Sunday when this prospect was first revealed. We know the result. There is no more "Battle of the Marne." The river lies peaceful under the sunshine, and the washerwomen are busy on its banks. The tide of war has ebbed over the northern hills, and the boom of cannon can now hardly be heard.

A long hospital train has just passed after it, and Mr. Atkins, in the market-place at the head of an incalculable line of motor-wagons, is examining his plugs and petrol-tins. In fact, the countryside is emptied of petrol, and almost of food. For the moment, the plight of the good folk of these little towns which have had two armies quartered upon them for a week is not a happy one. But they take it with true French gallantry; and you have only to be an Englishman to know that a bond has been sealed between the two nations stronger than any parchment treaties. Only those who have seen the British divisions in the field—not only the gunners, cavalry, and infantry, but the supply services and columns of communication with the base camps, the flying corps, the pontoon outfit, the field telegraph, and the rest—can appreciate how much their complete preparation and clockwork order contributed to the general result.

Before Soissons, Tuesday, September 15.

For three hours, I have been watching, from the hills to the south of the town, that part of the unending and terrific struggle which may be isolated in history as the Battle of Soissons. It has lasted for four days; and only now can it be said that victory is turning to the side of the Allies. The town itself cannot be entered, for it is still being raked both by artillery and rifle fire; and great columns of smoke mark several points at which the houses are burning.

The centre of the fighting lies where the British and French pontoon corps are trying to keep the bridges they have succeeded in throwing across the river—for, of course, the old bridges in the town and up and down stream were destroyed by the French on their retreat southward a fortnight ago. This Golgotha, for it deserves the name, is out of sight below the end of the plateau on which I am standing; but men who have come from the front line tell me that the combat there has been a positive slaughter, putting anything in the South African War, or anything else in modern warfare that they have heard of, altogether into the shade. The river-crossings are the great objective—on the one side to make and keep, on the other to destroy, and again to destroy. Several British regiments, some detachments of which were the first to get to the north banks of the Aisne, have suffered severely.

The first crossings were effected on Sunday; but the German big guns got the range, and yesterday it became necessary to withdraw. Last night, however, the Allies were able to bring up some heavier cannon; and these were set to work at an early hour this morning, when the prospect began to change. Several German batteries were soon moved backward; but one or two others, hidden in the woods that cap nearly all these hills, could not be exactly located until an incident of this morning's duel revealed them. The British had managed again to get a battery across the river, and into position. Apparently, the German artillery could not reach it from their hiding-place; and they therefore moved to a better pitch. Under heavy fire, the British had to retire, leaving six guns behind. But their assailants were now discovered. Covered by a heavy bombardment, two British batteries were got over, and were planted at the bridge-head. Very soon the six guns had been recovered, and two German batteries captured.

On the western side, the French succeeded in getting three batteries and a regiment of infantry over the water. About 1,500 prisoners have already been taken today. I can clearly trace the abandonment during the last three hours of a number of German positions, for the smoke from their guns—great white bubbles which fade away in less than a minute—is moving further and further away over the northern hills, and the dull boom and sharp bang grow slowly fainter. But even the aviators flying like great hawks overhead—a British biplane and a French monoplane—cannot see more than a part, and that uncertainly, of a modern battlefield. From Vic-sur-Aisne on the west to Rheims on the east is nearly fifty miles; and that is only a part of the line that is now being contested.

The lie of the land, which makes Soissons so important a place, also circumscribes any individual view. The town lies across the Paris-Laon road, mainly on the south side of the River Aisne, in a cup formed by the breaks of several ranges of southern hills; while the line of hills bounding it on the north appears to be more continuous. The French occupy the left, and the British the right, wings of the pursuit. I came up a more westerly road from Paris, and then moved, up hill and down dale, to the high plateau above the village of Belleu. All these villages are classic ground; they have wonderful old churches and *châteaux*, and the region is full of forgotten battlefields. The curious twelfth-century cathedral of Soissons, with its odd tower, and the still more ancient church of St. Jean-de-Vignes have not yet been damaged by the bombardment of the town.

A little geography may be a dangerous thing, but it is sometimes an incomparable help toward the solution of a military puzzle. Perhaps we do not yet know all the reasons for the sudden German *débâcle*, and even this local situation was very obscure yesterday. During the afternoon, the French War Office announced that the Germans had not been able to hold the defensive lines they had prepared to the north of the Aisne, between Compiègne and Soissons, and also above Rheims. At night, on the other hand, the official *communiqué* admitted that they were still holding out in these positions. The general fact that the Germans were resisting firmly this morning, and are now giving way, is beyond doubt. Now that I have seen the landscape, the whole affair is much more comprehensible.

The hillside closing on the north the Soissons gap, into which several southern valleys lead, was evidently a post to seize and hold, if possible. It is said, with great probability, that, in their march south, the Germans started entrenching a foothold here, and that the big siege guns destined for Paris got thus far and no further. There were two places of considerable natural strength on the course of their fifty-mile retreat. The first was above Meaux, the other above Soissons. At both points, it is now evident that they have fought very hard, despite a crushing discouragement. At the risk of being blamed for reiteration, I may express the belief that they never entertained the hope of getting back to Paris, but that their aim was to effect an easterly concentration and reconstitution of their armies, and, to this end, to delay the main advance of the Allies. The first object of the arrest at Soissons, therefore, was to cover the line of the retreat; and, as it has been to a large extent, so far, an affair of artillery, no doubt it has given some at least of the harried German cavalry and infantry a short breathing-time.

Let me repeat just one other word for the last time. There is an attempt to attribute the German collapse on the Marne to a withdrawal and transfer of troops in order to check the Russian advance. This was, no doubt, a factor. But the very character of the victorious Teutonic rush southward contributed to its sudden end and failure. It exhausted itself. It burst. It was a case of heartbreak—as though a runner who has to cover ten miles should put all his strength into the first three. It is important to realise that the Allies are winning because a rational, steady, and persistent spirit possesses them; that the invaders are failing because they were governed by the mad-bull infatuation of Prussian militarism, aided up to a point by technical skill and the endurance of the German rank and file.

Many British wounded are being sent today to Paris. Several whom I have seen have their hands and faces stained a horrid yellow. At first I thought it a peculiar form of jaundice; actually, it is the effect of the fumes of the lyddite shells which the Germans are using.

The Army Service Corps has done wonders in the rapid and fearfully trying northern pursuit. When they started out from home, there was more than a little doubt whether the petrol engine would be equal to this its first crucial test. There is no doubt now. Within the zone of fire, horse transport is still used, however, I suppose because the motor-wagons are too precious to be endangered unnecessarily, as well as because they are too heavy, for instance, for rough pontoon bridges. As to the British Flying Corps, nothing need be added to General Joffre's handsome recognition of the "precision, exactitude, and regularity" of their information.

My map marks the road to Soissons through the Forest of Villers Cotterets as "impassable for autos." So, indeed, it proved for the German army on its breakneck flight to the Aisne. At least, there are dozens of broken cars and wagons abandoned in the broad quagmires that bound the narrow cobbled causeway. There are still many fugitives in the woods; parties of them are brought in daily. At Berzy-le-Sec we witnessed one of these man-hunts. It was exactly like an October *battue* in the shires. Deep on the hillside below our road stretched fields broken by clumps of covert. On the other side of these thickets, a line of eight or ten men in civilian dress, looking exactly like gamekeepers, slowly advanced into and through the trees; while, on our road above, a score of soldiers watched the other side, with rifles ready. They did not interfere with us; but I could not bear to wait for the final "Hands up!"

Paris, September 16.

I have returned from a run of seventy miles through the country north of the Marne, by foul roads and over rickety plank bridges, to find that Paris has no exact news of the battle of the Aisne. The official *communiqué* of this afternoon does, however, give an important indication of the direction, and so it gives the character, of the German retirement as a whole.

The chief links of the chain from west to east are as follows: Noyon, Vic-sur-Aisne, Soissons, Rheims, Ville-sur-Tourbe, Varennes, and Forges, on the Meuse north of Verdun. The Germans are at, or to the north of, these points, and, despite the strain of a pursuit unprecedented in its speed and extent, the Allies are everywhere in close contact with them. It will be seen that the German positions form two groups, which, abandoning old definitions, we may call the German right and left. The former makes a double curve from Noyon, where the force recently in Amiens has arrived, round south to the heights above the Aisne, then up lo the hills around Laon, and then south again to the hills around Rheims.

This right wing gathers many, if not all, of the fragments recently scattered about the north-west of France into connection with the armies retreating from Paris and the Marne. The second, or German left wing, stretches in an almost straight line from Rheims eastward toward Metz, passing through the north of the Argonne and to the north of Verdun. A glance at the symmetry of these lines appears to me to dispose of the idea that the German armies are so much broken as to have no word in the choice of where they shall fight. They seem to have been as rapid in retreat as in advance; and it would be a mistake prematurely to call this, taking the vast field as a whole, a breakneck flight. They have got out of the barren plains of Champagne; their forces are no longer divided by the mazes of the Argonne Forest; and they now seem to be advantageously ranged along a series of railway lines interrupted only at a few points.

The armies of General von Kluck and General von Bülow have two, if not three, lines from Noyon round to Laon and Liège, as well as the line from Rheims to the Luxemburg frontier and north Lorraine. The eastern force, including the armies of the Duke of Würtemberg, and the crown prince, are less well served, the Verdun line being cut off; but they also can get north to Rethel by rail and river as well as road. How far these lines are now serviceable we do not know, but, until we know. General Cherfils is, perhaps, a little too positive in his view of the serious encumbrance the German heavy guns may be.

Chapter 18

Rheims Bombarded

Epernay, September 18.

The news that the Cathedral of Rheims has been struck and damaged during a bombardment of the city will be received, not only throughout France, but throughout the educated world, with a thrill of disgust and indignation. This vast edifice is one of the first glories of European architecture. The wonderful west *façade*, dating from the thirteenth century, with its three deeply recessed portals, containing more than five hundred statues of Scriptural personages and the kings of France, and its great rose window, has been described as perhaps the most beautiful structure produced in the Middle Ages. The church, which has almost completely escaped the hands of the enterprising restorer, contains or contained much splendid woodwork, valuable tapestries, reliquaries, and church plate, and several pictures, besides its superb old windows. It is the cathedral of the Capetian and later kings, an unequalled shrine of the faith, culture, and history of the French people. With but a little pardonable exaggeration, it has been called "the Acropolis of France." The greatness of Rheims began fourteen centuries ago, after the Vandals and Huns had gone. A general instinct recalls today the fearsome name of those olden practitioners of "frightfulness."

Although Rheims is firmly held by the French, it was still being cannonaded by the Germans this morning, and civilians cannot enter. I have got thus far, but cannot get further. Nor do the good folk of Epernay know much of what is occurring fifteen miles to the north. Rheims has suffered three separate bombardments—the first on the southward march of the Germans at the beginning of the month, the second when the French returned, and the third when the Germans had fixed upon the positions of the old French forts on the north, and entrenched themselves above the Vesle Valley. The French retirement from the town began on September 2, and was completed on the following day. The army returned at noon on the 11th; and, since then, they have been engaged in holding their ground, and in attempting to recover the fortified hills which had been lost. In the first bombardment, the destruction within Rheims was not large; and this is not surprising, for the forts, which lie in a semicircle from north-west to southeast at a distance of about four miles, were the chief objective of the German attack. The civil population was forewarned; and most of the houses and practically all business places were closed. Since the return of the French army, and the more desperate development of the struggle, however, there has been a great deal of damage, chiefly by shellfire.

A leading citizen of Epernay, to whose private diary I am indebted for many details, believes that, on the first German attack, the forts did not offer any substantial resistance; and he says that some of the big guns were brought away and taken to Paris, while others, too large to be transported, were destroyed. He adds that the Vitry-le-Rheims fort, on the north end of Mount Berru, and another were mined, and may, perhaps, have been blown up. The whole question of the fortresses—and Rheims. perhaps, chiefly—is so grave that sooner or later an inquiry is inevitable. This "entrenched camp," with its girdle of permanent works, was supposed to be one of the strong links in France's second line of defence. It was designed to block an invader coming either from the Ardennes or the Argonne, and to command the system of roads and railways that here find their centre.

If it was not immediately captured, it was immediately turned; for the Germans entered Epernay on September 4, and continued their advance the next day. Had Rheims been able to offer an effective and prolonged resistance, the southern march, both here and nearer Paris, if not impossible, would have been so dangerous that it might never have been attempted. That the Germans should now be defending positions the French abandoned is a fact that calls for explanation. Also, if forts do not serve their designed purpose, they are worse than useless, for they bring a terrible penalty upon the civil population.

The fate of Epernay offers a singular contrast. This pretty and almost completely modern industrial centre of Champagne, with its great mansions and many signs of wealth, has suffered all the anxieties of the double invasion—it is only today that the good citizens begin to breathe freely—but very little material damage. On September 2, the first French troops came into the town on the retreat from Rheims. On the morning of September 4, the redoubtable enemy appeared, and, overtaking the French rear-guard in the hilly and thickly wooded district to the south of Epernay, between Pierry and Brugny, opened fire upon them. A running fight followed, without great effect, except that several farms and country houses were destroyed. During the same afternoon, a large body of Germans who had crossed the Marne at Mareuil (eight miles east of Epernay) marched on the town by the Paris road. On this occasion, again, the first German cavalry patrols are said to have pretended to be British soldiers.

Some leading citizens went out to treat for the safety of the town, no doubt having in mind what a general sack of the world-famous wine cellars would mean. The *commandant* was brought to the mayor, and at once demanded supplies of tobacco and champagne for the troops, and 40,000 rations. This was an impossible requirement; and a curious bargain was struck. The amount of requisitions not yielded was estimated by Count von Moltke at 165,550 *fr.* (£7,102). This amount was demanded in gold, and was actually paid over by the mayor, and five municipal councillors (one of them, the editor of the *Reveil de la Marne*, told me the story), who were being held as hostages. But the great winegrower, M. Chandon (Moët and Chandon have over twenty miles of cellars here), happened to have a German general billeted upon him, and complained of the unfairness of this exaction. The general agreed. Another influence was even more valuable.

One considerate doctor remained in the town. The Germans had many wounded, and were anxious that they should be cared for. Dr. Veron undertook that this should be done, on condition that no damage should be done to the town. Between the general and the doctor it came about that, on their return, finding their wounded in good hands, the German commander returned the money that had been taken.[1]

This episode would be more pleasant to contemplate were it not that the supplies actually provided were not paid for, and tobacco stores and closed shops and houses were freely pillaged. The commandant warned the hostages he had taken that any inhabitants who attacked his soldiers in any way would be at once shot. With the German flag flying over the town hall and the railway station, the soldiers

---

1. Some later newspaper reports stated that one of the wounded soldiers was a nephew of the Duke of Mecklenburg. But see the later reference to this matter, Chapter 27.

ransacked the food shops, giving receipts for what they took. In the evening, a fire broke out in a granary, where several of them were stationed. Probably it had been caused by their own carelessness; but an officer informed the mayor that, if there were another fire, no matter who caused it, he and the other hostages would be shot.

At 6 a.m. on September 5, these troops left for Montmirail; and three hours later many new regiments, headed by bands, began to pass through the town. Some officers wished to have a German flag made, and sought out the daughter of the *concierge* of the town hall for the purpose. The girl was so much alarmed that she became insane, and is now in an asylum. With the second column were brought a score of French prisoners. After having been exhibited for some hours in the chief square of the town, they were lodged in a house under strong guard. They remained there till the first day of the evacuation of Epernay, and followed the Germans in their retreat.

A notable incident was the visit of the German Staff, including a son of the *Kaiser* (my informant believed him to be a younger son, not the crown prince) who stayed with other officers in the splendid mansion of M. Claude Chandon. On the day of their arrival, the prince entertained seventy persons, including the Staff, to a grand banquet. He took several walks in the town, and was enthusiastically acclaimed by the soldiers.

One of my informants showed me a copy of the following proclamation, signed by Count von Moltke, and printed in French, which appears to have been intended for general use during the invasion:—

> All the authorities and the municipality are informed that every peaceful inhabitant can follow his regular occupation in full security. Private property will be absolutely respected, and provisions paid for.
>
> If, on the contrary, the population dare, under any form whatever, open or hidden, to take part in the hostilities against our troops, the severest punishment will be inflicted on the refractory.
>
> The people must give up their arms. Every armed individual will be put to death.
>
> Whoever cuts telegraph wires, destroys railway bridges or roads, or commits any action whatever to the detriment of the German troops, will be shot on the spot.
>
> Towns and villages whose inhabitants have taken part in the

combat, or fire upon us from ambush, will be burned down, and the guilty shot at once. The civil authorities will be held responsible.

The Chief of Staff of the German Army,

Von Moltke.

It is certain that the promise to respect private property was not taken seriously.

At dawn on Sunday, the 7th, the population was wakened by a violent cannonade from the south, and this continued till nightfall. During that day, the Germans were very busy organising ambulances for the wounded, who were brought in by hundreds. The artillery duel seemed to be redoubled on the morning of the 8th, twelve batteries firing together and almost without interruption. Soon the ambulances were all full, and were sent off to the north. A French Alsatian nun has since reported a saying of a wounded German officer whom she was nursing in one of the hospitals of the town. Speaking of the battle in which he was wounded, he said, in accents of deep sadness: "It is the end of the world for us."

On the afternoon of September 9, the retreat of the Germans from Epernay began. The inhabitants were ordered to stay at home, doubtless that they should not witness the extent of the movement. At first, great convoys of ammunition came in by all the southern roads, and went on toward Rheims. All through that night the mixed procession of troops, wounded, and supplies continued. On the 10th, further regiments passed, singing dolefully. The retreat became more and more like a rout. All the vehicles that could be got in the town were taken; and still some wounded had to be placed on gun-carriages—the gunners tramping beside them. They all seemed exhausted, and some could be seen hungrily devouring chunks of bread. On Friday morning, September 11, the last detachment crossed the Marne, and blew up the road and railway bridges. A piece of stone thrown up by the explosion killed a child of fourteen. In their precipitancy, they had forgotten a convoy of 300 wounded, which remained in the hands of the French.

Three hours after the Germans had passed the river, a body of French *chasseurs* entered Epernay, and they were speedily followed by cavalry and infantry regiments. The inhabitants cheered them loudly, and brought bunches of flowers to show their delight. In a very short time, a bridge was thrown over the river, and the fighting on the road to Rheims began. But the Germans had already fixed their batteries on the hills, which rise sharply to the north of the town, and a long and costly effort has been required to drive them back.

During the ride of about ninety miles from Paris to Epernay, I saw something of the battlefields from Montmirail northward. In some places, the Germans had made strong positions, the trenches being deep and solidly covered, with resting-places and lateral approaches. A good many houses on the route showed holes and rents due to shell-fire, and a few had holes pierced in the walls for the use of riflemen. Several very large farmhouses had been burned down, evidently as punishment or revenge. A French sergeant tells me that 3,000,000 cartridges and several thousand shells were abandoned in the retreat to the south of Epernay.

Some bodies of the Allied troops were able to enter Soissons on Wednesday; but only at noon yesterday was the town completely held, the Germans falling back to the crest of the hills. Together with the reoccupation of Rheims, this success will be a great encouragement. Soissons is a point of concentration of the railways and roads of the Picardy and Champagne borderland. Rheims is of even greater importance for the immediate future; and these two towns make natural bases for the conduct of the struggle between the Forest of Laigle and the Craonne plateau. The question of the German lines of communication will assume increasing interest. Obsessed, as it always has been, by the value of turning movements, the German Grand Staff must be nearly as nervous just now about its west, north, and east flanks as about the host that is relentlessly pressing upon it from the south.

But this does not mean, unhappily, that any early conclusion of the war is to be looked for. New slaughter will be sown about the old battlefields; and if the German generals continue to show the agility in escape that they have so far exhibited, they may yet get the lager number of their men back to the line of their own fortresses. Perhaps, after all, it will be General Hiver and the gathering storm of economic ruin at home that will determine the issue.

A French cavalry officer says that the German cavalry has never dared to test on the battlefield the reputation it had gained in manoeuvres at home.

When it has shown itself it was merely to unmask our guns or to follow up a pursuit. The chivalry of the charge does not accord with the character of troops who even in their public proclamations put 'honour' after 'well-being.' In material preparation the Germans are very good. The officers are brave, but reckless in spending their men. The subaltern grades are competent. The rank and file are sheep, knowing neither why nor against whom they are lighting. The only strength they have had—and it is formidable—is that of numbers. Each in proportion to his rank, these officers follow the *Kaiser's* example and think themselves 'supermen.' Now that they have become more prudent—especially the African troops—our men are splendid. The lesson is learned, and now, with smaller losses, they do more work. As our 75-pieces (3-in. guns) can rake the trenches, and upset the enemy's field-guns, it is useless to throw the infantry forward till the way has been properly prepared."

I am informed, in fact, that the rules for opening action which were in effect at the beginning of the war have just been amended by General Joffre in an important particular. Instead of the infantry going in first, and being supported by the artillery, it will now be usual for the guns to make an opening, and the infantry attack to follow. This is evidently a result of experience of the effective quality of the famous French field-pieces.

Among the stories of the double bombardment of Soissons, not the least inspiring is that of Mme. Marcherez. When the Germans, on their southern advance, came into the town, it was found that the mayor had fled, along with nearly the whole of his fellow-citizens. But this plucky woman remained, and it was with her that the invaders talked as representative of the municipality. If they did not, for her sake, abandon their habit of breaking into and looting all closed houses, they seem not to have molested the remaining inhabitants.

Yet another type of heroine: The good folk of a little town on the Grand Morin were preparing for flight on the approach of the enemy. What to do with a swarm of cats and dogs and other small domestic animals? An old lady sent round the drummer, who, in French villages, takes the place of the English bellman, to say that she would look after the cats and dogs till their owners returned. And the others left her to keep this menagerie while the Germans came and went. It is often said that French people are less sensitive than we to the sufferings of animals. At a time which is as evil for the brute world as for its proud masters, let us remember this example to the contrary.

Paris, September 21.

The bombardment of Rheims continues. The cathedral and public buildings have suffered further damage; and several hundred civilians have been killed. The town is now closed to any but military and official persons; but the following further details of what has occurred have been obtained from soldiers and refugees.

German troops first arrived before Rheims on Wednesday, September 2. The neighbouring forts being incapable of resisting; the weight of the newest explosives, they were disabled and abandoned. Thus there was only a short resistance. Four thousand Saxon troops entered the city on the afternoon of the 4th, at parade step, singing the *Wacht am Rhein*, and lined up before the town hall. Some of the officers were actually there when the first bombardment began on September 5, and a hundred shells had been thrown in before the firing could be stopped. Regiments then took possession of the town; but the main body passed round it and went on to Epernay and Montmirail. In Rheims the German troops do not seem at first to have acted badly.

The inhabitants say that they then gave either receipts or money to the shopkeepers for the goods they took, and they gave a receipt for a million *francs* (£40,000), which they seized as a guarantee for the delivery of army requisitions of bread and other supplies. Dr. Langlet, the mayor, a fine and courageous old gentleman of seventy-six years, and other leading citizens were held as hostages. Those of the inhabitants who remained were warned that any of them resisting the troops would be shot and the city wholly or partially burned.

It was on Friday, the 11th, that the Germans came pouring back, with the French cavalry hard upon their heels. The town was reoccupied on the following day. The following narrative of its recapture was given to me by a young infantryman of Picardy who was wounded on September 15:—

> The German rearguard were still in Rheims on that Saturday evening when we decided to make a general assault on the town. We were in all about twelve regiments of infantry and a strong force of cavalry. We surrounded the town, and went in by all the roads that led into it. The Germans, who were in force, at first made some resistance; and for an hour or two sharp fighting took place in the streets. But soon the enemy abandoned their hurriedly built barricades, and took refuge in the houses and cellars. A number of their men were drunk, and were not in a condition to fight. We then started hunting for them. There was not a house or a wine-cellar in which we did

not discover German soldiers or officers hidden. The chase was a most extraordinary sight, especially at night-time. In a huge cellar I went to, I found a German hidden in a corner behind two big boxes. I thought my last minute had come, for he had a revolver in his hand and aimed at me. I was holding my rifle by the barrel, the bayonet behind me. I shouted to him, 'Surrender, or I will shoot you.'

He fired, but I had fortunately jumped aside and he missed me. Then I struck him with the butt-end of my rifle right on the mouth and nose. He dropped his revolver, and put his hand to his face. I had broken most of his front teeth. I did not want to kill him, so I took him up from the cellar and handed him to an officer. All the other soldiers who had been hunting in the houses came out similarly with one or two prisoners apiece. Some of them tried to escape and ran out into the streets, where they were pursued or shot by our men. The hunt lasted all night. Counting dead and wounded, we captured 5,000 Germans in all.

Perhaps it was the punishment the Germans had received that turned their obstinate pride into a wild savagery. Rheims is an open town, and cannot itself be defended; but the hills to the north and east, some of them the site of the dismantled French forts and batteries of Brimont, Fresnes, St. Thierry, and Nogent l'Abbesse, make a strong position, though not as strong as the hills above Soissons. It was absolutely essential that these hills should be held if the whole line of the Aisne was not to be turned. Here the beaten German army pulled itself together, and rapidly entrenched; and here, except for a few points which have been captured, it is still holding out. Rheims was evacuated at 4 p.m. on Saturday, September 12. The fact that at least 150 German wounded were left lying in heaps of straw in the nave of the cathedral would suggest that up to this time another bombardment was not contemplated. When the French entered the town, the long artillery duel, which is still proceeding, began. For the first few days it was rather of a preparatory nature—at least, its present intensity was not reached till the end of the week, when repeated attacks and counterattacks had been delivered in the hills around. From time to time shells fell into the town, and brought down a house like a pack of cards. All the time, the Red Cross flag flew from the cathedral.

The serious and deliberate bombardment of the town began on

Friday and continued on Saturday, being chiefly directed from the German batteries placed on the site of the old French fort on the hill of Nogent l'Abbesse. This position stands barely six miles from the centre of the city to the east; and the chief buildings would be clearly visible through field-glasses, so that there can be no question of accident. Either on Friday afternoon or early on Saturday morning, it had been the scene of severe fighting, the French making persistent attacks, and at last capturing the site of their old Pompelle battery, a couple of miles short of the main position at Nogent.

Was it in revenge for this audacity that shells were deliberately aimed at the wondrous fabric in which the artists of the Middle Ages enshrined their noblest conceptions of beauty and faith? Hundreds of shells were thrown into the city—one person says 1,500 in the two days. A whole block of buildings to the north of the cathedral was gutted. The northern (Laon) and eastern (Ceres) quarters show great piles of smoking ruins. During Saturday morning the city was on fire in several places, columns of smoke and tongues of flame leaping to the gloomy sky. A few firemen vainly tried to stay the conflagration. Most of the inhabitants had taken refuge in their cellars.

Several shells struck the cathedral, and some scaffolding around the left (north) tower, where repairs were being made, took fire, falling upon the roof, which was soon ablaze. This would be at about 4 o'clock on Saturday afternoon. The flames quickly spread to the rafters of the nave and transepts; and burning timber, falling upon the straw littered about the floors, the chairs, and choir-stalls, turned the shadowy interior into a furnace. An eyewitness tells me that most of the magnificent and irreplaceable windows were shattered and lay about in many-coloured fragments. The ancient Archiepiscopal Palace is burned down, with its prehistoric and ethnographic collections, its library, its tapestries, and its splendid "Hall of Kings," only the charred walls standing. The exact damage cannot be ascertained, for Rheims is now cut off from the remainder of the country, the roads of approach being forbidden except to the army.

The bombardment was resumed early on Sunday morning, apparently with the aim of completing the destruction of the city and its historical monuments. Of these the Abbey Church of Saint-Remi is a century older than the cathedral itself, and contained splendid stained-glass windows, marble statues, and other treasures.

The Town Hall, a fine building in Louis XIII style, dating from 1630, in which were also situated the town library and museum, is damaged, and the Protestant Church, the Hôtel Dieu, or hospital, the sub-prefecture, and some of the ancient houses of the town are destroyed. Many sick and wounded have been removed to the wine-cellars, the ambulances having been fired upon, and five nurses killed.

I will only add one comment to this grievous story. It is that of M. Maurice Harris, the eminent reactionary:—

> At least these shells have not fallen on our battalions, our brothers and sons, our defenders. Perish the marvels of the French genius rather than that genius itself. Let the most beautiful of stone be destroyed rather than the blood of my race. At this moment I prefer the humblest, weakest infantryman of France to our worthiest works of art. These we will recreate. The essential thing is that our nation remains. *Vive la France!* This is the only reply of believers, artists, and patriots to this deed.

I may mention that, at the height of the conflagration, the French army doctors, remembering that some German wounded remained in the cathedral, went in and brought them away to safety. It appears to me that in that act lies the finest revenge for this pitiless barbarism. Long after our little angers are silent and forgotten, it will be recalled in history that these wounded Germans were rescued from flames which their own brethren had kindled.

Chapter 19

The Eastern Barrier

It has been repeatedly pointed out that the whole plan of campaign of the Allies depended upon the maintenance of a successful defence on the east, from Verdun to Belfort. The efforts of the armies of Generals Sarrail, De Castelnau, and Dubail were not absolutely limited to the defensive, for they had to endeavour to win back ground, especially in the Woevre and Lorraine, that had been lost, and they had to hold as many German corps as possible on this front, in order to relieve the pressure elsewhere. But the first and supreme order was to stand firm. There must be no more blundering, and no further retreat. It is not the role that the French soldier of tradition favours; it may, however, be doubted whether men of any race could have fulfilled this hard service with greater courage, stouter endurance, or more persistent energy. Their success has not loomed so large in the world's eye, but it was as solid and important as that of the western armies. The defence of Verdun and the neighbouring region will be the subject of a later chapter; here we shall notice the outstanding events southward along the Heights of the Meuse, and in the gap between the fortresses of Toul and Epinal.

The chief attempt to break through the eastern barrier was made south of the Moselle, and centred upon the Grande Couronne of Nancy. At the height of this major attack, when General Sarrail's forces were engaged against the Crown Prince to the south of the Argonne, the army of Metz delivered a lesser assault upon the line of the Meuse, eighteen miles south of Verdun, where the Spada road is covered only by the small fort of Troyon, on the hills which bound the river on the east. On September 7, the gallant commander of Troyon, Captain Xavier Heym, had been out shooting partridges. Before another day was over, 400 large shells had been thrown upon the fort, seven guns being put out of action, and large parts of the building demolished. Nevertheless, resistance was maintained till September 13; and, in these five days, of 454 men, only 4 were killed and 45 wounded. Two infantry assaults were made on the nights of the 8th and 9th. They were discovered by the flashlights of the fort, and repelled by the fire of rifles and the remaining guns.

The besiegers were hidden in the wooded hills, and their positions could not be found: it was Liège over again on a smaller scale, but with hardly less at stake, for if Troyon had fallen, the German armies retreating from the Battle of the Marne could have been re-enforced. Verdun invested, and a permanent road opened to Metz. Two German officers and a trumpeter rode up to the fort, and demanded its surrender. "Never!" replied the commander; "I shall blow it up sooner." And finally: "Get out, I've seen enough of you. *A bientôt, à Metz!*"

At length, on the 13th, the 2nd Cavalry Division brought relief from Toul. The men were exhausted from lack of sleep; the fort showed ruins on every hand (largely the work of shells 3 feet long, of 305-mm. calibre). But Troyon had fulfilled its task.

A few days later, the effort to break the Meuse line was repeated a little further south, at a point where the Fort du Camp des Romains overlooks from the forest-clad hills the ancient town of St. Mihiel, on the left bank in a loop of the river. St. Mihiel is the converging point of roads from Pont-à-Mousson. Vigneulles, Heudicourt. and Woinville. It had a considerable garrison, whose barracks were situated on the other side of the river, in the suburb of Chauvoncourt. Along this west bank of the Meuse runs the railway from Verdun to Toul—of less importance since the Ste. Menehould line was recovered, but not lightly to be lost. Four German army corps, with heavy siege guns, under General von Strantz, were engaged in these operations; and, after a most hardy resistance, the fort of the Camp des Romains fell on September 22. The survivors of the garrison, 300 in number, were, said an American correspondent with the German Army, accorded the most honourable conditions.

On the following day, St. Mihiel was occupied, and a long foot-to-foot struggle, first on the west, then on the east of the Meuse. During October, the Verdun army was able to reach further to the south-east, and the Toul troops to the north-east, but with no more success than to stop the German advance, and to restrict and threaten constantly the German force pushed forward, like a spear-head, from Pont-à-Mousson and Thiaucourt to St. Mihiel. From its fastness on the Camp des Romains, neighbouring villages were bombarded, including Sampigny, and President Poincaré's villa therein. On November 17, the French troops silenced some German mortars which had been placed on the hills at Paroches, and seized the western part of Chauvoncourt. They then found that parts of the town had been mined. On the morning of the 18th, the mines were exploded; the French lost about 2,000 men, killed, wounded, and prisoners, on this occasion. The Metz army retained a bare foothold upon the Meuse at St. Mihiel, the only substantial piece of ground won since the battle of the Marne.

After its defeat at Morhange and Sarreburg, on August 20, General de Castelnau brought his army back to its prepared positions along the circle of low hills to the northeast of the picturesque town of Nancy, with the fortress of Toul behind. The retreat was so hard-pressed that it would appear extravagant to attribute its direction to a cool, strategic design. Nevertheless, important strategic consequences followed. The gap of Charmes-Mirécourt, between the fortresses of Toul and Epinal, was left open, save for minor forces which Castelnau and Dubail could spare for the work of obstruction and harassment in that direction. It was a temptation; and the German commanders never seem to have been quite certain what to do about it. The main French Army was drawn up in a semicircle from near Pont-à-Mousson, through the plateau of Amance, rising to 1,000 feet over the forest of Champenoux, to Dombasle and the forest of Vitremont. It was outnumbered, probably by two or three to one; but it held strong natural positions, improved by entrenchment.

The Crown Prince of Bavaria, in command of the Bavarian Army and certain troops from Metz, could probably have penetrated from Lunéville and Baccarat to Mirécourt, and thence to Châlons, had he concentrated upon this objective. But he would then have had not only two fortresses upon his flanks, but a great army behind. Lunéville, as we have seen, was occupied on August 22. Thence, the German left crossed the Rivers Meurthe and Mortagne, and advanced to the Moselle. They were received by a heavy artillery fire from the hills above Bayon on August 24; but their progress was more effectually arrested by the news that Castelnau was taking the offensive eastward of Nancy. Part of the force was brought back just in time to recapture the wood of Crévie.

The 59th and 68th French Reserve Divisions on the left, and the 36th Brigade on the right, now marched eastward along the roads from Nancy to Delme and Château-Salins, toward Amance and

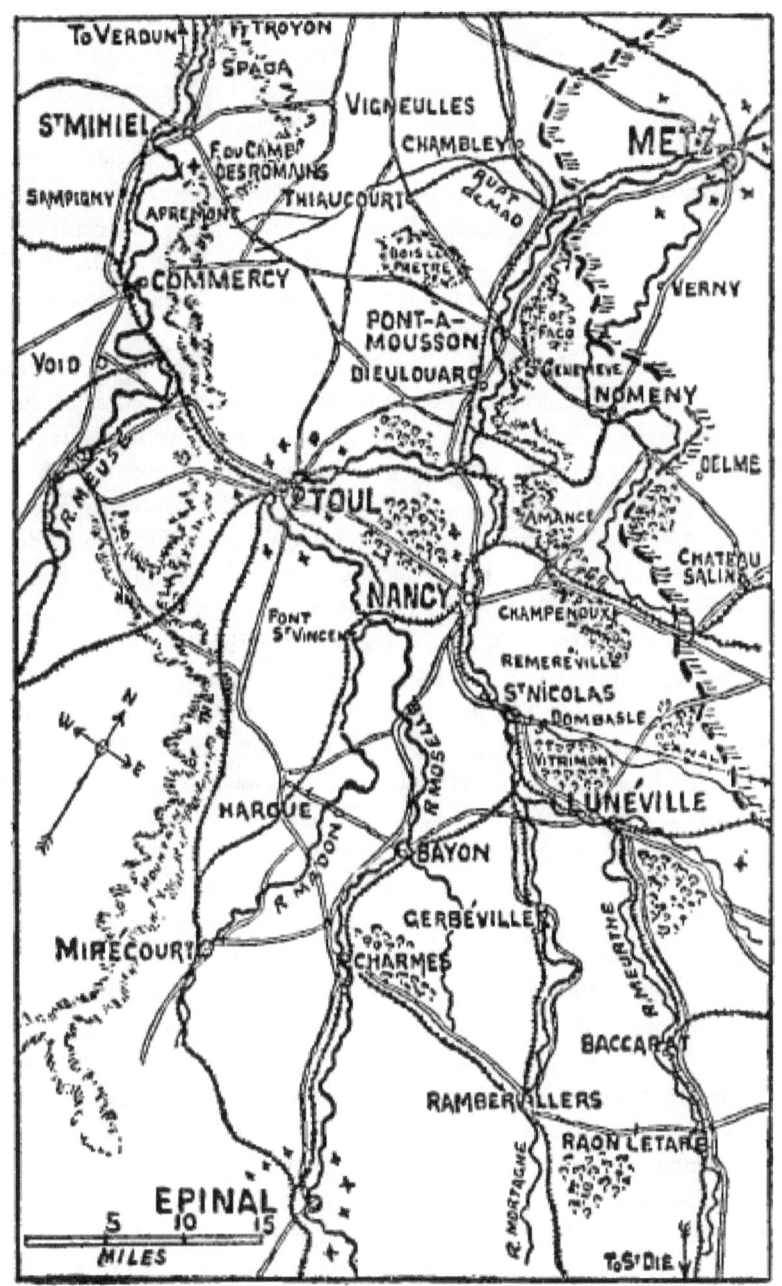

The defence of Nancy

Champenoux. For several days, only skirmishes took place. The object was not to cross the frontier, but to create a diversion, and to take up and entrench favourable positions which would make even a distant bombardment of Nancy impossible. By September 3 (they do not seem to have hurried—perhaps they were synchronising their movements with Von Kluck and Von Bülow), German re-enforcements particularly strong in artillery began to arrive. The great crisis was being reached in the west, and General Joffre did not want the added risk of adventures in Lorraine. De Castelnau was ordered, therefore, to hold himself on the defensive.

By this time, the German commanders had come to accept the necessity of a frontal attack upon the line of the army of Nancy. It began in force on September 4; and it is said to have been supported by no less than four hundred heavy guns, many of them borrowed from the forts of Metz and Strassburg. For a week, with hardly any cessation, the French positions on the Amance plateau were bombarded from behind and within the forest of Champenoux, and the positions further north, at Mont Ste. Genevieve, from the forest of Facq. On the latter wing, Pont-à-Mousson was occupied by the enemy, 12,000 strong, on September 5, the French soldiers blowing up the Moselle bridge behind them. The town was retaken on the 10th; and thereafter the French held the left, the Germans the right bank of the river. At the neighbouring village of Loisy, a single company of infantry posted itself in the cemetery, and, waiting till the Saxon attackers were quite near, opened a deadly fire upon them.

A night assault to the left, at Ste. Geneviève, held by a battalion of the 314th Infantry, with two batteries, was no more successful. The French claim to have found 933 dead at these points. But the brunt of the struggle occurred on the slopes of the Grand Mont d'Amance, a position of peculiar advantage for the defence. Their way prepared by a rain of shells, the Bavarian troops marched in massed columns upon Erbéville, defended by the French 344th Regiment, and on the village of Champenoux, held by the 212th. The battle continued through September 5 and 6. On the 7th, the French counter-attacked, but Champenoux was lost, the 206th Infantry suffering very heavily. On the 8th, a new attack was attempted—a single division against three army corps. Apparently, the Germans were as much exhausted as the French, for the 9th passed quietly, an armistice being granted for the burial of the dead. A mixed regiment was brought up from Toul to re-enforce the line. A French writer says:

But our soldiers, hungry, harassed, haggard, could hardly stand upright, and marched like spectres. Visibly, we were at the last breath, crushed by infinitely superior numbers. We could hold out only a few hours more. And then, O prodigy, calm fell, on the 12th, upon the whole of the stricken field. The enemy gave up, retreated for good, abandoned everything, Champenoux, so frantically contested, and the entire front he had occupied. He fell back in dense columns, without even a preens of further resistance.

One by one, Saint-Dié, Lunéville, Baccarat, and Raon-l'Etape were evacuated, and reoccupied by the French. Three divisions had defended against three times as many, for a fortnight, the whole crescent from Pont-à-Mousson to Dombasle. At the south end of this line, about the villages of Réméréville, Courbessaux, and Drouville, and the Wood of Crévie, the ground is lower; and here the fighting was of a dreadful stubborn fierceness, every farm and hamlet being contested to the last. Réméréville was captured, the French detachment of only a battalion and a half which held it being wiped out. A few shells were thrown into Nancy from this point—the only time it was reached by the enemy. The Crévie plateau was repeatedly lost and won, at a cost of thousands of lives.

The general result may be attributed to (1) De Castelnau's success in holding out in the hill trenches of Amance and Champenoux, which made any advance into the gap of Mirécourt highly dangerous; (2) exhaustion and heavy losses—the French claim to have found 40,000 German dead; (3) the fact that the retreat of the German western armies from the Marne deprived the Crown Prince of Bavaria of his objective. That great hopes were placed in this part of the campaign seems to be indicated by the presence with the Bavarian Army, for two or three days, of the Emperor William, to whom report attributed the expectation of entering as conqueror the capital of French Lorraine.

It has been said on an earlier page that the cruel treatment of the civil population which nearly everywhere marked the progress of the German armies did not in France reach the extent or depth of iniquity shown at Tamines, Aerschot, Louvain, and other towns and villages in Belgium. It is only with hesitation that this statement can be maintained in face of the report of the French Commission of Inquiry upon the devastation and barbarities wrought in the Department of Meurthe and Moselle. As though the destruction of hundreds of farmsteads and parts of scores of villages in course of the fighting were not sufficient penalty for this unfortunate countryside, the Bavarian infantry, in particular, are proved to have been guilty at many places of almost incredible acts of ferocity.

In the village of Nomeny, between Nancy and the frontier, the 2nd and 3rd Bavarian regiments seem to have sunk to the level of Abdul Hamid's *Bashi-Bazouks*. The place was first sacked, then burned; and, as the villagers fled from their cellars, they were shot down—old men, women, and children—fifty being killed and many more wounded. Generally speaking, the larger the place the less extreme was the lawlessness. But at Lunéville, during the three weeks' occupation, the Hôtel de Ville, the Synagogue, and about seventy houses were burned down, with torches, petrol, and other incendiary apparatus; and seventeen men and women were shot in cold blood in the streets. A notice to the population, signed "Commander-in-Chief, Von Fosbender," was posted on September 3, announcing that a "contribution" of 650,000 *francs* (£26,000) must be paid in three days, or "all the goods which are available will be seized," and "anyone who shall have deliberately hidden money, or shall have attempted to hide his goods, or who seeks to leave the town, will be shot."

The money was actually found and paid. In the neighbouring village of Chanteheux, the Bavarians fired twenty houses, and shot eight civilians, on August 25. A day earlier, practically the whole of the little town of Gerbéviller was destroyed by fire (more than 400 houses), and at least thirty-six civilians, men and women, were slaughtered. The Bavarian troops were here under the command of General Clauss. At Crévie, seventy-six houses were burned down; at Maixe, thirty-six, and nine men and one woman were murdered. At Baccarat, no civilians were killed; but 112 houses were burned down after the whole place had been pillaged, under the supervision of the officers, one of these being General Fabricius, commanding the artillery of the 14th Baden Corps.

These are a few of the graver cases; many other well-attested instances of wholesale and retail vengeance could be cited. No attempt to chronicle the outstanding facts of the great war can ignore this part of it. But I would add that I have touched upon it, even so briefly, with extreme reluctance. War itself is the uttermost barbarism, the all-inclusive atrocity beside which the most damnable of retail crimes sink into insignificance. Despite the long and earnest efforts of lawyers and humanitarians, we now know that its most dire penalties cannot be limited to the armies in the field. That the German Government and its captains entered upon their aggression, and maintained it, in the resolve that no gentle scruple should stand in their way, they have abundantly proved on the sea and in the air, as well as on the land. But that this diabolical spirit was shared by the common German soldier, or even the average German officer, would have been an implication as revolting to every fair-minded Frenchman, Englishman, or Belgian, as to find their own defenders playing the Apache or the Kurd in the beautiful cities and villages of the Rhineland.

Let us suggest no ideal tests in a field where the ideal is so discounted. Murder, arson, and rape are (if such things can be assessed) a small part of the evil that war unlooses. But the German armies boast of an iron organization and discipline; and with all their unquestioned courage and varied powers, it must be said that these savageries deeply and unforgettably dishonour them.

CHAPTER 20

The Battles of the Aisne

One of the surprises of the campaign of 1914 was the power of mass retreat and recovery after severe reverses given by modern organisation (based, it is well to remember, upon civil education, as well as upon specific military training). Von Kluck and Von Bülow had no such task after the Battle of the Marne as faced Sir John French after Mons. The re-establishment of a solid German line extending from the Oise across the Laon plateau. dipping toward Rheims, and then reaching over Champagne, through the Argonne, and around Verdun, to Metz was, nevertheless, one of the great achievements of the war. a success which the Allies had soon to admit their inability to do more than limit until time should give them a heavy supremacy of numbers and artillery power.

The bulwark of this unprecedented line was its western third, the crests of the hills above the lower Aisne; and the reckless waste of life in German charges which marked the height of the combat may have been supported by the feeling that they would never again have such good positions to defend. The Allies also sustained very heavy losses, the small British Army alone having 13,541 killed, wounded, and missing on the Aisne in less than four weeks, bringing their total casualties to the second week of October up to 33,000. It may be asked whether the end actually attained would not have been as well or better served by holding the hills of the south bank of the river defensively, and throwing more force into the parts of the field which offered less natural difficulties. It is sufficient here to reply that, when the 5th and 6th French and the British armies crossed the Aisne, it was not known whether they had to deal with a mere halt, or a definite arrest. A fortnight's hard fighting showed that the plateau was held resolutely, and with large re-enforcements; and a new plan of cam-

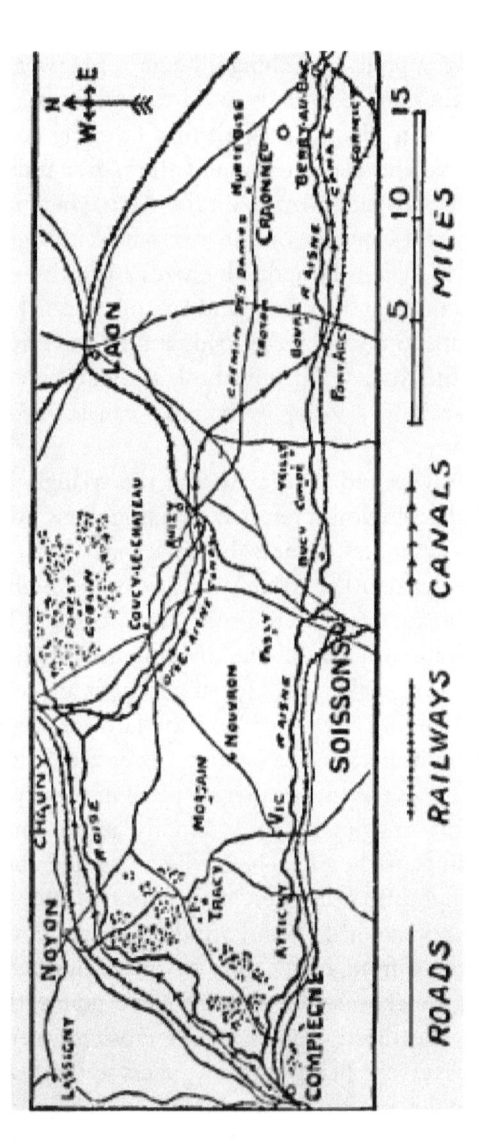

Triangle of the Laon Mountains

paign was then adopted.

Leaving till we come to that plan other features of the region, especially that of the northern railway communications, we may briefly note the physical conformation which makes the Laon plateau a natural fortress. It may be broadly described as a triangle of hilly and wooded country, sloping up gently from the north (a great advantage for the German supplies), reaching a height of between 600 and 700 feet, and breaking down to its base on the Aisne in a series of spurs and ravines, every roadway of which may be easily covered by cross-fires from above. The plateau is about thirty-five miles long from a line between Attichy and Noyon, on the west, where it falls gently to the Oise Valley, and Craonne on the east, where it drops abruptly into the plain. The triangle is bounded by roads and railways of which the angles are at Compiègne, La Fère, and Cormicy (north of Rheims). It is cut from south to north by the roads and railways from Soissons, in the middle of the base, to Chauny and Laon; and it is cut from north-west to south-east by a valley by which a canal is brought from the Oise to the Aisne.

The small towns and villages within the triangle are full of historical and archaeological interest, containing many twelfth and thirteenth century churches, ruined abbeys, *donjons*, and *châteaux*. Beside the main road through the Aisne Valley, there is a highway along the edge of the plateau, from the Soissons-Laon road to Craonne, which was to be for long months the line dividing the Allied from the German trenches. Originally built for the benefit of certain Bourbon princesses, and ending at Vanclere and the farm of Heurtebise on the scene of a famous victory of Napoleon over the Allies of 1814, the Chemin des Dames now takes a larger place in history in connection with a series of struggles yet more bloody and momentous. Finally, there is a feature of the river-bed which considerably affected the course of the fighting. It lies here only about 140 feet above the sea; and the Aisne pursues a slow and winding course through meadows having a width of from half a mile to two miles between the two hillsides, rising quickly by 400 feet. At some points, the river nearly approaches the northern spurs; here the crossings were of particular difficulty, the river not being fordable, because the bridge heads and camps were under fire from the heights immediately above. Where there is flat land on the north, the passage and the first stages of advance were made with comparative ease.

The Allied armies were thus divided: the 6th French Army (Maunoury), after driving Von Kluck's flank-guard back from the west of the Ourcq, pursued it northward to the Aisne between Compiègne and Soissons. The British army swept up the east of the Ourcq, touching Soissons on its left, and clearing the ground between the Vesle and the Aisne. To its right, the 5th French Army (D'Espérey) held the line eastward of Bourg, through Rheims, to its junction with the 7th Army (Foch) in Champagne. Of the German armies. Von Kluck was in the west. Von Bülow from about Craonne across the north of Rheims; and between these lay a force brought round from Lorraine under General von Heeringen, based upon Laon. The last named consisted of three, later on of four, army corps—12th (Saxon), 10th, and 7th and 10th Reserve.

Maunoury quickly cleared the Compiègne district, and crossed the Aisne by pontoons at Vic on Sunday, September 13, and at Fontenoy on the following day; while at Soissons, with the help of the British 4th Division, he drove the enemy across the river and occupied the southern part of the town. At the west end of this advance, progress was made through the Forest of Laigle toward Noyon, on the Oise; and, at the same time, with the French recovery of Amiens, the re-organization of resistance on the north-west began. In their advance northward from Vic toward Nampcel, Morsain, and Nouvron, Maunoury's columns felt severely the German superiority in heavy field-guns and in positions on the western spurs of the Laon hills. A daring attempt was made along this narrow valley to cut off some outlying forces; but numbers of men and guns prevailed, and a retirement to the river was effected with difficulty. At Soissons, the bridge was destroyed by the retiring Germans, who, from the quarries of Pasly and neighbouring heights, not only made a pontoon passage impracticable, but subjected the town to a continuous bombardment. At this point, the battle of the Aisne immediately reached the position of deadlock.

The British were more fortunate, partly because of the physical characteristic already indicated, partly because the section of the line at which they struck was less vital to the Germans than the Soissons-Laon road. From west to east, the three army corps under Sir John French (of which the 3rd consisted only of the 4th Division *plus* the 19th Brigade) made the crossing at the following points: the 3rd, immediately east of Soissons, at Billy, Bucy, and Venizel; the 2nd, at Missy and Condé; the 1st, at Chavonne, Pont-Arcy, and Bourg. The usual way was to raft over a covering detachment, and then construct a pontoon bridge; but the Germans probably found the Chauny-Rheims

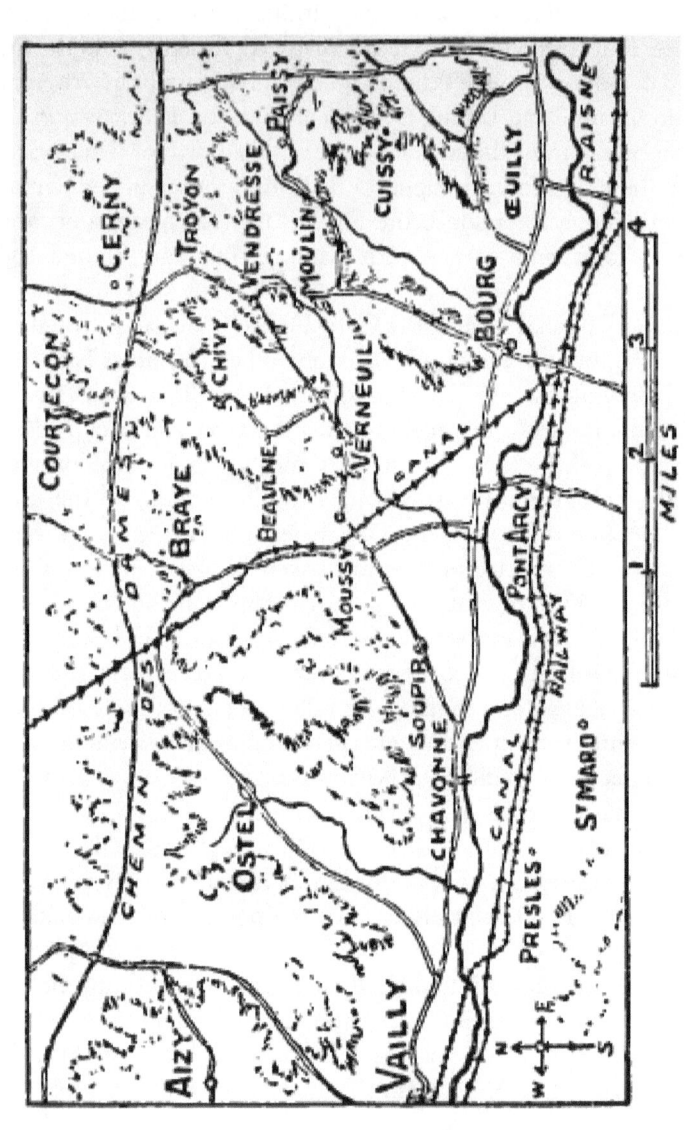

The British Right above the Aisne

Canal too useful to allow of the aqueduct which leads it over the Aisne at Bourg being destroyed. The 5th Infantry Brigade crept over a remaining girder of the Pont-Arcy bridge in Indian file, under heavy gunfire. The repairing and building of bridges was immediately begun; and, within three or four days, the engineers had thirteen passages made between Soissons and Villers.

Of the three positions, the two extremes, at Venizel and Pont-Arcy, are favoured by flat land on the north of the river; while the centre, from Condé to Vailly, immediately faces a crescent of hills whose defenders, already entrenched and hidden by thick woods, could make an approach almost impossible. Not only is the river-crossing easier at Pont-Arcy. but there opens here what we may call the valley of the canal, leading almost up to the Chemin des Dames at the villages of Braye, Chivy, and Troyon. This was evidently the most favourable line of advance, particularly as it was not served on the German side by any line of railway (as were the heights near Soissons).

Crossing here, then, the 1st Corps under Sir Douglas Haig and the Cavalry Division under General Allenby at once struck north. By nightfall on the 13th, the 1st Division had established itself in the villages of Moulins, Paissy, and Geny, with outposts in Vendresse. With more difficulty, the 3rd Corps, under Lieutenant-General Pulteney, reached the lower spurs of the Crouy and Vregmy hills on the same day. The 2nd Corps was hard put to it to maintain its river crossing; the British force, indeed, never succeeded in driving the German troops from the promontory above Condé, which is the site of a former French fort. Elsewhere, there was, on the night of the 13th, a withdrawal of the German main positions to the line of the Chemin des Dames, skilfully hidden batteries and entrenched rifle detachments being left at lower points of vantage. The deluge of fire that now broke, day and night, over the northern slopes of the Aisne Valley was such as utterly to eclipse the worst experience of the oldest soldiers in the field.

Apparently, the German commanders had recovered their lines of supply; they had all the advantages of position; and they had been able carefully to measure the chief gun-ranges. Including the 8-in. siege howitzers brought up from Maubeuge, which came into use on the 15th, they had a considerably greater weight of artillery; heavy rains aggravated the difficulty of getting the Allies' guns through the valley and into the hills. The work of the engineer, supply, and other subsidiary services in these trying circumstances is not less deserving of praise than the heroism of the actual combatants.

Sir John French says:—

> On the evening of the 14th it was still impossible to decide whether the enemy was only making a temporary halt, covered by rear-guards, or whether he intended to stand and defend the position. With a view to clearing up the situation, I ordered a general advance. The action of the 1st Corps on this day under the direction and command of Sir Douglas Haig was of so skilful, bold, and decisive a character that he gained positions which alone have enabled me to maintain my stand for more than three weeks of very severe fighting on the north bank of the river.

This action consisted of an advance up the valley of the canal, and over the neighbouring hills about Moussy and Moulins. On the right, held by the 1st Division (Major-General Lomax), the 2nd Infantry Brigade and the 25th Artillery Brigade, under General Bulfin, moved at daybreak through Vendresse, and attacked a considerable German force entrenched in and around a sugar factory north of Troyon, on the Chemin des Dames. This, it may be noted, was for the moment the most northerly point of the Allied front (twenty-six miles northwest of Rheims), there being as yet no western wing beyond the Oise. The King's Royal Rifles and the Royal Sussex regiment led the attack, supported by the North Lancashires; and, these being insufficient, the Coldstream Guards were brought up to the right, and the remainder of the 1st Brigade (1st Royal Highlanders, 1st Scots Guards, and the Munsters) to the left. By noon, the North Lancashires had seized the factory, and the two brigades, with the 3rd Brigade in support, were holding a line to the south of the Chemin des Dames, that is, along the southern crest of the plateau.

This was a threat the German commanders could not ignore. Moreover, D'Espérey's army was simultaneously assaulting Von Bülow's at Craonne, a few miles further east; while, on Haig's left, the 4th Guards Brigade had reached the south of the Ostel ridge, and the 6th Infantry Brigade was moving up the valley toward Braye, both with strong artillery supports. There was, however, a weakness in the line, a break in the attack due to the strength of the German hill entrenchments between Condé and Vailly, the British centre. Sir John French said:—

> At this period of the action the enemy obtained a footing between the 1st and 2nd Corps and threatened to cut the commu-

nications of the latter. Sir Douglas Haig was very hard pressed, and had no reserve in hand. I placed the cavalry division at his disposal, part of which he skilfully used to prolong and secure the left flank of the Guards brigade. Some heavy fighting ensued, which resulted in the enemy being driven back with heavy loss. About 4 o'clock the weakening of the counter-attacks and other indications tended to show that his resistance was decreasing; and a general advance was ordered. Although meeting with considerable opposition, and coming under very heavy artillery and rifle fire, the position of the (1st) Corps at the end of the day's operations extended from the Chemin des Dames on the right, through Chivy, to Le Cour de Soupir, with the 1st Cavalry Brigade extending to the Chavonne-Soissons road.

On the right, the corps was in close touch with the French Moroccan troops of the 18th Corps, which were entrenched in *échelon* to its right rear. Throughout the battle of the Aisne, this advanced and commanding position was maintained. Day after day, and night after night, the enemy's infantry has been hurled against the 1st Corps in violent counter attack, which has never on any one occasion succeeded, while the trenches have been under continuous heavy artillery fire.

Every part of the line was tested in course of these desperate assaults. Of one of the most serious, the British commander-in-chief reported:—

> On the afternoon of the 17th, the right flank of the 1st Division was seriously threatened. A counter-attack was made by the Northamptonshire Regiment in combination with the Queen's, and one battalion of the Divisional Reserve was moved up in support. The Northamptonshire Regiment, under cover of mist, crept up to within a hundred yards of the enemy's trenches, and charged with the bayonet, driving them out of the trenches and up the hill. A very strong force of hostile infantry was then disclosed on the crest line. This new line was enfiladed by part of the Queen's and the King's Royal Rifles, which wheeled to their left on the extreme right of our infantry line, and were supported by a squadron of cavalry on their outer flank. The enemy's attack was ultimately driven back with heavy loss.

> In course of the day, the Northamptons lost about 150 men by the treachery of a German company, which offered to surrender, and then

attacked its captors.

Between September 26 and 28, the Germans made what Sir John French calls "one last great effort to establish ascendency." This may be regarded as the end of the battles of the Aisne, for on the Laon plateau, as across Champagne and in the Argonne, the long deadlock of trench warfare, without a definite ascendency on either side, had begun, while a new phase of the struggle had been opened in the north-west. The French 5th Army could not reach level with the British 1st Corps, and the Chemin des Dames, therefore, could not be crossed. Maunoury made better progress in the Forest of Laigle, but could not drive the German gunners and riflemen from their stronghold above Soissons. For a few days it looked as though a dangerous breach might be made in the hostile lines at Berry-au-Bac, just beyond Craonne; this hope, also, soon disappeared, General von Bülow had been allowed to seize and strengthen the positions of the old French forts around Rheims, especially those of Nogent l'Abbesse and Mount Berru; and, although Brimont changed hands, and Pompelle was recovered, all attempts to pierce the crescent round the northeast of the city failed.

So in the plain to the east, between Souain and the ridge on the north of the River Suippes, only slight variations occurred in the opposed lines, and the campaign developed into a kind of double siege. In the Argonne, the closeness of the woodland and the scarcity of roads gave the fighting a special character; but, after an attempt by the crown prince to penetrate southward had been repulsed in the district of La Gruerie, on the road from Vienne-la-Ville to Varennes, at the beginning of October, a static condition was reached. By the middle of the month, the French southern army had recovered the crests and passes of the Vosges as far north as the Col du Bonhomme, and the Alsatian slopes as far as Thann. But the Metz field force still held the valley called the Rupt du Mad, with its railway to Thiaucourt, and, beyond, a narrow footing on the Meuse at St. Mihiel. Why they should maintain this spearhead so resolutely without further attempt to press it in was not clear—perhaps, as a future opportunity of offense.

There were many indications of a fatal dispersal of German strength over too many objectives. In all that could be done by long scientific preparation, the Imperial Staff had more than justified its reputation. Despite increasing pressure on the Russian frontier, it was keeping its numerical superiority in the west by an unexpected power of absorbing into the combatant ranks vast numbers of half-trained levies, who, if they were poor marksmen, repeatedly showed that they could meet the test of massed attack in close formation against first-class infantry. The German armies displayed courage, energy, and endurance of a high order; their organization, supply, and transport were beyond reproach; and in some respects their equipment was still better than that of the Allies. In the higher region of command, they were now as signally lacking as their political chiefs had been in moral sense and foresight. The battles of the Aisne confirmed the result of the battle of the Marne, though they did little more. The idea of an early conclusion of the war now disappeared. The main body of the new British armies could not be ready for six months; and till then the Allies could not hope to assume a general offensive. The invasion, however, was definitely contained; and in this fact the defenders of France found encouragement to bear the terrible trials of the coming winter.

All the time they were learning. The Boers had taught Mr. Atkins something of the art of taking cover under rifle fire. The French quickly picked up this lesson; but at the outset, both French and British showed a reluctance or incapacity for effective entrenchment against heavy artillery which, though it may be usual in novices, was particularly deplorable in this instance. The German infantry use the bayonet little, and their mass assaults are rarely successful before the modern magazine rifle. But against heavy guns, there is nothing for it but deep digging, until a counter bombardment brings relief. The art of entrenchment was recreated on the Aisne; and, with the elaboration of earth works for the firing line, the heavy rains of mid September dictated an unanticipated provision of covered shelters and rest-places. The German armies had learned, however, not only to entrench, but to subordinate this skill to offensive action.

After the Battle of the Marne, Sir John French asked that four 6 in. howitzer batteries should be sent out, as "our experiences in this campaign seem to point to the employment of more heavy guns of a larger calibre in great battles which last for several days." As the deadlock extended and hardened, this need became more and more evident, especially in the French armies, where faith had being placed almost exclusively in the remarkable "75" light field-pieces. During the autumn, the balance in heavy artillery was gradually rectified. Meanwhile, all sorts of expedients, old and new, were tried to break the stalemate of the buried lines—sapping and mining, the throwing of hand grenades, sniping from trees and other vantage points, the control and direction of massed gunfire by telephone from the extreme front, or by aeroplane signals.

CHAPTER 21

The North-West Turn

1. A Flank Blow that Failed

Sir John French says that, on September 15, his own and the French reports made it clear that the German armies were taking up "a determined stand" above the Aisne; and, on September 18, "information reached me from General Joffre that he had found it necessary to make a new plan, and to attack and envelop the German right flank."

Four considerations united to draw the attention both of the Allies and the German Staff to the north-west, as soon as the heat of the pursuit from the Marne was over: (1) There lay the most prolonged and the only vulnerable line of German communications; (2) there lay large, rich districts of France not yet effectively occupied by either party; (3) there, in the extreme north, at Antwerp, lay the still unconquered Belgian army; and (4) there lay the roads to the Channel ports, the only way by which England could be directly threatened, and the only remaining possibility of envelopment. The first two considerations gave birth to, and the third affected. General Joffre's "new plan," and the events dealt with in the present chapter; the fourth governed the development of the plan, and the events narrated in the next chapter.

Two more general conditions are to be borne in mind: (a) At the outset, the whole aim of the invasion had been to obtain a rapid result in the west, in order to turn with full force against Russia. Its authors clung obstinately to this hope, and the mass of German troops was kept in the west. But the strength of the Allies was steadily, though very slowly, increasing. Thus deadlock along most of a long, thin line, with violent attacks at promising points, became the only alternative to the abandonment of a large part of the occupied territory. The very success of the invasion now began to bring its punishment. All the monetary exactions from Belgian and French towns could not meet the cost of maintaining a front measuring, from Ostend to Basle, about 360 miles; and the military expense of holding this front effectually prevented an overwhelming attack upon Russia. We can now see that, in a defensive campaign—with a western front of only 170 miles—the German armies would have been invincible. It may be locally true that the best defence is by offense; in the larger picture, Germany appears from this time as doomed by the weight of her original aggression. (b) The Allies had reason ultimately to fear the deadlock of the trenches, if the territory thus held were to he recovered by local force. Otherwise, time was wholly on their side; and, from this point, the prospect of an exhaustion of the internal resources of the Germanic lands came more and more prominently into consideration.

We have seen that, of the two main lines of supply and communication of the German western armies, the chief ran up the western side of the Laon triangle—that is, up the Oise Valley—and then northwestward through St. Quentin and Maubeuge to Brussels and Liège; while the other ran from above Rheims, through Rethel, to Mézières, and then turned eastward to Luxemburg and the Rhineland. The failure of the French attempt to break through at Craonne and Berry-au-Bac left the latter line secure. The former, and more important, was at once threatened by the advance of General Maunoury's army from Compiègne through the Forest of Laigle, on the east of the Oise, and along the Ribécourt and Lassigny roads on the west of the river. While this advance was beginning to suffer a definite check around Noyon, a new army was being constituted on its left under General Castelnau. Between September 21 and 26, this new force established itself along a northward line from Lassigny, through Roye, to Péronne, with some Territorial divisions, under General Brugère, extending across the Somme north-westward to Albert.

A glance at the map further on will show that this rapid movement threatened the whole flank of the 1st and 2nd German armies, and in particular the vital railway junction of Tergnier, where, before the war, the Nord Company kept 1,200 men employed in their workshops. Roye and Lassigny are about twenty-five miles west of Tergnier; Péronne and Chaulnes are a little nearer to St. Quentin. By so narrow a margin were Brussels and Cologne connected with the Aisne. On the other hand, this new French front covered the great city of Amiens, and promised the re-establishment, through Abbeville and Boulogne, of the most convenient line of communications with England. The call for some effort to restore order in this region was emphasized by the revelation that it had been possible for a band of German engineers to keep an armoured automobile running for some days across Picardy and Normandy. The purpose was to destroy railway bridges; and the raiders, who worked by night and slept in the woods by day, had chosen their field of operation to include a part of the French railway system essential to the Allied movements. They were at last recognised and caught on the Paris-Rouen road, after an encounter in which three *gendarmes* and two of the audacious Germans were mortally wounded.

The promptitude of their reply suggests that the German commanders had anticipated this French movement, and had designed a westward enveloping movement of their own. Whether this be so, or fear for their homeward roads was the first motive, a large displacement of troops at once took place. French Lorraine was almost wholly abandoned. The forces in Alsace were reduced. A southward advance from Belgium was started; and the line of the Aisne was thinned by the gradual shifting westward of Von Bülow's, the Duke of Würtemberg's, and the Crown Prince of Bavaria's commands. From September 21 to the end of the month, efforts to break through between Castelnau's right and Maunoury's left, just west of Noyon, led to lighting of a sustained and desperate violence, a glimpse of which will be found in the story of the action at Tracy-le-Mont quoted in our final chapter.

On September 29, the Germans had seized Lassigny and Chaulnes, but the French held firm at Roye—midway between these towns—and at Ribécourt on the Oise. The blow at Tergnier had failed. And now began what was afterwards called "the race for the sea"—the reciprocal extension of the lines toward the north until, on the Belgian coast, no possibility of envelopment remained. By September 30, General Joffre had constituted a new army under General Maud'huy. one of the most brilliant of his assistants. This occupied the region of Arras and Lens, maintaining a frail connection with the garrison of Dunkirk and a body of Territorials still holding Lille. On October 2, fighting was reported as far north as Arras; on the 7th, the French bulletin noted that "the opposed front extends as far as the neighbourhood of Lens—La Bassée, prolonged by masses of cavalry which are engaged as far as the district of Armentières"; and on the 8th that "the cavalry operations are now developing almost as far as the North Sea coast."

2 From Amiens to Lille

Before we trace further this great displacement of the axis and centre of gravity of the campaign, a more particular reference should be made to the experience of the larger town of north-west France between the retreat to the Marne and the battles of Flanders. It will be remembered that, during the retreat, the French and British western wing stood fast for a moment at Cambrai, then again on the line Bapaume-Combles-Péronne. Next, the invaders were arrested for two days on the Somme between Amiens and Péronne, the Allies holding a strong position behind the marshes through which the river here flows. The two villages of Proyart and Framerville were the centres of the subsequent engagement, and were reduced to ruins. Péronne was reached by the Germans, victorious at Bapaume and the neighbouring village of Moislains, on the afternoon of August 25. For an hour or so, they were stopped by a body of dragoons and Alpine Chasseurs. Their batteries in the woods of Racogne, overlooking Péronne on the east, on the left bank of the Somme, bombarded the French positions on the opposite bank and in the suburb of Bretagne, where many houses and several neighbouring farms were destroyed As the German troops entered the town, they fired into the house-windows, apparently to intimidate the inhabitants.

The civil authorities had fled; the Germans therefore burned down the town hall and other public buildings using petrol sprays and grenades for the purpose The 'whole of the Grand Place would have been destroyed but for the intervention of a courageous priest, Canon Caron who, with other leading citizens, formed an administrative committee. Four hostages were also taken, but were released a few days later. All uninhabited houses and closed shops were broken open and sacked. On September 5 the major directing the German ambulance ordered the removal to Amiens of a large number of French wounded remaining in Péronne. The Red Cross accordingly sent twenty motor-cars from Amiens, and the doctors and nurses were preparing to return with their convoy, when Colonel von Kosser, the military commandant, ordered their arrest and the confiscation of the cars. For two days they were detained in the Péronne barracks; they were then released, after another four hostages had been taken in their place, but they had to walk to Amiens. From the 7th to the 14th, the hostages remained under arrest. On the latter day, the German retirement began. A German ambulance was left behind; and as some of the nurses were armed with revolvers they were arrested on the arrival of the French troops. On and after the 15th, the Germans tried to retake the town, but without success.

The first train for nearly a month reached Amiens from Paris on September 26. During this period the inhabitants had been practically isolated, hearing no news, having no postal or telegraphic communications, and practically no newspapers. Those who had fled now returned, and the city began to resume its normal aspect. It was on the night of August 30 that the approach of the enemy was signalled—after the Battles of Bapaume and Proyart. On the 31st, they appeared; but the German Staff and most of the troops were left on the hills beyond the Somme, at the end of the Beauville boulevard. A lieutenant with fifty men came to the town hall, and found there the venerable mayor, Senator Fiquet, who was seventy-three years old. The German flag having been hoisted, M. Fiquet and his colleagues were taken to the *commandant* of the corps of occupation. Von Stockhausen, who announced that the ransom of the city was fixed at 1,000,000 *francs* (£40,000) to be paid in money or kind. If this were found and no harm were done to German soldiers, the city would not suffer any other penaly; otherwise it would be bombarded. The requisitions in kind amounted to a value of about £34,000; the rest was to be paid in money.

M. Fiquet found the money; but his colleague, M. Francfort, an Amiens merchant, had great difficulty in getting together the various goods demanded—cigars, horses, petrol, bread, wine, etc. He asked for a short delay. Von Stockhausen then demanded twelve hostages—the mayor and eleven town councillors and the *procureur-general*, M. Regnault. volunteering, was added as a thirteenth. By way of stimulus, 40,000 troops were brought into the city, only 3,000 of whom, however, remained. One of the requisitions that could not be met was for 20,000 electric pocket-lamps. The commandant condescended to receive 20,000 *francs* instead. The hostages were then released; and it is to be noted that the only building in the city that was damaged was the post-office, where the telegraphic and telephonic instruments and cables were completely destroyed. But one morning all the men of the town liable to mobilisation were summoned to the military headquarters, where 1,200 of them were arrested and sent to Cambrai. Some escaped on the way; but most of them remained prisoners of the German Army. A regular procedure of the invasion was to carry off able-bodied civilians, and set them to digging trenches, mending roads, and other hard labour. On the morning of September 11, the troops left the city, and others, in full flight from the Battle of the Marne, followed them. Then the French arrived, and the citizens who remained hailed them with cries of joy.

A month passed, the Germans gradually concentrating toward the east. Then the northward movement of the left wing of the French began from Lassigny and Noyon, soon extending for ninety miles due north from Roye to Armentières. There followed a series of destructive struggles in which the little towns of Albert and Péronne and many villages were repeatedly taken and lost. Well named Santerre—not holy land, but land of blood—this flat region about the middle course of the Somme has been horribly ravaged. It was a country of large farms, much occupied with the growing of beetroot, and the manufacture of spirits and sugar. Not only were many distilleries and sugar factories destroyed by shell-fire; but at Roye, Lihons, and other places the churches and public buildings, as well as many houses, were bombarded, with grievous results. Albert is important as a junction of the highroads and railways between Amiens, Arras, and Cambrai, and between Doullens, Péronne, and St. Quentin, as well as be cause it covers the passages of the Somme. On his march toward Paris at the end of August, Von Kluck had sent a column as far as Poix, twenty miles to the south-west of Amiens on the Rouen road. On September 13, Amiens was abandoned; and the German front was then defined by the line Roye-Lassigny-Albert. These three places were soon little more than names, masses of smoking ruins showing where busy communities lately flourished.

In turn, Arras became the point of special pressure. It had been occupied by the Germans up to the middle of September and then evacuated, not very much damage having been done to the quaint old city. During the latter part of the month Douai, which cuts the Lille Cambrai railroad, was occupied by a French Territorial detachment, and patrols were sent out as far as Somain and Aniche, eight miles to the eastward, to attack bodies of the enemy. This led to reprisals: and, on September 30 and October 1, feeling their lines of communication threatened, the Germans, sending forward a dirigible and two aeroplanes to scout, attacked Douai with infantry and artillery. On the former day, the French held their own at Lewarde and Auberchicourt. During the night the enemy was re-enforced; but still the French stood their ground. On the afternoon of Thursday, October 1, however, Douai had to be abandoned. Meanwhile, feeling themselves threatened toward Cambrai, the heart of their western line, the Germans had brought up new bodies of troops, both from the north east and the south-west, against Arras.

The town was already occupied by French troops of all arms, and, as an important centre of roads and railways, it became the base of Maudhuy's attempt to hold out a helping hand toward Lille. On October 1 the German artillery came up from Douai, Vitry-en-Artois, and Cambrai, and heavy fire was exchanged along the surrounding hills. Evidently the enemy was in much stronger numbers; and on the 2nd and 3rd, although re-enforcements had arrived, it was thought well to retire behind the town, men liable to mobilisation being first warned to leave lest they should be made prisoners. This was the signal for a pitiful exodus to the coast. On the 6th and 7th, the town was bombarded from the hills, the splendid Hôtel de Ville, dating from 1501, the cathedral, and many houses being much damaged. Arras remained to the French; but in a later cannonade the town hall, with its superb clock-tower, was destroyed, and a large part of the town reduced to ruins. On October 31, a large German force, including a detachment of the Prussian Guard, was allowed to enter the suburbs of the town, where a trap had been prepared. A Guard battalion surrendered, and a military train containing one of the famous 42-cm. siege mortars was captured.

Already this second phase of the desperate struggle of the Germans to release themselves from the western grip had become merged—under pressure of the resolve of the French to move onward—in a third phase, the scene of which lay still further north, in the Black Country of the Franco-Belgian frontier. This is a very different region, a flat, gloomy land, with few trees, broken by coal-mines, canals, and a thick network of railways. Midway between Lille its capital, and Arras lies Courrières, the scene of one of the most terrible of colliery explosions, the suffering of which, it is odd to recall, was relieved by expert aid from Germany. A little later, in 1906, Lens, which stands just to the west, was the scene of another tragedy, when some strikers were shot down by the troops. Strikers and troops, in this day of the French-British-Belgian alliance, were the best of friends. La Bassée, to the north of Lens, is a pretty town on the Aire Canal.

A few miles further north, again, are Armentières and Lille. On Saturday, October 3, German patrols were reported on the outskirts of Lille which had so far suffered but little from the invasion. The mayor, M. Delesalle, at once distributed a notice warning the inhabitants to keep cool, not to gather in numbers, and to give no provocation. At midday on the 4th, rifle firing was heard near the station in the suburb of Fives; and during the afternoon some shells were thrown into the town, one striking the Hôtel de Ville. They came, in fact, from a new German force advancing southward from Belgium. It turned out that, during the morning, an armoured train bringing 300 *Uhlans* had entered the town. But an enterprising railway employee had switched the train into a siding, and here the French attacked it. The German soldiers, thus surprised, took refuge in neighbouring houses and workshops. Most of them were captured on the following morning. Another attempt to seize the town, made by about 3,000 infantry, entering on the other side from Tourcoing, was repelled by the French. On the same day, a body of German troops attempting to cross from the Belgian to the French side of the River Lys, between Armentières and Warneton, was repelled, and retired toward Tournai. The fighting continued on the 5th, when large numbers of German troops passed around the city to the south.

On the 6th, the cannonade continued all day on the west of Lille, in the direction of La Bassée. A regiment of French "Terriers" captured two cannon, after killing all the soldiers serving them. On the evening of Saturday, October 10, a company of *Uhlans* entered Lille. They were received with rifle shots, and several were dismounted. The others went to the town hall and, in a furious temper, arrested the mayor, M. Delesalle, and several other citizens, whom they promised to hold as hostages. In the nick of time some French *chasseurs* came up, set the prisoners free, and pursued the *Uhlans* along the Rue Nationale. Directly afterward, evidently in revenge for this insult, the town was bombarded by German batteries posted near. The first shell struck the roof of the town hall. A rain of shrapnel followed. Early on the morning of Sunday, the 11th, the bombardment was resumed; it continued until noon, then ceased, began again in the evening, and continued all that night. At several parts of the town buildings took fire. There was a further bombardment on the 12th, and an infantry attack began which the Territorials resisted for a time. Then they withdrew.

On Tuesday, the 13th, to save further destruction, the city was surrendered; and the German troops, some of whom had marched over 100 miles in five days, entered with bands playing. By this time, a large part of the best quarter of the capital of French Flanders was in ruins, many large commercial buildings and private houses having huge rents torn in their *façades*, and being then gutted by the flames. The Rue Faidherbe, Rue de Paris, Rue de Béthune, and Rue de l'Hôpital

Militaire were particularly damaged. The fire was quickly arrested, and the normal processes of German rule were established. The loss of life had been very small; yet this last week's resistance of Lille had vitally aided the Allies. It helped to conceal the western movements, and by diverting a considerable German force enabled the French and British troops to take up, just in time, the line of the Yser.

3. The Fall of Antwerp

The comparative neglect of the great port, city, and fortified position of Antwerp both by the German high command and by the major Allies up to the end of September, and the plans for the attack upon and defence of the city, have been so little explained, and are so much open on both sides to criticisms which may be quite undeserved, that we shall be content with a brief narrative of these events. It seems probable that the French and British commanders hoped to occupy and hold north-western Belgium; that the assault upon Antwerp came before they expected it; and that, in face of large new German re-enforcements, they abandoned the design; while the German Staff deliberately left the towns between Antwerp and the coast open, to tempt the Allies into a dangerous extension of their already very frail lines. General von Beseler does not seem to have had more than 100,000 troops available against Antwerp.

The slackness with which he completed his victory is in very marked contrast with the speed and power shown in the first stages of the war, and still shown by Von Kluck and Von Bülow further south. To this slackness, as well as their own energy and courage, the six Belgian divisions under General de Guise and the little British force under General Paris owed their survival. On the other hand, it must be placed to the credit of Von Beseler—as well as the vigilant activity of the representatives of the United States—that the beautiful city on the Scheldt did not share the fate of Louvain.

The first German approach was by the southwest; but, after repulses at Audeghem and Lebbekke, villages on the south-west and south-east of Termonde, on September 26 and 27, the western roads to Antwerp were left strangely free for movements of the Allies. On the following day, Malines having been once more bombarded, the direct advance upon the Scheldt from the south and south-east began. The outer defence works here extended at a distance of about nine miles from the city along a crescent formed by the Rivers Scheldt, Ruppel, and Methe, and included eight large forts, from that of Bornem on the

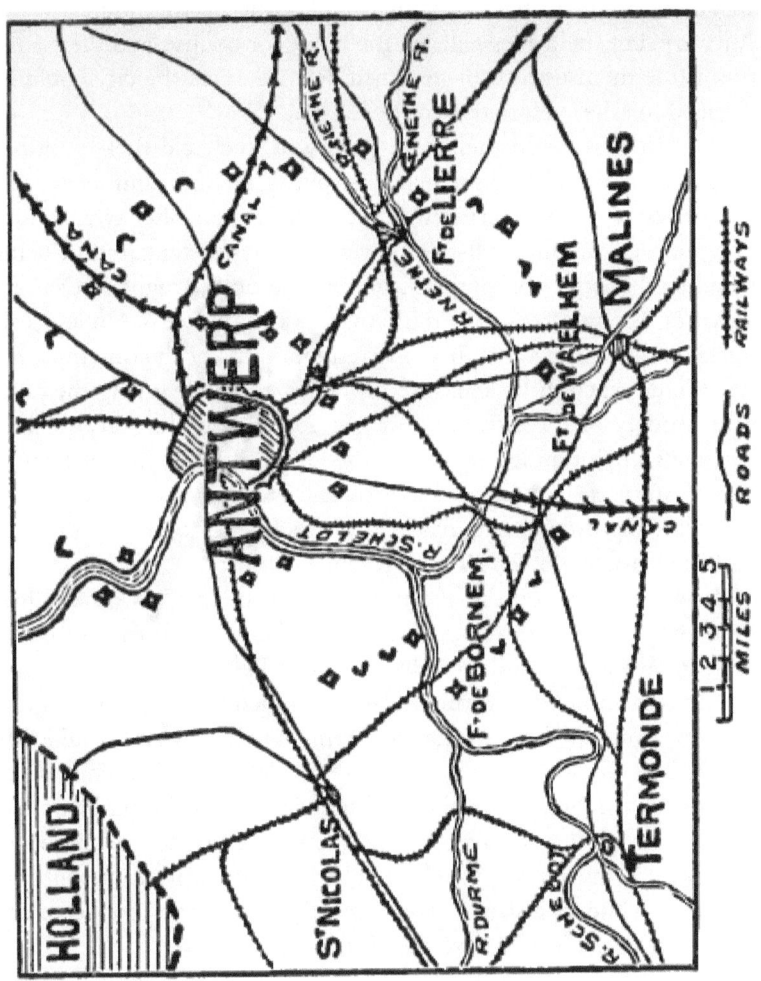

THE SIEGE OF ANTWERP

west, through Waelhem and Wavre Ste. Catherine (covering the Malines road), to that of Lierre, before the small town of the same name. The riversides were entrenched, and the roads blocked. There was an inner ring of forts, two or three miles outside the boundaries of Antwerp; but their guns had not the range for offense, and their position made them useless for sustained defence, since the city could be reduced to ashes before they were reached.

The Belgians used their field-guns well, and held their positions in the villages and river trenches despite a terrific cannonade. The fort of Wavre Ste. Catherine was put out of action, after twenty-four hours of continuous shell-fire, however, many of the garrison being killed by the explosion of the magazine; and on the night of October 1 that of Waelhem was little more than a heap of debris. No less serious than the loss of a fort (if a long resistance had been contemplated) was the destruction by shell-fire of a great reservoir giving the chief water supply of the city. On October 2, the defending troops were withdrawn behind the Nethe; and the flight of the wealthier inhabitants of Antwerp, including the British and French colonies, began. On the following evening, the first part of the British force, consisting of a Marine Brigade of 2,200 men, reached Antwerp.

It was followed on the afternoon of October 5 by two naval brigades, with six heavy naval guns, two of which served on an armoured train and were afterward brought south. The Belgian Government had asked for British aid; and rumour so multiplied these 8,000 men that the Anversois could hardly contain themselves for joy and confidence. General de Guise knew it was too late. Mr. Winston Churchill, when he stood with Jack Tar in the trenches, knew it, as he probably had done when they were sent; but he knew, also, that the detention of a German army on the Scheldt might save the position in southern Flanders, while British aid would greatly fortify the morale of the Belgian troops. He afterward stated that:

> The naval division was sent to Antwerp not as an isolated incident, but as part of a large operation for the relief of the city which more powerful considerations prevented from being carried through.

The First Lord explained that the naval brigades—largely consisting of new recruits, imperfectly equipped—were chosen because the need was urgent and bitter; because mobile troops could not be spared for fortress duties; because they were nearest, and could be embarked the quickest; and because their training, although incomplete, was as far advanced as that of a large portion not only of the forces defending Antwerp, but of the enemy forces attacking."

Repeated attempts to make the river-crossing at Waelhem and Lierre, on the nights of October 3, 4. and 5, were defeated with heavy loss; but, at dawn on the 6th. the Belgian line was forced by a concentration of artillery and infantry attack. The British marines about Lierre and the whole of the Belgian troops were then drawn back to the inner forts for a ftinal stand, in order to cover the retreat, and the flight of the civil population. That night, the withdrawal of the army commenced. Admirably covered by cavalry, armoured motorcars, and cyclist corps, it moved out by the narrow strip of territory between the Scheldt and Dutch Zealand, toward Ghent and Ostend. the Belgian and British trenches on the south of the city keeping up a full show of resistance. In the morning, the government and diplomatic corps left; the great oil-tanks on the Scheldt were blown up; and the machinery of many ships in harbour was disabled. The northern and western roads were now black with scores of thousands of people from Antwerp and the country around, flying to the sea and the Dutch frontier. Von Beseler's left wing was now crossing the Scheldt between Wetteren and Termonde; it would have gone very ill with the mingled masses of retreating soldiers and civil refugees had he boldly and immediately thrown his left wing forward to St. Nicholas and Lokeren.

A light bombardment of Antwerp began late at night on October 7. It is thought that 500,000 people left on the following day, the greater part to cast themselves upon the splendidly generous hospitality of the Dutch, many thousands to reach England, where homes were found for them. Amid this confusion, General de Guise's troops and most of the British contingent abandoned the forts and trenches, cut the Scheldt pontoon bridge behind them, and passed westward, successfully beating off flank and rear attacks. Unfortunately, three battalions of the 1st British Naval Brigade did not receive the orders to retire; and, ultimately, finding the Germans in possession of Lokeren and reaching near to St. Nicholas, they either crossed the Dutch frontier and were interned, or were captured. Beside this loss of about 2,500 men, a considerably larger number of Belgian soldiers gave themselves up to the Dutch frontier guards.

Antwerp formally surrendered at noon on October 9. Perhaps the German troops were exhausted; at any rate, not until the 12th were they ready to occupy Ghent, the 13th Bruges, and the 15th Ostend. At length, they saw the narrow sea that protects perfidious Albion. The Allies had decided to defend the coast along the course of the Yser. Part of the 4th British Corps—the 7th Infantry Division and the 3rd Cavalry Division—under Sir Henry Rawlinson, had been landed at Ostend and Zeebrugge without interference, and had advanced eastward to cover the Belgian-British retreat to the south. At Ghent, it found a garrison of eight squadrons of cavalry, a mixed brigade, a brigade of volunteers, and two line regiments, all of much reduced effectives, under General Clothen. Here also, on the evening of October 8, it met Admiral Ronarc'h's brigade of French Marine Fusiliers, 6,000 strong, which had been rushed north on the same errand.

This force, which was to play so remarkable a part in the next stage of the struggle, had been hurriedly organised in Paris, Creil, and Amiens, and only started north on the morning of October 7. Consisting for the most part of Breton naval reservists and recruits who had not the least experience of land warfare, its employment in such critical circumstances was a bold experiment, but, under a chief who was to prove himself one of the notable figures of the war—a big, broad-shouldered man, cool till the volcanic moment comes, obstinate, yet with reflection sitting in the eyes of Celtic blue—these sons of the sea, boys and gray-beards, proved themselves equal to the best soldiers in Europe. "The girls with the red pompon," the Germans called them. But that was before the Battle of Dixmude.[1]

The retreat from Antwerp, though we cannot dwell upon the story, is not unworthy of comparison, except that it was on a much smaller scale, with the retreat from Mons and Charleroi. The first stand was made, on October 9, 10, and 11, in the villages around the east and south of Ghent, when 45,000 German troops were held at bay, the French Marine brigade acting under Major-General Capper, commanding the British 7th Division. It was then decided to retire westward to Aeltre, on the way to Bruges; and the twenty-six miles' march was done during the night, under a wintry moon, the British force covering the rear. After a short rest, a south east turn was made, and Thielt was reached on the following evening.

It is stated that the mayor of one of the neighbouring towns misdirected the pursuers; the bold lie cost him his life, but gave the tired troops the first good night's sleep they had had for some days. On the 13th, they reached Thourout. Here Sir Henry Rawlinson's division

---

1. Dixmude by Charles Le Goffic is also published by Leonaur.

passed southward for Roulers and Ypres; while Admiral Ronarc'h's men and the Ghent force joined the main body of Belgian troops, which had come southward through Bruges to the Yser. King Albert at once rejoined his army, helped in its reorganisation between Calais and Nieuport, and thereafter stayed with it, Queen Elizabeth giving such aid as a woman may.

Chapter 22

The Battles of Flanders

1. The "Race for the Sea"

During this time, by a triumph of transport organisation, the main British Army was taken round from the Aisne to the north west. The convenience of such a movement has already been indicated. Sir John French says:—

> Early in October a study of the general situation strongly impressed me with the necessity of bringing the greatest possible force to bear in support of the northern flank of the Allies.

And, as there was no more danger on the Aisne, General Joffre readily agreed to the transfer. Instead of British reliefs, French infantrymen from the neighbouring armies crept into the trenches below the Chemin des Dames; and, one by one. the three British corps, the cavalry, and their various supports left the hillsides where a thousand or more of their bravest fellows lay buried. On October 3, General Gough's cavalry division marched for Compiègne, leading the way; and by the 19th, by train and motor-bus and taxicab, the whole force had reached the Black Country near the Belgian border. These were, indeed, exciting days on the great north road that passes through Amiens, Doullens, St. Pol, and Hazebrouck, to Calais, Dunkirk, and Ypres, for re-enforcements were being brought up simultaneously for the armies of De Castelnau and Maud'huy: and still another French Army was gathering, under General d'Urbal, which, with the British and Belgians, was to hold the pass from Ypres to the sea.

In order to co-ordinate the movements of this large tri-national combination, General Joffre sent the victor of the centre in the Battle of the Marne, General Foch, who as *generalissimo* of the French northern armies established his headquarters, on October 3, at Doullens. Here he was visited on the 8th by Sir John French; and the two commanders "arranged joint plans of operations."

Before tracing the development of these operations, it will be well to obtain a clear impression of the alignment of forces, as it was completed during October, in this new field between the Aisne and the North Sea. They fall into four zones:

(1) Compiègne-Péronne.—Here we have seen General Maunoury's left extended into the angle between the Aisne and Oise, connecting with General de Castelnau's army. This was holding the first northern positions from Lassigny to Péronne, being prolonged by General Brugère's Territorial units as far as Albert. Early in October, the French offensive directed against the critical point of the German line of communications at Tergnier Junction and St. Quentin had failed. It was followed by a German attempt to break through the corner of the French line which, in turn, failed no less signally. Here an entrenched deadlock similar to that of the Aisne and the eastern frontier was now being reached.

(2) Arras-Armentières.—The main body of General Maud'huy's army reached from Arras toward Lens and La Bassée, with the hope of relieving Lille. This offensive had also failed of its immediate object. By the end of the first week in October, the Germans were in force from Cambrai northward, through Douai, to the east of Lens, and were moving up the right bank of the Lys from Tourcoing to Armentières. We have seen that Lille fell to them on October 13. The joint plan of General Foch and Field-Marshal French was made, on the 8th, in the hope of better fortune. The British 2nd Army Corps, with the British and French cavalry on its northern flank, was to connect with Maud'huy's left, and there was then to be a general eastward advance, the British right being directed on Lille. When the 3rd and 1st Corps arrived on the northern front, they were to cooperate in this movement. Sir Henry Rawlinson's Division was for the present to support the Belgian Army, and a thin line, chiefly of cavalry, was to act between the Yser and the Lys. We shall see how, in this region, the course of events converted the intended Battle of Lille into the battle of the Lys.

(3) Ypres—The fall of Antwerp on October 9, followed by the German occupation of Ghent on the 12th, Bruges on the 13th, and Ostend on the 15th, was the prelude to a swooping attack of immense power upon the unprepared lines of the Allies between Ypres and the sea.

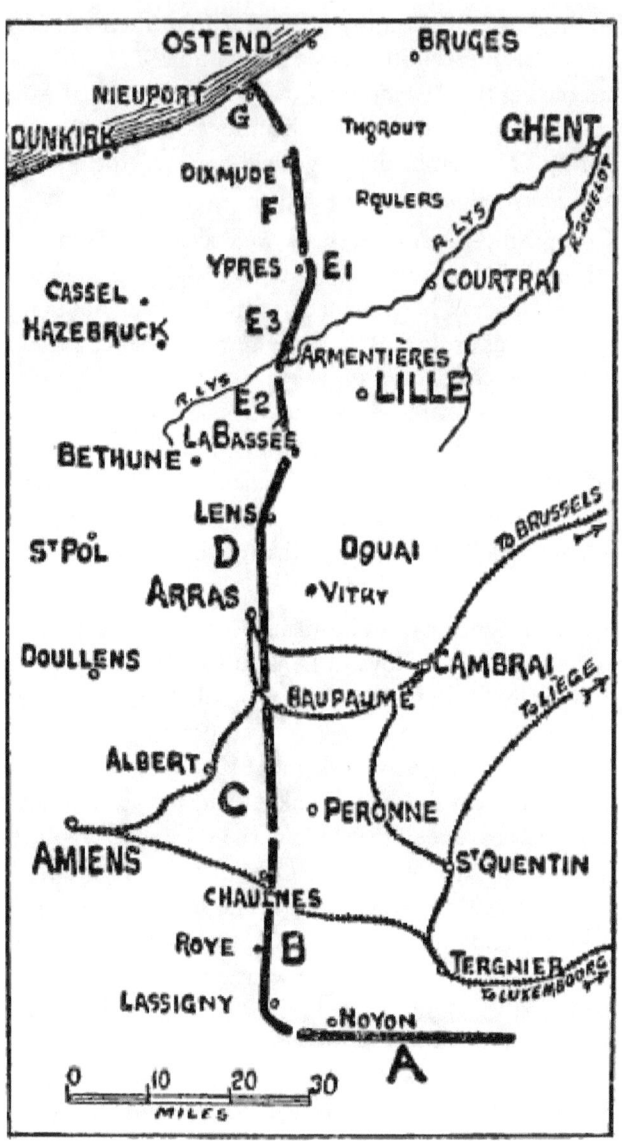

THE WESTERN ARMIES.

G, Belgian Army. F, General d'Urbal (French "Army of Belgium"). E, Field-Marshal Sir John French, 1st, 2nd, and 3rd Corps (with French Divisions under General Bidon). D, General Maud'huy. C, General Brugère. B, General de Castelnau. A, General Maunoury.

The German Staff neglected nothing to turn us. On the part of the front extending from the Lys to the sea. it threw, from the beginning of October to the beginning of November, four corps of cavalry and four armies comprising altogether fifteen army corps. Their heads, the Crown Prince of Bavaria, General von Fabeck, General von Deimling, and the Duke of Würtemberg, issued to their troops appeals and exhortations which agree in announcing 'a decisive action against the French left.' It must be pierced at Dunkirk, or at Ypres.., . Further, the Emperor was there to encourage his soldiers by his presence. He announced that he wished to be in Ypres on November 1, and everything was prepared for the proclamation on that date of the annexation of Belgium."

(*Bulletin des Armées.* November 25, 1914.)

The main weight of the latter attack fell upon the left wing of the British force; and we shall see, in the battle of Ypres, one of the most remarkable cases recorded in history of successful resistance against overwhelming numbers.

(4) At the same time, the remainder of the line of the Yser Canal was defended by the Belgian army and the newly organised French "Army of Belgium" under General d'Urbal, which included Admiral Ronarc'h's Marine Fusiliers. The attacks upon this line between the middle of October and the end of the year were like in character and aim, and they may be collectively regarded as the Battle of the Yser.

With the last three series of actions, we have now to deal. They began with the Allied armies hastening forward in scattered fragments to new positions that had for long lain behind the main German lines. The spirit of the offensive in which this new front was taken up is very marked in the dispatches of Sir John French. It was soon checked; but as much ground had been won back by this short forward rush as by the Battle of the Marne, and, speaking broadly, what was won was held. At Nieuport and Dixmude, at La Bassée, and at the outstanding bastion of Ypres between, the German aim was the same: to cut through to the English Channel, enveloping or piercing and routing the Allies on the way.

The effort made was gigantic. From the barracks where half instructed recruits and gray-headed reservists were drafted into the active line, through every stage of an organisation that still maintained much of its original speed and exactitude, to the battlefields where, week after week, through failure after failure, these raw levies sacrificed themselves in massed assault, the powers peculiar to the Prussian military system received a final demonstration. There is much to question, but not the bravery of these thousands of victims. Since they failed, however, despite the advantage of superior—at some points, vastly superior—numbers, and of interior lines of movement, we must conclude that the Allies possessed, beside a higher general inspiration, either greater intelligence in command or a stouter manhood in the resistant mass, or both. After failure on such a scale, what hope of success could remain when the superiority of numbers had passed away?

2. The Battle of the Lys

We have seen that, in the hope of relieving Lille, a general advance eastward had been decided upon, the British 2nd Corps. under Smith-Dorrien, with the British and French Cavalry Corps of Generals Allenby and Conneau, moving along the Lys Valley, and the French forces southward of the Béthune-Lille road. Sir John French speaks of "the great battle" as opening with a cavalry engagement amid the woods to the north of the Aire-Béthune Canal, on October 11. But a party of forty Bavarians had made a raid upon the station at Hazebrouck (presently to become a British base) on the 8th, killing two sentinels, a train-driver, two women, and a little girl; and on the 10th, Conneau's dragoons, having crossed the Lys from the north, between Merville and Estaires, had dispersed a body of *Uhlans*.

On the 11th, Smith-Dorrien's infantry crossed the Aire-Béthune Canal, eastward, with the intention of piercing the line of the Bavarian Army, which extended from the sharp hill called the Mont des Cats, near the Belgian frontier, through Bailleul, across the Lys at Estaires, and struck, between Béthune and La Bassée, southward to the west of Lens and the east of Arras. The 5th and 3rd Divisions became engaged east of Béthune, where they touched General de Maud'huy's left; and despite the obstruction of the ground with mine-heads, factories, and streets of workmen's cottages, and its flat and swampy character, some progress was made. On the 13th, General Smith-Dorrien commenced an attempt to get astride the La Bassée-Lille road, and thence to strike around the German flank. The Dorset regiment suffered heavily at the village of Pont Fixe; and on the following day the 3rd Division lost its commander. Sir Hubert Hamilton, who was struck by a shrapnel bullet while riding along the lines. Sir John French says:—

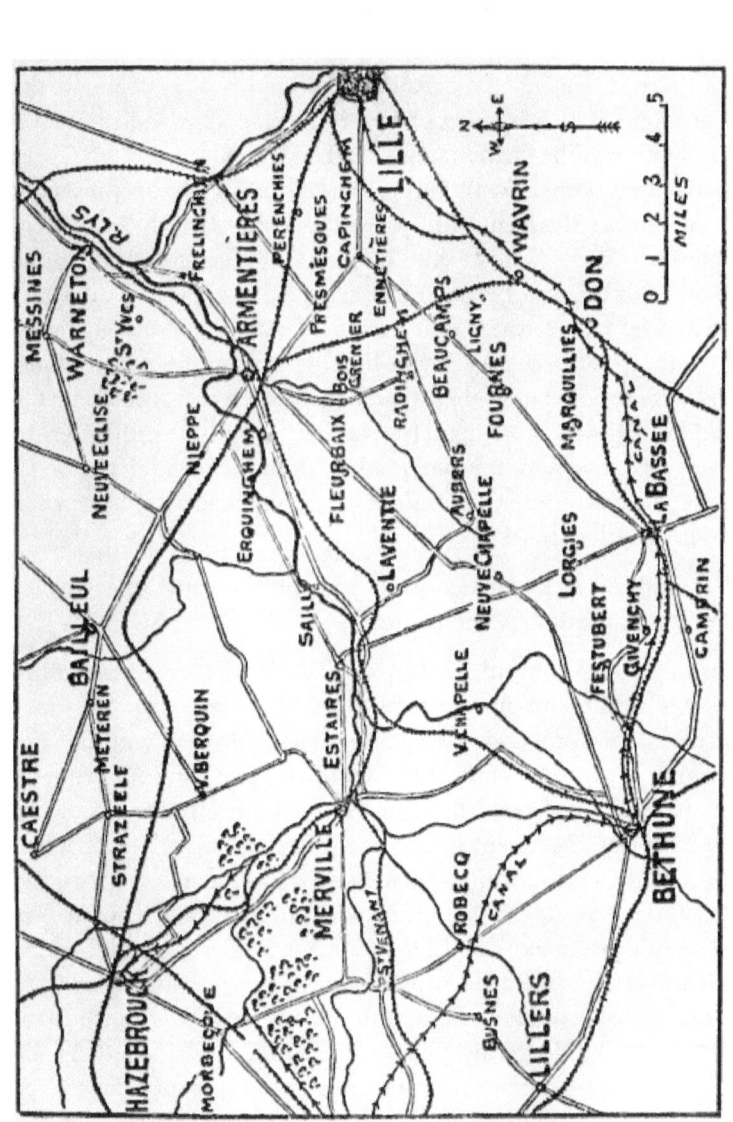

The Battle of the Lys

On the 15th, the division fought splendidly, crossing the dykes with which this country is intersected, with planks, and driving the enemy from one entrenched position to another in loop-holed villages, till at night they pushed the Germans off the Estaires-La Bassée road.

On the 17th, the villages of Aubers and Herlies were captured, the latter at nightfall by a bayonet charge of the Lincolns and the Royal Fusiliers. This was the furthest point reached. The German 14th Corps and parts of two others, with four cavalry divisions, had been brought north to protect this flank; and for ten days the British 2nd Corps (re-enforced on the 24th by the Lahore Division of Indian troops, and by the 8th Infantry Brigade) was subjected to a series of desperate counter-attacks. Once the Royal Irish were cut off and surrounded in a village they had occupied, losing heavily. Once the Gordon High-landers were driven out of their trenches; these were recovered by the Middlesex regiment. On the 21st, the left wing was withdrawn to prepared positions; and, thereafter, a line from Givenchy (west of La Bassée) to near Laventie was resolutely held. As Field-Marshal French wrote six months late:—

> This position of La Bassée has throughout the battle defied all attempts at capture by the French or the British.

Further north, the 3rd Army Corps, under General Pulteney—Conneau's cavalry linking it with the 2nd Corps—had advanced down the roads from Cassel and Hazebrouck eastward, with the aim of reaching Wytschaete (four miles south of Ypres) and Armentières (where it would threaten Lille). The German 4th Cavalry Corps was driven back from Meteren; and on the morning of the 14th, Bailleul was occupied. Next morning "in the face of considerable opposition and very foggy weather," the left bank of the Lys from Sailly to Ar-mentières was occupied; and on the 17th, when the 2nd Corps was at Aubers and Herlies, the 3rd Corps continued the line northward from three miles north to three miles south of Armentières. Unfortunately, the 2nd Corps could get no further. The 3rd Corps reached, on the 18th, through Armentières into the western suburbs of Lille—Cap-inghem and Premesques; then it, also, had to retire. Heavy German re-enforcements, delivering a series of determined attacks in which lines of trenches were repeatedly lost and recovered, immediately ex-plain this failure.

The two corps were being tried beyond human strength. The 2nd Corps was exhausted by very heavy losses. General Allenby had taken Warneton, but found the lower line of the Lys held in force, and had been unable to establish a permanent footing on the east bank. Yet the ranks of the 3rd Corps lay across the river, its over-long front of a dozen miles presenting many weak spots. Sir John French says:—

> It was impossible to provide adequate reserves, and the constant work in the trenches tried the endurance of officers and men to the utmost. That the corps was invariably successful in repulsing the constant attacks, sometimes in great strength, made against them by day and by night, is due entirely to the skilful manner in which the corps was disposed. . . . The courage, tenacity, endurance, and cheerfulness of the men in such unparalleled circumstances are beyond all praise.

The conditions had greatly changed since the advance upon Lille was planned. Antwerp had surrendered. The Belgian Army, with the British and French naval brigades, had drawn back to the Yser. The whole of the German forces in Belgium were now free to carry out the programme of their Imperial master. Whether the main blow should fall at Dixmude or at Ypres, its success would require the immediate abandonment of any positions gained by the Allies across the Lys. When the field-marshal directed General Rawlinson, on October 17, to march the 7th Division east from Ypres to Menin, the French cavalry to go north toward Roulers—with the idea of cutting the German communications between Courtrai and Lille—the commander of the 4th Army Corps replied that the whole position at Ypres was threatened by the advance of large hostile forces from the east and northeast. Sir John French was evidently reluctant to abandon the Menin passage and the line of the Lys. But when the 1st Army Corps reached Hazebrouck from the Aisne on October 19, the only question was whether Ypres or the east of the Lys—unless, indeed, playing for safety, both—should be given up. The decision was an heroic one. The commander in-chief says:—

> I knew that the enemy were by this time in greatly superior strength on the Lys, and that the 2nd, 3rd, Cavalry, and 4th Corps were holding a much wider front than their numbers and strength warranted. . . . To throw the 1st Corps in to strengthen the line would have left the country north and east of Ypres and the Ypres Canal open to a wide turning movement. . . . After

the hard lighting it had undergone, the Belgian Army was in no condition to withstand, unsupported, such an attack; and. unless some substantial resistance could be offered to this threatened turning movement, the Allied flank must be turned, and the Channel ports laid bare to the enemy. I judged that a successful movement of this kind would be fraught with such disastrous consequences that the risk of operating on so extended a front must be undertaken; and I directed Sir Douglas Haig to move with the 1st Corps to the north of Ypres.

The withdrawal of the 2nd and 3rd Corps to defensive positions followed upon this decision; and the battle of the Lys resolved itself, on the part of the Allies, into a struggle to hold a front connecting Ypres, through Armentières, with General de Maud'huy's positions before La Bassée and in Arras, with the knowledge that no considerable re-enforcements were possible, and that failure would be disastrous. At the end of October, severe attacks were made all along the line of the 3rd British Corps. During the night of the 25th, the Leicestershire regiment was driven from its trenches by shells blowing in the pit in which they were dug. Four days later, the Middlesex regiment lost its trenches at Croix Marechale, near Fleurbaix, in a midnight attack; but they were recovered, 200 Germans being bayoneted and forty made prisoners. On the 30th, the line of the 11th Brigade near St. Yves (between Neuve Eglise and Warneton) was broken. It was restored by a counter-attack by the Somerset Light Infantry, The Cavalry Corps, operating further north, around Messines and Hollebeke, was incessantly attacked.

Support was sent to Wulverghem from the 7th Indian Infantry Brigade; and part of the 2nd Army Corps and the London Scottish Territorial battalion were moved to Neuve Eglise. For forty-eight hours, the Cavalry Corps had to withstand the shock of two nearly fresh German army corps; it was then relieved by the French 16th Army Corps and General Conneau's cavalry. The London Scottish had particularly distinguished themselves at Messines by repeated bayonet charges against greatly superior Bavarian forces. About dawn on Sunday, November 1, they were caught in a cross-fire of rifles and machine-guns, and retired with the loss of nearly a third of one battalion killed and wounded, having, as the commander-in-chief afterward said, given "a glorious lead and example" to other Territorial units. The Indian troops also proved their steadiness in the strange and terrible conditions of western warfare. The Lahore Infantry Division was heavily engaged at Neuve Chapelle (three miles north of La Bassée; Sir John French mentions particularly the gallantry of the 47th Sikhs and the 3rd Sappers and Miners. After the arrival of the Meerut Division, the Indian Corps took over the line previously held by the British 2nd Corps, and repelled many assaults.

Throughout, the neighbouring French forces showed the most admirable spirit of co-operation. Both the French and the British cavalry learned to adapt their traditional methods to the new circumstances, and many a mile of trenches was held for periods by dismounted horsemen. When the Battle of the Lys was beginning, one of the French official bulletins reported "very confused" cavalry fighting. The term referred mainly, but perhaps not wholly, to the nature of the country, which is cut up in parts by pitheads and mining villages, and, further west, by canals and streams. Here the cavalry regiment would go out attended by a cartload of spades and picks to make trenches. Leaving their horses half a mile behind, half of the men formed a firing-line, while the other half went on in extended order to prepare a more advanced position. They might be for twelve hours in the trenches before they were relieved, and with only such cold food as they took out from camp. And, at any moment, the evil thing might come that happened to Lieutenant Wallon, a brilliant cavalry officer who was known outside of France, before the war, as a champion rider.

It was at the village of Sailly, on the Lys, near Merville. The day had broken with a thick mist lying over the flat, dull country, and a cold wind blowing. The French dragoons advanced over the fields to seize the river bridge, an important crossing. Two squadrons took their places in the trenches before a small farmhouse—to the left a road, to the right a long potato-field, in front the invisible enemy, and beyond them the village. The lieutenant, behind the wall of the farmyard, rose from time to time to scan the front through his field-glasses. Several times small bodies of German scouts came in view; thirty of them were shot down. A more substantial attack was made and repulsed. A short calm followed. Then, eleven men in peasants' dress, with picks and spades over their shoulders, were seen to be advancing toward the French lines. What could they be doing there? No one fired. At 40 yards' distance, as with one movement, they raised each a hand, and a volley of revolver shots rang out. This was a sign for general firing from the enemy's trenches.

A sergeant who stood with Lieutenant Wallon called out with a laugh, as a bullet whistled by, that another "Boche" had missed him. But the lieutenant had fallen, with the ball in his chest. The sergeant lifted him in order to get him away to a safe place. "See, Rossa," said the wounded officer, "leave me. You know a wounded man is worthless. Get back to the trench; they want you there." The trusty non-com. would not budge, and dragged his leader to the rear. Again the lieutenant begged to be left, saying he no longer needed anyone. Three dragoons found a little cart, and, putting the dying man upon a pile of straw, they took him away. The eleven disguised Germans were all shot. They were soldiers. The bridge was taken, and the village occupied. In the evening, around the camp fire, the men spoke of the good officer who had fallen before a neo-German ambush.

3. The Battle of Ypres

When the so-called 4th Corps, consisting of the 3rd Cavalry Division under Major-General the Hon. Julian Byng, and the 7th Infantry Division, under Major-General Capper, reached the neighbourhood of Ypres from Ghent, on October 16, Sir John French was still bent on pressing forward to the north-east. On that day, Capper's force was posted five miles east of Ypres, from Zandvoorde through Gheluvelt to Zonnebeke; while the cavalry lay as much to the north of the beautiful little city, about Langemarck and Poelcapelle. Two French Territorial Divisions under General Bidon were in Ypres and Poperinghe; and. on the following day, four French cavalry divisions under General de Mitry joined Byng's troops along the road to Dixmude, and drove back some German scouts beyond the Houthulst woods. When, on the evening of the 19th, the field-marshal decided to send the 1st Cops to Ypres, he thought that:—

> Sir Douglas Haig would probably not be opposed by much more than the 3rd Reserve Corps, which I knew to have suffered considerably in its previous operations, and perhaps one or two *Landwehr* divisions.

The 1st Corps, therefore, was to advance to Thourout and, if possible, to capture Bruges and threaten Ghent.

This ambitious programme came to nothing. On the 21st, Sir John French was in Ypres consulting with Haig and Rawlinson; and he then concluded that "the utmost we could do. owing to the unexpected re-enforcements of the enemy." was to hold the positions round Ypres for two or three days, by which time General Joffre had promised a relief of French troops. In fact, the Allies had again been taken unawares by one of the German lightning concentrations, so that they found themselves outnumbered by three or four to one at the critical point. The attempted advance came to a sudden stop early on the afternoon of the 21st, when the French Cavalry Corps was forced back to the west of the Yser Canal. No summary can do justice to the frightful series of struggles that ensued. Day after day, with an apparently inexhaustible energy, the gray-coated German columns of Generals von Deimling and von Fabeck were hurled against the thin lines of the defence; night after night, the exhausted survivors crept out to repair the broken parapets of their trenches, or the barbed-wire network in front.

Late in the evening of the 22nd, the part of the line held by the Cameron Highlanders was cut; it required hard fighting all the next day by the Queen's Northamptons, and King's Rifles, to recover the lost ground. At Langemarck, on the same day, after an attack upon the 3rd Infantry Brigade, the bodies of 1,500 dead Germans were counted on the field. A French line division and some Territorials were brought up; and on the 25th, an advance was made to the north-east. During a lull before the next grand attack, what was left of Sir Henry Rawlinson's command was absorbed in the 1st Corps.

The tide of battle ebbed and flowed, but the line was still held with little change. On October 29, a mass assault by the German 24th and 15th Corps was delivered on the Menin road east Gheluvelt; by dusk it had been repelled. This attempt to drive through to the south of Ypres was repeated on the following day, with more serious results. A slight ridge at Zandvoorde was seized, and the 3rd Cavalry and 7th Divisions had to withdraw to Klein Zillebeke, only three miles outside Ypres. Some French and British detachments were ordered round to the weak spot, with instructions to hold out at all costs. Sir John French says:—

> An order taken from a prisoner captured on this day purported to emanate from General von Deimling, and said that the 15th German Corps, together with the 2nd Bavarian and 13th Corps, were entrusted with the task of breaking through the line to Ypres, and that the emperor himself considered the success of this attack to be one of vital importance to the issue of the war.

When the crisis was reached, on the 31st, therefore, the two British

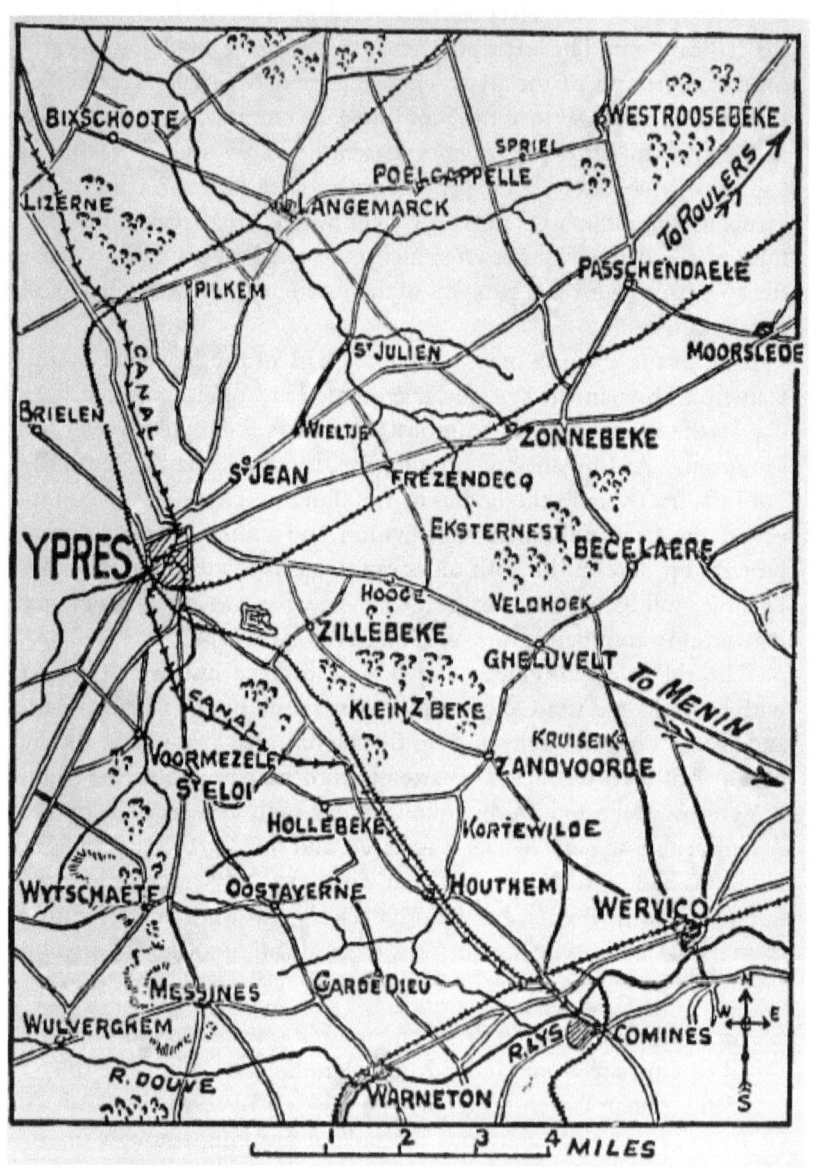

THE BATTLE OF YPRES

and one French divisions posted across Klein Zillebeke, between the Menin road and the Yser Canal, were not quite unprepared in mind and will, though grievously inadequate in numbers of men and guns. Before noon, the line of the British 1st Division, assailed by a force six or eight times stronger, was broken. Its retirement "exposed the left flank of the 7th Division; and, owing to this, the Royal Scots Fusiliers, who remained in their trenches, were cut off and surrounded." Another disaster of a very exceptional character followed. Early in the afternoon, the house in which the 1st and 2nd Divisions Staffs had made their headquarters was discovered and shelled, General Lomax, commander of the 1st Division, being wounded and three of his Staff officers, and three of the 2nd Division, being killed. Fortunately, the commander-in-chief and his staff were near, and joined General Haig within an hour.

Such a loss in such an emergency would have damped any but the most tried spirits. Moreover, the 22nd Brigade, on the right of the 7th Division, had been compelled to retire, and then the 2nd Brigade, next on its right. When all seemed to be lost, the 1st and 7th Divisions rallied. The former, helped by some of the 2nd Division, swung round against the German right flank, on the Menin road, and, the 2nd Warwickshires leading, recaptured the village of Gheluvelt at the point of the bayonet. This success enabled the 7th Division to bring its left back in touch with the 1st; and it liberated the 6th Cavalry Brigade, which, by a dashing attack, further helped to restore the front. Aid was also forthcoming, late in the afternoon, from the French cavalry. Field-Marshal French says:—

> Throughout the day the extreme right and left of the 1st Corps held fast, the left being only slightly engaged, while the right was heavily shelled and subjected to slight infantry attacks. In the evening, the enemy were steadily driven back; and by 10 p.m. the line as held in the morning had practically been reoccupied. As a result of the day's fighting, 870 wounded were evacuated.

So passed "the most critical moment in the whole of this great battle," the day that was to have made Belgium a German province. One more special effort was made to retrieve the Imperial fortunes before Ypres.

> About November 10, after units of several German corps had been completely shattered in futile attacks, a division of the

Prussian Guard, which had been operating in the neighbourhood of Arras, was moved up to this area with great speed and secrecy. Documents found on dead officers prove that the Guard had received the emperor's special commands to break through and succeed where their comrades of the line had failed. They took a leading part in the vigorous attacks made against the centre on the 11th and 12th, but, like their comrades, were repulsed with enormous loss.

The Prussian Guards numbered some 15,000 men, but they were no longer of the quality of those who had fallen in the marshes of St. Gond. They broke through the lines, but were enfiladed, and fled. The British losses included three commanding officers—Brigadier General FitzClarence, of the 1st Guards; Colonel Gordon Wilson, of the Horse Guards, and Major the Hon. Hugh Dawney, 2nd Life Guards. The last two were killed on November 7, when the 7th Cavalry Brigade was called to support the French troops near Klein Zillebeke.

The Battle of Ypres was followed on November 23 and subsequent days by a long distance bombardment of the town and the destruction of the famous Cloth Hall, a spiteful kind of confession of failure. The siege warfare of the trenches continued: the phase of acute and open struggle involving the fate of a large area, to which alone the word "battle" can now be applied, was finished, at least for the present. Its later stage had been the occasion not only for prodigies of valour on the part of the regular troops, and "quite extraordinary" services by the artillery, the engineers, the flying corps, signal corps and other special arms, but for the baptism of fire of the first units of the Territorial force—the Loudon Scottish and Hereford battalions, and the Somerset and Leicester Yeomanry regiments. Sir John French says:—

> They took a conspicuous part in repulsing the heavy attacks delivered against this part of the line. 1 was obliged to dispatch them immediately after their trying experiences further south, and when they had had a very insufficient period of rest; and, although they gallantly maintained these northern positions until relieved by the French, they were reduced to a condition of extreme exhaustion.

Regulars, volunteers, and the subsidiary services had all earned a share of their leader's tribute:—

> That success has been attained, and all the enemy's desperate

attempts to break through our line have been frustrated, is due entirely to the marvellous fighting power and the indomitable courage and tenacity of officers, non-commissioned officers, and men. No more arduous task has ever been assigned to British soldiers; and in all their splendid history there is no instance of their having answered so magnificently to the desperate calls which of necessity were made upon them.... Words fail me to express the admiration I feel for the conduct, or my sense of the incalculable services they rendered.

Sir John French says that the German losses in the Battle of Ypres were "at least three times as many" as the British. The French War Office estimated them as "at least 120,000 men." Four Victoria Crosses were afterwards granted for gallant actions during this battle; and it is notable that two of them were for life-saving, one of these taking the form of a clasp to a cross already gained, an unprecedented distinction. The official entries for these V.C.'s were as follows:

6535 Drmr. William Kenny, 2nd Bn. Gordon Highlanders. For conspicuous bravery on 23rd October near Ypres, in rescuing wounded men on five occasions under very heavy fire in the most fearless manner, and for twice previously saving machine-guns by carrying them out of action. On numerous occasions Drummer Kenny conveyed urgent messages under very dangerous circumstances over fire-swept ground.

Lieut. James Anson Otho Brooke, 2nd Bn. Gordon Highlanders. For conspicuous bravery and great ability near Gheluvelt on the 29th October, in leading two attacks on the German trenches under heavy rifle and machine-gun fire, regaining a lost trench at a very critical moment. He was killed on that day. By his marked coolness and promptitude on this occasion Lieutenant Brooke prevented the enemy from breaking through our line, at a time when a general counter attack could not have been organised.

Capt. John Franks Vallentin, 1st Bn. South Staffordshire Regt. For conspicuous bravery on 7th November at Zillebeke. When leading the attack against the Germans under a very heavy fire he was struck down, and on rising to continue the attack was immediately killed. The capture of the enemy's trenches which followed was in a great measure due to the confidence which the men had in their captain, arising from his many previous acts of great bravery and ability.

Lieut. Arthur Martin Leake, R.A.M.C, who was awarded the Victoria Cross on 11th May, 1902, is granted a Clasp for conspicuous bravery in the present campaign. For most conspicuous bravery and devotion to duty throughout the campaign. especially during the period 29th October to 8th November, 1914. near Zonnebeke, in rescuing, whilst exposed to constant fire, a large number of the wounded who were lying close to the enemy's trenches.

A thousand acts of zeal, skill, and heroic devotion by those whose duty it is not to take, but to save, life on the battlefield cry for mention. There was a French doctor attending to the wounded in the Civil Hospital during the bombardment of Ypres. For four days, with the help of volunteer assistants, he had been caring for fifty-four German wounded, and the hospital had been struck by shells, one of them an incendiary shell. The supply of bread was failing, but the doctor and nurses shared their portion with their patients. It was suggested to him that they should desert so dangerous a post. His reply deserves textual quotation:—

> Our superiority consists precisely in showing to this race of vandals that we possess those humanitarian feelings of which they seem to be devoid, and that we should do this because example is the only law which nations obey. If we imitate the Germans, there is no reason why the present state of things should not continue for ever, for we are merely descending to their level, whereas the mission of France is to elevate the Germans to our own. So long as I remain here, by your leave, I will continue to look after the wounded Germans, showing them that a French doctor laughs at their shells, and only knows his duty.

This hero did so continue until, on November 13 or 14, he was killed by a shell. The surviving wounded, in sole charge of two nuns, were then removed to a safer place.

Two personal events of political interest here call for notice. The first is the death of Field-Marshal Earl Roberts, on November 14, from illness due to exposure during a visit of inspection and farewell to the Indian Army in France. An official writer said:—

> Only one Englishman has attained to anything near the place

which Lord Roberts filled in the heart of the Indian soldier, and that was John Nicholson, (the hero of Delhi).

During the week November 30-December 5, King George, with the Prince of Wales, visited in succession the four British army corps in the field, the Indian troops, and the various headquarters of the connected services. On December 1, he met President Poincaré, M. Viviani, and General Joffre, who received the G.C.B. decoration. Field-Marshal French was afterwards invested with the Order of Merit; and on December 4 the king met King Albert at Furnes, and inspected some of the Belgian troops.

4. The Battle of the Yser

By this name we mean not chiefly the stream so called, but the canal which runs from Ypres, first beside the little Yperlee, then beside the Yser, which at length it joins to reach the sea amid the dunes by Nieuport. Halfway along this course of twenty-three miles, the Yser Canal touches Dixmude, a large village of 4,000 souls (before they fled, and it was destroyed), happy in their cottages of rosy brick and tile, prosperous in their surrounding beet-fields and grazing grounds, their flocks and herds, and proud of their ancient church of St. Nicholas. In this dead flat land, seamed with canals and dykes, man was ever doomed to a double struggle—against the reluctance of the earth, and the insidious aggression of the water. Between the hills of the French border and the dunes of the North Sea coast, it lay saturated, misty, saved from total submersion only by an intricate system of drainage maintained by farmers' associations under direction of the Belgian Government.

For a population scattered in villages and small towns, a few highroads served—narrow causeways of cobblestone, with broad bands of black mud on either side. A dismal land, under its frequent rains and white mists, though quaint enough in sunshine, with its turning mills, bulbous spires, white farmsteads, and everlasting lines of pollards and poplars: so the tourist might say. But it is the soul that counts, in nations as in men. The wounded spirit of this marshy land had cried its wrong to the world; and Britons and Bretons, Indians and Canadians, ranchmen from the Antipodes and tribesmen from the Atlas had answered the call to help a little nation defending the last miles of its hard-won soil.

Down in their ditches by Dixmude, 5,000 Belgians under General Meyser and 6,000 French marines under Admiral Ronarc'h, held out

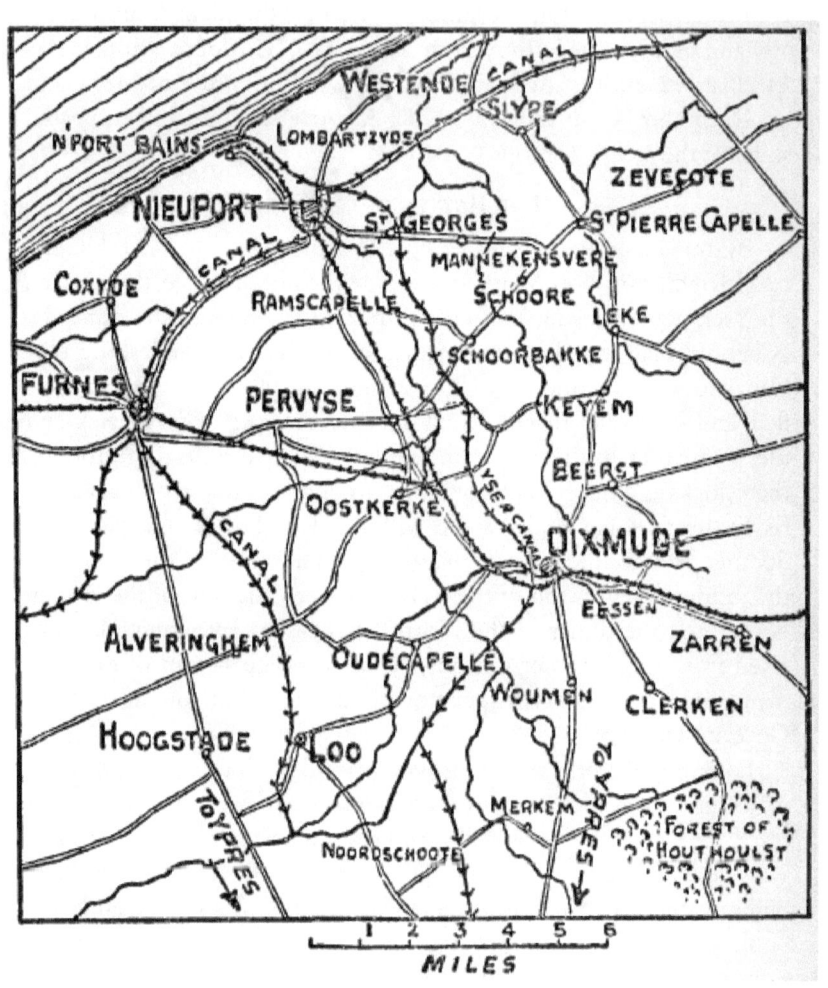

THE BATTLE OF YSER

against three corps of the Duke of Würtemberg's army from October 16 to November 10, in torrents of rain hardly less painful than the fire of the German guns. "You have to sacrifice yourselves to save our left wing," the admiral told them; "try to hold out at least for four days." The four days dragged on to a fortnight, and still these lion-hearted fellows held their place, with no heavy guns, and with no scouting service but that of a few Belgian cyclists. The line of defence ran .at first from Dixmude almost due northward, by the villages of Beerst, Keyem, Leke, to Slype, on the Nieuport-Ostend road, and almost due southward to Ypres—that is, it ran for most of the way two or three miles east of the Yser Canal. The French marines held the centre, in and north and south of Dixmude, with the help, in the end, of a few hundred Senegalese.

Four Belgian divisions, with badly depleted ranks, occupied the Ostend road, with rear trenches on the west of the Yser. South of Dixmude, a French cavalry corps and some Territorials kept touch with the British and French troops around Ypres. The first German attack was delivered at the village of Essen, to the east of Dixmude, throughout the night of October 16 and the morning of the 17th. Although the way was prepared by a lengthy bombardment (the heavy guns had not yet arrived, however), the close columns of infantry were at length driven back. Five Belgian batteries reached Dixmude on the 17th, giving the defence a total strength of seventy two g:uns. There was other cheering news. Field Marshal French had ordered his 4th Army Corps to try to advance from Ypres upon Bruges; and the cavalry of General d'Urbal's 9th Corps, co-operating, had ridden east from the Dixmude-Ypres road and occupied the village of Clerken, whence it was conducting a series of bold raids across the north o the Forest of Houthulst. Admiral Ronarc'h immediately endeavoured to aid this movement.

Re-enforced by two regiments of Moroccan horsemen, a party was sent out eastward toward Thourout. It found the churches of Eessen and Vladsloo in the condition of stables, but no other traces of the invaders. They seemed to have beaten a retreat. In fact, unfortunately, they had only gone along the Ostend road where, on the morning of October 19, they attacked simultaneously three points of the thin Belgian line, at Leke, Keyem. and Beerst. When he discovered this perilous diversion, the French commander sent three battalions, with artillery, to the rescue, one of which was to make a flank assault. Beerst was recovered after a bloody struggle lasting the whole day; but new

German forces had come up, and had captured Vladsloo. The Ostend road had to be abandoned; and, at midnight, the Allies, much exhausted, were back in Nieuport and Dixmude. and the trenches between on the west bank of the canal. All that could be kept—and that with great difficulty—of the northward advance nearer Ypres was the road from Bixshcoote, through Langemarck, to Zonnebeke.

And now the crucial moment had come; both sides must have known it, from the high commanders to the tired and tattered privates. If the line of the Yser were lost, not only would Dunkirk and Calais be imminently threatened; not only would the last thin strip of Belgian soil be lost; the Allied army at Ypres would have to retire rapidly or be surrounded, and all the bloodshed on the Lys would have gone for nothing. No "little band of brothers" ever had a sterner task, and none ever carried their duty to a more heroic triumph. The small Belgian force was being slowly strengthened, and provided with the munitions it had had to leave behind in the retreat. But, with the whole of the long line across France pressed to the utmost, neither the French nor the British Government was able to throw into this end of the field forces numerically equal, or nearly equal, to the new formations which the German Staff had rushed across Belgium for a conclusive effort to break through the extreme left of the Allies.

In this crisis, King Albert found two very powerful friends upon whose appearance the invaders had evidently not calculated. The first was the British fleet, now in fact, and not only in theory, supreme upon the seas, since its adversary had dared to essay nothing but a few trivial raids. On October 18, when the danger at Nieuport had become apparent, the Belgian Government again asked London for naval aid. A flotilla, under Admiral Hood, consisting largely of shallow-draught monitors, carrying powerful long-range guns, was immediately sent across the North Sea, and appeared before Nieuport on the morning of October 19. It was afterwards joined by several French destroyers. Before the German regiments had had time to settle down in the small seaside towns along the coast road south of Ostend—Lombartzyde, Westende, and Middelkerke—or the villages just beyond the dunes, they were overwhelmed with a raking fire much heavier than General Grosetti's artillery could bring to bear upon them. The gunners were directed by observations from naval balloons and aeroplanes, and by signals from shore; and, while their marksmanship proved remarkably accurate, the ships were enabled, by the superior range of their guns and constant movement, to evade all attempts to reach them effectively by ordinary field batteries.

Nor could the German troops easily protect themselves by entrenchment; for, if the trenches and gun-pits were directed toward the sea, they might be enfiladed from the canal, and vice versa. Hour after daylight hour, during the next week, the cannon blazed over the sandhills—one vessel fired a thousand lyddite and shrapnel shells in a day—reaching three miles inland between Middelkerke and Nieuport, destroying batteries, blowing up ammunition wagons. and dispersing infantry columns. On the 24th, heavier batteries that had been established on the sea-front at Ostend were bombarded, much to the discomfort of German officers who had their quarters in the large hotels there. Many fruitless at tempts were made by submarines to torpedo the fleet. By the end of the month. the British Admiralty was able to report that:—

> The opposition from the shore has practically ceased, and the preponderance of the naval gunnery seems to be established.

During this experiment in amphibious warfare, the Belgians and French were defending the river bridge and the three canal bridges at Nieuport, the passage at Dixmude, and their trenches between, against constantly repeated mass assaults. On the 24th, the Germans succeeded in getting across the Yser between Nieuport and Dixmude. The last defensive expedient of the Lowlander was then called into play: the lock-gates were opened, and the country around the high causeways was submitted to a slowly extending inundation. The Würtembergers had scarcely succeeded in destroying the little town of Nieuport by long-range artillery fire, they had scarcely set foot, at the cost of terrible losses in their close-formed ranks, in the village of Ramscapelle, commanding the road through Furnes to Dunkirk, when they found the expected triumph snatched from them. The Belgians and French could well protect the few raised highroads; they had no numbers for long lines of trenches extending inland to Ypres. What they could not do was effected by the floods, extending at first between the Yser and the Nieuport-Dixmude railway, and afterwards over part of the line between the latter place and Bixschoote.

On October 30, Ramscapelle was recovered by a night charge of French *Chasseurs* and Algerian Rifles; and on November 3, the lost passages were completely recovered. Lombartzyde, a mile north of Nieuport, was captured, and lost after several struggles; but generally the stress of the fighting now passed southward. On November 10, the

Germans succeeded in occupying the piles of broken walls and torn street that had once been Dixmude; but they could not cross the canal. Three days later, they secured two passages, only to be driven back on the 15th, when one German regiment was almost annihilated. An even more terrible carnage marked attempts to pierce the wall at Bixschoote and Pervyse.

This extremity of violence, damped by repeated snow and rain storms, soon exhausted itself. One of the last futile struggles raged, about December 5, around the ferryman's house at Poësele, a point of some importance that had been contested for a month. Then the fury of attack died down; the three armies turned to the strengthening of their trenches, not only against each other, but against the common enemies—rain and frost; while the British fleet went north, and bombarded Zeebrugge, now in process of conversion into a German naval station.

CHAPTER 23

Paris, the Austere

Paris. October 10.

Paris is coming to life again. Under the wonderful autumn sunshine, so pure and radiant, there is a fluttering activity that has long been absent from the boulevards and squares. Every day the railway services which, for civilians, had been almost completely suspended after the great flight, are pushed out a few miles further to the north and east. At some hours there are quite considerable numbers of people in the streets. Nearly a half of the shops in the centre of the city must now be open—one sees the tradesmen pluckily dressing their windows, or cajoling a shy customer. The *terrasses* in front of the *cafés* still present a forlorn array of empty chairs; but the chairs are at least a beginning. More restaurants are reopening, and the few that have never shut are fuller. In some mansions, the great gates stand wide, and the shutters are thrown back; one imagines that they have stripped the chandeliers and the pianos of their holiday covers, and that here, as in humbler homes, the family gathers in the evening to hear the "*communiqué*" read, and the little flags moved northward on the map of the battlefield.

At the beginning of August, each new alarm—were it only a tiny column of volunteers, with a flag and a trumpet—brought a crowd on to the pavement. The theatres were already shut, and the crying of newspapers was forbidden. But there was always a crowd, always a noise. Years seem to have passed since then. At the beginning of September came the flight of the half million, immediately followed by the first German defeats. But the invaders might yet return. Every approach to the city was barricaded; it was difficult to come in or go out, and impossible to remain without various kinds of permit. Impossible to get a meal after 8.30; by 10, nearly everybody was abed.

Paris—all, or nearly all, that is essential in the real Paris, save the men at the front—settled down to a stoical acceptance of the hard rules of General Gallieni and the Censorship, a splendid courage of silent waiting.

It was then I fell in love with the Parisian women. Outside their houses, they always seemed to be stitching or knitting, with a grim intentness. Inside, who knows? Marie, who brings me my morning coffee, and whose husband and brother are at the front, asked every morning, as she still asks, for the news; and presently she let fall an occasional complaint that it was impossible to find out whether her soldiermen were alive—not a single letter had come for a month. For the rest, not a tear, not a complaint—though she has sometimes said, like thousands upon thousands of others, no doubt, "God grant this may be the last war!"

When the crowd had gone, with its miserable fears and patent hypocrisies, a strange and blessed calm fell upon us. The blows of those terrible days of the long retreat had fallen too fast upon our hearts to be separately felt. We were stunned. We did the work we had to do, automatically. The swarming, surging masses added an element of squalor to our pain. When they departed, and a perfect quietude lay, defy and night, upon the city, something new was born in us as we became accustomed to the empty vistas, the unbroken silence, the pure air, the majesty of the sky, and—perpetual accompaniment—the familiar thought of Death.

At three o'clock, and again at eleven, we went to get the official bulletins. At first, they were given out, to those duly accredited, in a room full of ancient furniture and arms in the Ministry of War; then in a stable like hall, lit by a bad oil lamp, next door, in the Rue St. Dominique; and latterly in a boys' school taken over for such purposes, opposite the Invalides. For a score of us, 31, Rue St. Dominique, on the evenings after the street lamps had been extinguished or turned low, will be a sacred memory. Journalists do not carry their hearts on their sleeves; but perhaps they feel more than most, as they see more than most in following the threads of tragedy and comedy that colour the common stuff of life. With what fears and hopes we awaited the appearance of the sheets bearing a few typewritten lines, and then groped our way down the blackness of the narrow street to the wide, star-lit spaces near the river!

In the daytime we could sometimes get down to the riverside, or one of the public gardens, and watch the children at their play. For a week or two. it was even possible to make furtive expeditions through the beautiful countryside twice crossed by the two armies. Between the loveliness of such a summer and the rage of hatred and slaughter, can there be any reconciliation? One knows less as one grows older; mystery, the foe of youth, becomes our friend, and we are content to know less. I only knew that, in these still weeks, some secret spirit of the air brought us a new humility, and with it a new fortitude, a sure sense that the unspeakable evil of today must end. because it is only by beauty and love that mankind can live. The witness of the soul is hard to utter. Let the raucous voices pass—the future is not theirs. But there is many a child of good English homes now in the trenches, keeping his vigil under the bright, chill moonlight of early October, who has felt the spirit-finger touch him, and has whispered a prayer for his country not often to be found in the liturgies of the vulgar. It is not these who will blaspheme against the most certain of truths, the truth of the world's need of peace.

And now President Poincaré and the two chief ministers have spent a night in Paris. No doubt they will soon be back for good; and with them will come a swarm of tradesmen and deputies, officials, and *arrivistes*, trippers, and *cocottes*. The Chambers and the Bourse, the hotels and the theatres will reopen, Paris will become "Tout Paris" again. The fugitives will tell each other that it was hard to bear the provincialism of Bordeaux. Everybody will rejoice over the recovery of the only possible capital of France. And a few of us will listen with a silly jealousy, knowing they are robbing us of something of an infinite tenderness and charm that we shall never see again.

It is gone for ever—the austere city, the Paris that was to be besieged. But sometimes, as I walk home in the early morning under the shining purple vault, and breathe deep the frosty air, I may hear again, as I did once, from behind a shuttered window, a voice singing an old song of love and pain and the faith that is stronger than death.

BOOK 4: ROUND THE FRONT IN DECEMBER

CHAPTER 24

Behind the Western Wall

On the Belgian Frontier, November 21, 1914

As the powerful car drew out of the courtyard of the Foreign Office on to the Quai d'Orsay, crossed the city, and passed swiftly through the northern suburbs, I wondered how much our French hosts would allow us to see on this visit to the hidden and tragic land which we call the front. It was the plan to reach the Belgian border in a single long day's journey, a matter of 160 miles or more—as far as from London to Sheffield. On this first day, then, we evidently could see hardly anything of the actual fighting lines along the great wall by which the invasion has been stemmed in western France. But the country immediately behind is nearly as inaccessible as the trenches themselves; and we know, by hearsay and our earlier expeditions, that it teems with a multitudinous secret and peculiar life. In peace time a motor journey from Paris to Dunkirk would be of interest; how much more so when every change of landscape is related to the changing fortunes of a fearful conflict.

The old ramparts and the further forts and field-works of Paris were soon left behind. The thin, wintry sunshine of early morning sparkled on the hoar frost in the bracken of the Chantilly woods, and outlined the feathery larch-trunks and leafless undergrowth, but could not yet dispel the mist that hung in the valleys. This is one of the loveliest regions of northern France, showing from each hill-top far prospects of wooded heights and peopled valleys, fading away into purple horizons. Chantilly, with its great villas, parks, and racing-stables, did not suffer very seriously during the German occupation; but at Senlis, eight or nine miles to the east, foul deeds were done. In these towns there is a recommencement of normal life; in the neighbouring villages most of the white plaster houses are empty and shuttered. Here and there, in the fields and woods, squads of Territorials are busy digging new trenches against the possibility of the lines being broken through, or cutting saplings and young trees to build shelters against the more likely evil of frost and storm. At every town or large village, pickets stop us and carefully examine our papers. The unhedged fields are bare and empty. A cart drawn by bullocks, the yoke fixed behind their horns, with low-bent heads and slow gait, passes us. Only the beauty of the scene saves it from appearing desolate.

At Creil we stayed to examine the ruins of a dozen buildings destroyed by artillery tire during the German advance upon Paris. It soon becomes possible to distinguish the havoc of "legitimate" warfare from that of deliberate incendiarism. Creil is in the former category; the German retreat took a more easterly road. The bridge over the Oise was destroyed; and traffic now depends upon a rough plank structure. As we came up, a soldier's funeral was crossing, a priest at its head with two tiny acolytes, then the coffin covered with a flag, on which lay a small cross of thin wood, and, last, a file of the dead man's comrades-in-arms. The sad procession was too familiar a thing to attract much attention from the townsfolk.

Here we left the woods, and entered a region of vast, warm, rolling downs, cut periodically by the valley of a westward moving river—the Oise, the Somme, the smaller Authie and Canche, and, lastly, the Lys, which, however, runs north-eastward, between Hazebrouck and Lille, to join the Scheldt at Ghent. All these streams have played their part in the war—the Somme and Oise, in particular, by giving the British and French armies opportunities for delaying actions during the great retreat, and the Lys as the border-line of the effort to relieve Lille. After the battle of the Marne, or, rather, after the battle of the Aisne had ended in the deadlock which still continues, the geographical character of the campaign altered. The Allies turned the western corner between Montdidier and Compiègne, and hurried northward in an effort to outflank the German right, and to break across its lines of communication.

This effort failed—both sides extended their lines till, from above Paris, straight up to the North Sea coast in Belgium, there stood a double wall which could be pressed a little this way or that, but which neither side has yet been able to break down. A human wall, every brick of which is a sacred life, a wall needing daily repair at a cost that can never be measured, resting upon scores of thousands of new-made graves, and the ruins of ancient country towns—Lassigny, Roye, Chaulnes, Albert, Bapaume, Arras, La Bassée, Armentières—and villages whose sufferings will not win even the honour of a record in history.

Behind this fire-riven, smoke-crowned wall facing east and west through a hundred miles of northern France, the downs climb up from the river valleys, and roll away to the coast. The deadness of winter lies over the open lands; and in a belt twenty or thirty miles wide the small communities are living almost wholly on and for the army. In the few hotels and large inns, officers and the more substantial sort of refugee or displaced inhabitant crowd together in something almost approaching to comfort. Amiens, the only considerable city along the line, drags on a thin, dull kind of existence. The trams are running; the shop windows cry out for the return of the wealthier inhabitants, who fled when the Germans came, but did not like military and police rule well enough to come back when they left. Placards of September 4 may still be seen on the public buildings warning the citizens not to make hostile demonstrations, forbidding motorcars to leave the town, and stopping the sale of all newspapers.

Though the trenches are only twenty miles away, there is no fear of a new visitation of the enemy, with new lists of requisitions, tines, and hostages. But everything; is abnormal; all usual interests and duties have lost their weight; one single reality—typified in the ambulances and hospitals, and the trains of supply wagons—dominates the thoughts of every man and woman, and even of the urchins who crowd about us as though visitors from Paris were as rare as a thumping good dinner.

From Amiens, we went north eastward, getting off our route and too near the zone of fire below Arras. Between the scattered, solitary farms, on the fine highroad or the muddy bypaths, we met occasional wayfarers, carrying packs on their backs, or pushing a barrowful of household goods, and, more frequently, a Red Cross car, a column of cavalrymen taking up remounts. or a line of big, hooded supply wagons. Some of the villages are simply dead, only a few miserable old folk remaining. Others have been taken possession of for rest-camps or depots; and here you see the streets of cottages bustling with the come-and go of privates, petty officers, and transport drivers, the yards full of horses corralled under rough straw shelters. Then again, you are out upon the bare countryside, the expanse of fields broken only by clumps of trees, haycocks, or heaps of manure and ensilage—a ragged, afflicted scene.

The road runs down into Doullens, past the high brick wall of the old citadel, now a Red Cross station, and up over another plateau toward St. Pol. These two old-fashioned market towns are the chief points on two railways connecting the coast with Arras. Unfortunately the Germans have, on their side of the great wall, many small towns that must be very useful to them for supplies, and a close network of railways. Beyond St. Pol the air has a more northerly bite; on the bleak hills large farmhouses, with deep tiled roofs, are more frequent, and the fields, cut up by hedges and lines of trees, have a familiar look. To our right, towards Lens and La Bassèe, pithead dump-heaps stand up for all the world like the pyramids on the margin of the Egyptian desert. A few smoking chimneys show that some of the collieries are still at work in the rear of the French trenches. At Aire, we cross the little river Lys, which has seen so many hard fights. Then we reach the quietude and beauty of Cassel, on its sharp, lonely height, from which the sea is visible on the one hand, and the battle lines in Belgium on the other.

It is pretty certain that Calais never loomed in the mind of the German Staff as prominently as it did in certain parts of the British Press. Except as a scare centre, Calais would be useless to the Germans while the British fleet is free and France is unconquered. Dunkirk would have been as good and much easier to take and keep. At any rate, the northern battles have another significance. When the contending hosts turned the corner where the Aisne falls into the Oise, and stretched northward in the effort each to outflank the other, the attacks became more and more desperate as one part of the wall after another was solidified, and as the point was being reached, on the Belgian coast, where outflanking became impossible. On the German side, particularly, they became most violent about Ypres and Dixmude for reasons quite unconnected with any insane idea of attempting the invasion of England.

In the first place, railway communications with Germany are here more direct and abundant than further south, so that it was easier to concentrate masses of men for a smashing blow. Secondly, success here would automatically relieve the Allies' pressure upon Lille; and a considerable success would rob them of a strip of coast containing four important seaports in a space of only fifty miles—Dunkirk, Gravelines, Calais, and Boulogne. To seize that strip of coast would not really threaten England; but it would be a most useful agency of panic on the one hand and triumphant advertisement on the other; and it would materially hamper Anglo-French communications.

The northward progress, then, showed a continual aggravation of attack until a new stage of deadlock was reached. Deadlock, however, is only a relative term. In this case, it involves unceasing struggle for trivial advantages, under conditions the most trying warfare has ever presented—except that there is no actual starvation, and that a large proportion of the sick and wounded quickly recover, thanks chiefly to the excellent road and railway services on both sides. It is for the present, on the part of the Allies, a contest of endurance and organisation, preparatory to a more decided offensive. There is already a real resumption of the offensive, but it is more apparent in the spirit of the men than in the outlaid course of events. They know that there is a long, hard path before them; but there is no sign of wavering. One peculiarly damaging effect of the spirit of conquest is that it blinds its victims to the extraordinary power of will which it arouses in defence of a threatened fatherland. And a Prussian war of conquest excites this resistance in the highest degree, because the Prussian spirit of dominance combines so many odious qualities and is repugnant alike to all the nations, and every part of each, that is threatened by it. Differing in nearly everything else, they agree upon this, that a Prussian victory or Prussian rule are things utterly and finally intolerable.

It is a very simple frame of mind; but the faces we see, the talk we hear, the concentration of energy which seems to increase as we approach our destination at the end of the great north road of France, all impress afresh upon us the elementary truth that the Allies will win because the peoples know that European life would be unbearable without this victory. The khaki-clad Englishmen look younger, trimmer, more expert. The French in their long blue coats, so often ill-fitting and shabby, look more like fathers and citizens. There are differences more real than those of appearance, deep differences of experience and character. But, as the night comes up around us, with its great winds and its bitter cold; as the mighty wagons, with blazing headlights, loom up out of the mystery before us and pass into the darkness behind; as we catch a sound of song in passing through the shadows of a village camp, or meet the challenge of pickets on the edge of a town where larger movements are afoot, I reflect that there is being forged in this dreadful furnace of war a brotherhood of two races such as diplomatists could never conceive, a unity of heart and purpose that may last out our time, if we are wise, and far beyond.

Chapter 25

From Furnes to Ypres

At the Front in Flanders, November 28.
There is, in a certain village just behind the canal which runs southward, twelve miles, from Dixmude to Ypres, a certain trench from which, if ever, the Invisible War should become visible. It represents the advanced firing-line at a point where the battle of the Yser took, and may again take, a character of sustained violence. It is of a construction that has become familiar from newspaper photographs—not one of the extensive subterranean galleries with kitchens and rest rooms that are to be the winter quarters (perhaps) of the Allied lines further south, but a narrow alley cut deep in the brown, clayey soil, with transverse sections, and, in the front, an open gallery at which the riflemen stand. The opening is only about 18 in. deep, from the turfed and sanded roof, supported by pieces of tree-trunk, to the ledge on which the rifles lie in action. The nearest building of the village is within a stone's throw. The men have no need here for more extensive arrangements; they come down, and are relieved at intervals, and the line of communications is so good that the intervals need not be long. The German trenches are on the other side of the Yser Canal, no more than 300 yards away to the east. Imagine the excited interest with which we looked out upon this expanse of dead-flat land, fields of grass and stubble broken by hedges, dykes, and lines of polders, where one of the crucial stages of the mightiest conflict of modern times has just been settled.

There is no doubt about the bloody work that has been done Most of this village is in ruins—a few blackened walls, yawning over heaps of brick and plaster, mark what were lately its humbly prosperous homes; the church is a broken skeleton, the vane and tip of the steeple hanging over on a thread which I guess to be the lightning conductor.

It is still a mark for the German artillerymen-the *boo-o-m* of their big guns breaks out intermittently; and a battery of French field-pieces close to our right replies with its lighter *rat-tat-tat*. But all we can actually see from our trench can be put in a couple of sentences. A shell bursts rather uncomfortably near, with a sudden flash of fire and cloud of dust Further away, to the north, a small village is blazing yellow tongues of flame rising clear against the gray sky. *Not a single human being is visible at any point of the compass.*

The particular phase of the Battle of Flanders which has been and probably will continue to be called the Battle of the Yser—that is, the desperate effort of the Germans to get across the canal—is over. Fighting continues; but it has not yet revealed any new objective, and one has the impression that it is only a mischievous sort of marking time, a warning from each side that it is not to be caught unawares, that the last word is not yet said. The fighting however, does unmistakably continue, for we have watched the ammunition wagons going in at one end of the process, and the ambulances taking the wounded men out at the other end. But it bears hardly any resemblance to the product of heated imaginations which I have called the romantic illusion.

While we were hurrying through from Furnes to Ypres, along the highway which runs parallel with the Franco-Belgian lines, a breakdown in front brought us to a sudden stop The best of these Flanders roads consists of a cobbled centre not wide enough for two vehicles to pass, with broad bands of mud on either side. For twenty minutes we stood watching a dozen *Zouaves*, with several horses, trying to get a cart out of a hole in the road. The guns were banging away to north and south of us, and once a rain of shrapnel burst over a line of willows just across a field on our left. To me there was much more reality in the hogged cart than in the shrapnel. They say it is bullets, not shells, that the men fear. I can understand this now without being able clearly to explain. The one is a silent, multitudinous messenger of death; the other makes a noise and a show altogether disproportionate to the damage done—at least, in the open field. Among buildings it is another story.

We examined Pervyse and Ypres particularly. Pervyse lies six miles east of Furnes and half way between Nieuport and Dixmude. This large village was one of the points of stress in the second phase of the Battle of Flanders. The first phase may be counted as extending from the cavalry advance which protected the landing of the British Expeditionary Force to the rallying of the Belgian Army after the fall of Antwerp; and it consisted essentially in delaying the German advance. The second phase centred in the German attempt to get round the Allies by the coast way, between Nieuport and Dixmude, the former place being defended by the Belgians (to the point of absolute exhaustion), under General Grosseti, and the latter, with heroic obstinacy, by Admiral Ronarc'h and his Marines. These attacks being defeated, there followed what has been called the Battle of the Dykes, the defence by inundation which proved locally decisive; and the centre of pressure was then moved southward, the Germans trying to break through between Bixschoote and St. Eloi—that is to say, around Ypres.

If either Pervyse or Ypres had been lost, the effort to keep a hold upon at least a corner of Belgian territory would have failed, and the Allied line southward would have been imperilled. Both places are important road centres, and both are served by railways—matters of critical moment in this country of dykes and ditches. Both, therefore, were defended with desperate determination, and with such success that, after losing 120,000 men in three weeks, the German Army had no more strength to attack, and has now lain idle in its trenches for a week, apparently incapable of a new initiative.

We came to Pervyse along the cobbled causeway, under a faint winter sun that silvered the canals and the flooded meadows. The windmills, the white cottages, the bulbous church towers, which are the common features of the Flemish landscape, now look down upon no humdrum labours of home and field, but upon columns of bluecoated infantrymen marching to or from the front, batteries ingeniously hidden in the willow thickets, Red Cross vans *laagered* in the farmyards, upon pickets of dragoons and *cuirassiers* and parks of artillery, pitched and bivouacked in orchards and gardens, and upon all manner of convoys—interminable lines of ammunition wagons, supply wagons, and cars carrying or to carry the wounded to the nearest ambulance. Through hurly-burly such as this we came to Pervyse. I have seen ruins, south of the Marne and the Aisne, that hurt me more, because there was time to learn what such an agony of modest homesteads may mean. Pervyse cannot have been anything but a very modest townlet; and, as it is still under fire, and the courteous officers under whose guidance the French Government has placed us are unconscionably anxious for our safety, there was no opportunity to realize fully how this little community was destroyed.

Many of the houses show marks of rifle-fire, as well as the shattering effect of shells. There remains a part of the outer walls of a large building that seems to have been a convent, for, high above the central doorway, the figures of Virgin and Child still stand in their niche, overlooking the scene of desolation and blind fury. Threading our way over a litter of broken masonry, timber, and ironwork in the churchyard, we reach the entrance to the church, now blocked by a mass of rubble, on top of which lies a great bell, fallen from the tower. The transept and aisles are quite open to the sky; and the floor is buried deep in broken brick and glass and charred fragments of the roof. The tower stands, but it has a perceptible tilt, which is said to be due to the force of the shell fire.

They tell a story of a certain general sitting calmly in a chair at a street corner near Pervyse church for two hours, while shot and shell were showered upon the place. The French officers repeat these fables with the tolerant, take-it-or-leave-it air of the scientific man who knows that the mighty public must be entertained, but knows also that all popular fables are essentially true. I think there was an addition to the story—of a British officer passing; by who did not altogether approve of this sort of heroism. That, also, sounds true. The French greatly value what they call a *"beau geste."* We have not the word because we have not the thing. For a *"geste"* is more than a "gesture." The one is a trifling sign; the other is a dramatic symbol, given and received with equal sincerity. Many a thing is necessary to an army of two or three millions that has never been, and never needed to be. contemplated for professional troops. But the differences lie deeper down in the minds of the two peoples; and probably these differences, so far from being causes of misunderstanding, actually contribute to the affectionate interest that draws them together to day more closely than any political bonds can do. The martial Frenchman must have his *beau geste*. Atkins demands capable management. They are each getting what they want in full measure.

Ypres is not on all fours with Pervyse. The latter is a small place; and. if a small place is obstinately defended, the fact that its chief building is a church will not avail to protect it from bombardment. Ypres is, or rather was, a town of 18,000 inhabitants. Its unique historical and architectural interest was universally known. If ever a thought be given in war-time to the precious memorials of the past, to the beauty that genius has made and time has enriched, here and now was the occasion for such a restraining thought. The officers of the Allies say that there is no military excuse for this fifteen days' bombardment, and that, in any case, shrapnel would have been as effective as big shells, except for the purpose of sheer destruction.

What I saw for myself is, perhaps, more conclusive. It is that, while large parts of the town have suffered no injury, the famous Linen Hall and the equally ancient, though less rare and beautiful, Cathedral of St. Martin are practically destroyed, with a number of the quaint old houses around them, including the "Nieuwerck," a little two-storey building in Spanish Renaissance style, dating from 1620, attached to the east end of the Linen Hall, containing the municipal offices, and commonly called the Town Hall. This result could not be accidental. It stands as clearly against the German commanders as the less serious damage to Rheims Cathedral, and the destruction of Louvain. Here, as at Louvain, the injury to civilization is irreparable. The high roof of the Halles has gone completely; its charred fragments strew the pavement of the pillared naves, which formed the ground-floor of the vast building. The windows are all shattered, the tiny diamond panes lying amid the heaps of brick and mortar within, and on the pavement outside.

Of the "Nieuwerck," which was only slightly damaged by the earlier bombardment, nothing now remains standing. The delicate pinnacles at the corners of the Halles still point up naked to the sky—strangely naked without their familiar background. The fine rafters and the long gallery of the Cloth Hall have disappeared; and the remarkable wall paintings are hopelessly defaced. Nothing stands inside but the pillars—poor skeletons that cry aloud for pity, like the pillars at Pompeii, or the Propylea on the Acropolis of Athens. The great central tower shows a huge rent in the upper part where the clock was; and on both sides of the tower the *façade* of the Cloth Hall has been smashed in.

Opposite this side of the Halles, a number of houses have been gutted, fragments only of the outer walls standing amid piles of rubble. On the other side lies the cathedral. We could not get within, for the entrance is blocked by a mound of still smoking mortar and stone, the top of which was lit by a faint flame throwing out curious little sparks. This was the remains of the belfry. Of the interior we could only see that there was no longer a roof, and that the floor was a horrible chaos. Everybody notices the odd things that escape the common fate amid these calamities. The stone effigy of some local worthy stands in the path leading to the cathedral door of the cathedral, quite unhurt—as though to emphasise the greater glories that are gone for ever. In the street just outside, a shell has dug a hide large enough to swallow up a horse and cart: it happened to strike the top of one of the town sewers. The station was naturally the first mark for the German guns; and, in the neighbouring square, houses, a large factory, and a large school have been knocked to bits. But all this is nothing beside the loss of that which has been a joy and pride to good men for 600 years and having been demolished in a fortnight of frenzy, can now never be replaced.

Out to the north and south of Ypres as we left the now depopulated town, the infantry of the Allies were pushing their lines a little forward. They might have been a thousand miles away for all we could see of them. The boom and rattle of the guns, close, yet muffed like stage thunder, followed us as we passed through the dead streets, and reached the mud-bound causeway which is one of the main arteries of the war.

You want to go further out there to the east, to the trenches and bridge heads of the Yser, into the villages by Bixschoote (which was described to me as a furnace full of unburied bodies), and the mysterious woods toward Messines where the Germans have held so hard? So do we my dear sir. But we have a scrupulous guardian. The nature of things, not any human law, however, is the real obstacle. No one, save those who have lived in the trenches, will ever know what life there is really like. My impression is that nearly all the heroic stories falsify the facts. They crowd together into a small space and time incidents which were scattered widely and happened with undramatic slowness and inconsequence. The most real thing about the battlefield proper must be the long intervals of sheer boredom sordid labour which will not bear to be told, and silent dogged endurance. The occasional incidents—such is the universal passion for a stirring story-are incredibly magnified. Some eloquent sentences have been written about fighting amid snow during the last few days

There has certainly been some snow, but from Paris to Ypres I could not discover a teaspoonful of it remaining. I was told a thrilling story, reminiscent of the Beresina a century ago about several German regiments advancing across the ice-bound Yser and being swallowed up—the ice on the ponds today would not carry a dog. As though the hostelry of the Noble Rose, in Furnes, had not seen enough of high romance in the three centuries of its history, they say that on All Saints' Day, while the Belgian officers were at dinner in the little back room overlooking the yard, a German shell went clean through the upper part of the building and fell into the narrow street. I found perfect peace in Furnes, thus the tide ebbs and flows.

Some stories attain, as I have said, a sort of collective or symbolical truth. It is, I suppose, for that kind of value that soldiers themselves like the war pictures of Detaille. But in general, the romantic illusion is mischievous, because it hides the real life of war, which is not a picnic relieved by episodes of a peculiar sort of play-acting, but a perpetual round of labour incredibly hard, with spells of utter lassitude intermingled; of acute sufferings from hunger and thirst, cold which pierces the weak places of the body and pulls down the courage of the strong and, in a minority of cases, the pain of actual wounds. These things are not, in fact, shown up by any scene shifter's limelight; but, for him who has the eyes to see, they are irradiated from within by a spirit as high and strong as any reflected in our old story-books. I do not hesitate to press this view insistently, because you must empty the bottle of falsehood before you can fill it with truth. The parents and wives and brothers and children of those at the front want to know what sort of a life their men are living, and they have every right to know. Would that it were easier to tell them.

I remember tumbling into the midst of a French infantry regiment on the first day of the Battle of the Marne. It was my first glimpse of the edge of war; and I felt like W. T. Stead when, in his last years, he went to the theatre for the first time. Where was the regimental band? There wasn't one: and from then till now I have never seen one. There are no more bands and standards; they are beginning even to cover the blue and red uniforms of France with khaki, as they have already covered the too-brilliant helmets and *cuirasses*. War has become invisible, not by choice, but by necessity. Why could we not see the infantry pushing forward their lines just outside Ypres yesterday? Because they were underground, and their progress probably consisted only in the capture of a score of yards by mining. This is not the whole story of the front, but it is by far the greater, and an increasing, part of it. At the present moment almost the whole line from the North Sea into Alsace is stationary, and is underground. Battles in the olden sense are rare, and will become rarer. That sort of thing is disappearing, and with it the fierce pride of the old warriors, their professional habits, and their superstitions of glory. Whether we like it or no, so it is.

But courage does not disappear; it is impossible that men can ever have endured monstrous evils more cheerfully, and individual capacity and morale are infinitely higher than they can have been in any previous war. I have met in the last three months a number of bloodthirsty journalists, but not one bloodthirsty soldier (except a poor Tommy, half-mad from fatigue, who wanted to shoot me for a spy). The Frenchmen strike one as quick enough, when needed, for an adventure, and at the same time as serious citizens, fathers of families, factory and office workers, or owners of little shops and farms, whose inspiration, whatever the original responsibilities for the war may have been, is nothing less than duty.

The Britons are younger on the average; and a finer set of men you could not hope to see. Often shy, generally silent, hating heroics, if you want anything doing, here's your man. Though we crossed them repeatedly we were not officially taken to any part of the British lines. But, among various chances, the luck of a motor mishap gave me half an hour's talk with men of the Army Service Corps, and particularly with one of those sergeants in whom you have the average British stuff at its best—clean, straight fellows, now tanned and lined about the cheeks and jaw, but with the keenness of intelligent youth in their laughing eyes; all alive, and ready for anything, men to be proud of, men infinitely too good for this filthy business of war.

It was a dark, icy night, with the moon Hitting between banks of cloud over a village not a hundred miles from Hazebrouck. A hundred and thirty big motor-wagons, in charge of this company of the A.S.C., were ranged up the two sides of the village street—awkward, delicate, very precious beasts, that must be nursed and coaxed and watched if they are to do their work well; and the breakdown of a single wagon may mean that some hundreds of men needing all you can give them, and much more, must go short. So the wagons must have, like the men, not only food (and one wonders how all the wells in the world can produce enough petrol for them), but hospitals for when they are wounded. The company has three complete workshops on wheels, with each of its dynamo and full tool equipment; and it seemed to me there was hardly anything they could not do, in their narrow space under the tarpaulin covers.

The sergeant told me, while his men set our headlights going, that since the beginning of September, including the retreat from Antwerp, his company had not lost a man or a machine. He said it with the touch of proud affection with which an old rider speaks of his favourite horse. "*Necessity is the mother of invention.*" he quoted; and, 'pon my soul, the hackneyed proverb sounded all new and vital. It was bitterly cold among the wagons under the pale moonshine as we parted. I hope those fellows will get back home safely.

It is work, business, organisation, and nothing like stage play, with the officers also. In a certain curious little town which must not be named, we suddenly learned, by the fact that he invited us to meet him, that we were in the midst of the *etat-major* of the commander-in-chief of the four northern armies, General Foch. The general of today does not go about the battlefields on a prancing charger. He sits still in an obscure house, working out the plans of the war as though it were a particularly long, hard, and momentous game of chess. There was no sign whatever to mark this house out from its terrace neighbours; and, within, there was no sign of pomp or comfort. A short, quick-moving, clear-glanced man stepped out of an inner room—the engineer's office of the northern campaign—and stood for three or four minutes in our midst. After greetings, he uttered a sharp speech of about a hundred words, noting the critical character of the twenty days' battle, the endurance and gallantry of the men, and the greatness of the issue. We had not time to thank him ere he had said goodbye and returned to his work. I had been re-reading Ségur, and could not but contrast the new method with the theatrical comings and goings of the greatest of soldiers. General Foch is responsible for a host larger than any Napoleon led, with the possible exception of the disastrous Russian expedition. But no Napoleonic legend will gather around his person or memory; and to say this is not to shadow a distinguished name, but simply to record our passage into a new phase in the development of the world

We should think of the war in terms of the new facts. It is a narrow red line, some ten miles wide and 350 miles long, with, on either side, a hinterland whose colossal activities are directed into a number of channels—main roads, railways, and canals—connecting with the central line. There is never a dull moment at the chief points on this system of communications; and, even between the towns, from Creil into Belgium, the solitude of the wide plateaux of central France is broken day and night by a never-ceasing stream of traffic, all concentrated upon the one appalling task The great green-hooded country wagon of our ancestors still plays a modest part, but the typical vehicle now is the petrol car and lorry. Where have they all come from—the town buses and traders' vans, the powerful touring cars in which officers rush hither and thither; the hospital vans, the motor-cycles of the dispatch-riders, and, above all, the high, lumbering *camions* carrying incredible quantities of bread, meat, and other supplies?

The most trivial incidents of the road reveal something of the romance of this vast agitation behind "the front." There was an English boy standing sentinel at a railway crossing near the frontier, some mother's darling fresh from a public school, straight, and slight, and very clean against the universal mud and murk. His angel face showed his difficulty in understanding the language of the townsfolk, and his anxiety that it should not show. For him, too, I uttered my hurried prayer that he might come safely home out of this devilry.

A column of Belgian infantrymen were marching along a cobbled causeway, returning from the trenches to camp. As he passed me, one of them dropped into the mud a big book, six inches long and two thick, bound in solid brown leather. It was a Bible. Yet some men think all the Covenanters are dead.

An English lady was standing, as we passed, at the gate of a tiny cottage over which floated the Red Cross, watching the mushroom smoke of bursting shells, and awaiting her wounded. Down the road a company of Alpines, with their slouch caps, marched, singing a tune that lilted rarely. There was a handsome young devil of a *Zouave* officer sitting his horse like an image of chivalry. Some woman is waiting for him in a far distant village with a heartful of tears. Three Hindus crouched shiveringly on top of a big cartful of baggage.

We came through pollard-lined, flooded fields to a wayside inn called "Au Duc de Marlborough." The Duke!—and the name conjures up a hundred pictures of campaigns in which England spoke for interests less respectable than now.

The big hall of the goods station at Poperinghe has been made into an ambulance for cases awaiting the daily hospital trains. Three doctors move about in the dusk dressing and re-dressing wounds, and saying kindly words. One man lying by me on a stretcher has both feet bound up. Some of the patients can move about, and are drinking something from cups, with a long drawn enjoyment that shows it is not medicine. The air is full of a faint, sickening odour of disinfectant.

After these wanderings, a Parisian dinner was comforting. As I went to the pay-desk afterward. I observed that the young woman was softly crying her heart out.

"Forgive me, *madame*," I said, "is it a relative at the war?"

"My husband." she replied, "I have not heard of him for three months."

Chapter 26

The Defence of Verdun

Verdun, December 1.

Thousands of French and German soldiers must have noted, as I did, by the metal signposts, that the road to Verdun was, for the one, the road from Paris to Metz, and for the other, the road from Metz to Paris. It runs, broad and smooth like all the great French highways, along the hill vineyards of the Marne Valley, and over the edge of the Brie plateau at Montmirail, to Châlons, across the rolling plain of Champagne, and through the somewhat mysterious region now known to the reader of the French war bulletins as "the Forest of the Argonne."

It has sometimes been thought that the power of movement in modern times was such that physical conditions would never influence the course of warfare as they manifestly did of old. The more I see of the country, however, the more am I struck with the influence of physical conditions in the present war. Taking only the three clearly distinguishable sections of the route just named, it will be seen that the hills above and below the Marne, and the sub-Alpine region of which the Argonne and the Heights of the Meuse are twin portions lightly separated, formed most important barriers against the southward swarm of the German host; while, on the other hand, the relative flatness of the interval between the first two enabled the Würtemberg Army to get sooner to the south. It is, again, no inconsiderable fortune to France that, in the west, her rivers, and the hills defining them, mostly run westward while on the eastern frontier they mostly run northward. To the extent, then, that these features constitute an obstacle (and broken bridges and defensible heights are a real obstacle), both waves of invasion, the northern and the eastern, were hindered. So far as the Germans are now on the defensive, they in turn share these advantages; and that is one reason, which modern trenches do but accentuate, why the greater part of the front today is in a condition of deadlock.

You have only to see the hills above Soissons, the Craonne plateau, the forest clad slopes about Ste. Menehould, and the wonderful girdle of mountains around Verdun, to realise that any force, well-armed and supplied. must be exceedingly difficult to dislodge from such positions. Nearly all this country is of a great beauty that emphasises the horror of the scenes of which it is the theatre. Not the richly crowded, vivid beauty of the best parts of our English countryside; but something more softly swelling and spacious, the difference—is it fanciful to say?—between Mrs. Siddons and the typical figure of the Republic on a coin or in public statuary. One learns to love (I watch many a stranded Tommy, with a friendly astonishment in his eyes, learning to understand) the differences between peoples and the lands that have made them what they are. This, also, is a factor in the future of what I would still prefer to call the *Entente Cordiale*. But, if I attempt now to convey a sense of the landscape of eastern France, it is for its more material, its military significance.

After passing through what they call "*la Champagne Pouilleuse*" (poverty-stricken), from the relative infertility of its chalky soil, it was a grateful change to strike, at Ste. Menehould. the sudden rise of the Argonne, grateful as that first entry into the feet of the Swiss mountains which made a certain morning golden in our youth. A little town of low-roofed houses, perched on a rock on the upper Aisne, and surrounded by thick woods, it seems to have been accidentally dropped here by the giant who planted the villages between Basle and Berne. Its name, taken from a lady who died in the odour of sanctity in the year 600, marks its age. Its more recent history is scant but characteristic. Here Louis XVI was recognised by a postman in course of his fatal flight; Varennes, where he was stopped, lies on the other side of the Argonne ridge, to the north-east—that is, toward the nearest part of the German frontier. Ten miles west of Ste. Menehould (and just north of the road we followed) lies the battlefield of Valmy, where, in the following year, 1792, the soldiers of the Revolution won their first considerable success, driving back the invading Brunswickers by their stiff cannonade. The Brunswickers of today are more redoubtable; but the townlet of Ste, Menehould remains one of the gateways of France, important to take and to hold.

From this point, in pouring rain, we rose by roads that twined along the valley sides, always flanked by forests of smallish trees, close set with much undergrowth, and—this is the point—clearly impenetrable by bodies of troops. The Argonne is about forty-six miles long from north to south, and only ten miles across. The hills rarely rise to 1,000 feet; it is the woods that make them formidable. In the middle of its width, the large village of Les Islettes marks one of the two central cross-roads; and at Clermont we pass out of the mountain belt into lower land stretching to Verdun. We did not visit any part of the Argonne front, although it was only four or five miles away, and, among the burned and battered houses of Clermont, firing was clearly audible. After seeing the ground, however, it is much easier to realise the nature of the struggle that has been going on for the last two months.

The German lines have been pressed northward very slowly but surely; and now the trench and mine warfare wages around the second, more northerly, cross-roads, in the Bois de la Grurie. There are, in fact, only three main roads east and west across the forest; and there is only one main road through its centre connecting these, which comes down from the Bois de la Grurie, through La Chalade, to Les Islettes, and so on to Triancourt. The first east-and-west way is the Gap of Grand Pré, through which the Germans have useful railway, road, and river communications. The second has been, during the past month, and still is the scene of continuous fighting. Running from Varennes, on the east, to Vienne le-Château on the west, the German lines extend almost straightly thence through the Suippe Valley to just above Rheims. Throughout this stretch of country it is hard sapping and mining work between the closely ranged trenches, with small engagements between artillery and scouting parties in the difficult forest heights. The French are attacking this critical line of communications both from the Sonain road on the west, and the Les Islettes road on the south. The third cross-way is as solidly French as the first is, for the present, German; it is the one by which through Ste. Menehould and Clermont we came to Verdun.

Sentries stood in their thatched boxes in the dusk; munition wagons passed, taking out or coming for new supplies—six horses to each caisson, three drivers, and four or five sleepy fellows riding on the wagon. Gradually the woods broke up, the hills softened down; and, after narrowly escaping being cut up in the dusk on a level crossing, we groped our way into the great fortress town, through the frowning gates and walls of the ancient citadel.

Here we are, then, within a day's march (in happier times, not now) of the Lorraine frontier, and only forty miles from the great German stronghold of Metz. Verdun! What memories cling around the name, from that fateful day, over a thousand years ago, when the heritage of Charlemagne was divided, and the eternal Franco-German scission of western Europe began. It is not surprising that, with such a background of history, the old words should obsess our minds, and become rather a hindrance than a help. But time is really a revolutionary youngster, not a gray dotard. It never ceases to spring surprises upon us, and he who seeks facts must beware of the pitfall of words. Certainly Verdun is a "fortress," yet of a kind how unexpected and strange! It has been sealed fast for the last four months (during which time much of France has been overrun) against the Teutonic intruder, and no less against the prying journalist. I am one of the first of that suspected order to be privileged to penetrate into this fastness, and to see it as it is.

But what do I say? "Penetrate"? There was no more apparent difficulty in getting into Verdun than in going down to Brighton for the weekend. When the threat of capture fell upon Paris early in September, it suddenly became impossible to enter or leave the city without a special permit, extremely difficult to obtain. Each gate on the line of the old ramparts had its rifle-pits and *chevauix-de-frise*. Along the eastward and northward roads, there were barricades at which you were stopped, perhaps ten times in the course of a mile, to show your scrap of pink or yellow paper. In the daytime, a sergeant attended by a picket with fixed bayonets came up to your car, examined your pass as a bank clerk examines a dubious check, and generally made you feel that, if you were not a German spy, you looked precious like one.

At night, the sentries waved their red lanterns across the road, and woe betide you if you advanced a foot too far. The bivouac fire gleamed against the black depth of the neighbouring woods; and, far behind, the flashlights searched the sky for night raiders who never came. Such weird scenes, through which we passed to and from the battlefields of the Marne and Aisne, until we were warned off the road altogether, gave us a ridiculous sense of sharing in martial events and of belonging to a capital city which was also a modern fortress.

Verdun presents none of these theatrical effects to her rare visitors. It looks at first sight about as warlike as York or Chester. Its scarps and counterscarps, moat and crenellated towers, are a curiosity, not a terror. We came in after nightfall by the Porte St. Paul, and no bluecoated guards arrested us. We crept by dark and narrow ways through the upper town, past the Place du Gouvernement and the ancient cathedral, to General Sarrail's headquarters; then, after reporting ourselves, crossed the Meuse to our hotel beside the town hall. Verdun is normally a small place of only 22,000 inhabitants; and there are now probably not much more than half this number of civilians in it. At our orthodox dinner hour, everybody seemed to have gone to bed— no Early Closing or Daylight Saving Act ever operated as effectively as this war has done. I will not conceal that if we had depended upon the resources of the Hotel of the Three Moors we should have felt them to be meagre and uncomfortable.

At the Military Club, we had all we wanted for the inner man, and a charmingly cordial welcome. Also we saw the habiliments of, and heard much talk about, war. We quickly corrected our crude notions of military geography and defence organizations. We learned that the real Verdun is not a certain quaint little town, with gates and walls in the manner of Vauban, and old houses overhanging the Meuse. Nor is it this *plus* the old forts which held out for three weeks in 1870, and are now smoothed down into a picturesque promenade. It is not even this together with the circle of modern forts, marked upon the military maps, which have never been in action, and whose guns have been used to better purpose elsewhere. It is, in fact, a piece of country around this centre, protruding to the north-east from the general line of battle, like a vast bastion, with crescent face of seventy miles' length, and a solidly French hinterland for its support. Here, at the heart of this area, we do not hear even the distant boom of the guns, and a bomb from an aeroplane, which killed a woman, is the only German shell that has disturbed the security of the town. We had asked ourselves "What came ye out for to see?" Now we know that we have come to see the real bulwark of eastern France, the Heights of the Meuse.

Verdun, December 2.

The great central doorway of the Lorraine frontier is not only banged, barred, and bolted against the invader; it covers an area, if not of perfect peace, at least of perfect security. Verdun has been advertised by the German commanders as subject to a close investment. They have even claimed to have captured some of the forts. No doubt the German people imagine that it is besieged. I wish some of their representatives, if they have any free men who could tell them the simple truth, could have accompanied us in at least a part of our tour of inspection. Verdun has never been besieged. Its communications are unbroken. It is the centre of a district in which there is no menace. On the north, west, and east there is a space of twenty miles before the zone of German gunfire is reached.

The road to the city through the Argonne is as safe and quiet as the road from York to London. On the south, the Germans touch the Meuse at only a single point—St. Mihiel. To reach it from Metz, there is but one single difficult road, and all along that line the position of the invaders is exceedingly precarious. Around the semicircle north of Verdun, the French armies make slow but steady progress. They are prepared for the winter as well as any armies can be. I spoke to many of the men at different points; and there is not the least doubt about their high spirits and perfect confidence. I spoke also to a number of officers. They struck me as men of marked intelligence and vigour, possessed by a modern and liberal spirit, seeing the moral and political issues of the war very much as we see them ourselves, and watching closely over the safety and comfort of their men. They felt, and seemed to me justified in feeling, themselves invincible men enjoying an impregnable position.

The secret of this important success at the pivoting point of the western campaign is not the strength of the fixed defences of Verdun, for many of the forts have not fired a shot. It is that the army has never lost its freedom of action. All danger is now past on the eastern frontier.

In the course of our journey we have been privileged to meet and spend some hours with General Sarrail; and it seemed to me that the fullness and frankness with which he explained to us the course and character of the operations exemplified the new type of mind that modern conditions are producing even in places where the conservative spirit most obstinately lingers. A tall, slight man. with short, white beard and moustache, soft gray eyes, and a gentle manner, he looks a scholar and a thinker, rather than the man of action we know him to be. In answer to a question about the present morale of the German troops, he said. "*Que voulez-vous?* It is a ship in a tempest, and the sailors run hither and thither." There was no sound of hate or triumph in his tone; but I thought that, if a symbolical picture of the defence of France were needed, one could hardly find a better than the portrait of General Sarrail.

Winter has fallen upon France this year with merciful softness. There has been only a brief touch of frost so far, and, better still for the men in the trenches, much less rain than usual. They should now be fully preparing and those we saw appeared to be. A bright but fitful sunshine favoured me as I went up, under the best possible military guidance, to view the line of the front from three chosen positions on the hills amid which Verdun lies. The town left behind, a magnificent panorama, for whose beauty I was quite unprepared, revealed itself. In sweeping lines of clean fields, the heights rose, through endless grades of green and brown, to the blue forest masses on the edge of the scene. White roads and the shining baud of the Meuse—a narrower and shallower trench than I had expected—cut them; and here and there were scattered small villages, their short church spires rising above the red roofs and plaster walls. In the morning, heavy clouds increased this effect of richly varied colouring; later in the day, a burst of sunshine, falling now upon one and now another range of hills, seemed to enhance the spaciousness of the amphitheatre, an illusion due, doubtless, to some indefinable harmony of its outlines.

We took, first, the more southerly of the two roads which run eastward to Metz, as far as a hill nine miles out, immediately overlooking the village of Haudimont. At this point, we had passed two of the famous forts, those of Belrupt and Rozellier; but not a sign of the traditional kind of fortification was visible till, on our return, we passed over a small piece of concrete pavement with an iron chimney sticking up, down which one of the party shouted a jocular message. No sooner on the hills than we found thatched sentry-boxes and the huts and cabins which the troops are making, with much ingenuity, for winter quarters. In the woods, bedded with red leaves, soldiers were cutting logs for firing, or saplings of ash and birch to make trellis for new streets of huts. They all like this work under the open sky, the *commandant* told me; it is an immense relief from waiting in barracks.

In clearings among the trees, small bodies of troops were camped. They turned to gaze as we passed, wondering who these strange civilians could be. Standing upon a height overlooking the far-spreading plain of the Woevre, the general explained to us the course and rationale of the Verdun position, and the action of its army of defence since the beginning of the war. It was a most illuminating statement; and, as this section of the campaign has been shrouded from western readers, and a knowledge of it is necessary to an understanding of the present position, I will here sketch very briefly what has happened, basing myself upon his words, but not attempting textually to repeat them.

It will be remembered that France was really prepared only for an eastern and north-eastern campaign. Against such an attack, she had three great obstacles to offer—Verdun, the most northerly, Toul-Nancy in the centre (and I include Nancy with Toul, although it is not a "fortress," because its field-works have successfully served the same purpose), and Belfort, which has never been within range of German fire. If any of these three positions had given way, all the after-course of the war would have been different, and probably the Germans would now be firmly established in Paris. The Verdun position was one of particular stress, because it was threatened from the north as well as the east. As it turned out, it was also to be vitally affected by events taking place far to the west. It had already conducted some successful skirmishes against German forces from the north and east (its proper business), when, at the end of August, the evacuation of Belgium and the rapid retreat of the Allies on Paris gave it a new and very difficult task—that of preventing a breach of its connections with the western armies. This involved a south-westward inclination which—when the crown prince had got down as far as Revigny and Vitry-le-François—had to be extended to Bar-le Duc. Finally, when the Germans were beaten back into the northern Argonne, the Verdun Army returned to the intermediate position, with its communications safely established.

Such, very briefly stated, are the four phases of the Verdun defence; and, evidently, the complex task called for exceptional talent in the command, and great courage and tenacity in the body of the troops. British readers have naturally had their eyes chiefly upon the western campaign. The recoil after the battle of the Marne, the great turning movement toward and over the Belgian frontier, and then the desperate effort of the Germans to break through the Allied lines in Flanders, absorbed their attention, because these events were nearest, and their own men were engaged in them. Yet all the efforts of those men would have been in vain had not the eastern wall held firm. Of course, the difficulties were not on the one side only. The German retreat from the Marne involved the crown prince's retirement to a line on which he could keep contact with Rheims and the Suippe Valley on the west, and the Metz Army on the east. This brought him between the Argonne and Verdun; and the German positions here have since been pressed northward slowly to the Varennes road.

On the eastern side, strenuous attempts have been made from Metz and Thiaucourt to break through the Meuse defences between Verdun and Toul. The heroic defence of Fort Troyon is one episode of a succession of intermittent struggles in this thickly wooded mountain re-

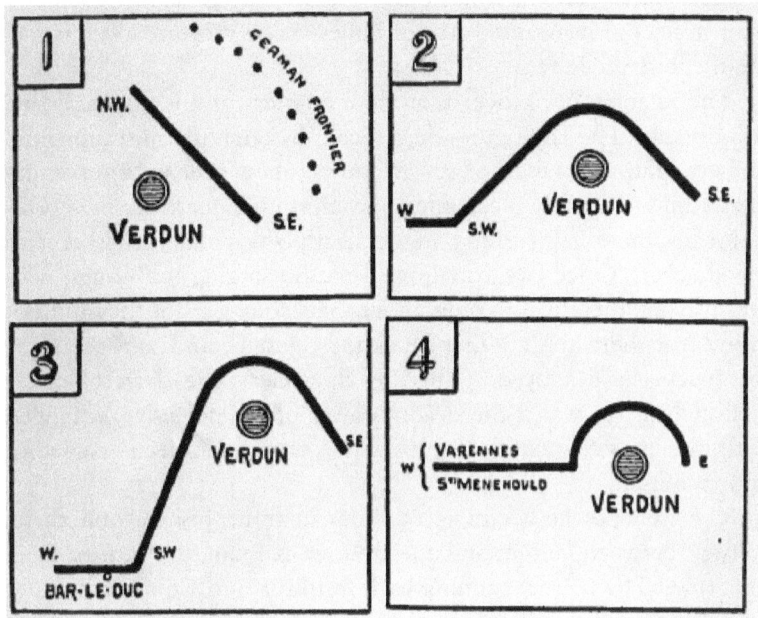

THE FOUR PHASES OF VERDUN

gion. Only at one point, where the hills fall and the woods thin off, have the Germans been able to obtain and keep a foothold upon the Meuse—at St, Mihiel. With forces much weaker than their assailants, the French have disposed of what the general called an "enormous bluff," held the integrity of the French lines, and freed Verdun from danger (an important thing for its moral effect, as well as in a military sense).

The point of the German lines now nearest to the town is the twin hills known as the Jumelles d'Orne, and that is ten miles from the town and four from the nearest fort (the infantry, however, are actually in touch). Generally speaking, the German batteries are about twenty miles from Verdun, and ten miles, or more, from where we stand, between the line of the forts and the French trenches. And now the struggle has undergone a double change. The Germans have fallen upon the defensive; the French have resumed the initiative of attack. But positions of such strength have been built up on either side that the progress is small and slow. "You are all safe here?" I heard an officer ask some men; and the answer was characteristic of the tactical position, as well as of the French spirit: "Yes, too safe!" It is a new sort of siege warfare, in which soft earth is found to give better protection than stone and iron, and a hail of bullets to be more deadly than all the melinite shells.

The infantry fire proceeds at close quarters, and is imperceptible at a distance. The large guns are directed by scientific measurements, not eyesight, at a range of several miles, often over an intervening line of hills—a purely mechanical and most undramatic business. Occasionally, there is a rushing attack, nearly always at terrible cost to the attackers. Once two battalions came on singing war-songs, with fifes playing; there is no doubt about their courage. But they did not know that there was another blockhouse just behind, and the force was practically destroyed by the French artillery. The clearest fact established in this war is the deadly power of the defensive, equipped with modern rifles and field-guns, when once it has been enabled to entrench itself.

The trenches lie a couple of miles in front. Just beyond them, halfway between Verdun and the frontier, is Etain, the nearest German town. The railway running back from Etain to Conflans is under French fire; and the Germans have had to improve their communications to the north-east by building a short line from a point near Spincourt to near the front. On the way from the east to the north-west of the French lines, we visited several batteries, one of which, receiving a message from either an aeroplane that soared ahead or a big yellow captive balloon that floated above a camp of white tents, began to bombard a German position. The sharp smack of the gun fell startling upon our ears; but there was nothing else impressive in the affair. They were firing over a line of wooded hills at some invisible objective two miles away; and I wondered when, if ever, they would hear of the result.

Montfauçon is an isolated hill, apparently only about 800 feet high, which would have presented no particular difficulties to the assailant a century ago. It was to this place that the Crown Prince withdrew his headquarters from Ste. Menehould after the Battle of the Marne; and for the last three months it has watched over the German trenches connecting the Imperial armies of Lorraine, the Argonne, and northern Champagne.

At any rate, Verdun is safe behind its seventy miles of field-works. As we returned to the city at nightfall, a man was quietly ploughing one of the hillsides, as though the war were not only invisible, but non-existent.

Chapter 27

Under Fire In Rheims

Rheims, December 4.

We were chatting over the luncheon table at our hotel in the Place Drouet d'Erlon, waiting for the coffee, when the first shell burst over the city. Others whistled over our heads during this afternoon; and, while a full inquiry was impossible, we learned that one of them had killed six men—street-cleaners—in a road beside the canal. We watched the columns of smoke rising from two separate parts of the south-eastern suburbs, set on fire by shells from the position still called after the old Fort Berru. The French artillery claim to have silenced the offending German guns.

The *gendarmerie* is essentially a romantic service, and the colonel in blue and silver expressed the opinion that, after all their efforts, there must remain somewhere in the city an underground telephone wire by means of which news of the arrival of particular visitors is signalled to the German batteries. I prefer the evidence of the Regulars. In any case, journalistic modesty and the horror of responsibility for the lives lost today would combine to make us wish to discredit this idea. Rheims lies, in fact, in a saucer between the "Mountain of Rheims," the Craonne plateau, and several outlying hills. I should suppose that every party entering the city is plainly within sight of the German gunners, and that every such party should expect to be potted at. Firing upon the city itself, which is unfortified and full of civilians, is quite another matter.

However that be, there had been no bombardment of Rheims for five days before we came, the last happening in precisely the same manner during the visit of a party of journalists representing neutral countries. No doubt, it is more sensible to bombard journalists than innocent townsfolk, who are not even armed with a pen, and are most of them women and children. But, generally speaking, one can discover no logical course at all in the conduct of the German campaign.

Many harmless and helpless communities have been pitilessly destroyed. Others have been inexplicably spared. I had the odd privilege of sleeping last night in one of the rooms occupied, while the Germans stayed in Epernay, by General von Bülow and his staff, in the house of M. Paul Chandon. The chalk marks of one "Hauptmann Brinckman" on my bedroom door are preserved as a curiosity, matching souvenirs of the visits of President Poincaré and the wife of Prince August Wilhelm to this palatial residence. Afterward, we walked through some of the seventeen miles of cellars of Messrs. Moët and Chandon, where about a million bottles of champagne per mile are stored. One of the most eloquent facts we had found in the devastated villages to the south-east was the litter of empty wine-bottles. Epernay, one of the richest and finest of French towns, was practically untouched.

The wine-cellars, in which the whole German Army could have been hidden, were not entered. During an earlier visit, immediately after the German retreat, I told how—whether by sheer whim or real sense of right it is impossible to say—the indemnity, extorted under pressure, was repaid in full. Turn now to Revigny on the south, or to Rheims on the north, and try to harmonize the sheer barbarity practiced there with the complete immunity of this wealthy town of Epernay, in which not a single house has been destroyed, and only trivial looting in the shops took place.

The official representatives of Germany, at the two Hague Conferences, and on other occasions, have pretty steadily resisted attempts to tighten the rules of warfare. But if they thus exiled themselves in advance from the comity of progressive nations, they claimed none the less to have rules of their own. What are they? Can some of the professors explain?

Let us try to state things precisely: Rheims is not "destroyed," like the villages and small towns burned from end to end by the army of the crown prince, Rheims Cathedral is not "in ruins" like the Linen Hall at Ypres. A considerable part of the city presents, if not its normal appearance, at least an air of quiet, solid security, under the radiant sunshine of this rare December. Here and there on the southern and western sides of the town, a building has been more or less badly damaged. Nearly all the larger houses are closed and shuttered, and the streets are deserted. Between the entrance by the Epernay road and the Fontaine Suby, a motor ride of ten minutes, I counted only five houses seriously damaged.

Nearer to the centre of the city, the shopping streets seem to have suffered more seriously, two or three houses in each block having the upper and middle storey broken in by projectiles. Immediately to the north of the Cathedral, a score or more of buildings, some of them very ancient, and a solid stone block facing the statue of Louis XV in the Place Royale, have been completely demolished. In the neighbourhood of St. Remi and what is called "The Seamsters' Quarters," where the Pommery and other wine-cellars lie, the worst mischief of all has been wrought, and many lives have been lost. It was impossible, in the circumstances, to examine this district.

At first I was surprised—such is the influence of promiscuous phrases—to find the vast pile of the cathedral standing majestic and seemingly whole. We approached it from behind; and, from below, the loss of the steep outer structure of the roof, essential though it be to the architectural scheme, is not immediately noticeable. Perhaps, also, the boom of guns is not favourable to close observation, and we had hardly an hour to view what it will require months to examine closely. But, when we came round to the front of the church, the injury to the most glorious of Gothic *façades* was grievously visible. One supposes that it must have been hit either sideways by shots from the German batteries at Nogent l'Abbesse, their most southerly position, or, more probably, by fragments of shells exploding immediately before the entrances.

Dozens of the beautiful statues and carved groups which fill the sides of the three deep doorways have been broken, the chipped stone showing white against the age-worn colour of the mass. The corner pillars of the front of the church are still more completely defaced, probably by the burning of the scaffolding which covered this part of the front before the first and most serious bombardment. Above the left porch, one of the long narrow windows of the west tower has lost a pillar. The range of about twenty gigantic statues of the Kings of France which runs across the *façade*, above the Rose Window, seems to be intact, as are the heads of the towers. But half of the fine balustrade between them has disappeared.

What the burning scaffolding did for the facade, blazing rafters did for the interior. In all, about forty shells are believed to have struck the cathedral. The direct damage thus done is relatively small—a hole in the wall of the north tower, several broken buttresses and pieces of parapet, and such like. The fire caused by the explosions has, on the other hand, done irreparable damage. All of the woodwork of the nave, transepts, choir, and apse has gone. Falling in upon piles of straw on which wounded German soldiers had been lying, it turned the vast interior for a short time into a furnace, shattering the stained glass windows, some of them dating from the thirteenth century; consuming doors, stalls, pulpit, chairs, and other woodwork, twisting iron and melting lead, sending the great bells crashing down from the belfry to the ground and partly melting them, corroding, and, In some cases, breaking the interior statues, pillars, and walls. The great Rose Window has lost a half of its wonderful glass. A few fragments only hang to the bars in the windows over the high altar and the three doors, in most of those in the aisles. The lesser rose window over the central portal is riddled.

It is a melancholy sight, though I will confess to having been more deeply shocked by the ruin of humble cottage homes, where the crime of murder was added to those of sacrilege and barbarous destruction. Most of the litter of masonry outside and within the cathedral has been swept into neat heaps; but there still lies all over the floor of the nave a sprinkling of fragments of coloured glass, and the riddled windows no longer temper the daylight to the soft gloom befitting hours of prayer. These are the remains of one of the glories of a heritage belonging, not only to the people of Rheims or to the Roman Church, but to all men who have a heart for the beautiful creations of the art and piety of the past. The priest who conducted us protested that the evil was not beyond repair. Rheims Cathedral is not, indeed, destroyed. But the work of restoration, where possible, will be difficult; the ancient glass can never be replaced; and in many lines and details of decoration the old loveliness can never be won back.

We came out of the cathedral into the small Notre Dame square; glanced at the blackened walls and debris of the old Archiepiscopal Palace; verified the odd fact that the statue of Joan of Arc on horseback in front of the cathedral has sustained no damage; and then looked around for evidence of some provocation for the bombardment, which was still proceeding. A very tame affair it seemed, not at all resembling the frightful splash of fire of the imaginative pictures. This was, no doubt, because no projectile happened to fall among or near our little party, and you cannot see through streets of brick and stone. In open country you may watch the puff of white or brown smoke from the guns, and the actual explosion; and, of course, the relatively small number of soldiers at the extreme front see it altogether too closely and too often for comfort.

Here we could only hear a heavy bang, a prolonged, soft screech, and once or twice a loud smash. For nearly everybody, the war obstinately continues to be invisible. But its bloody work goes on steadily. This particular cannonade lasted for about two hours, and I do not think that more than a score of German shells were fired in that time. I may be mistaken about this, for there were other things to think about.[1] It is the general testimony that for some time the Germans have been economizing ammunition, as they conspicuously did not at the outset.

We searched, but could find no sort of justification. Rheims completely answers to the military description of an open town. It is neither fortified nor occupied. The French army is either in the trenches two or three miles out, in a crescent from the north-west to the southeast, or it is in the camps to the south. There is not, and never has been, any military reason for the bombardment. A glance around the region from the southward heights shows that there can be nothing accidental about it. As from here, so from the German batteries, the city lies spread out in the plain between, every part of it clearly visible. The cathedral rises prominently from its centre, and, like St. Paul's in London, is a landmark for many miles around. The repetition of the bombardments proves their deliberate character.

Two justifications have been offered. On September 2, General von Bülow, commanding the Second German Army in its southward advance, sent forward two officers of the Imperial Guard (Von Arnim and Von Kummer) to treat for the surrender of the city. At the village of Neuvillette, they were met, and told that the governor-general was leaving Rheims, and it was useless for them to go further. From this moment, they inexplicably disappeared. Prince August Wilhelm (fourth son of the *Kaiser*) came into the city to make inquiries, and gave permits to the Mayor of Neuvillette and another Frenchman to go in search of the missing *parlementaires*. On the morrow, as they had not returned, the Guards' artillery, not knowing that General Zimmer and other Saxon officers were already in the town arranging for requisitions, bombarded it; and there are said to have been 200 killed and wounded on this occasion. General von Bülow then took hostages, and imposed a large fine on the city. The two French envoys, also, have not returned; they are believed to be prisoners in Germany. There is

---

1. The French official bulletin for the day stated: "Rheims has been bombarded with a particular intensity."

no need to enlarge further upon this incident, which evidently affords no justification for the bombardments following the northward return of the French.

The second excuse is that the cathedral has been used as a military signal station or observation post. The Abbé Thinot, chapel master of the cathedral, in a published statement, says that, for a single night before the opposed hosts had come into contact, an electric light was installed in the north tower, but that it was taken down, and never re-established. The military and ecclesiastical authorities agree in declaring positively that, since September 12, when the French returned and the Germans retired, leaving a number of their wounded behind, no military use of any kind has been made of the cathedral, and no military post has been established near it. I can only myself speak of the present time; and today there is certainly nothing in Rheims that can reasonably invite the attention of the German guns. We were ourselves absolutely refused permission to go to the roof of the cathedral to examine the damage there, lest we should be taken for soldiers making observations.[2]

Such are the main facts of an episode of the great war which will be a lasting stain upon the character of the German Army. It seems to me an episode calling urgently for a formal, open, and unmistakable protest from the public men of neutral countries. There is no mere question of passing judgment upon acts that are dead and done with. The interests of a great living community cry out for such a moral intervention. Of the normal population of 110,000 persons, there remain 60,000 in Rheims today. Why do they not clear out? I presume because they cannot. The rich have gone, and practically all the able-bodied men are away with the army. Some of the poor have probably been able to find a refuge with relatives beyond the region of the invasion. Most of them—women, children, old men and weaklings—stay here because they have no other home, and it is here that they receive their allowances of a shilling a day for soldiers' wives and 5d. a day for each child. On these pittances they drag out a feverish, pitiful existence, going down into their cellars during each bombardment, if they are in the quarters most open to it; or walking out on to the roads outside the town to watch the explosion of shells from behind

---

2. On October 19, the German Consulate-General issued a statement to the effect that French batteries were placed in front of the cathedral "in the direct line of the German fire." This tardy explanation has, I believe, no better basis than those examined above.

walls and haystacks.

How many lives have already been sacrificed to provide an entertainment for the German artillery officers, it is yet impossible to say. One substantial citizen whom I questioned thought a thousand civilians had been killed in the last three months, chiefly by the earlier cannonades. This is, perhaps, an over-estimate, but the death-roll is certainly a long one. The material destruction in this open town is a very serious matter, to be counted in millions of pounds sterling. There is no apparent reason why the city should not lie under fire for another three months. The Germans will certainly hold on here as long as they can, and when they have to let go they will not do so in a spirit of Christian submissiveness. Are another thousand innocent and helpless non-combatants to be slaughtered? A shipful of Christmas toys is a very jolly present; and I have seen Americans, men and women, working here in the ambulances, on the edge of the thin red line, with an energy and practical sense beyond all praise. There are, however, emergencies when a plain word from men who speak with authority, like the President of the United States, might effect more than all such individual devotion.

CHAPTER 28

The Lines of the Aisne

Paris, December 11.

The British reader early became acquainted with the more westerly portion of the Aisne Valley, from Soissons to Compiègne, not because this region was of exclusive interest, but because it was comparatively easy of access from Paris, during the exciting days of the first German retreat. The more easterly portion has been practically closed to civilians, except the remaining inhabitants, for the last four months. It is, however, an area of great interest, not only or chiefly because, before they were moved to the north, Sir John French's troops had here some of their hardest work, but because it is here that the military deadlock is seen in its fullest development. I rejoiced greatly, therefore, when I found that I should be able to visit, not, indeed, the trenches of the extreme front, but three points of vantage giving bird's-eye views of the whole field, and a number of points behind the Aisne lines, in addition to the city of Rheims.

Briefly, we came up from Epernay north-westward to Fismes, through what is called the Forest of the Mountain of Rheims, and the Ardre Valley. From Fismes, we went northward, to a point where the Aisne Valley, from Condé to Craonne, lay before us, a superb panorama. Returning to Fismes, we then took the eastward road to Rheims, and, just before reaching the city, obtained another remarkable view-point. Finally, from the terrace of Mme. Pommery's *château* to the south-east of Rheims, we viewed the positions on that side. During the journey, three generals and several staff-officers gave us explanations with a clearness and courtesy essentially French, and with a freedom that should have made certain censorial ears tingle.

It may be the obsession of current events, but I always seem to feel a contest, a rivalry, of beauty and martial qualities in these landscapes of central France. In the perfect clarity of the winter air, the waters sparkle; the scudding clouds, like prisms, filter the thin light in a thousand degrees of colour upon the hillsides; and in the bare fields and leafless woods there is only an enhancement, not an interruption, of the sweeping outlines of the scene. But, as we climbed through the vineyards and orchards above Epernay, into the heights of the Forest of Rheims, this sense of an incomparable loveliness in the Marne Valley was spoiled (ah! the wickedness of the mind of man!) by the thought: Why did not Von Bülow defend this ridge, instead of falling back beyond Rheims? Perhaps he did; there have been hundreds of engagements in this war that we have never heard of, and that may never be distinguished when its history comes to be written. Again and again the thought recurred, as we coasted the wooded slopes of this high, crumpled plateau. In a width of about seventeen miles, there are only three northward-running main roads.

Few, if any, of the Germans, in their haste, took the Ardre Valley way—the main body were making due north, for Rheims. So the small stone villages—Sarcy and Faverolles, Savigny and Serzy—lie uninjured, fat and smiling, doing their humdrum labour, with here and there a camp of wagons and huts, or a slow convoy column, to remind them of the younger men who are striving and dying for France just over the hills. But at Fismes we met the road from Paris through Château-Thierry, and the railway that runs to the front from Paris through Meaux—one of two lines, the other hugging the south bank of the Aisne, which, as an officer said, "seem to have been put here by Providence to help us." Now we heard the distant flap of gunfire; the bustle of all the supporting processes of a large army increased; and in a few minutes we reached a large farm, from which we could see right over to the Laon Mountains.

At our feet lay the villages, Revillon, Maizy, Villers, Arcy, where many British soldiers fell in the first fighting to secure the crossing of the Aisne, in mid-September. On the other side of the river stretched the Chemin des Dames and the hills from Vailly, on the west, through Soupir and Vendresse, to Craonne, which marks the eastern edge of the plateau—all names made famous in the official war bulletins of the last three months. Just under Craonne village, the farm of Heurtebise, and just behind it the farm of Vanclérc, were plainly visible—both doubly famous, for at these spots Napoleon directed some of the critical operations of the Laon campaign of 1814. Unknown to the modern tourist, it is all classic ground, full of the marks of Homeric strife.

There lie the ruins of the great Abbey of Vanclérc, built by Saint Bernard, and destroyed by the Revolution. Across the crest, an old farm called the Tower, now razed to the ground, dates back to the time of Charlemagne. Joan of Arc came with Charles VII by the Chemin des Dames to Vailly, now in ruins, to receive the keys of Laon, now the centre of the German position in France. Condé recalls the name of the great family whose two fortresses of Coucy and La Ferté-Milon were connected by a system of dungeons and underground tunnels. In the quarries of Bourg, where one of Caesar's lieutenants defended Gaul against the Northmen, a few wretched peasants hide from the newest phase of the same eternal conflict. At Heurtebise, Napoleon looked out upon his last great victory. Upon such ground the Hohenzollern has dared to tempt destiny. He may well be ill as he reads the omens.

The general told us that the French and German trenches, only 70 or 80 feet apart, were also visible through field-glasses. Perhaps they were; all I could make out, for my part, was some lines of white which might be walls or any kind of marks across the face of the fields on the slope five or six miles away. But one gained a new impression of the latest kind of warfare in seeing spread out before one like a map the theatre where it had been practiced with hardly any considerable movement for two months.

At the second point, just west of Rheims, we could follow more closely, because it was much nearer, the division between the two armies, broadly marked by the Rheims-Laon highroad, running northwest across the plain, past the edge of the Craonne plateau. Here, also, it was possible better to appreciate the part played by the dismantled French forts on the north of the city, those of Chenay, St. Thierry, Loivre, Fresnes, and, especially, of Brimont. From the Château Pommery, we could note how the strong positions above Berru and Nogent l'Abbesse dominate the east of the city and the neighbouring plain. The only part of the former semicircle of fortifications the French have been able to recover is the Pompelle battery, below Nogent. On this side, the front is pretty closely defined by the Aisne-Marne Canal, which runs between the Châlons road and railroad.

It is indescribably strange, looking out upon this fair margin of Champagne, to reflect that, within range of our eyes, there are hidden several hundreds of thousands of men engaged in an unremitting and deadly struggle. Save for some burning building, and occasional puffs of smoke followed by the peal of artillery, but for the hospital we have

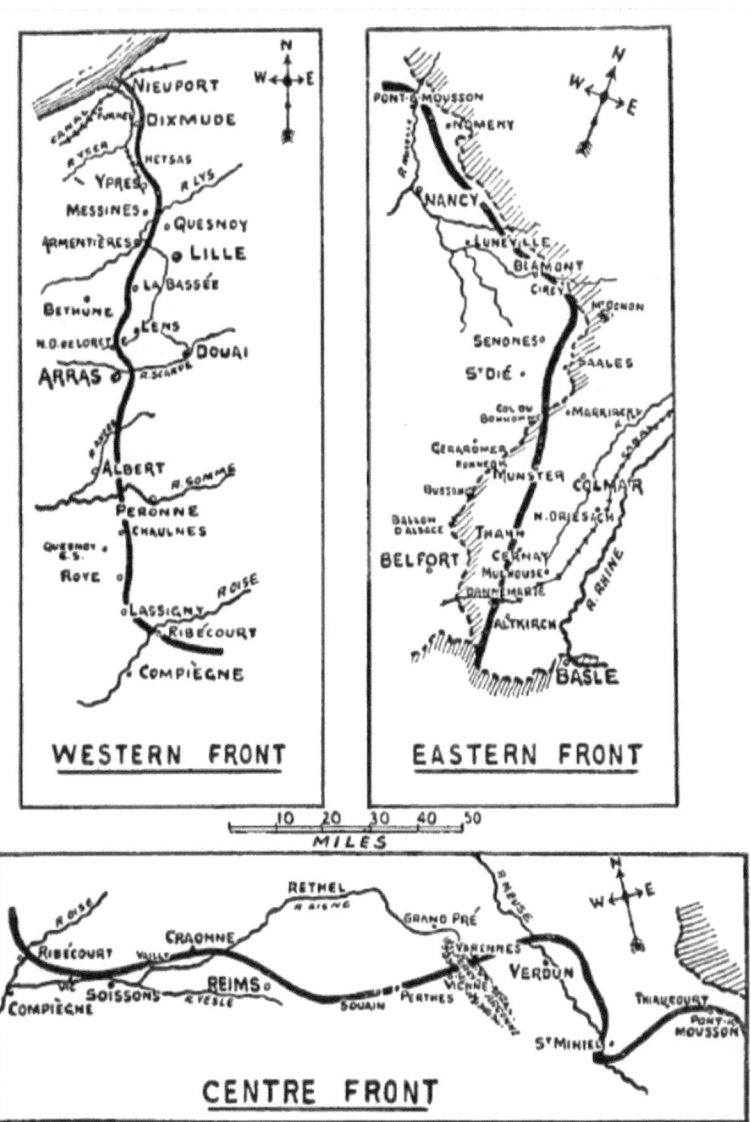

THE FRONT AT THE BEGINNING OF 1915

just left, and the encampments we have visited, it would be incredible. It is now, in the main, a test of endurance in this part of the field. The power of either side is such that open operations are impossible except at frightful cost, and offer hardly any chance of success. During the last three weeks Soissons and Rheims have been several times bombarded; the *château* of Soupir has been burned down; the French artillery has located and destroyed one or two German batteries; an advance of 500 yards has been won near Berry-au-Bac; on November 30, the artillery "scattered German infantry columns north of Fort Condé"; west of Presles and near Rouge-Maison, a German gun was destroyed and others silenced, and it is claimed that here "the growing activity of our artillery reduced our daily average of infantry casualties from 100 to 20"; a German attempt to blow up the bridge at Berry-au-Bac, by means of a barge laden with explosives and a time-machine, was repulsed. That is all that merits mention in the official reports. Both sides, in fact, have been largely occupied in preparing winter quarters. The Germans not only hold positions of great strength; they have, especially through Mezieres, very good lines of communications. And they hold on obstinately because this is a most critical point of their front.

Pending some diversion, the deadlock is complete. But there is not a sign of discouragement or restlessness among the French officers and men. Some frankly enjoy the rough, open-air life. "If it were not for the deaths," one of them said to me, "it would be splendid." The rest go to and fro with a quiet, sober resolution of which the civilian spirit seems to me as effective a part as any remnant of martial tradition. Their intelligence, their invincible wit, their camaraderie and robust democratic sense, the high manliness of these French citizens-in-arms, all cry shame upon the foul business into which they have been forced. I do not believe that any military adventurer could carry them into a war of conquest. They give their lives for the defence of their homes, for the land they always figure not as an armed man, but as a noble woman. No ocean bed can hold the tears of this sacrifice. But France is worth saving, at whatever cost must be saved. And from this agony the great Republic will rise nearer to the ideal than even her dreaming founders dreamed.

CHAPTER 29

The Government Returns

After the fall of Antwerp, the Belgian Government established itself at Havre, with all the honours the French Republic could offer it, with its own telegraphic and postal services, and every facility for carrying on such business as remains to ministers temporarily separated from their land and people. The local officials in Belgium in general were requested to remain at their posts so that, as far as possible, the country might be saved from anarchy; magistrates were asked to continue to act on condition that they were permitted to do so "in the name of the King of the Belgians," promising to do nothing that could be considered as an act of hostility to the invader while exercising his provisional authority.

In the last week of October, I learned with astonishment that the German Government had intimated to certain influential Frenchmen, through commercial-financial channels, that it was ready to negotiate a separate peace. Briefly, the message was that the Imperial Government recognised the quality of the stand made by the French armies, had never regarded France as its principal enemy in this struggle, and was ready to grant terms not merely honourable, but generous. They would include the transfer to France of Metz and the neighbouring portion of Lorraine, and perhaps, also, of at least a part of Alsace. Quite apart from the "scrap of paper" on which the Allies had undertaken, at the outset of the war, not to conclude peace separately, such an invitation could have no chance of acceptance. For dependence upon Berlin, even Metz would be no price. And what of Servia, of Russia, of England, above all, what of the martyr-land, Belgium?

Before these questions the would-be negotiators fell vague, shrugging a dubious shoulder, but opined that Germany would require an enclave on the Scheldt—in other words, Antwerp and northern

Belgium. Perhaps the offer was designed to aid the efforts of Count Bernstorff, Herr Dernburg, and Professor Mûnsterberg to influence American opinion. Intelligence, interest, and even lack of interest combined in the United States at this time to produce a vague feeling that the war should be brought to an end somehow, anyhow. It was a sentiment creditable to a great humane and neutral Power. But it was not then a very helpful sentiment, because, for Europe, the issue was one of life and death, and the "how" was everything, no less than in the Civil War of the States themselves fifty years before. Fortunately, the process of education furthered by men like President Nicholas Murray Butler, of Columbia University; President Starr Jordan, of Leland Stanford, and President Eliot, of Harvard, had gone far. Many misunderstandings had been removed.

The original aggression, the devastation of Belgium, the destruction of historic edifices, the aeroplane outrages, had made a deep impression across the Atlantic. Mr. Herrick, at the American Embassy in Paris, had been a courageous, able, resolute, and disinterested observer; and so, no doubt, would his successor prove. From one quarter and another. President Wilson had been truly and fully advised. He could not but be aware that even so powerful an influence as that of the United States must be carefully conserved; and he had himself said that peacemaking in such a case is no child's-play.

As though to remind the world of one of the characteristics of German warfare, there was about this time a new outburst of aerial raiding upon the civilian population of Paris. After a lapse of more than three weeks, there had been an aeroplane visit on September 27, when an aviator signing himself Von Decken had thrown four bombs on the city. The American Ambassador had just passed the spot where one of these fell, at the corner of the Avenue du Trocadero and the Rue de Freycinet. Two persons were seriously injured—a solicitor, who died on the way to hospital, and a little girl, whose leg was badly cut. They were on their way to church. A fortnight passed. Then another aviator arrived from the German lines, and threw two bombs, which wounded a policeman, his wife, and a child of seven years, in the working-class quarter of St. Denis.

On the following day, October 11, there were two raiders, and about twenty projectiles were thrown, three persons being killed and fourteen injured. Of these, fourteen were women, mostly of the working class, six of them being girls. One of the bombs struck the roof of Notre-Dame, without doing much damage, and two more fell close by. On October 12, a further attack was made, without serious results. A more effective air police was then organised around the city; and no more was heard of this particular pest.

With the passing of summer, the French people suddenly realized the need not only of an improvement of the services of care for the sick and wounded, but of ample supplies of warm clothing for their soldiers. M. Clémenceau— who, when the government moved to Bordeaux, had gone to Toulon, and then to Toulouse, as it was said, to keep an eye upon them—had conducted a characteristic campaign in his journal on the subject; and when, at the end of September, *L'Homme Libre* was suspended for eight days, because he refused to suppress certain passages in an article on the army medical services, the old statesman-journalist had restarted it under the title of *L'Homme Enchaîné*. Undoubtedly, the official provisions, and the energies of all the official staffs—doctors, nurses, stretcher-bearers, supplies, transport, and hospital accommodation—had been strained to the utmost. The government pleaded that there had been occasions when not only the wounded have had to be picked up under fire on the field, but those under treatment in the field hospitals had to be removed, because they were fired upon by the German artillery.

There were French hospital trains capable of carrying 100,000 wounded. But evidently very few of these could be concentrated upon any given battlefield, however great the need. The immense numbers of men gathered within such an area as that to the north of the Aisne, and the continuity of the fighting, must inevitably result in a strain upon hospital services altogether beyond anything that had been experienced in preceding wars. Hence the grievous scenes of which we saw so many, when the wounded soldier must be content with a pile of straw in a horse-truck of a slow-going train, and the charity of the villagers at the wayside stations which it passed.

Impatient people asked why civilian and even amateur assistance was not enlisted more freely, not understanding how difficult it is to combine military and civilian services, and to organise the help which, in the nature of the case, could not be submitted to the full rigor of official rules. Indeed, it was exactly the faculty of powerful organisation, one of the rare human faculties, that was most strained. Thousands and tens of thousands of women and men were devoting themselves gallantly to softening the blows of war. Perhaps a very small illustration will bring this fact home better than overwhelming statistics or *grandiose* eulogies. Trainloads of wounded were constantly arriving on the outskirts of Paris, whence they were shunted on to the lines for the south and west. Seeing that the State services could not at the time guarantee these convoys constant supplies of warm food and other comforts throughout what was often a long journey, the good folk of Argentenil organised a committee; and, after the Battle of the Marne, particularly, forty ladies, in day and night relays, were in constant attendance at this and the next station on the Grand Ceinture (Outer Circle) Railway.

They supplied freely to the wounded and their guardians bread loaves, sandwiches, coffee, tea, and boiling milk, packets of chocolate and cigarettes, and, sometimes, fresh fruit and pots of jam. A local baker put his bakery at the disposal of the committee; and they cooked large quantities of apples and pears presented by the inhabitants—portions of the stewed fruit being given to the suffering men between slices of bread. If you happened to be in the station watching curiously the happy scene, a girl would jog your elbow, present a little clinking bag, and tell you with a smile that, in this theatre, every man must pay for his place. So, in a hundred other spots. Every effort was made to coordinate the work of the two government departments—the health service and the "*Assistance Publique*"—the three societies constituting the French Red Cross, and other philanthropic groups. But to secure that at every point—from immediately behind the fighting line to the sanatorium on the Spanish frontier—good surgical aid, medical supplies, food, and competent nursing were always available was a gigantic if not an impossible task.

The provision of warm clothing against the cold and wet months was easier, for the millions of women and girls left at home were only too glad to knit vests, socks, mufflers, and gloves, and to make good shirts, too, when they were provided with the flannel. Evidently, however, the government itself must be chiefly responsible for clothing the men in the field. As a first measure, it was announced at the end of September that they might provide themselves with the following articles, and that they would be reimbursed on showing that they had them: two flannel shirts, two pairs of pants, one jersey, one flannel belt, two pairs of woollen socks, one blanket, one pair of woollen gloves. This provision was supplemented by an immense volume of voluntary effort; and, the stationary warfare of the trenches somewhat simplifying the problem of communications, it could be said during the autumn and winter not only that no armies had ever been better cared for, but that the sacrifice of many thousands of men was recognised by attention they would hardly have received in the trials of civil life.

The Chambers, which had been silent since the beginning of the war, reopened on December 22 for a short special session. This was formally necessary in order to postpone the elections that would have normally taken place before the end of the year, to vote supplies, and to ratify acts of the government done by decree during the war. The session had the more general, the unwritten, aim of marking the return of the government to Paris—an event heralded by various Presidential and Ministerial visitations, and now quietly completed—and of demonstrating the unity and resolution of the nation. The chief interest on such an occasion naturally centres in the popular assembly; and thither I betook myself soon after noon.

The lobby of the Palais Bourbon, called the "*Salle des Pas Perdus*," has, no doubt, presented in some past crises a spectacle fuller of the elements of dramatic surprise, but never, I should think, a more moving scene or one more finely reflecting the sufferings and anxieties, the capacities and courage, of a great people. Many of these men had come direct from the camps and trenches of the battle line, where votes do not count and another law than that of Parliament reigns supreme. They told each other weird experiences, laughed over hardships the thought of which would have been intolerable six months before, recalled their colleagues who had fallen on the stricken field—the deputies Goujon, Nortier, and Proust, and Senator Reymond, the gallant aviator—and three others, MM. Ghesquiere, Delory, and Basly, who were still hostages in the hands of the enemy. The Abbé Lemire, the only priest in this Chamber, told of the stirring events he had witnessed at Hazebrouck.

The two deputies for Valenciennes, MM. Durre and Melin, succeeded in escaping from that city when it was occupied, and had many curious and tragic incidents to relate. The eastern members were full of the advance in Alsace and the gallant actions by which Nancy and Verdun had been held immaculate. To an assembly 190 of whose members were in the army—they had received leave of absence from the front for the session, as the law provides, and, by the same obligation, appeared in civilian garb, not uniform—these experiences had a peculiar interest. So when, at 2 o'clock, they trooped into the Chamber to take each his accustomed desk in face of the tribune, from which fierce and fiery harangues had so often been hurled against this side or that, it was in a strange new spirit of gentleness and fraternity. Some day the old divisions must reappear, the old feuds revive. Today there was only one party in France, the universal party of national defence.

In the House of Commons, the dominant feature is the division of Government and Opposition benches, with Mr. Speaker paternally guarding the decencies. In Paris, parties grade off imperceptibly from Right to Left; the concentration of seats within the well-lighted amphitheatre, and of the vision both of deputies and visitors in the high galleries behind upon the tribune, or speaker's platform, gives a dramatic and modem quality to the scene quite absent at Westminster. There was, however, no theatrical note in these proceedings. After a quarter of an hour's hubbub of greetings and gossip, M. Deschanel read an admirably conceived presidential oration. He spoke, amid sharp volleys of hand-clapping, of the courage and powers of organisation that had carried the French colours back into Alsace, and had triumphed on the Marne and in the north; of the complete cessation of civil discords before the national peril; and of the spirit in which France was defending the respect for treaties, the independence of Europe, and human liberties.

In an incidental phrase, he spoke of Germany as treading underfoot the principle of nationalities which she had invoked for herself in earlier days, a principle truly illustrated by England, surrounded by a loyal family of daughter nations. A sentence of homage to Belgium, "the sovereign example in our days of moral grandeur," was received with a wave of applause, the whole assembly standing. "Right is greater than force," M. Deschanel protested; and no words uttered during the session reached higher than this simple denial of the Bismarckian maxim. The president then proceeded to the traditional eulogy of members of the Chamber dead since the last session. The seats of the three deputies who had fallen in action were marked with tricolour scarfs.

M. Viviani followed. He looked tired, and his voice was not at its best; but there was something impressive in the quietude and strong reserve of this civilian figure. His speech was not, he said, a declaration of policy, for there was that day only one policy—the unceasing combat for the definite liberation of Europe, guaranteed by a fully victorious peace. The complete unity of France had disturbed the drunken dream of a German triumph. The prime minister referred to the documents by which the German Government's attempts to rehabilitate itself had been destroyed. The Allies had been forced into this war, and would wage it to the end. France had shown that an organised democracy could, when necessary, support with vigour its ideal of liberty and equality. A nation that could show such heroism was imperishable. None doubted the supremacy of Parliament, but all must make sacrifices. Let them go forward with one cry—victory; one vision—the fatherland; one ideal—the right. It was an inspiring allocution, and the Chamber cheered its chief passages to the echo. Then the sitting raced to a conclusion.

M. Ribot appeared for about one minute in the tribune to lodge his budget. M. Viviani presented a number of bills, including a measure enabling the government to withdraw by simple decree the privilege of naturalisation from any person found guilty of trafficking with the enemy. M. Millerand, the War Minister, and M. Malvy, the Home Secretary, ran up the steps and down again, and, before anyone had had time to reflect that, in an assembly of nearly six hundred members, there might well be one dissentient voice, all the day's business had been finished, and the House had adjourned.

There was behind this short Parliamentary Session a powerful but hidden wave of anxious thought, which marked its importance. The Press said little about it, and leading politicians would not allow themselves to be interviewed on the subject. Yet it filled all intelligent minds; and to define it will help us to understand where lies the fundamental unity of Englishmen with the people of France, and how great was in this day of trial the difference of their immediate circumstances and sacrifices. They were, in this struggle, the two great champions of democracy and civil liberties. But whereas Britain lay safe within her girdle of sea, her ancient institutions unchallenged, and her habitual life little modified, the whole fate of France was cast into the scales of war. For the French Republic, it was no mere question of an expeditionary corps swelling slowly to the dimensions of a Continental army.

Like a lightning stroke, all her best manhood had to be thrown out to answer the hellish challenge of a Power openly contemptuous of democracy and Parliamentarism. At this moment, eight departments of France, including some of her richest industrial districts, the textile cities and half of the collieries of the north, lay under the heel of the invader. There was hardly a family in the land that was not already wounded in the prodigious effort by which his advance had been stayed. The army was now the nation, and so it must be till the day of victory.

The best English book on France—true, it was now ten years old—spoke of the French people's "incapacity for parliamentary government." Such was the failure of the conservative mind to see into the depths of national consciousness. In Germany, the same kind of deception was naturally encouraged, and went to ridiculous lengths. France was decadent, French parliamentary disputes were a preparation for conquest, Gustave Hervé and the Labour Confederation were worth so many army corps, the French Army was an army of lawyers, deputies, talkers. If our eyes had not been dazzled with the flashing succession of events, every man of us who had ever criticized French Parliamentarism would have stood still for a moment of sheer shame on August 4 to recognise the wonder of the miracle that German aggression had worked. There is a perpetual mingling of faith and scepticism in the French nature, which may easily be misunderstood by foreign observers.

Scepticism, for instance, of the motives of carpetbag politicians is almost universal. It leads to very large abstentions from voting at every General Election. It may easily be mistaken for disbelief in Parliament itself. So, again, many things one heard in private conversation in Paris when the Government moved to Bordeaux might be mistaken for scepticism as to the Republic itself. Now no such mistakes could be made. The Republic was more firmly founded than ever in the minds and hearts of the French people. There is not any alternative—we can say that now more positively than before the war. And even when the Chambers are only in brief and occasional session, when martial law and military dispositions are supreme, Parliamentarism has justified itself. It has passed through the supreme test, not a French voice challenges it, and it emerges purified of certain quarrelsome and unclean elements into a new strength, the voice of France, in danger one and indivisible.

Chapter 30

War as It is

1. The Costs in Life and Wealth

The deadlock of winter warfare across the trenches of Belgium and France gives a material reality to the chronological limit of this narrative. In costs and losses, in the anxiety and lab or of putting new forces into the field and maintaining those already there, there was, however, no breach of continuity; and, while it would be evidently foolish, in reviewing a portion of a war, to enter into a detailed discussion either of these major factors or its military lessons, it would be a yet graver error to omit the few faint indications that can be given of the dire injuries that the world in general, and Europe in particular, have suffered.

There is one fact of a wholly satisfactory kind, the result of modem surgical and medical skill and the advances in sanitary organisation. At the end of the year, Mr. Asquith stated in the House of Commons that, of 104,000 British casualties, about 60 *per cent*, of the wounded had recovered, and were again fit for service. On February 15, 1915, Mr. Tennant gave remarkable figures as to disease in the army during the first six months of the war. In that period, there had not been a single case of typhus or cholera, in either the Expeditionary Force, or the troops in the United Kingdom. For other diseases, the figures were:

	Expeditionary Force		Troops in U. K.	
	Cases	Deaths	Cases	Deaths
Typhoid Fever.......	625	49	962	47
Scarlet Fever........	196	4	1,379	22
Measles.............	175	2	1,045	65

Among the troops in the United Kingdom, there had been only one case of smallpox, and that not fatal. Six men had died of diphtheria, out of 783 cases. The highest mortality was from pneumonia—357 deaths out of 1,508 cases. Within this period, England had been called upon to multiply by four her land forces, apart from the Indian and Colonial contingents: thus—

Regulars and Territorials at the outbreak of the war	711,005
Increase on August 6, 1914	500,000
Do. on September 10, 1914	500,000
Do. on November 16, 1914	1,000,000
Total	2,711,005

These were numbers voted, not yet raised; the above figures of sickness apply only to the troops in being. But they may be taken broadly to represent the modem level of army health; and both in amount of sickness and rate of recovery they show a very marked improvement upon past war experience. It is highly probable that France and Germany could both exhibit equal proof of skill, devotion, and organisation, but that Russia and Austria-Hungary have suffered much more heavily, and Servia and Turkey most heavily of all, in proportion to numbers engaged.

The military position of these States involved for Germany the heaviest proportionate losses if she failed to effect an early success. She was able indeed, in the last resort, to throw eight or nine million men into the field, a number that would secure her, with the Austro-Hungarian army, an equality with any forces Russia and the Western Allies could enrol and arm for at least six months. But the Austro-Hungarian armies proved to be quite unequal to their share in the programme; and, simultaneously, the offensive which Germany had planned in the west failed. Every day thereafter must make their case more hopeless, for the difficulty of the Allies had been not the lack of men and other resources, but only the difficulty of quickly mobilizing them. In nearly every direction, their resources were much superior; among them was the power of imposing a naval blockade, and so limiting the German Empire almost wholly to its domestic production in agriculture and industry.

Hence the reckless desperation of those massed assaults by which it was sought to force an issue at one part after another of the front across France and Belgian Flanders. Only the Prussian casualty lists have been published. Approximately, however, it may be said that the wastage of the German armies up to the end of 1914, from death, permanent disablement, and constant sickness (allowing for those able to return to the ranks) and capture, amounted to about a million and a quarter men. The French Government says 1,300,000 (gross, 1,800,000, less 500,000 returned to the ranks); and it declares that this was double the French losses.

Something has been said of the great effort of charity to assuage the unspeakable pains of this world-wide calamity. It is, perhaps, not to be wondered at that no equivalent amount of thought was given to the larger economic problems of the war. In France, as in England, there was much talk of "capturing" German trade, which, in fact, was rapidly being destroyed. The thinking observer knew that trade is not to be caught as boys catch butterflies; and he knew, also, that the idea of any substantial compensation for this vast disturbance and arrest of production and exchange by way of war indemnities was a simple fantasy. At a meeting of the French Political Economy Society, on October 5, M. Yves Guyot estimated that, in six months, the war would cost the seven European belligerents, including loss of production and losses in human capital, more than 88 *milliards* of *francs*—£3,520 millions—or over seventeen times the amount of the indemnity imposed on France in 1871. M. Leroy-Beaulieu reckoned that £240 millions a month was being spent by the seven nations in immediate military costs. He thought that they would have to borrow from £1,400 millions to £1,600 millions at the end of a six-months' war, and that, considering the lowness of the real national debt of Germany, she could pay an indemnity of £800 to £1,000 Millions.

The current strain of the war upon State finances is illustrated by the account placed before the House of Commons at the beginning of March 1915, when the British. Government obtained two new Votes of Credit. The first of these brought the war expenditure for the eight months, August-March, up to £362,000,000, nearly tripling the normal national budget. As £441,000,000 had been borrowed for the war up to this time (£350,000,000 in the previous November, and the rest earlier), a margin of £86,500,000 was left in the Treasury toward a war expenditure which was being piled up at a rate of £543,000,000 a year, or about a million and a half per day.

The completest estimate of the costs of the war hitherto attempted was laid before the Royal Statistical Society on March 16, 1915, by Mr. Edgar Crammond, and showed a rate of expenditure and loss considerably in excess of that of M. Guyot's calculation. Mr. Crammond assumed a continuance of active and general hostilities up to the end of July 1915, and, for the period of twelve months, concluded that the direct and indirect costs to the six chief nations involved would amount to £9,147 millions, the larger half of this colossal sum falling upon the Allies. This does not include the losses of Japan, Servia, or Turkey, for which the data were insufficient, or the very heavy penalties falling upon the United States and other neutral nations. The cost to the six Powers, Mr. Crammond reckoned as follows:

	£
Belgium	526,600,000
Russia	1,400,000,000
Germany	2,775,000,000
France	1,686,400,000
British Empire	1,258,000,000
Austria-Hungary	1,502,000,000

These totals he divided into direct and indirect costs (in millions of pounds), as follows:

	Direct expenditure of Government	Destruction of property	Capitalized value of loss of life	Loss of production and other losses
Belgium	36.5	250	40	200
France	553.4	160	348	625
Russia	600	100	300	400
British Empire	708	—	300	250
TOTAL	1,897.9	510	988	1,475
Austria-Hungary	562	100	240	600
Germany	938	—	879	958
TOTAL	1,500	100	1,119	1,558

The loss of production, in the case of England, by the withdrawal of, say, two million workers, he placed at £200,000,000. He endeavoured to distinguish clearly between the permanent loss of capital—that is, the direct State expenditure and destruction of property—which he estimated at £4,000 millions, and the indirect losses, such as that of income and the capitalised value of lives lost, which was put at £5,150 millions. He gave reasons for believing that, although the larger half of these burdens would fall upon the Allies, the vast superiority of their resources would enable them to continue the war much longer than Germany and Austria could, and to recover much more quickly from its effects.

The chief value of calculations like this was to turn such competent minds as were not absorbed in the work of the war itself to the contemplation of the exceedingly grave problems which, if historical precedent goes for anything, must arise upon the resumption of normal economic life. The word "normal" is, indeed, out of place, for many years must elapse ere Europe reaches a stable condition in industry and business. Mr. Crammond's balance-sheet dealt with immediate penalties: it scarcely touched the neighbouring field of losses due to the world-wide dislocation of finance, commerce, and production that usually follows a great war. The political treaty of peace is merely the occasion, in the present anarchic condition of international society, for the opening of an undeclared economic war, in which the victims can find neither patriotic nor any other kind of consolation. Millions of soldiers and armaments workers are disbanded, and sent out to destroy the price-level of productive industry. For a time, a spasm of "trade reviva" may help them.

Floods of newly created wealth are suddenly poured into markets which are mere glass-houses in their delicacy. A fever of financial speculation aggravates the process. Prices, interest, and wages soar up, and up. Then the bubble bursts. The nexus of production and consumption is lost; there is what people call overproduction, a glut of commodities. Orders are restricted, and prices fall. Labourers are dismissed, and wages fall. Capital is cancelled, and interest falls. What should be the blessing of mankind, the power of producing new wealth, is turned into a curse. There is a widespread "trade crisis"; and riotous crowds of unemployed workmen ask angrily whether it was for this that they fought through the greatest war in history.[1] Nevertheless, the war taxes required by the bill of immediate losses have still to be paid.

Three schools of political thought may be said to have arisen from the long economic crisis following the war of 1870-71—those of Imperialism, of "Tariff reform," and of Labour-Socialism. We cannot foresee the changes the great war will work in the mind of the western world, except that there will certainly be a general demand for some better means of assuring European peace than those yet existing.

---

1. The writer may, perhaps, refer to an inadequate consideration of the economic effects of the wars of 1866 and 1871 in his *Industrial History of Modern England*.

But it should not be altogether beyond the power of the doctors of physical and social science to cope with the problems just indicated. It was the new power of steam, directed by Pitt as national financier, as really as the power directed by Nelson and Wellington, that broke Napoleon and saved England a century ago. Because the new means of producing wealth were not subjected by organisation to the general welfare, the mass of the people sank for many years into abject misery. Whether invention and science can again effect such a miracle as that of the "industrial revolution," we cannot say; we can, however, say that only second in importance to the conclusion of a lasting peace between the belligerent States is the task of so directing the resumption of common work that the injury shown in past trade crises may be reduced to a minimum.

2. The Deadlock of the Trenches

The chief military lesson of the first five months of the western war was the great power of the entrenched defensive. Not even in Napoleon's highest period had the doctrine of energy and concentration afterwards formulated by Clausewitz been illustrated as in the first month of the German campaign, and afterward in the persistence of mass attacks. Everything that superior numbers, filled with inspiration of the offensive, and backed by long scientific preparation, could attempt was attempted; and nearly always it broke upon the resistance of a thin line of magazine rifles and field-guns in a deep ditch.

In 1902, before the aeroplane and the motor-wagon—perhaps the most important of the new implements of war—had appeared, the writer summarised as follows the chief thesis presented in the writings and conversations of the late John de Bloch, the Russian military economist: "The resisting power of an army standing on the defensive, equipped with long-range, quick-firing rifles and guns, from ten to forty times more powerful than those employed in 1870 and 1877, expert in entrenching and in the use of barbed wire and other obstacles, and highly mobile, is something quite different from that which Napoleon, or even later aggressors, had to face. Not only is it a much larger force, the manhood of a nation, instead of its hooligan surplus; it is also a body highly educated, an army of engineers.

Its infantry lines, and battery positions will be invisible. Reconnaissances will be easily prevented by protecting bands of sharpshooters; and no object of attack will offer itself to the invader till he has come within a zone of deadly fire. His cavalry cannot charge entrenched infantry; and, while the direction of an attack against a hidden foe has become extremely difficult, owing to the immensity and dispersion of the two forces, the morale of the attacking army will be weakened by the absence of all the bracing elements of ancient warfare, and the open order now necessary. The most heavy and powerful shells, which are alone of use against entrenched positions, cannot be used in great number, or brought easily into action; while the defenders have their ammunition at hand in unlimited quantities.

While the defenders are more safe than ever in their trenches, the attackers are necessarily exposed over an immensely enlarged field, to a heavier and more accurate fire than has ever been known in earlier battles. Artillery shares the advantage of a defensive position. If the attackers have a local superiority, the defenders can delay them long enough to allow of an orderly retirement to other entrenched positions. The attacker will be forced to entrench himself, and so the science of the spade reduces battles into sieges. Battle in the open would mean annihilation; yet it is only by assault that entrenched positions can be carried.

Warfare will drag on more slowly than ever. Frontier defences will give time for a concentration of national resources; while, on the other hand, the invader will have greater difficulty than ever in provisioning his enormous hosts. A conqueror cannot reward himself as he once did, nor can be hope for compensation for the expenses he will have to bear. While an invading army is being decimated by sickness and wounds, and demoralised by the heavy loss of officers and the delay of any glorious victory, the home population will be sunk in misery by the growth of economic burdens, the stoppage of trade and industry. The small, mobile, elastic, and manageable army of the past was capable of making quick marches, sudden changes in its line of operation, turning movements, movements on interior lines, strategical demonstrations in the widest sense; in a word, it was capable of performing all the acts in which the genius of a great captain could show itself.

But massed armies of millions, like those of today, leaning on fortresses, entrenched camps, and defences which have been prepared for the last thirty years, must perforce renounce all the more delicate manifestations of the military art. Armies as they now stand cannot manoeuvre, and must fight in directions indicated in advance. The losses of today would be proportionately greater than in past wars, if it were not for the tactical means adopted to avoid them. The diminution in the losses arises from dispersion and the great distances over which battles are fought. But the consequence of distance and dispersion is that victorious war—the obtaining of results by destroying the enemy's principal forces, and thus making him submit to the conqueror's will—can exist no more.

De Bloch was prejudiced by inaccurate summaries of his work *La Guerre*; and much has happened since the closing years of the nineteenth century, when he wrote it. He did not say that war had become impossible—if he had believed that, proof in six volumes would, indeed, have been a labour of supererogation—but that an aggressive war could not now give the results aimed at as between States of nearly equal resources. Whatever errors of detail he made, he was a true *savant*; it can no longer be denied that he foresaw the main track of military development; and, at a time when western readers are encouraged by many republications to test German military theory by its results, it cannot be ill to challenge comparison with a radically opposed school of thought. The new instruments of war have not invalidated his thesis, because, generally, they are the property of both sides. The aeroplane has greatly succeeded in scouting and signalling work, revealing concentrations of troops behind the lines, and hidden gun positions.

The motor-wagon has exceeded all expectations, and, with the motor-bus, car, and cab (1,300 motor-buses were requisitioned in Paris alone), has revolutionised the conveyance of men and supplies. To these and the railways, we owe the marvellous rapidity with which the extension of lines is now carried out. The searchlight, field-telephone, "wireless," and the trench periscope must be mentioned as important parts of the modern equipment But neither side has a monopoly of these scientific auxiliaries; and the most characteristic tools of the newest armies are still the oldest of all tools, the spade and pick for digging trenches—and graves. This is due above all to the fact that trenches are so easily dug and moved in obedience to local conditions, and that they offer so narrow a mark (2 or 3 feet) to the enemy's artillery. The stoutest steel and concrete coverings give no compensation for the fixity of the fort, whose position cannot be long concealed.

Even if its guns have the advantage of number, range, and power, the besiegers may be able to steal near without being located, or they may get protection behind a range of hills; if the fort does not possess these advantages, it is doomed, except for the purpose of a short arrest, by the weight of high explosives the new mobile, heavy howitzers can pour upon it, by high-angle fire, from their protected and frequently changed emplacements.

It will be said, and with truth, that, when his aggression has been checked, the would-be conqueror can still fall back upon the advantages of the entrenched defensive. But he does so with forces relatively as well as positively, reduced by his heavier losses in the aggressive campaign. The following estimates of comparative strength, put forward at various times, with much supporting evidence, by the French Government, have not, so far as I know, been challenged. On a peace footing, the German Empire had 25 army corps. At the opening of the war this number was increased to 61; and by the end of the year, it had reached 69 (Active corps, 25½; Reserve, 21½; Ersatz brigades, 6½; Reserve corps of new formation, 7½; *Landwehr* corps, 8½). This represented, very nearly, if not quite, the maximum of the German effort. For, assuming original resources (minus railway men, police, etc.) of about 8½ million men, there being on the two fronts, at the end of the year, about 4 millions; and the net losses in five months having been 1,300,000, there remained a margin of only 3,200,000, or, if inefficients and men over thirty-nine years of age be deducted, only 2 millions. This would compensate for wastage at the same rate for about eight months; if more new corps were formed, the margin available would be used up proportionately sooner.

On the other hand, Russia and England had only just begun to bring their main forces into action; while France, with 2,500,000 men at the front, and every unit at war strength, had still 2 million men to call up. In quality, the comparison favoured the Allies still more markedly. The new German levies were largely untrained. Most of the old regiments had had to be entirely renewed; and the lack of officers was already seriously felt. Depressed by the knowledge of repeated failure in both fields, and the rumour of approaching famine at home, they saw France reforming her generalship and conserving her energies; they saw new hosts gathering on both flanks, better trained and commanded, better equipped and supplied—already definitely superior in artillery—and unboundedly confident in their rising strength. The moral difference between a genuine national defence and a defensive which is only the bankruptcy of an outrageous aggression is enormous. Added to the material difference in the balance of forces which began to show itself when winter sealed the deadlock in the west, it warranted the high hopes with which the Allies entered upon the new year's operations.

3. The Farm of Quennevières

On the first of October, the French official bulletin contained the following phrase:—

> Between the Oise and the Aisne, the enemy has vigorously attacked Tracy-le-Mont, to the north-east of the Forest of Laigle, but has been repulsed with heavy loss.

Tracy was a village of 600 inhabitants, between Noyon and Vic-sur-Aisne. It did not share the fame of these larger neighbours (Noyon is reputedly the birthplace of Charlemagne, as well as of Calvin, and Vic has an eleventh-century church and a thirteenth-century donjon). Nor was any war correspondent present to chronicle the conflict of which the above sentence is the only direct record. But there was present on the battlefield a corporal stretcher-bearer, who, being wounded, has since put down some notes of his experiences. In printing them, the *Temps* says, not too strongly, that, "while written by a man who has no literary pretensions, they may be compared with the most striking pages of some Russian authors."

The writer is concerned to expose the current idea that the Army Medical Service begins to work when the firing ceases, resting meantime at the rear. This is only true of the special divisions of nurses and stretcher-bearers charged with the removal of the wounded to hospital. The regimental doctors, on the contrary, work on the field and under fire, and cannot even take shelter in trenches, like the firing-line. On the day in question, when the duel of gun and rifle fire had begun in earnest, they were advised that many French and German wounded needed help in the large farm of Quennevières; lying between the lines. It was a journey of the utmost peril, but two doctors and the writer started off without hesitation. The trio reached the farm. Around it, the trees were torn and cut, deep holes showed in the soil, and gaps in the walls of the farmyard. Probably the Germans thought it sheltered the French artillery, and had deliberately bombarded it

> We now heard again the *whizz-z-z* that those who have once heard it can never forget. The shell was coming straight toward us. We fell flat, in the twinkling of an eye, our noses to the ground. Happy he who finds a drain or ditch at such a moment! Yet we had time to ask ourselves whether it would pass over, or catch us in this ridiculous posture; and I saw the past and the future.

Four, five, six shells tore over them.

We got up, muddy and peevish. A faint smell of dynamite filled the air. We passed through the gateway. The yard, surrounded on three sides by the farmhouse and servants' quarters, was quiet and trim. Through the open shed doors, we could see cows peaceably ruminating. But a horribly thin dog was barking grievously, as he turned round and round something on the soil—a great red patch of clotted blood. The poor beast bayed without cessation, in lamentable appeal to his master, who had fallen there.

We entered the kitchen, and found three ground-floor rooms full of wounded—French and German uniforms pell-mell; a few officers. Six unwounded German soldiers, three carrying the Red Cross armlet, are taking care of both—we must say it to their honour—with equal solicitude. There are also a French doctor and nurses. Many of the unfortunates, lying on the blood-marked straw, had horrible wounds. The farm had seemed to them a last refuge; and they had dragged themselves as best they could to what for many of them would be only a tomb. . . . A soldier asks for a drink; as he rises, with hand stretched out for the glass of water, a bullet comes through the window, and strikes him full in the heart. The poor fellow sinks without a sigh.

Most of the wounded are taken away in a lull of the combat. Drs. A. and T. remain with the last of them, and with the Germans, who help them with a real courage. It is three in the afternoon. Firing recommences, more violent than ever. The shells whistle ceaselessly. An adjutant, terribly wounded, begs to be put into the cart, which seems to him a guarantee that he will be among the next to be removed. Scarcely is he laid there than shrapnel bursts over the cart, killing him. The firing sounds more clearly. I watch the doctors, indifferent to the approaching danger, tending the wounded. Most of the living rooms of the farm are now in ruins. In the sheds, the cows low piteously.

A wounded man in the kitchen calls me. Struck by a ball in the chest, the poor fellow pants for breath. He is supporting himself by one arm, which slips on the bloody straw. With the other hand he feels in his overcoat pocket, which is glued up with congealed blood, for a letter which he hands to me, his eyes full of tears. 'It will soon be over,' he says, perhaps for both of us. But if you should escape, look, here's a letter.' He stopped. A shell passed, burying itself in the road twenty yards away. The lad looked at me, smiling sadly through his tears. I take the letter. 'My sweetheart,' he murmurs. And I see in his bloodstained fingers a little lock of black hair which he presses tenderly to his lips.

Raising my eyes to the ceiling, I see the plaster break into a huge star, and through a gaping hole the end of a great shell appears. The ceiling sinks funnel-wise; at the same moment the roof cracks, and the shell explodes. Then all is dark.... Presently I come to myself, half suffocated with dust and the fumes of dynamite. The house is riven from top to bottom, and we can see the calm blue sky through the broken roof. The least seriously wounded men disengage their fellows. One of the Germans, half mad, gesticulates and wails, '*Zum keller, zum keller!*' ('To the cellar!') His contortions throw a comic note into the terrible scene. Nearly all of ns are bleeding. The poor lover is dead, disfigured. Shells have struck the house on two sides. In a part that is still standing, a sergeant, mortally wounded, with indifferent gaze watches the ceiling cracking and sinking above him.

They manage to get into the cellar; and here the German wounded, hungry and desperate, burst out into complaints of this war of pains incalculable into which they have been driven. "'My poor wife! My poor children!' cries one of them, wounded in the stomach by a fragment of shell. Another says that his wife was a Frenchwoman, and he had seen his brother-in-law in a group of prisoners. At this moment, in a dark comer, we heard a sob, and a woman's voice rose out of the shadow: 'All my own children are dead, and my husband was killed up there in the yard.' It was the farmer's wife. She had watched, helpless, the work of destruction. Children, husband, goods, she had lost everything.

And I saw once more the emaciated dog up there baying in the yard before the clotted blood of his master.

Another cartful of wounded was removed. The remaining woman and two men spent four more hours in the cellar, under the faint light of a smoky lamp. It was 9 p.m. when they got away from the ruined farm. As they passed over the battlefield, they saw the dim forms of ghouls robbing the dead.

The writer signs himself "Pierre de Lorraine." It Is doubtless a pseudonym. And the official record of one day of this "anonymous war" merely records that "the enemy has attacked Tracy-le-Mont, but has been repulsed with heavy loss."

4. The Christmas Truce

Sometimes, not often, there comes to hand a simple soldier's letter that reflects more faithfully than any but the highest art the facts of an obscure corner of the vast battlefield. A Lorrainer, wounded and made prisoner by the French, writes:—

> To tell you what I have suffered is impossible. The marches, the nights in ditches, the fever of fighting, the lack of food—I lived for three days on tinned stuff that I took from the knapsacks of dead soldiers—the burning villages—what horrors! It was frightful; my heart bled. I was with one section for six hours under artillery fire. The first shell killed the man on my right, and a long string of blood dripped from his ear; he died after an hour and a half of acute suffering, during which he cried out like one of the damned. We lay there, our heads buried in the soil, without stirring, waiting for death. What moments! Every day was like that.
>
> The dead bodies blocked the trenches. Although bullets and projectiles fell like hailstones about us, I was preserved from them until the morrow of the terrible battle of ——, when I was given the mission of reconnoitring a village. We were received with a storm of fire. I was struck by a piece of shell which tore my arm. Sitting under a hedge, I tied my handkerchief round it, but the blood ran down in a stream, staining my breeches and boots, and falling drop by drop on to the grass. Completely exhausted, I yet managed to walk a couple of miles to the ambulance. Then I was made prisoner; but we of Alsace or Lorraine were separated from the Germans, and everywhere welcomed with open arms.

M. Georges Berthoulat gives an account of a visit he paid to one of the camps of wounded behind the centre of the French fighting line. The men spoke to him of the horrible conditions of trench warfare, with the air poisoned by dead bodies that cannot be removed, because directly a head is lifted above the earthworks it is a mark for the sharpshooters. Without naming it, he refers to a jolly suburb of a large town, in the villas of which some British officers had installed themselves during the interval of rest He was very much struck to find them occupying themselves with golf, football, boating, and swimming; and, after speaking of their clean-shaved faces and carefully brushed uniforms, he observes: "The British troops fight like ours, but they dress and wash better."

He tells two of the best stories of the war. The army corps whose base he was visiting has two chaplains—a Catholic priest and a Jewish *rabbi*. They seemed to be very good friends, as well as the best of fellows. One evening, they were kept on the battlefield looking after some wounded, and found it impossible to get back to the lines. After looking round, they found an abandoned farm, with a single ragged pallet. Here they spent the night, side by side; and, as they went off to sleep, the priest remarked to the *rabbi*:—

> If there were only a photographer here!—the Old and the New Testaments as bedfellows.

An officer told the writer that the carnage on the Craonne plateau was such that, owing to the mass of German corpses, the aviators have now to fly high to avoid the pestilential odour. The same officer narrated the following piece of heroism:—

> After the fighting on September 15-17, an infantry regiment was defending the village of P——, which the Germans were shelling from a higher level. The French troops had to evacuate a large farm, called, I suppose symbolically, "Cholera Farm," standing between the two firing-lines. In it had been left a number of French wounded. The colonel asked for a volunteer to bring them back over the 300 yards of intervening plain, which was swept continually by the enemy's fire. A cart and horse would be at his disposal. For a moment, there was silence. Then a simple soldier named Expert stepped out of the ranks, and said, "I'll go." For three days, he made the journey to and from "Cholera Farm," alone, putting the wounded in his cart, and taking them, with others whom he picked up on the road, to the ambulance in the rear.
>
> He never budged under the storm of the big guns. But, on the evening of the third day, his horse was shot. Expert at once stepped into the shafts, and began to drag the cart himself. On the road, however, meeting a carriage belonging to another regiment, he commandeered one of its horses, for the supreme

sake of his precious wounded. This was a military offense, and Expert received, almost simultaneously, the military medal for his heroism, and a sentence of fifteen days' imprisonment for having taken a horse without authority. But he did not serve the term.

I have no heart to collect humorous stories of the war; but this incident told by a returned soldier is characteristic. An infantryman walked into his trench eating a pear. The whizz of a shell was heard; then it burst, throwing the man to the ground amid a cloud of dust. Before his comrades could speak, he was on his feet, shouting angrily: "The pigs! They've made me drop my pear!"

A cavalry patrol was reconnoitring the edge of a wood. There was deep silence; the place was believed to have been evacuated, and nothing suspicious could be seen. Suddenly, a wounded infantryman half-rose from the beetroot field, and, with his last strength, called out : "Take care ... machine-guns!" The patrol turned and galloped off, pursued by a volley which did not touch them. The wounded soldier fell dead.

Eighty years ago, Alfred de Vigny reproached his con- temporaries by comparing the soldier's life with the gladiator's: "The people are the easy-going Caesar, the laughing Claudius, whom the soldiers endlessly salute as they pass—'Those about to die salute thee!'" There was no easy-going Caesar in England, or France, or Belgium when the great war began; and it was in no gladiatorial spirit that the millions of reservists and volunteers offered their lives to their country. For them, war was a hateful means to a necessary end. I have spoken to hundreds of them, and have not met one who would not have prayed, with me, that the end might come soon, and the means be then abandoned and broken for ever. How else shall their sacrifice honoured?

One of the strangest and most significant events of the marked Christmas on a long line of trenches held, on one side, by a body of Saxon troops, on the other by the Leicestershire Regiment, the London Rifle Brigade, and the other British units. Darkness fell at about 7 o'clock Christmas Eve, and with it a sudden calm. The German snipers seemed to have disappeared. Then the sound of carol-singing rose from the trenches; and, at that, the British snipers in turn ceased. The magic chorus sank and swelled again to the black sky. Some of the British soldiers raised an experimental cheer. An officer of the R.F.A wrote:

Shouts from the Germans: 'You English, why don't you come out?'—and our bright knaves replied with yells of 'Waiter.'

Nevertheless, they came out; and, very soon, fires and candles were burning along the parapets hitherto guarded with ceaseless vigilance, and the men were fraternising in a crowd between them, exchanging gifts and experiences, and agreeing that the truce should continue till midnight of Christmas Day.

It was all arranged privately, and started by one of our fellows going across. You can hardly imagine it. The only thing forbidden was to make any improvement to the barbed wire. If by any mischance a single shot was fired, it was not to be taken as an act of war, and an apology would be accepted; also, that firing would not be opened without due warning on both sides.

Officers came out to see "the fun." A chaplain gave a German commander a copy of *The Soldier's Prayer*, and in return received a cigar, and a message for the bereaved family of a certain British officer.

He had been killed; and, as he was dying, the German commander happened to pass, and saw him struggling to get something out of his pocket. He went up, and helped the dying man, and the thing in the pocket was a photograph of his wife. The commander said, 'I held it before him, and he lay looking at it till he died, a few minutes after.'

Christmas Day passed in burying the dead, whose bodies lay in scores between the trenches; in carol-singing, each side cheering the other; and in a football match, which the Saxons won. "War was absolutely forgotten," says one soldier's letter; "they weren't half a bad lot, really." An officer wrote:—

The sergeant-major has not got over it yet; his remarks were, 'It is 'ardly credible,' and 'I never would 'ave believed it.'

God bless you, comrades, say I. Such acts, such men, give us back our faith in the virtue of life and the common human heart. No earthly Majesties or Excellencies sanctioned, no pale-faced dreamer invited them to, this high experiment. The vision of their hours of reconciliation will last when many a day of dear-bought but necessary victory has sunk into oblivion. The men who went back to their guns, if they survive, will recall it as the day when Christmas became real for them. Bereaved mothers and wives will cherish the memory. We who sit in a security we have scarcely helped to make will remember with twinges. "Its logic?" Thou grub, to set logic against prophetic love! And you, pundits and sergeant-majors of our ruling spheres, read and mark well this humble, yet most imperatively credible, omen. Our sons' ways will not be as ours. They will make a new Europe. At your peril, do not hinder them. Many will have died for liberty. The rest, and their sons, and their sons' sons, will live for peace.

ALSO FROM LEONAUR
AVAILABLE IN SOFTCOVER OR HARDCOVER WITH DUST JACKET

THE FALL OF THE MOGHUL EMPIRE OF HINDUSTAN *by H. G. Keene*—By the beginning of the nineteenth century, as British and Indian armies under Lake and Wellesley dominated the scene, a little over half a century of conflict brought the Moghul Empire to its knees.

LADY SALE'S AFGHANISTAN *by Florentia Sale*—An Indomitable Victorian Lady's Account of the Retreat from Kabul During the First Afghan War.

THE CAMPAIGN OF MAGENTA AND SOLFERINO 1859 *by Harold Carmichael Wylly*—The Decisive Conflict for the Unification of Italy.

FRENCH'S CAVALRY CAMPAIGN *by J. G. Maydon*—A Special Correspondent's View of British Army Mounted Troops During the Boer War.

CAVALRY AT WATERLOO *by Sir Evelyn Wood*—British Mounted Troops During the Campaign of 1815.

THE SUBALTERN *by George Robert Gleig*—The Experiences of an Officer of the 85th Light Infantry During the Peninsular War.

NAPOLEON AT BAY, 1814 *by F. Loraine Petre*—The Campaigns to the Fall of the First Empire.

NAPOLEON AND THE CAMPAIGN OF 1806 *by Colonel Vachée*—The Napoleonic Method of Organisation and Command to the Battles of Jena & Auerstädt.

THE COMPLETE ADVENTURES IN THE CONNAUGHT RANGERS *by William Grattan*—The 88th Regiment during the Napoleonic Wars by a Serving Officer.

BUGLER AND OFFICER OF THE RIFLES *by William Green & Harry Smith*—With the 95th (Rifles) during the Peninsular & Waterloo Campaigns of the Napoleonic Wars.

NAPOLEONIC WAR STORIES *by Sir Arthur Quiller-Couch*—Tales of soldiers, spies, battles & sieges from the Peninsular & Waterloo campaingns.

CAPTAIN OF THE 95TH (RIFLES) *by Jonathan Leach*—An officer of Wellington's sharpshooters during the Peninsular, South of France and Waterloo campaigns of the Napoleonic wars.

RIFLEMAN COSTELLO *by Edward Costello*—The adventures of a soldier of the 95th (Rifles) in the Peninsular & Waterloo Campaigns of the Napoleonic wars.

AVAILABLE ONLINE AT **www.leonaur.com**
AND FROM ALL GOOD BOOK STORES

ALSO FROM LEONAUR
AVAILABLE IN SOFTCOVER OR HARDCOVER WITH DUST JACKET

ESCAPE FROM THE FRENCH by *Edward Boys*—A Young Royal Navy Midshipman's Adventures During the Napoleonic War.

THE VOYAGE OF H.M.S. PANDORA by *Edward Edwards R. N. & George Hamilton, edited by Basil Thomson*—In Pursuit of the Mutineers of the Bounty in the South Seas—1790-1791.

MEDUSA by *J. B. Henry Savigny and Alexander Correard and Charlotte-Adélaïde Dard* —Narrative of a Voyage to Senegal in 1816 & The Sufferings of the Picard Family After the Shipwreck of the Medusa.

THE SEA WAR OF 1812 VOLUME 1 by *A. T. Mahan*—A History of the Maritime Conflict.

THE SEA WAR OF 1812 VOLUME 2 by *A. T. Mahan*—A History of the Maritime Conflict.

WETHERELL OF H. M. S. HUSSAR by *John Wetherell*—The Recollections of an Ordinary Seaman of the Royal Navy During the Napoleonic Wars.

THE NAVAL BRIGADE IN NATAL by *C. R. N. Burne*—With the Guns of H. M. S. Terrible & H. M. S. Tartar during the Boer War 1899-1900.

THE VOYAGE OF H. M. S. BOUNTY by *William Bligh*—The True Story of an 18th Century Voyage of Exploration and Mutiny.

SHIPWRECK! by *William Gilly*—The Royal Navy's Disasters at Sea 1793-1849.

KING'S CUTTERS AND SMUGGLERS: 1700-1855 by *E. Keble Chatterton*—A unique period of maritime history-from the beginning of the eighteenth to the middle of the nineteenth century when British seamen risked all to smuggle valuable goods from wool to tea and spirits from and to the Continent.

CONFEDERATE BLOCKADE RUNNER by *John Wilkinson*—The Personal Recollections of an Officer of the Confederate Navy.

NAVAL BATTLES OF THE NAPOLEONIC WARS by *W. H. Fitchett*—Cape St. Vincent, the Nile, Cadiz, Copenhagen, Trafalgar & Others.

PRISONERS OF THE RED DESERT by *R. S. Gwatkin-Williams*—The Adventures of the Crew of the Tara During the First World War.

U-BOAT WAR 1914-1918 by *James B. Connolly/Karl von Schenk*—Two Contrasting Accounts from Both Sides of the Conflict at Sea D uring the Great War.

AVAILABLE ONLINE AT **www.leonaur.com**
AND FROM ALL GOOD BOOK STORES

ALSO FROM LEONAUR
AVAILABLE IN SOFTCOVER OR HARDCOVER WITH DUST JACKET

OFFICERS & GENTLEMEN *by Peter Hawker & William Graham*—Two Accounts of British Officers During the Peninsula War: Officer of Light Dragoons by Peter Hawker & Campaign in Portugal and Spain by William Graham.

THE WALCHEREN EXPEDITION *by Anonymous*—The Experiences of a British Officer of the 81st Regt. During the Campaign in the Low Countries of 1809.

LADIES OF WATERLOO *by Charlotte A. Eaton, Magdalene de Lancey & Juana Smith*—The Experiences of Three Women During the Campaign of 1815: Waterloo Days by Charlotte A. Eaton, A Week at Waterloo by Magdalene de Lancey & Juana's Story by Juana Smith.

JOURNAL OF AN OFFICER IN THE KING'S GERMAN LEGION *by John Frederick Hering*—Recollections of Campaigning During the Napoleonic Wars.

JOURNAL OF AN ARMY SURGEON IN THE PENINSULAR WAR *by Charles Boutflower*—The Recollections of a British Army Medical Man on Campaign During the Napoleonic Wars.

ON CAMPAIGN WITH MOORE AND WELLINGTON *by Anthony Hamilton*—The Experiences of a Soldier of the 43rd Regiment During the Peninsular War.

THE ROAD TO AUSTERLITZ *by R. G. Burton*—Napoleon's Campaign of 1805.

SOLDIERS OF NAPOLEON *by A. J. Doisy De Villargennes & Arthur Chuquet*—The Experiences of the Men of the French First Empire: Under the Eagles by A. J. Doisy De Villargennes & Voices of 1812 by Arthur Chuquet.

INVASION OF FRANCE, 1814 *by F. W. O. Maycock*—The Final Battles of the Napoleonic First Empire.

LEIPZIG—A CONFLICT OF TITANS *by Frederic Shoberl*—A Personal Experience of the 'Battle of the Nations' During the Napoleonic Wars, October 14th-19th, 1813.

SLASHERS *by Charles Cadell*—The Campaigns of the 28th Regiment of Foot During the Napoleonic Wars by a Serving Officer.

BATTLE IMPERIAL *by Charles William Vane*—The Campaigns in Germany & France for the Defeat of Napoleon 1813-1814.

SWIFT & BOLD *by Gibbes Rigaud*—The 60th Rifles During the Peninsula War.

AVAILABLE ONLINE AT **www.leonaur.com**
AND FROM ALL GOOD BOOK STORES

www.ingramcontent.com/pod-product-compliance
Lightning Source LLC
Chambersburg PA
CBHW030228170426
43201CB00006B/142